Collins

Key Stage 3
Science

Teacher Pack 2

Series editor: Ed Walsh
Authors: Tracey Baxter
Sunetra Berry
Pat Dower
Anne Pilling

William Collins' dream of knowledge for all began with the publication of his first book in 1819. A self-educated mill worker, he not only enriched millions of lives, but also founded a flourishing publishing house. Today, staying true to this spirit, Collins books are packed with inspiration, innovation and practical expertise. They place you at the centre of a world of possibility and give you exactly what you need to explore it.
Collins. Freedom to teach

Published by Collins
An imprint of HarperCollins*Publishers*
77 – 85 Fulham Palace Road
Hammersmith
London
W6 8JB

> Browse the complete Collins catalogue at
> www.collins.co.uk

© HarperCollins*Publishers* Limited 2014

10 9 8 7 6 5 4 3 2 1

ISBN 978-0-00-754022-8

Tracey Baxter, Sunetra Berry, Pat Dower and Anne Pilling assert their moral rights to be identified as the authors of this work.

All rights reserved. No part of this publication may be reproduced, stored in a retrieval system, or transmitted in any form or by any means, electronic, mechanical, photocopying, recording or otherwise, without the prior written permission of the Publisher or a licence permitting restricted copying in the United Kingdom issued by the Copyright Licensing Agency Ltd., 90 Tottenham Court Road, London W1T 4LP.

British Library Cataloguing in Publication Data
A Catalogue record for this publication is available from the British Library

Commissioned by Letitia Luff
Project managed by Jane Roth
Series editor Ed Walsh
Managing editor Caroline Green
Project editor Amanda Redstone
Editorial assistant Lucy Roth
Edited by Elizabeth Barker, Hugh Hillyard-Parker, Sophia Ktori, Jane Roth, Ros Woodward
Proofread by Tony Clappison, Hugh Hillyard-Parker, Nigel Rumble
Illustrations by Ken Vail Graphic Design
Cover design by Angela English
Cover photograph by Irina1977/Shutterstock
Production by Emma Roberts
Printed and bound by RR Donnelley

Health and Safety: The publisher and authors have made every reasonable effort to ensure that the experiments and activities in this book are safe when conducted as instructed. However, the publishers assume no responsibility for any damage or injury caused or sustained while performing the experiments or activities in this book to the full extent permitted by law.

Many thanks to Andrew Young, Head Science Technician of Stewards Academy, for his safety testing and reviewing of all practical activities.

Acknowledgements
Every effort has been made to trace copyright holders and to obtain their permission for the use of copyright materials. The publishers will gladly receive any information enabling them to rectify any error or omission at the first opportunity.

Contents

Introduction	1
Planning the learning process	3
Assessment of learning	6

1 Getting the Energy your Body Needs
1.1 Introduction	8
1.2 Exploring the human skeleton	10
1.3 Analysing the skeleton	12
1.4 Understanding the role of skeletal joints	14
1.5 Investigating muscle strength	16
1.6 Analysing muscle strength	18
1.7 Examining interacting muscles	20
1.8 Exploring problems with the skeletal system	22
1.9 Applying key ideas (The bare bones of space travel)	**24**
1.10 Understanding how muscles get energy	26
1.11 Investigating respiration	28
1.12 Analysing adaptations for respiration	30
1.13 Examining links between respiration and body systems	32
1.14 Exploring respiration in sport	34
1.15 Understanding anaerobic respiration	36
1.16 Investigating fermentation	38
1.17 Comparing aerobic and anaerobic respiration	40
1.18 Checking students' progress	**42**
1.19 Answers	**44**

2 Looking at Plants and Ecosystems
2.1 Introduction	46
2.2 Understanding the importance of plants	48
2.3 Exploring how plants make food	50
2.4 Looking at leaves	52
2.5 Exploring the role of stomata	54
2.6 Investigating photosynthesis	56
2.7 Exploring the movement of water and minerals in plants	58
2.8 Investigating the importance of minerals to plants	60
2.9 Investigating chemosynthesis	62
2.10 Applying key ideas (Down at the allotment)	**64**
2.11 Understanding food webs	66
2.12 Exploring the importance of insects	68
2.13 Looking at other examples of interdependence	70
2.14 Understanding interactions in the environment	72
2.15 Learning about ecological balance	74
2.16 Understanding the effects of toxins in the environment	76
2.17 Exploring how organisms co-exist	78
2.18 Checking students' progress	**80**
2.19 Answers	**82**

3 Explaining Physical Changes
3.1 Introduction	84
3.2 Using particles to explain matter	86
3.3 Understanding solids	88
3.4 Exploring Brownian motion	90
3.5 Understanding liquids and gases	92
3.6 Changing state	94
3.7 Understanding evaporation	96
3.8 Exploring thermal expansion	98
3.9 Making sense of models	100
3.10 Applying key ideas (Explaining heat packs)	**102**
3.11 Explaining the density of solids and liquids	104
3.12 Explaining the density of gases	106
3.13 Explaining concentration and pressure	108
3.14 Exploring diffusion	110
3.15 Conserving mass	112
3.16 Deciding between physical and chemical changes	114
3.17 Explaining the properties of mixtures	116
3.18 Using particle models	118
3.19 Checking students' progress	**120**
3.20 Answers	**122**

4 Explaining Chemical Changes
4.1 Introduction	124
4.2 Exploring acids	126
4.3 Exploring alkalis	128
4.4 Using indicators	130
4.5 Using universal indicator	132
4.6 Exploring neutralisation	134
4.7 Explaining neutralisation	136
4.8 Understanding salts	138
4.9 Exploring the reactions of acids with metals	140
4.10 Exploring the reactions of acids with carbonates	142
4.11 Applying key ideas (Ever-changing urine)	**144**
4.12 Investigating the effectiveness of antacids	146
4.13 Understanding the importance of acids and alkalis	148
4.14 Exploring combustion	150
4.15 Understanding combustion and the use of fuels	152
4.16 Exploring the effects of burning	154
4.17 Understanding acid rain	156
4.18 Checking students' progress	**158**
4.19 Answers	**160**

5 Exploring Contact and Non-Contact Forces
5.1 Introduction	162
5.2 Exploring magnets	164
5.3 Understanding magnetic fields	166
5.4 Investigating static charge	168
5.5 Explaining static charge	170
5.6 Understanding electrostatic fields	172
5.7 Applying what we know about electrostatics	174
5.8 Exploring gravity on Earth	176

Contents

5.9 Applying our understanding of gravity to space travel — 178
5.10 Applying key ideas (Exploring Earth's atmosphere and beyond) — 180
5.11 Exploring pressure on a solid surface — 182
5.12 Calculating pressure — 184
5.13 Exploring pressure in a liquid — 186
5.14 Explaining floating and sinking — 188
5.15 Exploring gas pressure — 190
5.16 Working with pressure — 192
5.17 Checking students' progress — 194
5.18 Answers — 196

6 Magnetism and Electricity
6.1 Introduction — 198
6.2 Looking at the history of magnets — 200
6.3 Exploring magnetic materials — 202
6.4 Testing the strength of magnets — 204
6.5 Describing the Earth's magnetic field — 206
6.6 Investigating electromagnetism — 208
6.7 Using electromagnets — 210
6.8 Exploring D.C. motors — 212
6.9 Applying key ideas (How can magnets be used to operate trains?) — 214
6.10 Investigating batteries — 216
6.11 Describing electric circuits — 218
6.12 Understanding energy in circuits — 220
6.13 Explaining resistance — 222
6.14 Investigating factors affecting resistance — 224
6.15 Explaining circuits using models — 226
6.16 Describing series and parallel circuits — 228
6.17 Comparing series and parallel circuits — 230
6.18 Applying circuits — 232
6.19 Checking students' progress — 234
6.20 Answers — 236

Scheme of work — 238

Concept teaching route diagrams — 269

Extra resources on CD-ROM

All pages from this print book available as PDF and editable Word files

Student worksheets in 2 formats; reusable and write-on (all available as PDF and Word files)

Practical sheets (as PDF and Word files)

Technician's notes (as PDF and Word files)

Each type of resource sheet collated in chapter batches to enable easy printing

Scheme outline for Teacher Pack 3

Introduction

Purpose of the Collins Key Stage 3 Science course

This course has been developed to provide support to teachers in planning and delivering exciting, engaging and effective lessons. The overarching priorities have been to:

- ensure that the requirements of the National Curriculum Programme of Study have been responded to
- support teachers in teaching lessons in which students make good progress and are on track to achieve well at the end of KS4
- offer ways of tracking, reporting on and responding to progress given the move away from levels in the National Curriculum
- enable schools to select the period of time they decide to devote to KS3 before starting on KS4 courses
- address the need to challenge and engage students working at different levels of attainment
- focus on the development of skills and processes as well as content
- provide teachers with clear guidance as to how learning can be managed during the lesson, from initial engagement to consolidation and application.

Overview of changes at Key Stage 3

Some concepts previously associated with GCSE are now in KS3, such as:

- the role played by Watson, Crick, Wilkins and Franklin in the development of the DNA model
- the chemical properties of metal and non-metal oxides with respect to acidity
- the properties of ceramics, polymers and composites
- heating and thermal equilibrium
- the superposition of waves
- resistance as the ratio of potential difference to current
- the concept of electrostatic fields
- the light year as a unit of astronomical distance.

How Science Works has been replaced with Working Scientifically, which covers a similar range of skills and processes but which moves away from the social and economic implications of scientific developments.

There are no levels or any descriptors of progression. Nevertheless, schools are expected to track progress, report accordingly and respond with further challenge or support.

Organisation of the Collins Key Stage 3 Science course

There are two biology, two chemistry and two physics chapters in each year. This means that science can be delivered as one subject or by subject specialists. A scheme of work shows both 3-year and 2-year routes though the course to aid long-term planning, see page 238. Support and strategies for building and assessing progress are embedded throughout. For more details please see *Planning the learning process* on pages 3-7.

How the lesson plans work
Chapter introductions
These:

- give an overview of the of the content and skills covered in the chapter
- help in assessing prior learning and identifying misconceptions
- list the overarching learning objectives to help medium-term planning.

Introduction

Learning objectives and outcomes

- Learning objectives for each topic are shared with students in the Student Book for short-term planning.
- Learning outcomes at three levels are listed, and it is shown which learning activities contribute to achieving each outcome.

These help in tracking the progress of all students, identifying those making good progress and who are on the right trajectory for sound results at GCSE, those who are making better than expected progress and are headed for the top results at GCSE, and those making less progress and for whom some intervention is needed.

Skills development

Ensuring progression in skills has underpinned the development of the course. There are three skill sets used, developed from a range of sources including PLTS, SEAL and APP in Science:

- **Thinking scientifically** relates to the relationship between evidence, ideas and theories, and has a strong role to play in science generally and in KS4 courses. It includes asking questions, considering the quality of evidence, understanding how theories develop, evaluating risks, using units and nomenclature, using equations and analysing data.
- **Working scientifically** relates to conducting practical investigations and includes making predictions, designing investigations, recording evidence, presenting evidence, interpreting evidence, developing explanations and evaluating data.
- **Developing as learners** is not a science-specific set of skills, though science can play a strong part in developing the skills, and they are recognised by the Ofsted school inspection framework. They include planning progress, acting responsibly, developing resilience, asking questions, communicating effectively, respecting others and collaborating effectively.

Resources needed gives an overview of all the resources needed for a lesson. More detailed guidance for practicals is given in student practical sheets and technician's notes on the accompanying CD-ROM.

Common misconceptions highlight specific misconceptions for the topic.

Key vocabulary is highlighted throughout to support literacy.

Teaching sequence

The lesson plans all use the same learning sequence. This is based on the idea that learning develops in stages during a lesson and that different parts of the lesson have different functions.

Engage This section draws students in to thinking about the ideas, and includes possible starter activities. Here students encounter ideas that will make them want to find out more.

Challenge and develop Students meet something that will challenge their existing understanding. It might be questions, ideas, demonstrations or experiments that make them realise the inadequacy of a simpler explanation.

Explain Students are encouraged to develop a good explanation and supported in capturing ideas in words or graphically. Differentiation ideas are given for students making less or more than expected progress.

Consolidate and apply Students realise how the new learning is to be consolidated and applied, including real-world applications. Again, differentiation ideas are given for students making different levels of progress.

Extend Addresses how the ideas of the topic can be extended to stretch students able to progress further.

Plenary suggestions Varied activities help in gauging student progress.

Answers All answers to Student Book questions and worksheet questions are provided.

Extra resources on the accompanying CD-ROM

Every lesson has an associated differentiated worksheet to support written work. These are provided as write-on versions with lines for student responses, and reusable versions without lines that can be used again and again to reduce photocopying costs. Practical sheets are provided to give support for planning, carrying out and analysing practical work. Technician's notes are provided to explain the materials and setup and help with planning.

Collins Connect is a linked publication of digital resources to enhance lessons. The resources are listed by lesson in the scheme of work on page 238 and in each lesson plan.

Planning the learning process: The thinking behind Key Stage 3 Science

Outstanding lesson plans

Each of the lesson plans is designed to support the delivery of high quality interactive lessons. They have a common structure that is transparent, making it easy for teachers to see what is suggested and make decisions about whether to use the plan as it stands or to customise. Sequences of lessons are planned to cover the requirements of the Programme of Study for Science (2013).

Objectives and outcomes

Each of the statements from the Programme of Study has been built into the plan and identified as 'overarching objectives'. From these authors have developed learning objectives for individual lessons; these draw upon processes as well as content. These objectives use the stem of 'we are learning how to' as it is important that students develop abilities as opposed to just learning facts.

From these, outcomes were developed; there is a strong relationship between objectives and outcomes. Outcomes use the stem 'what I'm looking for' (in which 'I' is the teacher) and indicate the evidence the teacher should see that indicates that learning has occurred.

The outcomes also play a critical role in the **assessment of progress**. The 2013 Programme of Study has no level descriptors but the importance of tracking progress hasn't diminished. Part of the function of the outcomes is to enable the teacher to decide if students are making good progress. The outcomes are differentiated; students who are making good progress will be, generally speaking, achieving at least two out of the three outcomes. Students regularly achieving all three may need, on occasions, more challenging activities. Those struggling to achieve more than one may need additional support. However the Teacher Pack materials are designed to be used in a flexible way, to be selected from and adapted to meet the needs of students.

Skills

Each lesson has two or three focus skills selected. The three sets of skills are as follows:

- **Thinking scientifically**. These are the skills that scientists use in a variety of contexts, such as asking questions, using equations and analysing data. Although these are used in practical activities their role is much wider than that. All lessons have such a skill identified; this skill will also be reflected in the learning activities and often feature in the objectives and outcomes.

- **Working scientifically**. These skills are strongly based on the 'Working Scientifically' aspect of the Programme of Study and are selected where practical activities form part of the lesson. Although students may well be developing and using a number of these skills there is always one in particular that is highlighted. This is designed to make it easier for teachers and students to focus upon particular aspects. Over a sequence of lessons the focus will change so that all are covered over a period of time. Obviously the teacher can select a different focus if their view is that this better serves students' learning needs. However what is less effective is a lesson in which a range of skills are ostensibly targeted but what happens in practice is that the same few (often gathering data and writing conclusions) are emphasised repeatedly.

- **Learner development**. Science has the power to develop a wider range of skills than those which are subject specific; it also draws upon these wider skills. In every lesson one of these is focused upon and reflected in the learning activities, providing an opportunity for the lesson to be placed in the wider context of the development of the student as a learner.

None of these skills are radical or original in nature, either in their form or function. Schools familiar with APP, PLTS or SEAL will recognise many of the components. However what the writing team have done is to present these in a form that is both manageable and integrated with the delivery of content.

The learning cycle

The main part of each lesson plan forms a common sequence as part of a 'learning cycle'. The basic idea behind this can be traced back to an inquiry lesson planning model developed for the Science Curriculum Improvement Study (SCIS) program in the USA, a K-6 science program in the early 1970s. In its original form the learning cycle model had 3 stages (exploration, invention and discovery). The idea was that the teacher would develop the science concept in the second stage, rather than defining it at the outset of the lesson as in the traditional approach. The introduced concept subsequently enables students to incorporate their exploration in the third stage and apply it to new examples. It thus has a strong link to a constructivist model of learning, in which students are challenged to develop ideas rather than being presented with a body of content to accept 'as is'. Many examples of learning cycles have since been developed; one current version is the 5E Learning Cycle, which is used in the new BSCS (Biological Sciences Curriculum Study) science programmes as well as in other texts and materials. The Collins KS3 Science sequence consists of the following stages:

- **Engage**, in which the teacher draws students into thinking about certain ideas. Here a student encounters ideas that will make them want to find out more.
- **Challenge and develop**, in which a student meets something that will challenge their existing understanding. It might be questions, ideas, demonstrations, experiments, etc., that make them realise the inadequacy of a simpler explanation.
- **Explain**, in which students are encouraged and supported to develop a good explanation. This draws upon the previous section and supports students to capture ideas in words or graphically.
- **Consolidate and apply**, where students realise how the new learning is to be consolidated and applied. Real world applications are often drawn upon at this point.
- **Extend**, in which ideas can be extended by students making greater than expected progress.

Throughout, the emphasis is upon students' active learning. Authors have identified what students should be doing to engage with each phase, and the purpose of the component, as well as the nature. This is designed to present the teacher with an open, easily assimilated structure which shows what is intended at each point. A teacher wishing to substitute their own activity will therefore be supported in knowing what it should do to support progress. Similarly a teacher using the plan as it is can see the reasoning behind what they are doing.

Encouraging discussion

Discussion is important for exploring ideas and evidence in science and for developing an understanding of concepts, as well as improving literacy. There is a wide variety of ways of organising small-group discussion. Eight of these are used extensively in the lesson plans:

- **Pair talk** This is easy to organise even in cramped classrooms. It is also ideal to promote high levels of participation and to ensure that the discussions are highly focused, especially if allied to tight deadlines. It can be used in the early stages of learning for students to recall work from a previous lesson, generate questions, work together to plan a piece of writing or take turns to tell a story. Pairs can also be used to work as reading partners with an unfamiliar text. It is also ideal for quick-fire reflection and review, and for rehearsal of ideas before presenting them to the whole class.
- **Pairs to fours** Students work together in pairs – possibly friendship, possibly boy/girl, etc. Each pair then joins up with another pair to explain and compare ideas.
- **Listening triads** Students work in groups of three. Each student takes on the role of talker, questioner or recorder. The talker explains something, or comments on an issue, or expresses opinions. The questioner prompts and seeks clarification. The recorder makes notes and gives a report at the end of the conversation. Another time roles are changed.
- **Envoys** Once groups have carried out a task, one person from each group is selected as an 'envoy' and moves to a new group to explain and summarise, and to find out what the new group thought, decided or achieved. The envoy then returns to the original group and feeds back. This is an effective way of avoiding tedious and repetitive 'reporting back' sessions. It also puts a 'press' on the envoy's use of language and creates groups of active listeners.
- **Snowball** Individuals explore an issue briefly; then pairs discuss the issue or suggest ideas quickly; then double up to fours and continue the process into groups of eight. This allows for comparison of ideas, or to sort out the best, or to agree on a course of action. Finally, the whole class is drawn together and a spokesperson for each group of eight feeds back ideas.
- **Rainbow groups** This is a way of ensuring that students are regrouped and learn to work with a range of others. After small groups have discussed together, students are given a number or colour. Students with the same number or colour join up, making groups comprising representatives of each original group. In their new group, students take turns to report back on their group's work and perhaps begin to work on a new,

combined task.

- **Jigsaw** A topic is divided into sections. In 'home' groups of four or five, students allocate a section each, and then regroup into 'expert' groups. In these groups, they work together on their chosen area, then return to original 'home' groups to report back on their area of expertise. The 'home' group is then set a task that requires the students to use the different areas of 'expertise' for a joint outcome. This requires advance planning, but is a very effective speaking and listening strategy as it ensures the participation of all students.
- **Spokesperson** Each group appoints a spokesperson. The risks of repetition can be avoided if:
  - one group gives a full feedback, and others offer additional points if not covered;
  - each group is asked in turn to offer one new point until every group 'passes';
  - groups are asked to summarise their findings on A3 sheets which are then displayed – the class is invited to compare and comment on them.

From: Literacy in Science, DfES © Crown copyright 2004

Starter and plenary toolkit

Authors have drawn on an varied selection of learning strategies, bringing ideas from lessons they have given or observed themselves, and drawing extensively from the following list:

- **Silent animation** Show students a short video clip without sound and ask them to say what they think is happening. They could either suggest the ideas or do a 'voice over' for it.
- **Ideas hothouse** Ask students to work in pairs to list points about what they know about a particular idea. Then ask the pairs to join together into 4s and then 6–8s to discuss this further and to come up with an agreed list of points. Ask one person from each group to report back to the class.
- **Where's the answer?** As students enter the room, give them a card with a word written on it. Then ask a question, ask them if they think they are the answer and why.
- **What's in the picture?** Have a complex picture such as the water cycle or a photo of an industrial process concealed by rectangles, each of which can be removed in turn. Ask for suggestions as to which tile should be removed and what the partially revealed graphic shows. Encourage speculation and inference; ask for suggestions as to which tile should go next and continue until a full explanation has been produced.
- **Learning triangle** At the end of a lesson ask students to draw a large triangle with a smaller inverted triangle that just fits inside it (so they have four triangles). In the outer three ask them to think back over the lesson and identify (and write in the respective triangles):
  - Something they've seen
  - Something they've done
  - Something they've discussed
  - Then to add in the central triangle: something they've learned
- **Heads and tails** Ask each student to write a question about something from the topic on a coloured paper strip and the answer on another colour. In groups of 6–8, hand out the strips so that each pupil gets a question and an answer. One student reads out their question. The student with the right answer then reads it out, followed by their question.
- **What do I know?** Ask students to each write down one thing about the topic they are sure of, one thing they are unsure of and one thing they need to know more about, being specific. Ask them to work in groups of 5–6 to agree on group lists, ask each group to say what they decided and agree as a class about what they are confident about, what they are less sure of and what things they want to know more about. This is a good way towards the end of a topic of identifying topics for revision.
- **Freeze frame** Ask students to create a 'freeze frame' of an idea in the topic. This involves 3–4 pupils arranging themselves as static image and other pupils to suggest what it represents.
- **The big ideas** Ask students to write down three ideas they learnt during the topic. Then ask them to share their facts in groups and to compile a master list of facts, with the most important at the top. Ask for ideas to be shared and find out which other group(s) agreed.
- **Ask me a question** Ask students to write a question about something from the topic and then a mark scheme for the answer. Encourage them to come up with ones worth more than 1 or 2 marks and to try out their questions on one another.
- **Hot seat** Ask each student to think up a question, using material from the topic. Select someone to put in the hot seat, ask students to ask their question and say at the end whether the answer is correct or incorrect.

Assessment of learning

There is a need for teachers to be able to assess the effectiveness of the learning and, indeed, for students to assess their own progress. This needs to be done for three reasons:

- Teachers need to gauge the effectiveness of a lesson, or sequence of lessons, to judge what the next steps should be.
- Student progress needs to be reported upon, both for accountability purposes but also to inform a whole school perspective on providing challenge and intervention.
- Teachers need to be able to assess whether the design of the lessons was effective for the next time they teach it.

This has, of course, been done previously using a system of levels. When the 2013 Programme of Study was published, it contained no level descriptors and the DfE indicated that it was dropping this calibration of progress. This doesn't mean that schools are not expected to assess progress, use it to plan next steps in learning or report on how individuals are doing. At the time of publication, levels are still being widely used, though this is likely to change as KS2 outcomes move to a new reporting system, GCSE outcomes move to a new set of grades and schools gain confidence in assessing progress.

Trajectories of Progress

Progress in KS3 Science can be represented by Trajectories of Progress based on what individual students need to achieve to be 'making good progress'. The three differentiated outcomes in each lesson plan (and the three coloured levels in the student book) correspond to three model trajectories for lower, average and higher attaining students.

An average student who studies the materials, encounters the ideas, tries the assessment activities and gains 40-70% of the marks is deemed to be progressing well. The materials enable the teacher to gather evidence to this effect, report accordingly and plan subsequent lessons effectively. Students gaining full (or close to full) marks may need additional challenge; those scoring half marks or under may need intervention.

However, schools may be using tracking systems still based on levels and it may be that data from the materials in these resources has to be used to support this. As a rule of thumb, assessment data from the books can be used to inform a levels based system as follows:

	Old NC level	KS3 Book 1	KS3 Book 2	KS3 Book 3	KS4 Yr 10	KS4 Yr 11
Student responses to broad range of assessment evidence, including Applying key ideas activities and end of topic Questions:		10	10	10	10	A*
		9	9	9	9	A
		8	8	8	8	B
		7	7	7	7	C
		6	6	6	6	D
Higher ToP: scores above 70%	5	5	5	5	5	E
Average ToP: scores 40–70%	4	4	4	4	4	F
Lower ToP: scores below 40%	3	3	3	3	3	G

FIGURE 1 Trajectory of Progress (ToP) the Collins Key Stage 3 Science progress tracking system

The Collins KS3 Science scheme has a number of assessment devices available to students and teachers. As well as questions in each spread which will give rise to written and spoken outcomes, there are also:

- **Ideas you have met before** summarises ideas that students will have met previously at the start of each chapter. These provide an opportunity for discussions around prior learning so that the teacher can gauge what is already understood and plan teaching accordingly.
- **Applying key ideas** sections near the centre of each chapter. These provide an opportunity for students and teachers to assess how well key ideas from the earlier part of the topic have been mastered. The Teacher Guide suggests how additional support can be provided if responses are not as good as expected.

Assessment of learning

- **Checking progress** sections at the end of each chapter showing how the key ideas progress. This supports students in assessing their own progress and targeting areas they need to focus on. The teacher could get students to suggest why they've assessed themselves as they have.
- **Questions** at the end of each chapter, with a balance of style and focus. The styles of questions include objective test questions, short written answers and longer responses. The focuses include knowledge & understanding, application and evaluation. This means that responses can be analysed against these criteria as well as against area of content.

Chapter 1: Getting the Energy your Body Needs

1.1 Introduction

When and how to use these pages

The Introduction in the Student Book indicates some of the ideas and skills in this topic area that students will already have met from KS2 or from previous KS3 work, and provides an indication of what they will be studying in this chapter. *Ideas you have met before* is not intended to comprehensively summarise of all the prior ideas, but rather to point out a few of the key ones and to support the view that scientific understanding is progressive. Even though students might be meeting contexts that are new to them, they can often use existing ideas to start to make sense of them.

In this chapter you will find out indicates some of the new ideas that the chapter will introduce. Again, it isn't a detailed summary of content or even an index page. Its purpose is more to act as a 'trailer' and generate some interest.

The outcomes, then, will be recognition of prior learning that can be built on, and interest in finding out more.

There are a number of ways this can be used. You might, for example:

- Use *Ideas you have met before* as the basis for a revision lesson as you start the first new topic.
- Use *Ideas you have met before* as the centre of spider diagrams, to which students can add examples, experiments they might have done previously or what they found interesting.
- Make a note of any unfamiliar/difficult terms and return to these in the relevant lessons.
- Use *In this chapter you will find out* to ask students questions such as:
  - Why is this important?
  - How could it be used?
  - What might we be doing in this topic?

Overview of the chapter

In this chapter, students will learn about the ways in which we generate the energy that we need to move. Students learn about aerobic respiration and how it relies on breathing to provide oxygen, and digestion to provide glucose as a reactant. They will learn that the process takes place in mitochondria and consider how these organelles are adapted to this function – the students will also learn about anaerobic respiration. The reactants and products of each type of respiration will be compared as well as the amount of energy released in each process. Students will learn about situations where each type of respiration takes place. The roles of the skeleton and muscles will be explored. Students will learn how movement is brought about at joints by muscles working in pairs. Different types of joint will be considered, as well as the consequences when things go wrong with the skeletal system.

This chapter offers a number of opportunities for students to plan investigations and to analyse data – this includes the analysis of both primary and secondary data. Students are encouraged to develop scientific explanations – for example to explain how a chosen factor affects anaerobic respiration.

Obstacles to learning

Students may need extra guidance with overcoming the following common misconceptions:

- **Movement** All joints allow movement. Muscles can push as well as pull.
- **Respiration** Respiration is the same as breathing. Plants don't respire – they only photosynthesise. Energy is 'made' during respiration, just like another product of the reaction. Anaerobic respiration doesn't release any energy. Anaerobic respiration only takes place when you hold your breath.
- **Reactions** During reactions, new products are made that may not contain the same atoms as any of the reactants.
- **Microbes** All microbes cause disease. Microbes cannot make useful products.

Chapter 1: Getting the Energy your Body Needs

	Topic title:	Overarching objectives:
2	Exploring the human skeleton	The structure and functions of the human skeleton, to include support, protection, movement and making blood cells
3	Analysing the skeleton	The structure and functions of the human skeleton, to include support, protection, movement and making blood cells
4	Understanding the role of skeletal joints	Biomechanics – the interaction between skeleton and muscles, including the measurement of force exerted by different muscles
5	Investigating muscle strength	Biomechanics – the interaction between skeleton and muscles, including the measurement of force exerted by different muscles
6	Analysing muscle strength	Biomechanics – the interaction between skeleton and muscles, including the measurement of force exerted by different muscles
7	Examining interacting muscles	The function of muscles and examples of antagonistic muscles
8	Exploring problems with the skeletal system	The structure and functions of the human skeleton, to include support, protection, movement and making blood cells Biomechanics – the interaction between skeleton and muscles, including the measurement of force exerted by different muscles
10	Understanding how muscles get energy	Aerobic and anaerobic respiration in living organisms, including the breakdown of organic molecules to enable all the other chemical processes necessary for life The word equation for aerobic respiration
11	Investigating respiration	Aerobic and anaerobic respiration in living organisms, including the breakdown of organic molecules to enable all the other chemical processes necessary for life The word equation for aerobic respiration
12	Analysing adaptations for respiration	Aerobic and anaerobic respiration in living organisms, including the breakdown of organic molecules to enable all the other chemical processes necessary for life
13	Examining links between respiration and body systems	Aerobic and anaerobic respiration in living organisms, including the breakdown of organic molecules to enable all the other chemical processes necessary for life
14	Exploring respiration in sport	Aerobic and anaerobic respiration in living organisms, including the breakdown of organic molecules to enable all the other chemical processes necessary for life
15	Understanding anaerobic respiration	The process of anaerobic respiration in humans and micro-organisms, including fermentation, and the word equation for anaerobic respiration
16	Investigating fermentation	The process of anaerobic respiration in humans and micro-organisms, including fermentation, and the word equation for anaerobic respiration
17	Comparing aerobic and anaerobic respiration	The differences between aerobic and anaerobic respiration in terms of the reactants, the products formed and the implications for the organism

Chapter 1: Getting the Energy your Body Needs

1.2 Exploring the human skeleton

Lesson overview

Learning objectives

- Identify bones of the human skeleton.
- Explain why we have different shapes and sizes of bones.
- Communicate effectively to investigate the structure and function of bones.

Learning outcomes

- Describe some examples of bones with different shapes and different roles. [O1]
- Share ideas to describe examples of bones with different roles and describe observations of the effect of acid on bones. [O2]
- Work effectively in a group to learn about the structure and function of bones and make a conclusion about the effect of acid on bones. [O3]

Skills development

- Thinking scientifically: ask questions
- Working scientifically: make predictions
- Learner development: communicate effectively

Resources needed skeleton model; information about structure and function of bones; clean, cooked chicken bones (e.g. leg bones); vinegar; 500 ml glass beaker; bones pre-soaked for 3–4 days in vinegar; Worksheet 2.1.2

Digital resources Quick starter; Interactive activity: drag the bones to the correct part of the body; Slideshow: An introduction to the human skeleton, its evolution and uniqueness

Common misconceptions All bones in the human skeleton have the same role.

Key vocabulary bones, skeleton, calcium, marrow

Teaching and learning

Engage

- Display a model of a skeleton without any discussion or explanation. Challenge the students to **estimate** the number of bones in the human body. Record some of their estimates for use later in the lesson. [O1]

Challenge and develop

- Use the skeleton model to demonstrate the different shapes and positions of the bones in the human body. [O1]
- The students **answer** verbal questions to establish the roles of some of these bones – for example the bones in the legs for support, the bones in the arms and the backbone for movement, the bones in the skull for protection. [O2]
- Ask the students to choose some words to **describe** how bones vary – such as size, length and shape. [O1]
- Students could name the parts of the skeleton in task 1 of Worksheet 2.1.2. [O1]
- Return to the estimates of the number of bones and tell the students that there are 206 bones in the human skeleton. Ask the students to **suggest** why it is very difficult to count all the bones and explain that some tiny bones are found inside the ear. [O1]

Chapter 1: Getting the Energy your Body Needs

Explain

- **Jigsaw activity** Arrange the students in groups of four to **learn** about the structures of different bones. Assign individual students a number between 1 and 4 linking them to the topics listed in task 2 (1 structure of bones; 2 how bones grow; 3 bones of the head; bones of the back 4). [O1&2]

    Differentiation can be achieved by assigning lower-attaining students topics 1 or 2.

- The groups should then split into 'expert groups' made up of students having the same topic number across the class. Provide each new group with relevant information containing both text and illustrations. Allow them 10 minutes to **assimilate** information and to **write** notes using only 10 words, supported by diagrams. Groups could be given access to the skeleton model at this stage. [O1, 2&3]

- The original groups re-form and each student spends two minutes **teaching** their group what they have learned. The rest of the group should **complete** Worksheet 2.1.2 as a summary of the work. [O1, 2&3]

Consolidate and apply

- Show the students some clean, cooked chicken bones. Allow them to feel the bones and ask them to **describe** the bones. Put the bones in a beaker of vinegar. Ask the students to **predict** what will happen to the bones. [O1&3]

- Leave the bones for 3 to 4 days before examining them or, preferably, have some bones pre-soaked in vinegar. Wash the bones and ask the students to **examine** and **describe** how the bones have changed. [O1&3]

- Tell the students that acids dissolve calcium. Ask them to **think** of an explanation as to why the bones became bendy and then to **discuss** this with a partner. Share ideas across the class, giving more clues if necessary. [O1&3]

Extend

- Ask students able to progress further to **design an investigation** linked to the effect of acids on bone. If they choose a question that can be investigated (such as how the length of the bone or the length of time affects how bendy it becomes), they could do the investigation at home. [O3]

Plenary suggestions

Sharing facts Ask the students to work individually to write down facts that they have learned today. Choose students at random to **share** one fact with the rest of the class – each must share a different fact. Encourage others to **correct** any misconceptions. [O1, 2&3]

Answers to Student Book questions

1. a) cranium b) clavicle c) scapula d) ulna
2. some of the bones are too small to show; others are hidden, such as bones in the ear
3. The backbone is made up of individual bones called vertebrae.
4. a) calcium b) milk, cheese etc.
5. to prevent them breaking easily
6. it makes bones lighter than if they were solid
7. a) long and wide; gives strength to support the body weight
    b) many small bones with joints; allows the hand to bend in different directions
    c) curved; to protect lungs inside the chest cavity
8. a) not symmetrical; unlike other bones
    b) allows vertebrae to fit together; but still move

Answers to Worksheet 2.1.2

1. A: skull (cranium); B: jaw; C: collarbone (clavicle); D: shoulder blade (scapula); E: breastbone (sternum); F: ribs; G: humerus; H: backbone (vertebrae); I: radius; J: ulna; K: pelvis; L: femur; M: tibia; N: fibula
2. A summary of some of the key points provided by the group work exercise.
3. a) without calcium, bones become bendy
    b) bones contain calcium; if there is not enough calcium in the blood, it is taken from the bones

Chapter 1: Getting the Energy your Body Needs

1.3 Analysing the skeleton

Lesson overview

Learning objectives

- Describe the roles of the skeleton.
- Explain the evidence for each of the roles of the skeleton.
- Estimate height using bone-measurement calculations and suggest reasons for differences between people.

Learning outcomes

- Describe most roles of the skeleton and give evidence for some of these. [O1]
- Describe the roles of the skeleton giving evidence for each role; make simple comparisons of body measurements. [O2]
- Explain the roles of the skeleton; calculate accurate proportions of body measurements and suggest reasons for differences between people. [O3]

Skills development

- Thinking scientifically: use units and nomenclature
- Working scientifically: interpret evidence
- Learner development: respect others

Resources needed skeleton model; beef bone, cut to show the marrow; glass rod; tape measures or metre rules; graph paper; a model femur (or a length of wood to represent a femur); calculators; Worksheet 2.1.3; Practical sheet 2.1.3; Technician's notes 2.1.3

Digital resources Quick starter; Interactive activity: drag the functions to the correct bone(s); Video

Key vocabulary support, protect, blood cells, joint, cartilage

Teaching and learning

Engage

- Display the skeleton model. Tell the students that there are four main roles of the skeleton – ask them to work in groups of four to **identify** the four roles. [O1]
- Ask the students to **give feedback** on their ideas about the roles of the skeleton one group at a time; build a list of suggestions. [O1]

Challenge and develop

- Demonstrate a cut beef bone, showing the marrow in the centre. Explain that marrow is where red and white blood cells are made. Ask the students to add to the list of roles of the skeleton, if necessary. Agree on the roles of the skeleton across the class. [O1]
- **Group work** Ask groups of students to **find evidence** for each of the roles (using the first section of the Student Book). Encourage students to **share** the task and for each to take on a specific role. Each group then **explains** the evidence in writing. Worksheet 2.1.3 task 1 could support this. [O2]

Explain

- Ask the students to **consider** the role of the skeleton in movement. Ask them to **suggest** how our skeleton helps us to balance. Draw out the idea that the proportions of the bones and the symmetry of the skeleton help us to maintain balance. [O1]
- Arrange the students in pairs and ask them to **measure** some bones and to **calculate** predicted heights using Practical sheet 2.1.3. [O3]

Chapter 1: Getting the Energy your Body Needs

- Students **draw graphs** to **compare** the predictions given by each of the measurements to their actual height. [O3]
- Ask the students to **evaluate** each of the methods used to predict height and to **suggest** any factors that may affect the accuracy of the predictions. [O3]

Consolidate and apply

- **Group work** Tell the students that the police have found a femur and a humerus. They need to estimate the height of the victim to help in making an identification. Ask the students to **agree** in their group which bone should be used to estimate height. [O3]
- Take a vote on the method to use and choose groups on each side to **explain** their reasoning. [O3]

Extend

- Ask students able to progress further to develop another way of predicting height, based on a different skeleton measurement. They should work out what the measurement should be multiplied by when estimating the height. [O3]

Plenary suggestions

Learning triangle The students work individually to construct a learning triangle. They should draw a large triangle with a smaller inverted triangle that just fits inside (making four triangles). In the outer triangles, the students write:

- something they've seen
- something they've done
- something they've discussed.

Then, in the central triangle, they write something they've learned. [O1, 2&3]

Answers to Student Book questions

1. support the body; protect organs; allow movement; produce blood cells
2. a) lungs   b) brain
3. knee, elbow, shoulder, etc.
4. carrying oxygen
5. transferring living tissue from one person to another
6. 65.91 cm
7. 65.91 cm
8. because these people are growing quickly

Answers to Worksheet 2.1.3

1. a) iii) b) iv) c) i) d) ii)
2. a) lack of oxygen; may be tired; short of breath
   b) unable to fight infection; get ill more often than normal
   c) blood unable to clot well; carry on bleeding if cut
3. a) outside
   b) inside
   c) for example 'exothermic'; with definition(s)
   d) for example 'endothermic' with definition(s)

Chapter 1: Getting the Energy your Body Needs

1.4 Understanding the role of skeletal joints

Lesson overview

Learning objectives

- Describe the roles of tendons, ligaments, joints and muscles.
- Compare different joints in the human skeleton.
- Collaborate effectively to interpret how we use joints.

Learning outcomes

- Describe the role of tendons, ligaments, muscles and joints with help; recall that there are different types of joints. [O1]
- Describe and explain the role of tendons, ligaments, muscles; recall different joint types and identify some uses of joints. [O2]
- Analyse the roles of tendons, ligaments, muscles and compare the movement allowed by different joints. [O3]

Skills development

- Thinking scientifically: ask questions
- Working scientifically: n/a
- Learner development: collaborate effectively

Resources needed model of skeleton; chicken leg quarter (uncooked with skin in place); scalpel; sharp scissors; plastic gloves; disinfectant; dissection board; camera; Worksheet 2.1.4; Practical sheet 2.1.4; Technician's notes 2.1.4

Digital resources Quick starter; Interactive activity: Drag the example of joints to the correct group; Slideshow: Introduction to the joints of the thumb, as new born baby and the pelvis; Hangman: Key vocabulary game

Common misconceptions The skull is one complete bone with no joints. Joints always allow movement.

Key vocabulary ligament, muscle, tendon

Teaching and learning

Engage

- Explain that many animals have skeletal systems similar to humans. For example, a chicken leg is similar to one of ours because it also has a femur, tibia and fibula and a joint at the knee.
- Explain that a human leg is very much like a chicken leg in structure. Both have a femur, knee, fibula and tibia. They also both have other tissues such as ligaments, tendons, muscles and fat.
- Dissect a raw chicken leg (instructions provided in Technician's notes 2.1.4) – the students could take photos/videos of this. Demonstrate the presence of muscle, cartilage, tendons, ligaments and a joint. Encourage the students to **discuss** the function of each tissue during the demonstration. [O1]

Challenge and develop

- Ask the students to read the second section of the Student Book and **make notes**. Ask them to **consider** the movement that each type of joint allows. [O2&3]
- **Pair talk** Ask the students to work with a partner to **compare** notes, **discuss** any differences and **amend** their own notes as necessary. [O2&3]

Explain

- The students work in pairs to **match up** types of joints, the movement that they allow and give one example for each – they could use task 2 of Worksheet 2.1.4. [O3]

Chapter 1: Getting the Energy your Body Needs

- Ask the students to **consider** other joints in the body. A skeleton model may be useful during this activity. They should group these joints into the correct joint category. [O2&3]
- **Pairs to fours** Student pairs can join to form fours and then **share** the examples of joints that they have grouped. [O2&3]

Consolidate and apply

- **Charades** The students play a class game of charades – ask a volunteer to come to the front and then whisper an activity to **act out**. Alternatively these activities could be written on cards for students to choose at random. (Examples include throwing a football, dribbling a basketball, doing press-ups, hopping on one leg, skipping, doing star jumps, kicking a football, swimming breaststroke.) [O3]
- The other students guess what the activity is and write down the answer. They then **identify** at least three bones and two joints involved in the activity. [O3]

Extend

- Encourage students able to progress further to **consider** the interaction between the skeletal system and other parts of the body. For example:
  - How do the skeletal system and the muscles depend on each other?
  - How do the bones and the blood depend on each other?
  - How do the skeletal system and the breathing system depend on each other?

Plenary suggestions

Questions and answers Arrange the students in groups of four. Ask each group to **devise** a question for another group. Groups pair up and take turns to **answer** the planned questions. Ask the students to **give feedback** about any good questions that they heard. [O1, 2&3]

You can differentiate by specifying the number of marks the question should be worth for different groups.

Answers to Student Book questions

1. *ligaments*: attach bone to bone; *tendons*: attach muscles to bones
2. to allow muscles to contract
3. accelerating/ decelerating quickly; changing direction quickly; landing hard/ awkwardly
4. fixed; pivot; hinge; ball and socket
5. a) ball and socket   b) hinge
6. table should show: ball and socket allowing forward, backward, circular; hinge allowing backward and forward movement; pivot allowing movement around a point
7. a) knee, ankle, foot   b) thumb, wrist, hand   c) elbow, shoulder, wrist
8. you utilise the nervous system/ nerves

Answers to Worksheet 2.1.4

1. A: bone; B: cartilage; C: synovial fluid; D: ligament
2. a) with iii); e.g. hip, shoulder   b) with ii); e.g. elbow, knee   c) with i); e.g. neck;   d) with iv); e.g. skull
3. a) *Tendons* attach bones to muscles; as the muscle contracts, the bone moves. We could not move without tendons.
   b) *Ligaments* attach bone to bone; joints would be loose without ligaments. Without them our movements would be less well controlled.
   c) *Cartilage* protects the ends of bones; stops them rubbing together. Without it movement would be painful and bones would wear out.

Chapter 1: Getting the Energy your Body Needs

1.5 Investigating muscle strength

Lesson overview

Learning objectives

- Identify muscles used in different activities.
- Plan an investigation to compare the strengths of different muscles.
- Make a prediction about which muscles are stronger than others.

Learning outcomes

- Carry out an investigation to compare muscle strength and identify the muscles used in some simple movements. [O1]
- Plan and carry out an investigation to compare muscle strength and identify muscles used in some complex movements. [O2]
- Make a prediction about which muscles are strongest, and plan and carry out a fair test of the prediction. [O3]

Skills development

- Thinking scientifically: consider the quality of evidence
- Working scientifically: make predictions
- Learner development: collaborate effectively

Resources needed simple fitness equipment such as steps, hand weights, handgrip strengtheners, etc. for students to choose from; stopclocks; Worksheet 2.1.5; Practical sheet 2.1.5; Technician's notes 2.1.5

Digital resources Quick starter; Interactive activity: Order the muscles of the human body, from head to toe; Interactive activity: Match the actions to the muscles involved

Common misconceptions Muscles 'pull'. Muscles contract and then stretch, rather than contracting and then relaxing.

Key vocabulary contracted, relaxed, force, newton

Teaching and learning

Engage

- Ask the students to **think** about where their muscles are – they then **share** their ideas in pairs. Encourage feedback. [O1]
- Reinforce that we have muscles all over our bodies. Ask the students to **recall** what attaches muscles to bones. [O1]

Challenge and develop

- Carry out a simple class activity (such as writing on the whiteboard or picking up a drink) and ask the students to **describe** the muscles they are using. Encourage the students to use scientific names where possible. [O1]
- Ask the students to work individually to **identify** the muscles used during a range of activities (they could use task 2 of Worksheet 2.1.5). They then **compare** their answers with a partner and **discuss** any differences. [O1]

Explain

- Use volunteers to demonstrate some simple fitness equipment as an introduction to **developing a plan**. For example step-ups, grip strengtheners, bicep curls using a small hand weight, calf-raises holding on to a desk for support.

Chapter 1: Getting the Energy your Body Needs

- **Group talk** Arrange the students in groups of three. Ask them to **brainstorm** ideas about how they could compare the strength of different muscles. Either collect feedback across the class or visit each group in turn to listen to their ideas. Some suitable ideas are to compare the strength of left- and right-calf muscles by counting how many calf-raises per minute on each leg are possible, or comparing the strengths of right- and left-hand muscles by timing how long they can squeeze a handgrip-strengthener for. [O2]
- The groups then **plan** their investigation, **considering** variables and making a **prediction**. The students could use Practical sheet 2.1.5. Assess the safety and suitability of each procedure. [O2&3]
- The students **carry out** their investigation and **record** the results. [O2]

Consolidate and apply

- Ask the groups to **summarise** what their investigation showed, in one sentence. The groups **share** this with the rest of the class. During the next lesson, they will have an opportunity to evaluate the investigation. If this 'next lesson' will not be delivered, they could **evaluate** their own investigation now. [O2&3]

Extend

For students able to progress further:

- Ask them to **research** how muscle strength is measured accurately in sportspeople.
- Ask them to **consider** some different methods, such as testing the strength of the muscle directly, testing how quickly the muscles tire and testing agility.

Plenary suggestions

Thinking up ideas Allocate each group one muscle referred to during the lesson. Ask them to **identify** an activity that uses that muscle that has not already been mentioned during the lesson. Encourage them to **devise** an exercise to train that specific muscle. [O1&2]

Answers to Student Book questions

1. cardiac – heart; smooth – other body organs; skeletal – bicep
2. bicep, tricep, forearm
3. muscles contract, pull on a tendon, and move a bone
4. *contracted muscle*: shorter; fatter
5. the calf muscle contracts, pulls on a tendon attached to a bone in the heel and lifts the heel
6. quadriceps; calf; abdominal; bicep; forearm
7. both; squeeze the handgrip strength tester as hard as possible; compare the force of each; higher force indicates stronger muscles
8. basketball player; uses arm muscles more than a footballer
9. sensible suggestion such as measuring the size of mass that can be lifted using the thighs

Answers to Worksheet 2.1.5

1. A: jaw muscles; B: shoulder muscles; C: pectoral muscles; D: bicep; E: tricep; F: forearm muscles; G: abdominal muscles; H: quadriceps; I: calf muscles
2. a) calf; quadriceps b) forearm c) face; tongue d) forearms; biceps; triceps
3. a) swimming; you use arm muscles more; using these muscles strengthens them
   b) it depends on the type of training that they do; there may be a genetic factor

Chapter 1: Getting the Energy your Body Needs

1.6 Analysing muscle strength

Lesson overview

Learning objectives

- Display data in a suitable graph.
- Analyse data to draw conclusions about muscles.
- Explore the use of scientific ideas in identifying and treating muscle conditions.

Learning outcomes

- Use data to reach a simple conclusion about muscle strength. [O1]
- Draw and analyse a graph of muscle strength data. [O2]
- Select a way of displaying muscle strength data independently, analyse it and evaluate the investigation. [O3]

Skills development

- Thinking scientifically: analyse data
- Working scientifically: record evidence
- Learner development: plan progress

Resources graph paper; scissors; glue; Worksheet 2.1.6a (copied onto card) and Worksheet 2.1.6b

Digital resources Quick starter; Slideshow: A look at steroids and their side effects; Video

Key vocabulary electromyography (EMG), anabolic steroid

Teaching and learning

Engage

- Give the students cards made from Worksheet 2.1.6a. Alternatively, they cut out the descriptions before starting. They work in small groups to **sort** the six people into rank order from most strong to least strong. Emphasise that the students may rank people as equally strong. [O1]
- Ask the students to **record** their solution by sticking their descriptions on plain paper. [O1]

Challenge and develop

- Ask the students to look at the first section of this topic in the Student Book. Ask them to **discuss** in pairs how the results in Table 2.1.6 could be displayed on a graph. [O2]
- The students work individually to **draw a graph** of the data. [O2]
- Ask them to **answer** questions 1–3 in the Student Book. [O1&2]
- If they have their own data from the previous lesson, they could also **display** this as a graph. [O2]
- Students work in pairs to **devise** another question linked with this data – they test this question on another pair. Collect feedback across the class on what made a question a good one. [O1&2]
- Ask the students to **reflect on** the solutions to the 'Engage' activity. Did their ideas agree with the data? [O1]

Explain

- **Group work** Arrange the students in the same groups as in the previous lesson where they tested muscle strength. If they did not carry out the investigation, arrange them in groups of three. Groups should select a recorder, a presenter and a chairman for their group. Ask the students to **evaluate** the investigation that they carried out into muscle strength. They should **consider** whether results were accurate, whether the investigation was fair, whether the conclusion was valid and how the investigation could be improved. They should record their ideas in a report. [O3]

Chapter 1: Getting the Energy your Body Needs

- Alternatively, for those students who did not carry out the investigation, they could **describe** an investigation into muscle strength, demonstrating how it would be carried out if possible. (You could use Worksheet 2.1.6b as an example.) Students then **evaluate** this investigation. [O3]
- Each group **shares** their report verbally with the class. [O3]

Consolidate and apply

- Ask the students to **imagine** that a volunteer was tested for hand and arm strength, and the results suggested that the volunteer had very weak muscles. The volunteer did not believe the result and thought that the test was not carried out properly – ask the students to **write** a reply for the volunteer. [O2&3]
- Read the information about electromyography in the second section of the Student Book as a class. Ask the students to **role-play** in their groups. One student should be the volunteer, who believes that the test was not carried out properly, and another should be the strength tester who is confident that the test was carried out accurately and fairly. [O2&3]

Extend

- Ask students able to progress further to **consider** why males generally have stronger muscles, and why strength decreases with age, particularly in men. They could follow up their ideas with **research**. [O3]

Plenary suggestions

Giving advice Each group should **develop** a piece of advice for the male and the female who have the lowest muscle strength from the sorting activity done at the start of the lesson. [O1]

Answers to Student Book questions

1. a suitable bar chart of muscle strength for each patient
2. yes (but it's a small sample)
3. no
4. checking if muscles are receiving electrical impulses and are contracting
5. the results would be similar if they were reliable
6. muscle tear will heal
7. steroids increase muscle mass, increase strength and improve performance
8. healthy diet; refrain from drug use

Answers to Worksheet 2.1.6b

1. a) Ali
   b) Daniel
   c) affected by factors such as how much training they have done, how tired they are, whether they are injured or not.
2. a) repeat the investigation and compare the results
   b) use masses with smaller differences between them
   c) subjects could injure themselves by lifting weights that are too heavy
3. a) Information should include the fact that steroids are taken because they increase muscle mass and increase strength.
   b) however, they cause problems such as heart failure and infertility

Chapter 1: Getting the Energy your Body Needs

1.7 Examining interacting muscles

Lesson overview

Learning objectives

- Describe antagonistic muscles and give examples.
- Explain how antagonistic muscles bring about movement.
- Evaluate a model of antagonistic muscles.

Learning outcomes

- Describe how muscles work in pairs and make a simple model. [O1]
- Describe what antagonistic muscles are; give some examples and a simple explanation of how they bring about movement. [O2]
- Explain clearly how antagonistic muscles bring about movement; evaluate a model of antagonistic muscles. [O3]

Skills development

- Thinking scientifically: ask questions
- Working scientifically: evaluate data
- Learner development: develop resilience

Resources needed cardboard; long rubber bands; sharp pencils; scissors; rulers; Plasticine; paper fasteners; sticky notes; Worksheet 2.1.7; Practical sheet 2.1.7 (second page copied onto card); Technician's notes 2.1.7

Digital resources Quick starter; Interactive activity: Match the muscles that work together in pairs

Common misconceptions One muscle of a pair pulls, and the other pushes. Muscles that work on their own can pull and push.

Key vocabulary antagonistic muscles, bicep, tricep, quadricep

Teaching and learning

Engage

- Ask the students to put a hand around their own bicep and tricep. Now ask them to bend and straighten their arm at the elbow. Ask the students to **describe** what they notice. [O2]
- Ask them to feel the quadricep muscle (at the front of their thigh) and the hamstring muscle (at the back of their thigh) as they bend and straighten their leg at the knee. [O2]
- Now ask them to feel the calf muscle (at the back of their lower leg) and the shin muscle (at the front of their lower leg) as they bend and flex the foot at the ankle. [O2]
- Ask the students to **discuss** what they notice about muscles with each of these movements. Collect class feedback. [O2]
- Explain that muscles that work together are called antagonistic muscles. Ask the students to **list** the antagonistic muscles from the activity they did. [O1]
- The students work in pairs to **explore** briefly any other antagonistic muscles. Tell the students that most of our skeletal muscles work in pairs. [O1]

Challenge and develop

- Ask the students to **think** individually about what would happen if we did not have paired muscles for the bicep, quadricep or calf muscles. They then **share** their ideas with a partner. Take feedback across the class and draw out the idea of needing antagonistic muscles to move bones in both directions. [O1&2]

Chapter 1: Getting the Energy your Body Needs

- The students work individually to **make a model** of the arm from card and rubber bands, using the template on Practical sheet 2.1.7. [O2]
- Ask the students to **explore** their model to ensure that they understand how movement is brought about at the elbow. Using sticky notes, the students work in pairs to **write** the steps involved in causing the muscles of the arm to bend at the elbow and then straighten. It may help if each stage is written on a separate sticky note. The students then **arrange** these notes into a logical order. [O2]

Explain

- Ask the students to **suggest** why scientists use models. Give other examples of models that they have come across to stimulate the discussion. For example, ball models of particles in solids, liquids and gases; bell-jar and balloon model of the lungs; modeling-clay or bead models of molecules digested by enzymes. [O3]
- **Pairs to fours** Ask the students to work in pairs to **evaluate** the model of the arm. Give an example of what makes a model good – such as being representative of what happens in the real world. Give an example of what makes a model bad – such as not being representative of what happens in the real world. [O3]
- Pairs then form fours and they **share** their ideas. As a group, they **list** the good and bad features of the model and **suggest** any improvements. [O3]
- Ask each group to **share** one idea. Repeat these across the class with each group giving a different idea until there are no more new ideas to share. [O3]
- The students could use Worksheet 2.1.7 here in preparation for the extended writing task. [O1, 2&3]

Consolidate and apply

- Ask the students to work individually to produce an extended piece of writing to **explain** the importance of antagonistic muscles. Provide the students with key words to include in the writing – such as 'antagonistic', 'contract', 'relax', 'joint'. [O1&2]

  Include some new words for higher-attaining students – ones that they need to find the definition of first, such as 'agonist', 'flexor', 'extensor'.

Extend

- Ask students able to progress further to **explore** some movements, suggesting where the antagonistic muscles that control the movement are found. Encourage them to explore tiny movements as well as more obvious larger ones. [O1&2]

Plenary suggestions

What have we learned? Ask groups of four to **agree** and **list** three things that they have learned about muscles during this topic. Display the lists while groups **share** their feedback. Compile and display a master list using ideas from all groups. [O1, 2&3]

Answers to Student Book questions

1. bicep and tricep; quadriceps and hamstring; calf and shin
2. bicep contracts, tricep relaxes, arm bends; tricep contracts, bicep relaxes, arm straightens
3. We need antagonistic muscles to move bones back to their original position.
4. muscles
5. *good*: rubber bands show how muscles contract and relax; *poor*: shoulder joint is fixed in the body but not in the model
6. use thicker rubber band; or more rubber bands
7. a) muscle at front of neck feels harder as it contracts   b) muscle at back of neck feels harder as it contracts
8. yes or no; with a suitable explanation

Answers to Worksheet 2.1.7

1. a) antagonistic   b) tendons; joint   c) bicep; tricep   d) contracts; relaxes
2. a) a with ii); b with iii); c with i)   b) front of the neck   c) back of the neck
3. a) Ideas such as the muscles contract and pull to bend the fingers, just as the string pulls to bend the fingers in the model; the fingers bend at joints just as the fingers on the model bend where the tape is added.
   b) Ideas such as the model do not show the other muscles of the antagonistic pair that straighten the fingers; the strings do not shorten and fatten as muscles in the hand do.

Chapter 1: Getting the Energy your Body Needs

1.8 Exploring problems with the skeletal system

Lesson overview

Learning objectives

- Recall some medical problems with the skeletal system.
- Describe treatments for some skeletal system problems.
- Communicate effectively to learn how treatments have changed over time.

Learning outcomes

- Describe some medical problems in different parts of the skeletal system. [O1]
- Research and describe treatments for problems with the skeletal system. [O2]
- Research and describe how treatments for some skeletal system problems have changed over time. [O3]

Skills development

- Thinking scientifically: understand how theories develop
- Working scientifically: n/a
- Learner development: communicate effectively

Resources needed information on skeletal system problems; science (or medical) dictionaries; Worksheet 2.1.8

Digital resources Quick starter; Interactive activity: Match the picture to the type of broken bone; Slideshow: A look at osteoporosis; Hangman: Key vocabulary game

Key vocabulary skeletal system, fracture, osteoporosis, arthritis

Teaching and learning

Engage

- Show pictures of some skeletal problems but with no explanation. These could be shown as a rolling presentation, as web-based images or as paper images. The images could include an X-ray of a broken bone, a fractured limb in plaster, an artificial hip used for replacement, an illustration of joint to show cartilage worn away (as in arthritis), a curved-spine X-ray of scoliosis, a photo of a muscular dystrophy sufferer in a wheelchair, bruising from a muscle tear, etc. The students try to **work out** what the lesson is about. [O1]
- Ask the students to **share** their ideas, asking others to comment on these without saying whether a guess is correct or not. [O1]
- Return to each image when the theme of the lesson has been established and ask the students to **comment** on the significance of each image. [O1]

Challenge and develop

- **Pair work** Provide pairs of students with a list of problems linked with the skeletal system (you could use the list in Worksheet 2.1.8). Ask them to **sort** the problems into 'problems related to bones', 'problems related to muscles' and 'other problems'. [O1&2]

Explain

- **Group work** Arrange the students in groups of four. Give each member of each group a topic to **research** – for example 'fractures', 'arthritis', 'osteoporosis' and 'muscular dystrophy'. [O2]

    You could differentiate by assigning a lower-attaining group the fracture topic.

- Provide each group with information in textbooks (such as the Student Book) or from the internet. Ask each group to **assimilate** the information and to **summarise** in notes. Remind them to **research** the cause of the problem, its treatment and how the treatment has changed over time. [O1, 2&3]

Key Stage 3 Science Teacher Pack 2

Chapter 1: Getting the Energy your Body Needs

- Approximately halfway through the research task, ask each group to **nominate** one team member to become a 'spy'. The spy visits other groups researching the same topic and looks for good practice and ideas to take back to their own team. They return and **share** what they have seen. [O1, 2&3]
- **Envoys** At the end of the research time (approximately 10–15 minutes depending on the lesson length), each team nominates a different team member to become an 'envoy'. The envoy moves to a group researching a different topic and **teaches** that group what they have learned. [O1, 2&3]
- The envoys return to their original group and the rest of the group **teach** the envoy what they learned from the visiting envoy. If time allows, another envoy could be selected to teach a different group. [O1, 2&3]

Consolidate and apply

- Ask the students to work in their groups to produce an information leaflet to be displayed in a doctor's waiting room. The aim of the leaflet is to inform patients about their skeletal system disorder and also to explain the treatment possibilities. Each group should focus on their research topic. [O1, 2&3]

Extend

- Ask students able to progress further to **create** a loop card game based on skeletal system problems. Encourage them to include questions and answers related to all the topics researched during the lesson. If time allows, test the loop card game with the class. [O1, 2&3]

Plenary suggestions

Mind map Ask the students to work in pairs to produce a mind map/concept map linked to the skeletal system. Encourage them to **refer back** to work completed earlier in this topic for prompts about what to include.

Answers to Student Book questions

1. by (large) impacts
2. using plaster of Paris and/or pins
3. there is a higher risk of infection
4. the density of bones decreases; and they become weaker
5. bones rub togethe
6. it mimics a ball and socket joint
7. more precise X-rays; improved surgery; increased knowledge of avoiding damage
8. scientists are learning more about all areas, including genetics

Answers to Worksheet 2.1.8

1. a) osteoporosis, arthritis, fracture, scoliosis
   b) torn muscle, muscular dystrophy
   c) tendonitis, torn ligament
2. a summary of the ideas shared during the group task, as guided by materials provided
3. a) *joint replacements* to replace damaged or diseased joints; *X-rays* to examine bones; *genetic screening* to estimate possibility of inheriting or passing on a genetic condition
   b) ideas about how each has improved; with examples from research
   c) all likely to improve, as science understanding and technology improve

Chapter 1: Getting the Energy your Body Needs

1.9 Applying key ideas

The bare bones of space travel

Objectives

- Extract ideas about the skeleton and muscles from the text, including earlier sections of the topic.
- Apply ideas about maintaining muscle and bone mass in relation to the effects of space travel.
- Suggest how an understanding of the effects of space on the skeleton can be applied on Earth.

Outcome

- Making clear and effective responses to questions, indicating understanding and the next steps in learning.

The purpose of this activity is to provide an opportunity to see how successfully students are grasping the key ideas so far. It is not designed to be used as a formal test – it might be that students work on the questions collectively. It does provide an opportunity for you to look at written work, engage students in discussions and form ideas about progress being made.

The tasks are progressive. Lower-attaining students should be able to tackle the first two or three and higher-attaining students will find the later ones more challenging.

Resources needed large sheets of paper and pens; small hand weights or other resistance equipment (e.g. exercise bands); Worksheet 2.1.9

Teaching and learning

Engage

- Challenge the students to think back over the last few lessons to **identify** some of the key ideas they have met. Draw out some responses about these ideas and say that it is important as learners that they develop a sense of their own progress.

- Show a web-based video clip of astronauts exercising in space. Ask the students to **discuss** why astronauts may do this.

- Ask them if they have ever broken a limb. Collect feedback from those who have been injured about how the limb changed as it was healing. Next ask all the students to **suggest** how the limb could be increased in strength again. You could give out hand weights or other resistance equipment as a stimulus here.

Challenge and develop

- Arrange the students in pairs or groups of three. Ask each group to draw a spider diagram with 'musculoskeletal system' at the centre. If necessary, support the students in interpreting what this phrase means. Encourage them to **refer back** to the Student Book and/or notes from previous lessons.

Explain

Ask the students to read the passage 'The bare bones of space travel' in the Student Book. Depending on their ability to assimilate text, you may need to adopt strategies such as:

- Having students working in pairs, with copies of the text (available on Worksheet 2.1.9) and highlighters. One student **highlights** key ideas and the other (with a different colour) any words they do not understand.

- Work with a group of students who have difficulty with reading to support them in **decoding** the text and **accessing** the ideas.

Consolidate and apply

- Now ask the students to **attempt** the tasks. They might do this individually or collaboratively – in either case, encourage them to **identify** and **record** their ideas.

- Ask them to **present** their responses to the various tasks, either orally or by displaying their work.

Chapter 1: Getting the Energy your Body Needs

Extend
- For students able to progress further, the later tasks give opportunities for extension work.

Plenary suggestions

How well did you do? Ask the students for **responses** to questions such as:
- How well were you able to approach these tasks?
- Did you manage to present some high quality responses?
- Are there some ideas that you need to strengthen in the later part of this topic? If there are, make a note of which.

Provide the students with some overall feedback, indicating ideas that they have grasped effectively and those that may need developing further.

Likely responses and next steps in learning

1. Students identify which muscles and bones carry the largest load on a daily basis. They then have an opportunity to apply this to the effects of a lack of load-bearing during space travel.
2. This task gives students an opportunity to refer to the text and to summarise information. This also gives an opportunity to recall some of the ideas discussed in previous activities. This checks if students understand how reduced gravity affects muscles and bones and if they are able to assimilate information from throughout the text.
3. In this task the students need to find relevant information from the text and then carry out multiplication. For this purpose, it is sufficient for students to multiply 1.5 × 12 for the total percentage loss. The students have to assuming that the bone is lost at a constant rate.
4. This task gives the students the opportunity to use their wider knowledge to predict the effects of decreased bone and mass on returning to Earth. They may also link the flight duration with the size of the effect. This activity also requires students to consider the discussion about the use of resistance training to build up muscles.
5. Extra calcium in the diet of astronauts would not prevent the loss of bone – it is the lack of weight-bearing that causes the loss. Increased calcium in the diet could have a negative effect and could increase the effect of kidney stones. This provides some cognitive conflict because students have previously learned that a calcium-rich diet is necessary for healthy bones. This task also requires students to carry out some independent research.
6. This task requires the students to make suggestions about building up muscle and bone. Sensible plans would include reference to gradually increasing the load and the time spent exercising, as well as to their diet providing glucose for respiration and minerals such as calcium for bones. The students should recognise that a similar format should be adopted as for astronauts returning to Earth, but may also identify that patients may not have had the opportunity to prepare for their time spent in bed because at least astronauts can prepare for their mission – for example by increasing muscle mass before they set off.

Chapter 1: Getting the Energy your Body Needs

1.10 Understanding how muscles get energy

Lesson overview

Learning objectives

- Recall the equation for respiration and describe what it shows.
- Explain the importance of respiration.
- Apply what we know about respiration.

Learning outcomes

- Recall that energy is released in our bodies by aerobic respiration, which uses oxygen and glucose. [O1]
- Recall the word equation for aerobic respiration and describe it as a way of releasing energy from food. [O2]
- Explain the importance of respiration in releasing energy and in building up complex molecules. [O3]

Skills development

- Thinking scientifically: use equations
- Working scientifically: n/a
- Learner development: ask questions

Resources needed equipment and materials as detailed in the Technician's notes; Worksheet 2.1.10; Practical sheet 2.1.10; Technician's notes 2.1.10

Digital resources Quick starter; Interactive activity: Match the words that are associated with proteins or carbohydrates; Slideshow: A comparison of the two life essential processes – photosynthesis and respiration

Common misconceptions Respiration takes place in the lungs. Respiration is the same as breathing.

Key vocabulary energy, respiration, glucose, aerobic respiration

Teaching and learning

Engage

- Ask the students to **share** ideas about how we get energy to move. Link the discussion back to muscles contracting as we move and needing energy to do this. [O1]
- Either show the real-life video of the screaming jelly baby experiment (internet search 'screaming jelly baby experiment') or perform a practical demonstration – see Practical sheet 2.1.10 and Technician's notes 2.1.10.) [O1]

Challenge and develop

- **Pair talk** Tell the students that the demonstration relates to the way that we generate energy in our bodies. Ask them to **discuss** in pairs how these processes are similar. They may discuss ideas such as in the demonstration, the jelly baby food is burned in oxygen and a lot of energy is generated; in our bodies, glucose from digestion reacts with oxygen from breathing and energy is released. This gives an opportunity to refer back to breathing and digestion (Student Book 1 Chapter 2 – Eating, Drinking and Breathing). [O1&2]
- Ask pairs to **share** their ideas with the class. [O1&2]
- Tell the students that the reaction in the body is much more controlled than in the screaming jelly baby demonstration. Ask them to **predict** the consequences of the reaction in the body releasing energy as explosively as in the demonstration. [O1&2]
- Ask pairs to **share** their ideas with the class. [O1&2]

Chapter 1: Getting the Energy your Body Needs

Explain

- With the students still in pairs, give each pair a set of cards from Worksheet 2.1.10, with the reactants and products of respiration, plus symbols and arrow. Ask the students to **arrange** the respiration equation correctly using the cards. [O2]
- Ask the students to **describe verbally** what the equation shows. [O2]
- The students should then work individually to **write an explanation** of the respiration equation. [O2]

Consolidate and apply

- Still in their pairs, ask the students to **devise** a question about respiration. Encourage them to create questions worth more than one mark and to generate a mark scheme to support their question. [O1, 2&3]

    You could differentiate by asking different pairs to devise questions worth differing numbers of marks.

- **Pairs to fours** Then two pairs work together to attempt to **answer** each other's questions. Each pair then uses the mark scheme to mark their own work. [O1, 2&3]
- Ask the students to **discuss** if the questions and mark scheme were well written. Take feedback across the class, ensuring that reasons are given for opinions. [O1, 2&3]

Extend

- Ask students able to progress further to **find the symbols** for each of the reactants and products of respiration, then to **explain** what each formula tells us (Task 3 of Worksheet 2.1.10). They could use building bricks or beads that stick together to explore the molecules. [O3]

Plenary suggestions

Why do we need energy? Ask the students to work in groups to **list** our bodies' uses of energy. Encourage them to **consider** processes inside the body as well as more obvious activities (for example contraction of muscles, making proteins from amino acids). [O1&3]

Ask one group at a time to **state** a use – each group should give a different example. Move around the groups until there are no new ideas. Reinforce that without respiration we would not be able to do any of these things. [O1&3]

Answers to Student Book questions

1. to move; to grow; to keep temperature constant
2. glucose
3. to keep temperature constant; in digestion; to keep the heart beating etc
4. 'with oxygen'
5. it carries oxygen to cells for respiration; and carbon dioxide from cells
6. glucose and oxygen react to form carbon dioxide and water energy is released
7. it gives strength to cell walls
8. protein used to grow bigger (e.g. muscles)
9. by arranging amino acids in different orders

Answers to Worksheet 2.1.10

1. glucose + oxygen → carbon dioxide + water + (energy)
2. a) a chemical process that releases energy from glucose
    b) gives the capacity for activity
    c) a process that uses air
    Glucose reacts with oxygen to release energy and carbon dioxide and water. This is aerobic respiration.
3. a) i) $C_6H_{12}O_6$; carbon, hydrogen and oxygen   ii) CO_2; carbon and oxygen   iii) H_2O; hydrogen and oxygen
    b) carbon has become part of carbon dioxide; hydrogen has become part of water; oxygen forms part of carbon dioxide and water

Chapter 1: Getting the Energy your Body Needs

1.11 Investigating respiration

Lesson overview

Learning objectives

- Recall that respiration takes place in plants and animals.
- Describe some experimental evidence for respiration.
- Consider the quality of evidence for respiration.

Learning outcomes

- Recall that plants respire; describe how to demonstrate that water is produced during respiration. [O1]
- Describe some practical experiments on plants that provide evidence for respiration. [O2]
- Evaluate the quality of evidence for respiration. [O3]

Skills development

- Thinking scientifically: consider the quality of evidence
- Working scientifically: evaluate data
- Learner development: collaborate effectively

Resources needed equipment and materials as detailed in the Technician's notes; cards from Worksheet 2.1.10 (as used in the previous lesson); Worksheet 2.1.11; Practical sheets 2.1.11a–d; Technician's notes 2.1.11

Digital resources Quick starter; Interactive activity: Drag the respiration and photosynthesis phrases to the correct box

Common misconceptions Plants do not carry out respiration. Plants only carry out respiration at night.

Key vocabulary reactant, photosynthesis, product, germinating

Teaching and learning

Engage

- Give each student a card from Worksheet 2.1.10 (as used in Topic 1.10) with either a reactant or a product of respiration. Ask the students to arrange themselves with other students to make a group that contains all the reactants and all the products of respiration. Increase engagement by making this a competition. [O1]
- When the students are arranged correctly, give each group three 'plus signs' and one 'arrow'. Ask them to **construct** the respiration equation as quickly as possible. [O1]
- Follow this activity with a discussion to establish that both plants and animals respire all the time. [O1]

Challenge and develop

- Ask the students to **observe** a series of demonstrations linked with respiration. As they watch, ask them to **make notes** to remind themselves later what they saw. Some students may need support with this activity and you could either model note taking during the first demonstration or arrange the students in mixed ability pairs for this activity. [O2]

  The demonstrations are: (see Practical Sheets 2.1.11a–d and Technician's notes 2.1.11)
  - Is water released during respiration in animals?
  - Is water released during respiration in plants?
  - Is oxygen used during aerobic respiration?
  - Is carbon dioxide released during aerobic respiration?
  - Is heat released during aerobic respiration?

  The latter three need to be set up well before the lesson, preferably the night before.

Chapter 1: Getting the Energy your Body Needs

- During each demonstration, ask the students to **suggest** what the experiment shows and to **explain** the use of any controls. Explore the links with photosynthesis during a discussion of the demonstrations. Leave the demonstrations set up for the next activity. [O2]

Explain

- **Group talk** Arrange the students in small groups. Allocate each group one of the demonstrations from the previous activity.

  You could differentiate by allocating lower-attaining students the demonstrations of water release or heat release. [O2]

  Ask each group to **evaluate** the evidence for respiration from the demonstration. Ask them to **consider** what the demonstration shows, whether or not this is evidence for respiration, and whether or not the evidence could be interpreted in any other way. [O1, 2&3]

Consolidate and apply

- Ask groups that evaluated the same demonstration to join together. Ask the new groups to **prepare** a short presentation to **summarise** the demonstration and also if it shows evidence for respiration. [O1, 2&3]
- Each group **presents** their summary. [O1, 2&3]
- Worksheet 2.1.11 could be used to reinforce ideas here. [O2&3]
- Discuss and agree the rank order of the demonstrations in terms of clear evidence for respiration. [O3]

Extend

- Ask students able to progress further to **consider** the energy changes in respiration starting from the energy stored in food or in plants. Encourage the students to consider any energy changes they have observed during the demonstrations and the energy changes in humans.

Plenary suggestions

Learning triangle The students work individually to construct a learning triangle. They should draw a large triangle with a smaller inverted triangle that just fits inside (to make four triangles). In the outer triangles, the students write something they've seen, something they've done, and something they've discussed. Then in the central triangle, they write something they've learned. [O1, 2&3]

Evaluate group work You could also ask the students to consider how well they worked as a group. [O1, 2&3]

Answers to Student Book questions

1. to grow; to repair tissues; to reproduce; to absorb nutrients
2. plants make their own glucose; animals take glucose in
3. it is a starting material in a reaction
4. water droplets are formed when you breathe onto cold glass
5. put a plastic bag over the leaves; allow time for water to condense; or similar
6. Germinating seeds give off carbon dioxide; because the 'air' leading from these seeds turns limewater milky.
7. *photosynthesis*: reactants – carbon dioxide, water; products – glucose, oxygen
   respiration: reactants – glucose, oxygen; products – carbon dioxide, water
8. because the products of one are the reactants of the other
9. a) both b) respiration only

Answers to Worksheet 2.1.11

1. *Picture A*: animals produce water during respiration
   Picture B: plants generate heat during respiration
   Picture C: plants produce carbon dioxide during respiration
2. *B: production of heat* – same set-up with boiled seeds
   C: production of carbon dioxide – same set-up with boiled seeds
3. a) suitable mind map with respiration at the centre; including equation, definition
   b) link made to photosynthesis; identifying that plants do both or by comparing equations

Chapter 1: Getting the Energy your Body Needs

1.12 Analysing adaptations for respiration

Lesson overview

Learning objectives

- Describe where in the cell respiration takes place.
- Explain how mitochondria are adapted for respiration.
- Compare and explain the numbers of mitochondria in different cells.

Learning outcomes

- Identify mitochondria as the sites of respiration. [O1]
- Describe some adaptations of mitochondria; compare the numbers of mitochondria in different cells using a graph. [O2]
- Explain adaptations of mitochondria; analyse data on the numbers of mitochondria in different cells. [O3]

Skills development

- Thinking scientifically: analyse data
- Working scientifically: interpret evidence
- Learner development: communicate effectively

Resources needed image of mitochondria; graph paper; Worksheet 2.1.12

Digital resources Quick starter; Interactive activity: Match the mitochondria-rich cells with their energy consuming function

Common misconceptions Mitochondria are found only in muscle cells. Mitochondria are found only in animal cells.

Key vocabulary mitochondria, membrane, enzymes

Teaching and learning

Engage

- Remind the students of what they learned about cells in Book 1. Revisit the structure of cells, briefly, with an overview of the organelles found within cells and the specific role of each. [O1]
- Ask the students to **explain** why we need mitochondria. Then ask them why both plant cells and animal cells have mitochondria and remind them that both types of cell carry out respiration. [O1]

Challenge and develop

- Display an image of a mitochondrion either from the internet or Figure 2.1.12a in the Student Book.
- Ask the students to work in pairs to **describe** the structure. Collect feedback across the class and ask a student to **record** some of the main ideas for the class to see. [O1&2]

Explain

- Ask the students to work individually to '**text mark**' some information about mitochondria. (You could use the information in task 2 of Worksheet 2.1.12.) Students should find and mark:
  - information about the structure of mitochondria
  - information about the role of mitochondria
  - information about how mitochondria are adapted to their role (respiration). [O1&2]

  You can differentiate this task by asking higher-attaining students to **mark** all three different types of information themselves in different colours, and arranging lower-attaining students in groups who divide the task.

Chapter 1: Getting the Energy your Body Needs

- The students work in pairs or small groups (depending on how they were arranged for the text marking activity) to **construct** a table to **summarise** how the structure of a mitochondrion makes it well adapted for respiration. [O1&2]

Consolidate and apply

- Ask the students to use the data about numbers of mitochondria in different cells in Table 2.1.12 in the Student's Book to **draw a graph**. [O3]
- Ask the students to work individually to **explain** what the data tells us. They then **share** their conclusion with a partner. [O3]
- Ask the students to **share** feedback about whether they drew similar conclusions and **address** any misconceptions. [O3]

Extend

- Ask students able to progress further to **predict** the consequences of any mitochondrial disease based on what they have learned about the role of mitochondria. They could then **research** mitochondrial diseases to test their prediction. [O3]

Plenary suggestions

What have we learned? Ask groups of three to choose three sentences to **summarise** the lesson. Encourage the students to focus on the *way* that they learned as well as *what* they learned. [O1, 2&3]

Answers to Student Book questions

1. in cells
2. they are the site of respiration; where energy is released
3. this increases the surface area of membrane; where respiration takes place
4. comments such as red blood cells have no mitochondria; most in muscle cells; comparison of numbers
5. the muscle was inactive
6. when more energy is needed; for example when muscle becomes active
7. they cannot release enough energy
8. this disease is due to inheritance; it is not an infectious disease
9. the brain controls all parts of the body

Answers to Worksheet 2.1.12

1. A: outer membrane; B: inner membrane; C: matrix; D: cristae
2. a) Identify text such as 'have two membranes', 'outer membrane surrounds the organelle'; 'inner membrane is highly folded'; 'inside ... is called the matrix'.

   b) Identify text such as 'where respiration takes place inside the cell'; 'inside mitochondria that glucose and oxygen react to produce water and carbon dioxide, releasing energy'.

   c) Identify text such as 'inner membrane highly is folded'; 'folds increase the surface area so that more respiration can take place'; 'contain special proteins called enzymes'; 'can increase in number if more energy is needed'.
3. Table should include features identified in question 2c) and give an explantion of how they make mitochondria well adapted – for example, 'folded membrane increases surface area for respiration to take place'; 'presence of enzymes speeds up respiration reaction'.

Chapter 1: Getting the Energy your Body Needs

1.13 Examining links between respiration and body systems

Lesson overview

Learning objectives

- Describe some systems in animals and plants that are linked with respiration.
- Explain how some systems and respiration are dependent.
- Suggest the consequences of a failure in linked body systems.

Learning outcomes

- Name some of the body systems that are associated with respiration, such as the breathing system. [O1]
- Explain how the breathing system, the digestive system and the circulatory system are linked with respiration. [O2]
- Suggest the consequences of a failure in any of the body systems for other systems. [O3]

Skills development

- Thinking scientifically: ask questions
- Working scientifically: n/a
- Learner development: ask questions

Resources needed information about digestive, circulatory and breathing systems for the collective memory task; large sheets of paper and pens; card of two different colours; Worksheet 2.1.13

Digital resources Quick starter; Interactive activity: Match the body systems to their function; Slideshow: A look at the importance of body systems in respiration and the role of the liver; Hangman: Key vocabulary game

Common misconceptions Breathing and respiration are the same. The systems of the body are separate, with no crossover to other systems.

Key vocabulary digestive system, breathing system, circulatory system, phloem, stomata

Teaching and learning

Engage

- Arrange the students in groups of four for a collective memory task. Give each group a large sheet of paper and some pens. Display images containing information about the breathing system, digestive system and circulatory system (all on one poster) spread around the room. [O1]
- The first student moves to a poster and **studies** it for 30 seconds. On returning to their group, the first student **records** some information on the group sheet. The next student goes to the poster as soon as the first one returns and again **memorises** for 30 seconds.

  Continue the process until all team members have had at least two turns to memorise and record. [O1]
- Ask the students to move around the classroom to **observe** the work of each group. Then ask the students to **vote** for the group who transferred the information most accurately. [O1]

Challenge and develop

- Ask the students to **summarise** the role of each of the three body systems. [O1]
- **Pair work** Ask the students to work in pairs to **describe** the links between respiration and each of the digestive system, circulatory system and breathing system. They could **record** these as bullet points or short notes. Collect some feedback across the class. [O1&2]
- Next, ask each pair to **predict** what the effects would be of any of the systems failing and the link breaking. Conversely, they should **discuss** what the effect of a lack of respiration would be on each of the systems. [O3]

Chapter 1: Getting the Energy your Body Needs

You could differentiate this task by asking lower-attaining students to consider only one system and respiration.

Explain

- **Pairs to fours** Ask pairs of students to **devise** questions and a mark scheme based on what they have learned this lesson. Encourage them to design questions worth more than one mark. Worksheet 2.1.13 could be used to support this activity. [O1, 2&3]
- Pairs form fours and try to **answer** each other's questions. Pairs then **mark** their own answers using the mark scheme provided. [O1, 2&3]
- Ask the pairs to **share** feedback about the questions and the mark scheme. [O1, 2&3]

Consolidate and apply

- Ask the students to work in pairs to **create** a concept map linking respiration with each of the body systems. Encourage students to **consider** any other links between each of the body systems. [O1, 2&3]
- Again, pairs form fours and each pair **explains** their concept map. [O1, 2&3]
- Pairs **add to**, or **amend**, their concept map and based on discussions with another pair. [O1, 2&3]

Extend

- Ask students able to progress further to **consider** links with other body systems that are more difficult to understand, such as the nervous system. They could also consider how respiration is linked with homeostasis. [O1, 2&3]

Plenary suggestions

Loop card game Arrange the students in groups of approximately eight. Each student **writes a question** related to the lesson on a piece of coloured card and writes the answer on a piece of different coloured card. The cards are mixed up and then each student **chooses** one question and one answer. The students then play a loop card game – one student **reads** out a question and the student holding the correct answer identifies him or herself. This student then reads out their question and so on. [O1, 2&3]

Answers to Student Book questions

1. digestive; circulatory; breathing (etc.)
2. *from* digestive system (intestines) *to* cells
3. the purpose of respiration is to release energy; these are by-products
4. the system would not get the oxygen needed for respiration; or remove the carbon dioxide formed by respiration
5. the energy; from respiration; is needed for muscles in stomach; and intestines during digestion
6. suitable table to summarise the effect of each system
7. circulatory system
8. through stomata

Answers to Worksheet 2.1.13

1. a) breathing b) circulatory c) digestive d) skeletal
2. a) *breathing* – takes air in and out of the body to allow us to take in the oxygen that we need and to excrete waste carbon dioxide
   circulatory – carries blood around the body, containing oxygen and nutrients
   digestive – breaks down food molecules so that we can make use of them
   skeletal – supports the body and allows movement
   b) *breathing* because it provides the oxygen needed for respiration and removes the carbon dioxide produced by respiration
   circulatory because the blood carries the oxygen needed for respiration to cells and carries the carbon dioxide produced from cells
   digestive because it provides glucose from food for respiration
   skeletal because muscles need energy from resipration to make bones move
3. a) the digestive sytem would not have the energy it needs; for example, the muscles of the intestine and stomach would not be able to contract
   b) a suitable question with a relevant mark scheme

Chapter 1: Getting the Energy your Body Needs

1.14 Exploring respiration in sport

Lesson overview

Learning objectives

- Describe what is meant by anaerobic respiration.
- Explain why some sports involve more aerobic or more anaerobic respiration.
- Explain what is meant by oxygen debt.

Learning outcomes

- Describe anaerobic respiration as requiring no oxygen; know that some sports rely mainly on anaerobic respiration. [O1]
- Explain why some sports rely on anaerobic respiration while others can use aerobic respiration; describe some of the effects on the body of anaerobic respiration. [O2]
- Explain what is meant by oxygen debt and why it occurs. [O3]

Skills development

- Thinking scientifically: understand how theories develop
- Working scientifically: n/a
- Learner development: collaborate effectively

Resources needed access to computers and the internet for research (optional); Worksheet 2.1.14

Digital resources Quick starter; Interactive activity: Match the sport to the main type of respiration that occurs; Interactive activity: Place into the correct order to describe how the body obtains and stores glucose; Video

Key vocabulary anaerobic respiration, lactic acid, oxygen debt, glycogen

Teaching and learning

Engage

- Show the students a video of a stamina sportsperson in action – such as a cyclist in the Tour de France or a long-distance swimmer. Ask them to **discuss** in pairs how these athletes gain enough energy to keep going through a long race. [O1]

Challenge and develop

- Show photos or videos of other sports such as weightlifting and sprinting, and ask the students to **suggest** how these sports differ from the sports in the real-life video. Students should **discuss** whether or not these sportspeople gain energy in the same way. [O1]
- Ask the students to **share** their ideas across the class and lead a discussion to draw out the idea that these sports use larger amounts of energy in shorter bursts than stamina sports. [O1&2]

Explain

- Ask the students to **recall** the respiration equation and reinforce that this is respiration with oxygen, which is called aerobic respiration. Ask a volunteer to write the equation on the whiteboard.
- Explain that during exercises such as weightlifting and sprinting, the body cannot gain oxygen quickly enough to carry out aerobic respiration continually. Ask the students to work in pairs to **discuss** what may happen when we cannot get enough oxygen. [O1]
- Describe what is meant by anaerobic respiration in terms of reactants and products and ask the students to **write** an equation for anaerobic respiration based on what you have told them. Do not worry too much about the students understanding the equation at this point – this activity is used as a way of reinforcing how we write equations with reactants forming products. [O1]

Chapter 1: Getting the Energy your Body Needs

- Refer to the second and third sections of the Student Book. Use the text as a stimulus for class discussion. For example, ask the students to **predict** what is meant by 'oxygen debt' prior to reading about this in the book. [O1, 2&3]
- Ask the students to work individually to **answer** the questions in the 'The results of anaerobic respiration' section of the Student Book. Worksheet 2.1.14 could also be used here. [O1, 2&3]

  You could differentiate this task by selecting specific questions for students to answer or by asking them to work in pairs.

Consolidate and apply

- Ask the students to **imagine** that they are sports scientists employed to work with a football team. They must **educate** the footballers about the way that their bodies work to generate energy, and the effects that this may have on them. Ask the students to **consider**:
  - how energy is generated during football matches
  - the effects of anaerobic respiration on the body
  - ways of treating any adverse effects of anaerobic respiration. [O1, 2&3]
- The students could **present** their work as a script or a slideshow, for example. They work in pairs and take turns to **share** their presentation. [O1, 2&3]

Extend

- Ask students able to progress further to **consider** why it is important that stamina sportspeople, such as marathon runners, train by running long distances rather than just training by sprinting. Encourage them to **suggest** other benefits to the body of stamina training, in addition to considering respiration. [O2]

Plenary suggestions

Share a comment Ask each student to **share** one interesting comment about the presentation of their partner. [O1, 2&3]

Answers to Student Book questions

1. a) jogging; swimming long distances; etc.
   b) sprinting; weightlifting; etc.
2. Aerobic respiration uses oxygen; anaerobic respiration does not.
3. any sports that require steady exercise as well as short bursts of high energy – e.g. football, basketball
4. the oxygen that needs to be used after anaerobic respiration; to get rid of lactic acid
5. because it releases less energy than aerobic respiration; and causes muscle cramp
6. both use glucose; aerobic respiration uses oxygen as well. Aerobic respiration produces carbon dioxide and water; anaerobic respiration produces lactic acid. Both release energy
7. so they can release it as and when more energy is needed
8. protein from organs and muscles can be used; which results in these tissues being damaged

Answers to Worksheet 2.1.14

1. in order: oxygen; energy; glucose; sprinting
2. a) produces carbon dioxide; releases more energy; releases energy more slowly; uses oxygen
   b) produces lactic acid; releases less energy; releases energy more quickly; results in oxygen debt
3. a) breaking down lactic acid; deep breathing is used to get as much oxygen as possible into the body. The oxygen needed to break down the lactic acid is the 'oxygen debt'
   b) lactic acid causes aching in the muscles; this would remain if we did not pay back the oxygen debt

1.15 Understanding anaerobic respiration

Lesson overview

Learning objectives

- Recall that plants and microbes carry out anaerobic respiration.
- Describe some evidence to show that anaerobic respiration can produce carbon dioxide.
- Construct a method to show what is produced in anaerobic respiration.

Learning outcomes

- Recall some examples of microbes and know that they carry out anaerobic respiration. [O1]
- Describe a piece of evidence to show that anaerobic respiration produces carbon dioxide. [O2]
- Write a logical method for an investigation of what is produced in anaerobic respiration, taking safety into consideration. [O3].

Skills development

- Thinking scientifically: evaluate risks
- Working scientifically: design investigations
- Learner development: communicate effectively

Resources needed potted plant with damp or wet soil; equipment and materials for class practical as detailed in the Technician's notes; Worksheet 2.1.15; Practical sheet 2.1.15; Technician's notes 2.1.15

Digital resources Quick starter

Common misconceptions Microbes only include bacteria. Microbes are bad for us.

Key vocabulary fermentation, microbe, yeast

Teaching and learning

Engage

- Show a potted plant with damp or wet soil. Tell the students that there may be aerobic respiration, anaerobic respiration and photosynthesis all taking place in this plant. Ask students to **discuss** in pairs where each of the three processes could be taking place. Ask some students to **share ideas** across the class. If there is some disagreement about whether or where anaerobic respiration would be taking place, explain that respiration in the roots could be aerobic if the soil was aerated enough, but if the soil were waterlogged the roots would be respiring anaerobically. [O1]

Challenge and develop

- Ask the students to **recall** the product of anaerobic respiration in animals – one student could **write** the equation on the board. [O1]
- Ask the students to **comment** on the differences they have observed in plants this lesson. Establish that anaerobic respiration in animals and plants results in different products. [O1]
- Write the fermentation equation on the board. Ask the students to work in pairs to **explain** what the equation shows. Take some feedback across the class. [O1]

Explain

- Show some pictures of microbes – different types of bacteria (including thermophiles found deep under the ocean, viruses, fungi) with the final picture showing yeast. Discuss what each picture shows during the presentation. Explain, for example, that some bacteria are found deep under the ocean where oxygen is absent. [O1]

Chapter 1: Getting the Energy your Body Needs

- Demonstrate how to set up a yeast experiment using a balloon to collect the gas (see Technician's notes 2.1.15). Students work in pairs to **set up** the experiment. [O2]
- While the experiment is incubating, ask the students to **think about** what should be included in a good method. Agree a list of success criteria as a class – these should include ideas such as a list of equipment, numbered steps, logical order of instructions, diagram, and references to safety. [O3]
- Students work individually to **write** a method. They can use Practical sheet 2.1.15 to support this task. [O3]

  You could differentiate this task by providing the steps on pieces of card for lower-attaining students to **sequence**.

- Students who complete this should attempt tasks 1 and 2 of Worksheet 2.1.15. [O1, 2&3]

Consolidate and apply

- **Pair work** Each student **peer-assesses** the method written by their partner, using the success criteria as a guide. Ask them to **write feedback** – for example, using the 'two stars and a wish' format. You could display some examples of good work and explain what is good about them – for example using a visualiser or by asking individuals to read out their method. [O3]

Extend

For students who are able to progress further:

- Show them a syringe and ask how they could measure the production of carbon dioxide more accurately. [O3]
- Ask them to complete task 3 of Worksheet 2.1.15. [O3]

Plenary suggestions

Finding the correct equation Ask the students to write the anaerobic respiration equation for animals on one piece of paper, and the anaerobic respiration equation for plants and microbes on another. Read out the names of plants, animals and different types of microbes. For each, students hold up the correct equation. Allow some students to suggest examples of organisms for the rest of the class to respond to. [O1&2]

Answers to Student Book questions

1. boggy; waterlogged
2. fermentation
3. glucose → lactic acid + carbon dioxide
4. tiny organisms including bacteria and viruses
5. they can survive even when oxygen levels fall
6. they would probably die
7. fermentation; anaerobic respiration
8. source of glucose
9. Carbon dioxide gas is produced during fermentation; and collects in the balloon.

Answers to Worksheet 2.1.15

1. a) ii) b) i) c) iv) d) iii)
2. a) microbe (fungus)
   b) sugar is needed for respiration, so no gas produced
   c) respiration takes place, and carbon dioxide gas is produced
3. a) Suitable description, such as use water at different temperatures but with same apparaus and set-up as task 2. Measure how much gas is produced in a certain time. Plot a graph using the results.
   b) Choose the temperature that resulted in most gas being produced.

Chapter 1: Getting the Energy your Body Needs

1.16 Investigating fermentation

Lesson overview

Learning objectives

- Describe some applications of fermentation.
- Identify dependent, independent and control variables in an investigation.
- Analyse data and identify next steps.

Learning outcomes

- Explain simply what is meant by fermentation; follow instructions to investigate the effect of sugars on fermentation. [O1]
- Manage variables in an investigation into the effect of different sugars on fermentation, and make a conclusion. [O2]
- Evaluate an investigation carried out into the effect of different sugars on fermentation. [O3]

Skills development

- Thinking scientifically: consider the quality of evidence
- Working scientifically: design investigations
- Learner development: plan progress

Resources needed dried yeast; warm water; a variety of sugars (e.g. sucrose, sweeteners, different fruit juices); boiling tubes; bungs and delivery tubes; balloons; stopclocks; limewater; Worksheet 2.1.16; Practical sheet 2.1.16; Technician's notes 2.1.16

Digital resources Quick starter; Slideshow: A look at how humans use yeast cells; Interactive activity: Match the products which are made by fermentation with the microbe involved; Interactive activity: Drag the phrase to the correct box – does it speed up reactions, slow them down, or both?; Video

Key vocabulary brewing, fossil fuel, independent variable, dependent variable

Teaching and learning

Engage

- Show some pictures of bread, cheese, yoghurt; some pictures of fuels, water treatment (or other images linked to fermentation). Ask the students to **suggest** what the lesson is about. [O1]
- Re-visit each of the pictures and discuss the relevance of each as an application of fermentation. [O1]

Challenge and develop

- Share the title of the investigation (Practical sheet 2.1.16) to be carried out: 'Investigating the effect of different sugars on yeast fermentation'. Ask the students to **think** about how they might measure this. After two minutes, ask them to **discuss** their ideas with a partner. Then collect some ideas across the class. [O2]

Explain

- Demonstrate the basic apparatus for the investigation and how to set it up. Students may **choose**, for example, to count bubbles, or time how long it takes for limewater to turn milky, or compare the size of balloons over time – but encourage them to ask for anything additional. [O2]
- The students work in pairs to **identify** the variables that they will change, measure and control. [O2]
- Check the plan of each group and then the pairs **carry out** the investigation and **record** their results. [O2]

   You could differentiate this activity by providing lower-attaining students with a plan or a results table to fill in.

Chapter 1: Getting the Energy your Body Needs

Consolidate and apply

- The students **plot a graph** of their results. Share results from another pair for those not collecting sufficient data. [O2]
- Ask the students to **explain** the conclusion made from their results. Encourage them to **refer back** to the title of the investigation when making a conclusion. [O2]
- Ask the students to **consider** the next steps in this investigation:
  - Would they repeat any measurements?
  - How could they improve accuracy?
  - How could they ensure reliability?
  - Is there a follow-up investigation that they would do? [O3]

Extend

- Ask students able to progress further to **suggest** any other factors that might affect the rate of fermentation. They should **write a list** and **decide** how each could be investigated. You could remind them that respiration is controlled by enzymes and ask them to **suggest** what would affect these enzymes. Alternatively, task 3 in Worksheet 2.1.16 could be attempted. [O2&3]

Plenary suggestions

What have we learned? Ask each group to **summarise** what their investigation showed using just one sentence. Encourage the use of scientific language and referral to the investigation title. [O2&3]

Answers to Student Book questions

1. baking; brewing; fuel
2. a) baking – carbon dioxide causes bread to rise; be light   b) brewing
4. a) temperature   b) number of bubbles
5. amount of glucose; length of counting time
6. as temperature increases, number of bubbles increases up to 40 °C; but the number of bubbles decreases after that
7. repeat the investigation
8. 40 °C; most bubbles are produced at this temperature to make bread rise

Answers to Worksheet 2.1.16

1. in order: anaerobic; microbes; yeast; brewing; baking
2. a) glucose → ethanol + carbon dioxide; yeast produces alcohol (ethanol)
   b) glucose → ethanol + carbon dioxide; carbon dioxide causes bread to rise
   c) yeast needs sugar for respiration
3. a) i) wine; beer   ii) antibiotics; enzymes   iii) yeast; other fungi; bacteria
   b) produces useful products such as carbon dioxide and alcohol, which can be used for baking and brewing; no need to keep in an oxygen-free environment

Chapter 1: Getting the Energy your Body Needs

1.17 Comparing aerobic and anaerobic respiration

Lesson overview

Learning objectives

- Describe some similarities and differences between aerobic and anaerobic respiration.
- Work responsibly within a team to summarise respiration.

Learning outcomes

- Describe one similarity and one difference between aerobic respiration and anaerobic respiration. [O1]
- Describe several similarities and differences between aerobic respiration and anaerobic respiration. [O2]
- Compare the implications of aerobic respiration and anaerobic respiration for the organism. [O3]

Skills development

- Thinking scientifically: ask questions
- Working scientifically: n/a
- Learner development: act responsibly

Resources needed large sheets of paper; highlighter pens; Worksheet 2.1.17

Digital resources Quick starter; Interactive activity: Drag the correct respiration phrases into the correct groups; Slideshow: Explores the importance of enzymes in respiration; Hangman: Key vocabulary game

Key vocabulary catalyst

Teaching and learning

Engage

- Show web-based clips of sports that require mainly aerobic respiration (e.g. marathon running) and those that require mainly anaerobic respiration (e.g. sprinting) – show the clips without sound. Ask the students to watch the clips and then **discuss** with a partner what was happening. Alternatively, ask them to work in pairs to agree five words linked with aerobic respiration and five linked with anaerobic respiration. [O1&2]
- Ask the pairs to **share** their ideas across the class. They should **identify** where aerobic respiration and anaerobic respiration are featured. [O1&2]

Challenge and develop

- **Pair work** Ask the students to work in pairs to **sort** some statements about respiration into 'aerobic respiration', 'anaerobic respiration' or 'both' (Task 1 of Worksheet 2.1.17). [O1, 2&3]
- The pairs should then **plan** another two statements (at least) to add to their groupings. [O1, 2&3]
- The pairs form fours and these **share** the statements that they planned. [O1, 2&3]

Explain

- **Group work** Arrange the students in groups of three or four. Ask them to produce a visual display to **compare** and **contrast** aerobic respiration and anaerobic respiration. They should allocate each group member a specific role. These roles could include responsibility to compare and contrast 'respiration equations', 'when each takes place' and 'applications of each type' – but the students may want to divide the workload in a different way. Encourage the students to refer to their work and to the Student Book for help. [O1, 2&3]

Consolidate and apply

- Ask each group to **present** their display to the rest of the class. [O1, 2&3]
- Ask all groups to make one positive comment about each presentation. [O1, 2&3]

Chapter 1: Getting the Energy your Body Needs

- Ask the groups to **reflect** on the way that they worked as a team and whether anything could be improved for group work next time. Collect some feedback across the class. [O1, 2&3]

Extend

- Ask students able to progress further to **create a list** of common misunderstandings or difficult concepts about respiration. They should **suggest** an explanation or a way of remembering the information. [O1, 2&3]

Plenary suggestions

Alphabet game Working in groups of three, the students try to suggest a word linked with respiration for each of the letters of the alphabet. Set the activity up as a competition and give them a time limit. The group with relevant words linked to the most letters of the alphabet wins. [O1, 2&3]

Answers to Student Book questions

1. aerobic respiration is 19 times more efficient
2. energy is released more quickly anaerobically
3. any other example of an activity using anaerobic respiration; such as weightlifting
4. diagram of: a cell with mitochondria labelled with 'aerobic respiration'; cytoplasm labelled with 'anaerobic respiration'
5. more energy is produced in mitochondria than in cytoplasm
6. catalysts speed up reactions; but are essential for some reactions
7. enzymes for respiration found in mitochondria, where aerobic respiration takes place. Anaerobic respiration takes place in the cytoplasm where not as many enzymes are located
8. any suitable example, such as digestion

Answers to Worksheet 2.1.17

1. *aerobic*: steady jogging; takes place in mitochondria
   anaerobic: ethanol is produced; lactic acid is produced; sprinting; leads to oxygen debt
   both: glucose is used; animals; yeast; plants; energy is released; football match
2. Suitable quiz questions to include questions and answers about both aerobic and anaerobic respiration.
3. Discussion to include such points as: both aerobic and anaerobic use glucose; aerobic uses oxygen, anaerobic does not; anaerobic in plants produces ethanol, in animals it produces lactic acid; anaerobic in plants produces carbon dioxide, so does aerobic but not anaerobic in animals; all types release energy; aerobic releases most energy; but anaerobic releases energy more quickly.

Chapter 1: Getting the Energy your Body Needs

1.18 Checking students' progress

The 'Checking your progress' section in the Student Book indicates the key ideas developed in this chapter and shows how students progress to more complex levels. It is provided to support students in:

- identifying those ideas
- developing a sense of their current level of understanding
- developing a sense of what the next steps in their learning are.

It is designed either to be used at the end of a chapter to support an overall view of the progress, or alternatively during the teaching of the unit. Students can self assess or peer assess using this as a basis.

It would be helpful if students can be encouraged to provide evidence from their understanding or their notes to support their judgments. In some cases it may be useful to explore the difference in the descriptors for a particular idea so that students can see what makes for a 'higher outcome'.

It may be useful with some descriptors to provide examples from the specific work done, such as an experiment undertaken or an explanation developed and recorded. If marking and feedback uses similar ideas and phrases this will enable students to relate specific marking to a more general sense of progress.

Chapter 1: Getting the Energy your Body Needs

To make good progress in understanding science students need to focus on these ideas and skills:

Students who are making modest progress will be able to:	Students who are making good progress will be able to:	Students who are making excellent progress will be able to:
Identify the main bones of the skeleton.	Describe the functions of the skeleton.	Explain how different parts of the skeleton are adapted to carry out particular functions.
Describe the role of skeletal joints.	Identify some different joints and explain the role of tendons and ligaments in joints.	Compare the movement allowed at different joints and explain why different types of joints are needed.
Recall that muscles contract to move bones at joints.	Identify muscles that contract to cause specific movements.	Explain how muscles work antagonistically to bring about movement and evaluate a model.
Investigate the strengths of different muscles and draw a conclusion.	Plan and carry out an investigation to compare strengths of muscles and analyse the results using a graph.	Plan and carry out a fair investigation, analyse the data and evaluate the procedure.
Describe some medical problems that can arise with the skeletal system.	Describe some treatments for a range of problems with the skeletal system.	Explain how diagnosis and treatment of problems with the skeletal system have changed over time.
Describe the purpose of respiration.	Describe and explain aerobic respiration using a word equation.	Explain the role of respiration in building up complex molecules.
Describe aerobic respiration in plants.	Identify evidence for aerobic respiration in plants and animals.	Evaluate the quality of evidence for aerobic respiration in plants and animals.
Describe where in a cell respiration takes place.	Explain how mitochondria are adapted for respiration.	Analyse data to compare and explain the numbers of mitochondria in different cells.
Define anaerobic respiration and give examples of sports that use anaerobic respiration.	Explain why some sports rely mainly on aerobic respiration while others require anaerobic respiration.	Describe and explain the effects on the body of anaerobic respiration and explain 'oxygen debt'.
Identify some living things that carry out anaerobic respiration and identify some applications.	Describe and explain some evidence to show the products of anaerobic respiration and plan an investigation into fermentation.	Plan an investigation to test a hypothesis about anaerobic respiration, analyse the data and evaluate the investigation.

Chapter 1: Getting the Energy your Body Needs

1.19 Answers to Student Book Questions

This table provides answers to the Questions section at the end of Chapter 1 of the Student Book. It also shows how different questions assess attainment in terms of the focus and style of a question as well as the context. Question level analysis can indicate students' proficiency in approaching different aspects of scientific understanding and different types of answer.

Q	Answer	Marks available	Focus: Knowledge & understanding	Focus: Application	Focus: Evaluation of evidence	Style: Objective test question	Style: Short written answer	Style: Longer written answer	Context: Skeleton	Context: Muscles	Context: Aerobic respiration	Context: Anaerobic respiration
1	a	1	x			x			x			
2	b	1	x			x			x			
3	c	1	x			x			x			
4	d	1	x			x			x			
5	The bones are curved and form a cavity	1	x				x		x			
	in which the lungs are protected	1	x				x		x			
6	Muscles are attached to bones	1	x				x		x	x		
	As muscles contract, they move the bone	1	x				x		x	x		
7	Any four from: • Aerobic respiration releases more energy (or converse) • Aerobic respiration uses oxygen (or converse) • Aerobic respiration takes place in mitochondria (anaerobic in cytoplasm) • Aerobic respiration produces carbon dioxide and water (anaerobic produces lactic acid or ethanol, for example) • Sensible example of different sports requiring each	4	x					x			x	x
8	b	1		x		x					x	
9	a	1		x		x					x	x
10	b	1		x		x				x		
11	b	1		x		x					x	X
12	There would be a bigger range of movement/ circular movement as well as backwards and forwards	1		x			x		x			
	Because the elbow joint is a hinge joint/ hinge joint it only allows forward and backward movement	1		x			x		x			

Chapter 1: Getting the Energy your Body Needs

Q	Answer	Marks available	Focus: Knowledge & understanding	Focus: Application	Focus: Evaluation of evidence	Style: Objective test question	Style: Short written answer	Style: Longer written answer	Context: Skeleton	Context: Muscles	Context: Aerobic respiration	Context: Anaerobic respiration
13	Plants carry out both respiration and photosynthesis	1		x			x				x	
	Animals just carry out respiration	1		x			x				x	
14	Biceps and triceps are antagonistic muscles/ a pair	1	x					x		x		
	When the bicep muscle relaxes, the tricep contracts	1	x					x		x		
	Each time the arm is moved downward, this works/ contracts the tricep	1	x					x		x		
	Muscles won't heal while using them	1		x				x		x		
15	The animal cannot bend its back	1			x		x		x			
	Humans can bend the back because the backbone is made up of many smaller bones	1			x		x		x			
16	B is most likely to produce more alcohol because it only respires anaerobically	1			x			x				x
	Any three from: • Explanation using the respiration equations • Consider if the microbes are disease-causing • Consider the cost of growing each microbe • Consider how quickly each microbe grows/ reference to yield • Any other sensible suggestion	3			x			x				x
	Total possible:	30	12	12	6	8	10	12	12	7	9	10

Chapter 2: Looking at Plants and Ecosystems

2.1 Introduction

When and how to use these pages

The Introduction in the Student Book indicates some of the ideas and skills in this topic area that students will already have met from KS2 or from previous KS3 work, and provides an indication of what they will be studying in this chapter. *Ideas you have met before* is not intended to comprehensively summarise of all the prior ideas, but rather to point out a few of the key ones and to support the view that scientific understanding is progressive. Even though students might be meeting contexts that are new to them, they can often use existing ideas to start to make sense of them.

In this chapter you will find out indicates some of the new ideas that the chapter will introduce. Again, it isn't a detailed summary of content. Its purpose is more to act as a 'trailer' and generate some interest.

The outcomes, then, will be a recognition of prior learning that can be built on, and interest in finding out more.

There are a number of ways this can be used. You might, for example:

- Use *Ideas you have met before* as the basis for a revision lesson as you start the first new topic.
- Use *Ideas you have met before* as the centre of spider diagrams, to which students can add examples, experiments they might have done previously or what they found interesting.
- Make a note of any unfamiliar/difficult terms and return to these in the relevant lessons.
- Use ideas from *In this chapter you will find out* to ask students questions such as:
  - Why is this important?
  - How could it be used?
  - What might we be doing in this topic?

Overview of the chapter

In this chapter, students will learn about life processes in plants and relationships in ecosystems. They will explore why plants are so important to the survival of all living organisms and will learn about the process of photosynthesis and the factors that affect it. They will study the movement of water and minerals through plants and the effects of mineral deficiencies on their growth. The students will learn about the adaptations in plants that allow them to carry out their life processes effectively. Chemosynthesis by bacteria at ocean vents will be explored and compared to photosynthesis in green plants.

The students will study the interdependence of organisms in ecosystems – including food webs and insect-pollinated crops and their importance to human food security. They will learn how organisms affect, and are affected by, their environment – including the accumulation of toxic materials in food chains and the role of variation in enabling living organisms to inhabit the same ecosystem.

This chapter offers opportunities for students to investigate photosynthesis, model the impact of relationships in ecosystems and and use evidence to construct explanations.

Obstacles to learning

Students may need extra guidance with the following common misconceptions:

- **How plants make food** Plants get their food from the soil. Plant food is added to the soil. Light is a reactant in photosynthesis. Minerals are plant food. Some students may confuse photosynthesis with respiration or think that plants breathe in carbon dioxide.
- **Leaf structure and stomata** Cells are like particles or atoms. Cells are two-dimensional. All cells are the same shape. All plant cells contain chloroplasts. Guard cells close when they fill with water. Plants do not respire.
- **Movement of water** Water enters the leaf through stomata.
- **Chemosynthesis** Bacteria feed on hydrogen sulfide.

Chapter 2: Looking at Plants and Ecosystems

- **Food chains and interdependence** The arrows in food chains go from consumer to consumed. Food security is guaranteed.

    Students need to be clear that food chains show the energy flow through an ecosystem. The concept of a niche is very difficult. They may find it difficult to understand that humans have had such disastrous impacts on the environment, and have only relatively recently started trying to correct these. Bioaccumulation in food chains is another very difficult concept.

	Topic title:	Overarching objectives:
2	Understanding the importance of plants	The dependence of almost all life on Earth on the ability of photosynthetic organisms, such as plants and algae, to use sunlight in photosynthesis to build organic molecules that are an essential energy store, and to maintain levels of oxygen and carbon dioxide in the atmosphere
3	Exploring how plants make food	The reactants in, and products of, photosynthesis, and a word summary for photosynthesis Plants making carbohydrates in their leaves by photosynthesis
4	Looking at leaves	The adaptations of leaves for photosynthesis
5	Exploring the role of stomata	The adaptations of leaves for photosynthesis The role of leaf stomata in gas exchange in plants
6	Investigating photosynthesis	The reactants in, and products of, photosynthesis, and a word summary for photosynthesis
7	Exploring the movement of water and minerals in plants	Plants gain mineral nutrients and water from the soil via their roots
8	Investigating the importance of minerals to plants	
9	Investigating chemosynthesis	The interdependence of organisms in an ecosystem, including food webs
11	Understanding food webs	
12	Exploring the importance of insects	The interdependence of organisms in an ecosystem, including insect-pollinated crops The importance of plant reproduction through insect pollination in human food security
13	Looking at other examples of interdependence	How organisms affect, and are affected by, their environment, including the accumulation of toxic materials
14	Understanding interactions in the environment	
15	Learning about ecological balance	
16	Understanding the effects of toxins in the environment	
17	Exploring how organisms co-exist	

Chapter 2: Looking at Plants and Ecosystems

2.2 Understanding the importance of plants

Lesson overview

Learning objectives
- Identify the importance of plants to life on Earth.
- Use evidence to explain that plants do not use soil to grow.
- Evaluate secondary data to start to explain how plants make food.

Learning outcomes
- Identify the various ways in which plants are essential to life on Earth. [O1]
- Explain the evidence that van Helmont obtained from his experiment. [O2]
- Critically evaluate secondary data showing plants growing in different habitats. [O3]

Skills development
- Thinking scientifically: understand how theories develop
- Working scientifically: design investigations
- Learner development: collaborate effectively

Resources needed bean and sunflower seedlings; plant pots; compost; plastic 50 cm^3 measuring cylinder; large plastic bags; Worksheet 2.2.2; Practical sheet 2.2.2; Technician's notes 2.2.2

Digital resources Quick starter; Interactive activity: Sort trees into the products they are used for; Slideshow: Looking at the discovery of photosynthesis; Video

Common misconceptions Plants get their food from the soil. Plant food must be added to soil.

Key vocabulary carbon dioxide, oxygen

Teaching and learning

Engage
- **Group talk** Ask the students to work in groups of three to **brainstorm** and **discuss** why plants are useful and important. Take feedback, one point from each group in turn, until ideas are exhausted. [O1]
- Alternatively ask the groups to study the pictures of plants in Worksheet 2.2.2 and **think about** how they are useful to us – ask them to **classify** the plants into groups and **discuss** the criteria they have used. [O1]

Challenge and develop
- Ask the groups of three to **consider** and **explain** how plants grow. Ensure that the students can recognise that plants use sunlight to build organic molecules (glucose and starch), and that these are a stored-energy source that can be used by consumers. [O1]
- Ask 'What happens to the oxygen released in photosynthesis?'. Discuss how plants use the carbon dioxide released by respiration (covered in Chapter 1) to photosynthesise and release oxygen that is then used in respiration, and so on. This cycle maintains the levels of oxygen and carbon dioxide in the air. [O1]
- Ask the students to work in pairs to list what is needed to help plants to grow well and to **justify** each idea. Take feedback from some groups and discuss it. [O1&2]
- Introduce van Helmont's background and experiment. Stress how he built on previous ideas about plant growth using evidence from his experiment. [O2]

Explain
- All the original groups of three should **discuss** the questions about the experiment. Each student **records** these ideas in a table. [O2]
- **Rainbow groups** Arrange the students in groups of six and assign each student in a group a number between 1 and 6. The groups should then split into 'rainbow groups' made up of students given the same

Chapter 2: Looking at Plants and Ecosystems

number across the class. The new groups **share** and **discuss** their ideas to develop their understanding. [O2]

Consolidate and apply

- **Pair work** The students work in pairs using their shared ideas to **plan** and, if possible, **set up** an investigation to see whether or not the increase in the mass of a plant is from water alone. Practical sheet 2.2.2 gives guidance on planning this investigation. [O2]
- Ask each student to **devise** a question that they would ask van Helmont about his work [O2]

Extend

Ask students able to progress further to:

- **calculate** how much the soil should have weighed at the conclusion of van Helmont's experiment if plants did indeed get their food from the soil. [O3]
- study the pictures of plants from other habitats in Worksheet 2.2.2. They should **discuss** their observations and **decide** if the evidence supports van Helmont's conclusions. [O3]
- **research** 'hydroponics' using the internet and to **write a short explanation** of the advantages and disadvantages of this process. [O2&3]

Plenary suggestions

Hot seat Elect one student to sit in the 'hot seat' and **role-play** van Helmont. The other students ask their questions and say at the end whether the response was correct or not. [O2]

Mind map The students work in pairs and start to **develop a mind map** for the topic, which they can then update at regular intervals. [O2&3]

Answers to Student Book questions

1. for food; building; textiles; medicine; oils; dyes; rubber; biofuels etc
2. Wood from trees is used to build boats, houses and furniture. Palm leaves are woven into baskets, hats and mats. Flax, hemp and cotton are woven to make textiles.
3. plants absorb (remove) carbon dioxide from the atmosphere and release oxygen; which animals use to respire
4. temperature; humidity; light intensity; disease; amount of water; amount of minerals
5. a) 80 − 2 = 78 kg; b) 100 − 99 = 1 kg
6. the soil lost only 1 kg; but the tree gained 78 kg
7. a) the tree used other materials to grow – e.g. water and carbon dioxide
   b) set up repeats; use a control with no plant; use different types of plants
8. Many plants grow naturally without soil.
9. no; van Helmont did not measure the amount of water he added, so he could not know if water caused the growth
10. to prevent: the evaporation of water; materials being added to or taken from the soil

Answers to Worksheet 2.2.2

1. a) *Oak*: building, fuel, furniture. *Pine*: building, fue, furniture. *Lavender*: herbal medicine, aromatherapy. *Cotton*: fabric. *Banana*: food, leaves for roofing, baskets, brushes etc. *Rubber tree*: resin to make rubber, fuel, leaves for roofing. *Cherry tree*: fruit, fuel, furniture. *Palm tree*: fruit, fuel, furniture, leaves for roofing, baskets etc.

   b) any groups based on type of plant, location or uses – e.g. trees; not grown in UK or abroad; used to provide food

   c) a list of the criteria used to group the plants – trees or not; grown in UK or abroad; any other sensible grouping

2. see answers to Student Book questions 4–7

3. a) some plants are growing in sunshine; some are in growing in rain; they appear to be growing in soil although the lavender is on very rocky ground and we can't tell about the banana tree

   b) no; because not all plants have all the conditions; yet they still grow

   c) yes; he did not measure the water he added; he only used one tree; he did not have a control (he could have used distilled water; grown the plant in the absence of air)

   d) any sensible experiment based on their knowledge – e.g. do plants need light?

   e) any sensible observations – e.g. that plants need manure/fertiliser/plant 'food', but explain that these are plant nutrients and not actually food

Chapter 2: Looking at Plants and Ecosystems

2.3 Exploring how plants make food

Lesson overview

Learning objectives

- Identify the reactants and products of photosynthesis.
- Plan and predict the results of investigations.
- Evaluate the risks of a procedure.

Learning outcomes

- Identify carbon dioxide and water as reactants, and glucose and oxygen as products of photosynthesis. [O1]
- Predict that plants will only photosynthesise in the light and that photosynthesis will only occur in the green areas of leaves where chlorophyll is present; draw up a good plan for an investigation. [O2]
- Critically evaluate the risks involved when testing a leaf for starch. [O3]

Skills development

- Thinking scientifically: evaluate risks
- Working scientifically: make predictions
- Learner development: act responsibly

Resources needed two geranium plants; plant with variegated leaves; sticky labels; equipment and materials for testing a leaf for starch as detailed in the Technician's notes; Worksheet 2.2.3; Practical sheet 2.2.2; Practical sheet 2.2.3; Technician's notes 2.2.3

Digital resources Quick starter; Interactive activity: Rearrange the steps in a method to explain how to test a leaf for the presence of starch

Common misconceptions Light is a reactant in photosynthesis. Photosynthesis is the same as respiration.

Key vocabulary glucose, photosynthesis, starch, iodine, chlorophyll

Teaching and learning

Engage

- The students work in pairs to **draw** a labelled diagram showing what they already know about how plants make their food. [O1]
- Ask different pairs to **present** their ideas and encourage the other students to **ask questions**. [O1]

Challenge and develop

- Develop the students' ideas and introduce photosynthesis as a chemical reaction in which carbon dioxide and water are the reactants, and glucose and oxygen are the products. Using Worksheet 2.2.3, students **discuss** and **agree** on the correct word equation for the process. Correct any misconceptions. [O1]

    For an increased challenge, higher-attaining students can use symbols for the reactants and products in the equation.

- **Think, pair, share** Ask the students to work in pairs to answer questions 1–4 in the Student Book and to construct agreed answers. Take feedback. [O1]

Explain

- Demonstrate testing a leaf for starch, highlighting the safety issues (e.g. ethanol boils at a low temperature). Explain the reasons for each of these steps in the process:
    - Place a Bunsen burner on a heatproof mat. Position the tripod and gauze over the Bunsen.
    - Heat the water in the beaker until it boils.
    - Place the leaf in a beaker of boiling water for 30 seconds.
    - Turn off the Bunsen burner.

Chapter 2: Looking at Plants and Ecosystems

- Half fill a boiling tube with ethanol. Place the leaf in it using forceps and then put the boiling tube in the beaker of hot water and leave it for 5 minutes. This will decolourise the leaf.
- Using forceps, take the leaf out of the boiling tube and rinse it in the water in the beaker.
- Put the leaf on a white tile; add three or four drops of iodine solution onto it. A blue-black colour means that starch is in the leaf. Starch is only made in the leaf as a result of photosynthesis.
- Ask the students to **think about** questions 5 and 6 in the Student Book, then **discuss** them as a class. [O2]
- The students work in groups to **plan** how to investigate the effect of light on photosynthesis, **predict** the outcome and **set up** a simple investigation (keeping one plant in the light and one in the dark for at least 24 hours before testing). Practical sheet 2.2.2 can be used again as a planning guide. [O2]

Consolidate and apply

- **Snowball** Show student pairs a plant with variegated leaves. They **discuss** why some parts of the leaves have different colours and **predict** what would happen if they tested these leaves for starch. Merge the pairs to fours to agree an answer and then take feedback. [O2]
- The students work in pairs to **test** a variegated leaf for starch, following the instructions on Practical sheet 2.2.3. Task 2 of Worksheet 2.2.3 supports them in **understanding** the purpose of each step of the process. [O2]

Extend

Ask students able to progress further:

- to **identify** the risks involved in testing a leaf for starch and then take feedback. [O3]
- to work in pairs and **decide** which risks were the greatest and **explain** the steps taken to control these. They **make suggestions** for improving the process if they were to do it again. [O3]

Plenary suggestions

What do I know? Give each group of four students a large sheet of paper – each student has a different coloured pen. Give them one minute to **write down** one fact they have learned in the lesson in turns. No one is allowed to speak, and facts must not be repeated. [O2]

Mind map Alternatively students work in pairs and **develop** their mind map for the topic, which they began last lesson. [O1, 2&3]

Answers to Student Book questions

1. a) carbon dioxide and water   b) glucose and oxygen
2. light is needed to give the energy for the reaction; at night there is no light energy for the reaction
3. it will increase
4. light does not take part in the reaction; it provides the energy needed
5. a) blue-black   b) orange; starch only forms when light is available to provide the energy for the reaction
6. orange
7. the leaf would stay orange in the white areas; and turn blue-black in the green areas; showing that starch is only made in the areas containing chlorophyll
8. *risks*: using boiling water; ethanol catching fire (it is flammable); iodine splashing and staining
   safety precautions: wearing safety glasses; turning the Bunsen off before using ethanol; using gloves to protect the hands; using forceps to remove the leaf from the hot water

Answers to Worksheet 2.2.3

1. the correct equation is: carbon dioxide + water → glucose + oxygen; do not allow any other symbols
2. 1 with E; 2 with D; 3 with C; 4 with B; 5 with A.
   a) some parts are a green colour and some are not; will depend on the leaf used
   b) the green parts have chlorophyll in the plant cells; the non-green parts have no chlorophyll in the cells
   c), d) the parts that were green will turn blue-black (indicating starch); the parts that were not green will turn orange
   e) the parts that were green turned blue-black (indicating starch); the parts that were not green turned orange; only cells containing chlorophyll (i.e. are green) can photosynthesise

Chapter 2: Looking at Plants and Ecosystems

2.4 Looking at leaves

Lesson overview

Learning objectives

- Relate the size of a leaf to the availability of light.
- Relate the function of the leaf to its structure and the types of cell.
- Evaluate the structure of a cell related to its function.

Learning outcomes

- Name the common features of leaves that are adaptations to photosynthesis; explain how the size of leaves relates to the availability of light. [O1]
- Explain the functions of the different cells in a leaf; identify the different cells found in the leaf. [O2]
- Critically evaluate the structure of different cells related to their function. [O3]

Skills development

- Thinking scientifically: develop explanations
- Working scientifically: record evidence
- Learner development: communicate effectively

Resources needed variety of leaves; microscopes; slides of transverse sections of leaves; equipment and materials for class practical as detailed in the Technician's notes; Worksheet 2.2.4; Practical sheet 2.2.4; Technician's notes 2.2.4

Digital resources Quick starter; Slideshow: A detailed look at the different components of a leaf; Interactive activity: Match the adaptations of the leaf to its function; Hangman: Key vocabulary game

Common misconceptions Cells are two-dimensional. All cells are the same shape. Cells are like particles or atoms.

Key vocabulary cuticle, epidermis, palisade cell, spongy cell

Teaching and learning

Engage

- Give each group a selection of leaves of different sizes and shapes. Ask the students to **discuss** what features all leaves have in common and why these features might be important. Take feedback, one point from each group at a time, and discuss with the class. [O1]
- Alternatively ask the students to work in pairs to **construct** a large annotated diagram of a leaf to show how it is designed to photosynthesise. Discuss why leaves are green – they contain chlorophyll, which absorbs light energy needed for photosynthesis. [O1]

Challenge and develop

- The students use a microscope to **observe** prepared slides of transverse sections of a leaf. They **draw** and **identify** the layers of cells. Ask the students to **compare** the leaf cells close to the darker upper surface with other cells. Make sure they identify that there are more chloroplasts near the upper surface. [O1]

Explain

- The students work in pairs following the instructions on Practical sheet 2.2.4 to extract chlorophyll from leaves and separate the pigments using chromatography. Discuss why the chlorophyll contains more than one pigment (simply to absorb more light at this stage) and how being able to absorb more light will be an advantage to the plant. [O1]
- Ask the students to use the Student Book and the internet to **research** and **explain** the functions of the different cell types. Take feedback. [O2]

Key Stage 3 Science Teacher Pack 2 © HarperCollins*Publishers* Limited 2014

Chapter 2: Looking at Plants and Ecosystems

Consolidate and apply

- The students use Worksheet 2.2.4 to **complete** a table explaining the functions of the different cell types. [O2]
- Ask the students to **discuss** and **explain** why water-lily leaves float on the surface of water. Take feedback. [O2]
- The students work in pairs to complete task 2 of Worksheet 2.2.4 and **identify** the adaptations of each cell type that help it to carry out its functions. [O3]

Extend

- Ask students able to progress further to work in pairs to **evaluate** the structure of each cell type related to its function (task 3 of Worksheet 2.2.4). [O3]

Plenary suggestions

An ideal leaf Ask the students to **draw** and **label** an 'ideal leaf' incorporating as many of the adaptations studied in this lesson as possible. [O1, 2&3]

Ask me a question Alternatively the students work in groups to **develop questions** starting 'How, where, when, why and what' on the topic, providing answers as well. Students **peer-assess** another group's work. Take feedback. [O1, 2&3]

Answers to Student Book questions

1. leaves are thin, broad and flat; they are green and contain chlorophyll; they have a network of veins
2. they are thin to allow fast gas exchange by diffusion; broad and flat to give a large surface area to absorb light; the chlorophyll absorbs light energy; the veins transport water, sugar and minerals
3. palisade cells
4. plants on the forest floor have very large leaves; leaves on the trees are much smaller
5. Plants on the forest floor receive much less light than those on the tall trees; the larger surface means they can absorb more light to photosynthesise.
6. Larger leaves contain more chlorophyll; to absorb all the light that reaches them.
7. Carbon dioxide moves into the leaf in daytime; and oxygen moves out; by diffusion.
8. see answers to Worksheet 2.2.4 below ('Adaptations' column)
9. see answers to Worksheet 2.2.4 below (final column)

Answers to Worksheet 2.2.4

Name of cell/ layer in the leaf	Function of the cell/layer	Adaptations of the cell	How do these adaptations allow the cell to carry out its functions?
Cuticle	Protects leaf from water loss	Made of wax	It is waterproof
Epidermis	Allows light to reach palisade cells	Thin and transparent	Light is able to pass through
Palisade cells	To absorb light	At the top of the leaf Cells are long and narrow Contain many chloroplasts Chloroplasts are concentrated at the top of the cell	So light does not have far to travel So more cells are at the top of the leaf To absorb the light energy To absorb as much light as possible
Spongy cells	To absorb remaining light To allow gases to pass in/out of the leaf	Contain chloroplasts Large air spaces between the cells	To absorb all the remaining light To allow gas exchange in and out of the leaf

Chapter 2: Looking at Plants and Ecosystems

2.5 Exploring the role of stomata

Lesson overview

Learning objectives
- Describe how stomata control gas exchange.
- Explain how gas exchange occurs in leaves.
- Analyse how stomata density is affected by different conditions.

Learning outcomes
- Describe the movement of gases into/out of a leaf. [O1]
- Explain how stomata open and close to control the movement of gases. [O2]
- Analyse stomata density in different temperatures and different concentrations of carbon dioxide. [O3]

Skills development
- Thinking scientifically: analyse data
- Working scientifically: interpret evidence
- Learner development: collaborate effectively

Resources needed equipment and materials for the optional starter, the class activity in Practical 2.2.5a and the optional activity in Practical 2.2.5b, as detailed in the Technician's notes; Worksheet 2.2.5a; Worksheet 2.2.5b (second page copied onto card); Practical sheet 2.2.5a; Practical sheet 2.2.5b; Technician's notes 2.2.5

Digital resources Quick starter; Interactive activity: Which of the sentences about stomata are true, and which are false?

Common misconceptions Plants do not respire. Water enters the leaf through the stomata.

Key vocabulary pore, stomata, stoma, guard cell

Teaching and learning

- Ask the students to work in groups and **discuss** the question 'How do you think the carbon dioxide needed for photosynthesis enters a leaf and how does the oxygen produced leave it?' Take feedback and guide them to establish that there may be holes in the surface of the leaf. Explain that the holes are called stomata. [O1]

- Alternatively show the students two geranium plants set up the day before. One has both sides of the leaves smeared with *Vaseline* and the other has no *Vaseline* on its leaves. Each has a plastic bag secured over the leaves. Water will be present in the bag around the plant with untreated leaves. Ask them to **discuss** 'Where has the water come from?' Take feedback from the groups as above. [O1]

Challenge and develop

- The students work in pairs to **describe** what stomata are, where they are found and why there are always two guard cells – they complete task 1 of Worksheet 2.2.5a. [O1]

- The pairs then use Figure 2.2.5a in the Student Book to **describe** the movement of carbon dioxide from the air to the palisade cells, and the movement of oxygen from the palisade cells to the air. [O1]

Explain

- Working in groups of three, the students **plan** and **draw** an annotated diagram to **explain** how stomata control gas exchange in a leaf. Then they complete task 2 of Worksheet 2.2.5a. [O2]

- In the same groups the students use Practical sheet 2.2.5a to **compare** the use of clear nail varnish and *Germolene* 'New Skin' to make impressions of the stomata. They use a microscope to **observe** the impressions and **draw** annotated diagrams. They say which method is best and **explain** why. [O2]

Chapter 2: Looking at Plants and Ecosystems

Consolidate and apply

- Ask the students to **discuss** and **explain** why there are more stomata on the underside of leaves. Extend this by asking them where the stomata would be found on a water-lily leaf (the surface) and why. [O3]
- Optional activity: the students **observe** stomatal density on the upper and lower surface of geranium leaves that have been kept in the dark or in the light for an extended period. Using their preferred method from the previous practical, they follow the instructions on Practical sheet 2.2.5b. You would expect to see more stomata on the leaves kept in the light. [O3]

Extend

Ask students able to progress further to **discuss** how the stomata of plants in very hot/cold climates might be different from those of plants in the temperate UK. They could also **discuss** whether or not water plants, such as pondweed, have stomata and **explain** their answers in completing task 3 of Worksheet 2.2.5a. [O3]

Plenary suggestions

Running game The students work in teams of four to **complete the questions** in a 'running game' activity. Worksheet 2.2.5b has the instructions and the questions. [O1, 2&3]

The big question Alternatively students work in groups to **develop an explanation** for the question 'Why do plants have stomata?'. Take feedback and develop an exemplar explanation using the student responses.

Answers to Student Book questions

1. pores; on the underside of leaves
2. Carbon dioxide diffuses into the leaf through the stomata and moves through it in the air spaces in the spongy mesophyll. Oxygen passes through the air spaces and out of the stomata.
3. Guard cells; there is one either side of the stoma.
4. To form the hole, and to open and close the stomata. They fill with water and open the stoma; when the guard cells contain a little water, they close.
5. Diagram should show open and closed stomata (as Figure 2.2.5b); labelled similarly explaining water concentrations.
6. There would be too much evaporation of water; from the leaf if the stomata were on the upper surface.
7. temperature; availability of light
8. High light intensity (high rate of photosynthesis) and low carbon dioxide concentration may favour high stomatal density. Temperature is more difficult to predict; in high temperatures leaves could have more stomata to increase evaporation to cool the leaf *or* they may have a lower density to prevent water loss.

Answers to Worksheet 2.2.5a

1. a) Stomata are small pores on the surface of the leaf surrounded by two guard cells. b) on the underside of the leaf
   c) to form the opening, allowing the stoma to open and close
   d) Use one plant; smear some wax on the undersurface of one leaf; and enclose it in a plastic bag/sealed conical flask; repeat on an untreated leaf enclosing it as before; water vapour should form on inside of this bag/flask.
2. a) as in the Student Book with guard cells labelled: open stomata 'guard cells full of water' and closed stomata 'guard cells containing little water'
   b) the underside
   c) To protect the plant; if stomata were on the top side, the plant would lose too much water. The guard cells are partially light activated; so plants under direct sunlight would constantly have their stomata open and would lose too much water – the plant would wilt and die.
3. a) no b) temperature; amount of wind; amount of available water (lower-attaining students may include the size of the leaf and the type of plant)
   c) With more light, more photosynthesis would take place; hence more gas exchange. With more wind, more gases can pass out of the leaf, so more photosynthesis could take place. In a dry environment, more water would need to be saved from evaporation from the leaf for photosynthesis.
   d) Water-lily leaves have stomata on the top side.
   e) easier access to carbon dioxide; easier for oxygen to pass out of the leaf

Answers to Worksheet 2.2.5b

1. stomata
2. guard cells
3. two
4. they allow substances to pass in and out of the leaf
5. they swell with water
6. on the underside
7. on the top surface
8. light intensity; humidity; temperature
9. water
10. too much water would evaporate

Chapter 2: Looking at Plants and Ecosystems

2.6 Investigating photosynthesis

Lesson overview

Learning objectives
- Identify the factors that can affect photosynthesis.
- Predict results of investigations.
- Interpret secondary data about photosynthesis.

Learning outcomes
- Identify the factors that affect the rate of photosynthesis. [O1]
- Accurately predict the results of investigations of photosynthesis. [O2]
- Analyse secondary data and apply learning to new situations. [O3]

Skills development
- Thinking scientifically: analyse data
- Working scientifically: making predictions
- Learner development: act responsibly

Resources needed graph paper; metre rule; pondweed; scissors; forceps; bench lamp; filter funnels; test tubes; 500 cm^3 beakers; thermometer; water baths at different temperatures; Worksheet 2.2.6a; Worksheet 2.2.6b; Practical sheet 2.2.6a; Practical sheet 2.2.6b; Technician's notes 2.2.6

Digital resources Quick starter; Interactive activity: Complete the sentences about photosynthesis

Key vocabulary rate, concentration

Teaching and learning

- Ask the students to work in pairs to answer question 1 in the Student Book, about the equation for photosynthesis, identifying the reactants (water and carbon dioxide) and the products (glucose and oxygen). They **identify** the conditions needed for photosynthesis to occur (presence of chlorophyll and light) and use this to **suggest** the factors that might affect the rate of photosynthesis (Student Book question 2). [O1]

- Alternatively ask them to add new learning to their mind map that was started in an earlier lesson. They should **underline/highlight** the reactants in photosynthesis in green, the products in orange and the conditions needed in blue. [O1]

Challenge and develop

- The students work in pairs to apply their knowledge by **discussing** if trees growing in hot and cold environments will photosynthesise at the same speed. For example, they know that heating up chemicals makes a reaction happen faster – or is it just that plants grow faster in summer than winter? The students complete task 1 of Worksheet 2.2.6a. [O1]

- The students use Figure 2.2.6b in the Student Book to illustrate how increasing the available carbon dioxide increases the amount of photosynthesis that occurs. They work in groups to **discuss** and **predict** the answers to questions 5 and 6 – they may find it helpful to **sketch** graphs showing these predictions. [O1&2]

Explain

- Use the example of a student's investigation in the 'Factors affecting photosynthesis' section in the Student Book to talk through a simple method of measuring the rate of photosynthesis. Discuss question 7 as a class to help the students to understand the next stage in the lesson.

- Using Practical sheets 2.2.6a and 2.2.6b, the students work in pairs to **carry out** an investigation into the effect of *either* temperature (for lower-attaining students) *or* light on the rate of photosynthesis. [O2]

Key Stage 3 Science Teacher Pack 2 © HarperCollins*Publishers* Limited 2014

Chapter 2: Looking at Plants and Ecosystems

- The students **analyse** their data and **compare** their results to the predictions made earlier. Were their predictions correct? Ask them to explain their results, and to identify sources of error and any risks in the procedure. [O2]

  Ask higher-attaining students to complete the tasks in Worksheet 2.2.6b, **analysing data** from the investigation presented.

Consolidate and apply

- **Pairs to fours** The students undertake a 'think–pair–share' activity and then merge to a 'fours' activity, to **explain** how the rate of photosynthesis changes from sunrise to sunset during a warm sunny day by producing an annotated graph (task 2 of Worksheet 2.2.6a). Take feedback from the different groups and discuss their ideas. [O3]

- The students work in pairs to decide what temperature the 'student's grandfather's greenhouse' should be kept at (question 9 in the Student Book) and any other conditions necessary to maximise the growth of tomatoes. [O3]

Extend

- Ask students able to progress further to do task 3 of Worksheet 2.2.6a. They should **discuss** whether or not the rate of photosynthesis can be increased indefinitely by continuing to increase the light intensity and/or the temperature. Ask which factor will have the biggest impact on the rate of photosynthesis. [O3]

Plenary suggestions

In a nutshell Ask the students to work in pairs to **summarise** this lesson in 30 words or fewer. Take feedback and **peer-assess** the statements. [O1, 2&3]

Two stars and a wish Alternatively the students work individually to name two 'stars' (things they have done well, learned, understood or enjoyed) and one 'wish' (something they could improve, need to complete or need help with). [O1, 2&3]

Answers to Student Book questions

1. carbon dioxide + water → glucose + oxygen (accept a correct symbol equation)
2. amount of carbon dioxide; light; water; the temperature
3. The tree in the warmer climate will photosynthesise more; because heat speeds up reactions.
4. Plants grow less; it is colder in winter; there is less daylight; the light intensity is weaker.
5. 'The stronger the light, the more photosynthesis' is sufficient.
6. 'As the temperature increases, photosynthesis increases' is sufficient.
7. a) Oxygen gas is released in the reaction.   b) temperature and the amount of carbon dioxide; (the plants are in water so this does not need to be controlled)   c) Heat is given off by the lamp; the closer the plant is to the lamp, the more heat will reach it; before it dissipates.
8. There is no photosynthesis when there is no light. As the Sun rises and the temperature increases, the rate of photosynthesis increases to a maximum when the Sun is highest in the sky. The rate then fall until the Sun sets.
   (At this stage do not bring the concentration of carbon dioxide into the explanation.)
9. 21/22 °C; photosynthesis is at its fastest

Answers to Worksheet 2.2.6a

1. a) no; it will depend on how much light they have access to, the amount of available water etc

   b) availability of light, water and carbon dioxide; temperature. Light provides the energy needed for the reaction; water and CO_2 are reactants in the reaction; temperature speeds up reactions.

2. a)–e) No light means no photosynthesis. As dawn breaks, photosynthesis starts to happen; it rapidly increases to a maximum when the Sun is at its highest in the sky. It then starts to decrease; when the Sun sets, it stops.

3. a) no; when all the chloroplasts are photosynthesising at their maximum rate, the rate will be steady

   b) depends on the response, but they should grasp that light is a limiting factor; because no light means no photosynthesis. Once light is available, it will also be limited by the amount of carbon dioxide, the temperature and amount of water; it depends on the environment where the plant grows.

Answers to Worksheet 2.2.6b

1. 10 cm = 47 bubbles; 20 cm = 25; 30 cm = 12; 40 cm = 7; 50 cm = 6
2. As light intensity decreases; the rate of photosynthesis decreases.
3. Light energy is needed for photosynthesis; the less light there is, the less energy for the reaction, so the rate decreases.

Chapter 2: Looking at Plants and Ecosystems

2.7 Exploring the movement of water and minerals in plants

Lesson overview

Learning objectives
- Identify how water and minerals move through a plant.
- Explain how water and minerals move through a plant.
- Evaluate the cell structures that allow the movement of water and minerals through a plant.

Learning outcomes
- Identify the passage of water and minerals through a plant; summarise the inputs and outputs for plant growth by a diagram. [O1]
- Explain how water and minerals are taken in and move through a plant. [O2]
- Evaluate cell structures that allow the movement of water and minerals through a plant. [O3]

Skills development
- Thinking scientifically: analyse data
- Working scientifically: interpret evidence
- Learner development: communicate effectively

Resources needed equipment and materials as detailed in the technician's notes; Worksheet 2.2.7a, Worksheet 2.2.7b; Technician's notes 2.2.7

Digital resources Quick starter; Interactive activity: Rearrange the sentences to describe the movement of water through a plant

Common misconception Water enters a leaf through the stomata.

Key vocabulary transpiration, xylem cells, root hair cell

Teaching and learning

Engage
- Ask the students the questions 'How, where, when, why is water lost from a plant?' and 'What adaptations do plants have to prevent water loss?'. [O1&2]
- The students work in pairs to **draw** a labelled picture showing the passage of water into and through a plant (task 1d of Worksheet 2.2.7a). Take feedback and discuss any misconceptions at this point. [O1]

Challenge and develop
- Show the students a potted plant with the soil washed off its roots. Ask them to look at the roots under a microscope, **draw** what they see and then **discuss** in groups how root systems are adapted to take in water. They can then read the 'Taking water in' section in the Student Book, answer questions 1–3 and complete task 1 of Worksheet 2.2.7a. [O1]
- The students read the 'Keeping the water' section in the Student Book and answer questions 4–7, working in pairs. [O2]
- Show two potometers set up with leafy shoots – one in still air and one in front of a hair dryer. Explain the set-up. Ask the pairs to **discuss** and **predict** which plant would experience the bigger water loss. After 10–15 minutes compare the water loss from the two plants. Which pair's predictions were correct? [O2]
- Show the students a celery stem (with leaves) that has been placed for one to two hours in a beaker containing a dye solution. Discuss how water is transported from the roots to the leaves, emphasising the role of transpiration. Give the students pre-cut thin slices of stem to **examine** with a hand lens and **draw**. [O2]

Key Stage 3 Science Teacher Pack 2 © HarperCollinsPublishers Limited 2014

Chapter 2: Looking at Plants and Ecosystems

Explain

- The students **make a model** of xylem cells using pieces of dried macaroni (to represent cells), threaded to form a 'pipeline' using the cotton. Ask what the pieces of macaroni represent. Is this a good model? [O3]
- The students work in pairs to answer the questions in task 2 of Worksheet 2.2.7a, including an explanation of why increasing the temperature and wind speed increases the rate of transpiration. [O2]
- They answer Student Book question 8 and **evaluate** how the adaptations of the specialised cells involved in transpiration help the plant to carry out the process (task 3 of Worksheet 2.2.7a). [O3]

Consolidate and apply

- The students work in pairs to answer the questions about a transpiration investigation on Worksheet 2.2.7b. They should **draw their graphs** individually. [O2]

Extend

- Ask students able to progress further to **suggest** some ways in which the potometer demonstration procedure could be improved. [O2]

Plenary suggestions

Picture summary The students work in pairs to draw an annotated diagram **summarising** the requirements for healthy plant growth. [O1&2]

Mind map Alternatively the students work in pairs to add their new learning to their growing mind map for the topic. [O1, 2&3]

Answers to Student Book questions

1. Roots take up water and minerals; and anchor the plant. 2. to get water from different parts of the soil
3. for photosynthesis 4. movement of water through a plant until it evaporates from the leaves
5. cold; wet; no wind 6. by closing the stomata; some have small or needle-like leaves
7. arrows going from soil water into the roots; up the stem; into the leaves; then showing water evaporating
8. The root has not got a large enough area to take up enough water, so the root hairs increase the surface area. They have no chloroplasts; because they receive no light to photosynthesise. In the xylem, there are no cell walls at the ends, so it makes a tube to allow quick transport of water and minerals.

Answers to Worksheet 2.2.7a

1. a) *Functions*: to take up water and minerals; to anchor the plant. *Adaptation*: have root hair cells to increase the area for absorption of water (and minerals).   b) Roots have adapted; to get water from different parts of the soil.
   c) the movement of water through the plant; until it evaporates from the leaves
   d) arrows going from soil water into the roots; up the stem; into the leaves; then showing water evaporating
2. a) it is needed for photosynthesis, and helps support the leaves and stem
   b) there is more or faster diffusion or evaporation or transpiration; the molecules move faster; it keeps water concentration low in the air or brings in more dry air or removes damp air/water
   c) plants close the stomata, some have small or needle-like leaves
3. a) i) The root has not got a large enough area to take up enough water, so the root hairs increase the surface area; they have no chloroplasts because they receive no light to photosynthesise.
   ii) There are no cell walls at the ends, so it makes a tube to allow quick transport of water and minerals.
   iii) Stomata have two guard cells that swell with water; they open to let excess water leave the leaf; when the guard cells contain little water, they close the stomata.
   b) to cool the plant through evaporation; to allow nutrients to be absorbed (with the water); to allow carbon dioxide to enter the plant.   c) decreases; it becomes harder for water to move through a thicker and waxier layer

Answers to Worksheet 2.2.7b

1. to stop water evaporating from the soil in the pot 2. dried out/lost water
3. correct curves on one pair of axes 4. this plant still had leaves; so more transpiration occurred
5. between days 6 and 7; because the combination of wind and sun increased the rate of transpiration'
6. transpiration happens from the leaves 7. hHot/windy/dry weather increases transpiration (or reverse)
8. use plants with different numbers of leaves

Chapter 2: Looking at Plants and Ecosystems

2.8 Investigating the importance of minerals to plants

Lesson overview

Learning objectives

- Identify the minerals essential to healthy plant growth.
- Explain the effects of a deficiency in essential minerals.
- Evaluate the limitations of evidence.

Learning outcomes

- Identify nitrogen, phosphorus and potassium as essential for healthy plant growth. [O1]
- Explain the roles of nitrogen, phosphorus and potassium in plant growth. [O2]
- Evaluate the limitations of collected evidence. [O3]

Skills development

- Thinking scientifically: consider the quality of evidence
- Working scientifically: design investigations
- Learner development: develop resilience

Resources needed equipment and materials for the class activity in Practical 2.2.8 as detailed in the Technician's notes; examples of packaging for different fertilisers; Worksheet 2.2.8a copied onto card; Worksheet 2.2.8b; Practical sheet 2.2.8; Technician's notes 2.2.8

Digital resources Quick starter; Slideshow: An introduction to plant mineral deficiencies; Interactive activity: Match the mineral deficiency to its effect on a plant; Video

Common misconceptions Minerals are plant food.

Key vocabulary deficiency, fertiliser, manure

Teaching and learning

Engage

- **Think, pair, share** Ask the students to **think about** what the following have in common – nitrogen, phosphorus, potassium, magnesium, sulfur and calcium. They form pairs and **share** their thoughts with their partner. Take feedback of their ideas and lead them to agree that minerals are needed by both humans and plants in order to be healthy. [O1]

- Alternatively remind the students that both plants and people are made of cells and that cells need nutrients to be healthy. Ask the pairs to **discuss** what happens to us if we don't get enough of an essential nutrient. What do they think might happen to plants if they are lacking in nutrients? [O2]

Challenge and develop

- Ask the students to work in groups of four. First, they read the 'Mineral deficiency' section in the Student Book. Put around the room pictures and information about plants with mineral deficiencies (using the cards on Worksheet 2.2.8a). The groups **organise themselves** to look up the information (5 minutes) and **share** it between them (10 minutes). [O2]

- The students work in pairs to answer questions 1 and 2 in the Student Book. [O1&2]

Explain

- Ask the students to read the 'Essential minerals' section in the Student Book and then answer questions 3–5. [O1&2]

- Working in pairs, using their information on minerals, they **complete a table** to explain why plants need the different minerals and what happens if they have a deficiency in each (task 1 of Worksheet 2.2.8b). [O1&2]

Chapter 2: Looking at Plants and Ecosystems

Consolidate and apply

- Ask the students to work in a group of four to **plan** and **carry out** an investigation into the effects of different concentrations of fertiliser solution on the growth of mung bean seedlings. They can use Practical sheet 2.2.8 to support their planning. They may need some help with how to control variables that are not being investigated. They will also need guidance on how to set up the different containers with the seeds in – see Technician's notes 2.2.8. If students recognise that repeat tests should be used to improve reliability, they can join with another group and agree their plan together. Students will need to leave the seedlings for 1–2 weeks and add more solution as required. [O1, 2&3]
- Later, allow time for the students to **produce a report** of their investigation and **contribute conclusions** to a class summary. [O1, 2&3]
- The students can work in pairs and use the examples of different fertiliser packaging and other sources to **find out about** nutrients – e.g. which nutrients each fertiliser provides, how much a plant requires, the cost and application rate). They then **summarise** the information in a table (task 2 of Worksheet 2.2.8b). [O2]

Extend

Ask students able to progress further to:
- **read** the 'Putting it right' section in the Student Book, answer questions 6–9 and complete task 3 of Worksheet 2.2.8b. [O2].
- **discuss** whether or not they have confidence in what they found out in their investigation and to **explain** why. Are there any limitations/errors? What would they do differently if they were to repeat it? [O3]

Plenary suggestions

Writing a guide The students work in pairs to **make a guide** to mineral deficiencies (NPK only). They should include an explanation of what the minerals are, what each one is used for, and the symptoms of deficiency including a picture. They conclude by writing how they can make the plants healthier. [O1&2]

Picture summary Alternatively the students work in pairs to **make an annotated drawing** of a plant detailing what they have learned about minerals and mineral deficiency. [O1&2]

Answers to Student Book questions

1. a lack of a particular mineral 2. with yellow leaves 3. absorb them (dissolved in water) through their roots
4. the most important minerals for plant health 5. nitrogen, phosphorus and potassium
6. a natural or man-made material added to soil; containing one or more essential minerals for plant growth
7. one containing nitrogen, phosphorus and potassium 8. to replace the minerals used up by crops
9. Some farmers prefer to use natural materials; manure is readily availableand releases the minerals over a period of time; others may not have animal stock so have to buy commercial fertilisers; or they need the fertiliser to act quickly.

Answers to Worksheet 2.2.8b

1.

Mineral deficiency	Description of the plant with this deficiency	What is the mineral used for?
Potassium	Yellow leaves with dead spots	Helps chemical reactions Needed to make proteins; to open and close stomata; to promote root growth
Phosphorus	Poor growth (including root growth) Bluish patches on leaves Small acid-tasting fruits Undersides of plant leaves; the veins and stems may turn purple	Used for energy transfer, photosynthesis, nutrient movement and reproduction
Nitrogen	Pale green or yellow leaves	Used to make chlorophyll
Magnesium	Yellow leaves Premature ageing	Production of chlorophyll for photosynthesis Helps in making proteins

2. Answers will depend on the samples used.   3. If farmers have cattle, pigs or horses, it is a good way of using the animal waste. Natural manure breaks down slowly and releases minerals back into the soil over a period of time. With natural manure there is no danger of chemicals (i.e. those found in artifical fertilisers) causing problems in the environment. Commercial fertilisers are always available, easy to store and the amount of each mineral added to the soil is known.

Chapter 2: Looking at Plants and Ecosystems

2.9 Investigating chemosynthesis

Lesson overview

Learning objectives

- Describe how ocean vent communities survive.
- Describe the adaptations of tubeworms.
- Compare and contrast chemosynthesis and photosynthesis.
- Evaluate models of chemosynthesis and photosynthesis.

Learning outcomes

- Describe an ocean vent community. [O1]
- Describe the adaptations of tubeworms. [O2]
- Compare chemosynthesis and photosynthesis, and evaluate models of these. [O3]

Skills development

- Thinking scientifically: ask questions
- Working scientifically: develop explanations
- Learner development: collaborate effectively

Resources needed equipment for making chemical models (equations); coloured blocks/craft pompoms; large sheets of paper and coloured markers; video clip of the ocean floor and deep-sea vents; Worksheet 2.2.9

Digital resources Quick starter; Interactive activity: Which of the statements are true for photosynthesis, and which are true for chemosynthesis?; Hangman: Key vocabulary game

Common misconceptions Bacteria feed on hydrogen sulfide.

Key vocabulary chemosynthesis, hydrothermal vent

Teaching and learning

Engage

- **Think, pair, share** Ask the students to **discuss** the questions 'Is there life in the depth of the ocean?' 'Would green plants survive there?' 'If there are no green plants, how would other organisms get their energy and survive?' Take feedback, discuss ideas and record the students' responses on the whiteboard. [O1]

- Alternatively ask the students to **brainstorm** what they think 'chemosynthesis' might be. If they need a hint, remind them of the word 'photosynthesis' – what does it mean? [O2]

Challenge and develop

- Show the students a video clip of the ocean floor and deep-sea vents. [O1]

- **Group talk** Ask the students to work in groups of three to **discuss** what they now know about the conditions on the ocean floor. Take feedback and refer to the original ideas that were recorded on the board. Were they correct? Ask them to read the 'Chemosynthesis' section in the Student Book. They **discuss** and **agree** on answers to questions 1 and 2. Ask the students to **share** their answers and **discuss**. [O1]

Explain

- Ask the groups to read the 'Chemosynthesis vs photosynthesis' section in the Student Book and to answer questions 3–5. They then **discuss** the questions 'How are tubeworms adapted to their environment?' and 'What is symbiosis?' [O1&2]

- The students continue to work in groups. Their task is to **research** and **prepare** index cards on the major organisms found in ocean vent communities (task 1 of Worksheet 2.2.9). Groups peer review each other's index cards, identifying at least one thing that has been done well and one that 'would be even better if...' Ask them to **summarise** what they now know about these organisms. Take feedback. [O2]

Chapter 2: Looking at Plants and Ecosystems

Consolidate and apply

- Using the index cards created in the previous activity, each group **makes food chains**. Ask 'What is the producer?' 'What are the consumers?' 'What are the scavengers?' [O2]

    Higher-attaining students may compile a simple food web.

- The students use the information about ocean vent ecosystems and work collaboratively to **make models** representing chemosynthesis and photosynthesis, and to **create posters** comparing them. They can use chemical models (equations), coloured blocks/craft pompoms etc. or just draw the coloured circles to represent the different elements. The groups **present** their posters and the other students **peer-assess** the models. [O3]

- The students then complete task 2 of Worksheet 2.2.9, **analysing** the growth rate of tubeworms. [O2]

Extend

- Ask students able to progress further to read the 'Life on Mars?' section in the Student Book and to **explain** why chemosynthesis may be more likely to support life on distant worlds than photosynthesis (task 3 of Worksheet 2.2.9). [O3]

Plenary suggestions

Marine chemist's diary Ask the question 'What must it have been like to be a marine chemist discovering the existence of chemosynthesis and these communities?'. Ask the students to write a diary entry as it might have appeared in the scientist's diary. [O1&3]

Summary display Ask the students to **summarise** the lesson using a maximum of 15 words along with pictures, numbers, symbols and acronyms – display these. [O1, 2&3]

Answers to Student Book questions

1. *similarities*: conversion of carbon compounds into sugars, source of energy
2. *differences*: photosynthesis is carried out only by plants, while a variety of organisms are capable of chemosynthesis; the source of energy for photosynthesis is light, whereas the energy for chemosynthesis comes from other chemical reactions in bacteria; chemosynthesis uses hydrogen sulfide
3. the bacteria absorb hydrogen sulfide, oxygen and carbon dioxide from the water. They break down the hydrogen sulfide to get energy. They use the energy and oxygen to convert carbon dioxide into sugars
4. organisms that live near the vents depend on them for food (and energy)
5. the tubeworms use some of the sugars produced by the bacteria as food; they provide the bacteria with hydrogen sulfide and oxygen that they take up from the water
6. the other planets do not have an atmosphere containing oxygen; they do have available sulfur compounds for chemosynthesis; planets further away from the Sun may not get sufficient light for plant life to photosynthesise
7. idea that: bacteria or other simple life forms were able to use the energy from chemosynthesis using the sulfur around hydrothermal vents

Answers to Worksheet 2.2.9

1. **Tubeworms**
    Habitat: live at the boundary where hot hydrothermal fluid mixes with cold seawater
    Adaptations: can grow up to two metres long and ten centimetres in diameter. They stay in their tubes, which are made of a hard material called chitin. The gill-like red plumes absorb hydrogen sulfide from the hot water and oxygen from the cold water. The tubes help protect the worms from toxic vent chemicals and from predators, e.g. crabs and fish
    Food source: Tubeworms have no mouth or stomach and do not eat. Billions of symbiotic bacteria live inside them and produce sugars from carbon dioxide, hydrogen sulfide and oxygen. Tubeworms use some of these sugars as food
    Microbes – Hydrothermal vent microbes include bacteria and archaea
    Habitat: grow on every surface including rocks, animals and the inside of vent chimneys
    Adaptations: some bacteria live inside tubeworms, clams and mussels, forming symbiotic relationships with them
    Food source: these are the start of the food chain. They are chemosynthetic, using the energy to manufacture sugars from carbon dioxide. Different species extract energy from different chemicals, including hydrogen, hydrogen sulfide and iron
2. c) Small tubeworms grow at a faster rate than longer tubeworms.
3. Must include reference to the atmospheres of other planets not having oxygen or carbon dioxide to support plant life, so they would need microbes to synthesise chemicals to produce energy.

Chapter 2: Looking at Plants and Ecosystems

2.10 Applying key ideas

Down at the allotment

Objectives

- Extract ideas about plant adaptations and nutrition from the text, including earlier topics.
- Apply ideas about plant nutrition to explain evidence.
- Apply ideas and information about plant nutrition to propose the outcome of a situation.

Outcome

- Clear and effective responses to questions, indicating understanding and the next steps in learning.

The purpose of this activity is to provide an opportunity to see how successfully students are grasping the key ideas so far. It isn't designed to be used as a formal test – it might be that students work on the questions collectively. It does provide an opportunity for you to look at written work, engage students in discussions and form ideas about progress being made.

The tasks are progressive. Lower-attaining students should be able to tackle the first two or three tasks, and higher-attaining students will find the later ones more challenging.

Resources needed highlighters; coloured pencils; Worksheet 2.2.10a; Worksheet 2.2.10b

Teaching & learning

Engage

- Challenge the students to **reflect** back over the last few lessons and identify some of the key ideas they have learned about. Draw out responses about these ideas and say that it's important as learners that they develop a sense of their own progress.
- **Back to back** The students work in pairs to complete the 'Back-to-back' activity using Worksheet 2.2.10a. The members of each pair sit back-to-back. One student **describes** the photosynthesis diagram to their partner, who has to replicate the diagram without seeing it. Have coloured pencils on the desks. Take feedback – how well did they do?

Challenge and develop

- Give each pair a key idea from the topic and a sheet of flip-chart paper. Ask them to summarise everything they can remember about the idea in 30 seconds. Each pair passes their work on to the next pair. Repeat the process three or four times. Return the work to the original pairs and give them time to read it through. Each pair then presents their ideas to the class. Encourage students to **ask questions** and **discuss** the ideas.
- Ask the pairs of students to draw a plant and to annotate it to describe and explain what they have learned about plant structure and nutrition.

Explain

Ask the students to read the passage 'Down at the allotment'. Depending on their ability to assimilate text, you may need to adopt strategies such as:

- Have students working in pairs using copies of the text (on Worksheet 2.2.10b). One student highlights key ideas and the other (with a different colour) highlights any words they do not understand. Take feedback and ask other students if they can **explain** the difficult words identified.
- Using the text as a source of ideas, draw a concept map with 'allotments' at the centre and ideas, evidence and explanations around it.

Consolidate and apply

- Now ask the students to attempt the tasks in the Student Book – they might do this individually or collaboratively. In each case, encourage them to **identify** and **record** their ideas.
- Ask them to **present** their responses to various tasks, either orally or by displaying their work.

Extend

- For higher-attaining students, the later tasks give an opportunity for extension work.

Plenary

How did you do? Ask the students for responses to questions such as:

- How well were you able to approach those tasks?
- Can you improve on some of these responses by working together as a class?
- Are there some ideas that you need to return to at a later stage? (If there are, make a note.)

Provide the class with some overall feedback, indicating ideas that they have grasped effectively and those that may need developing further.

Likely responses and next steps in learning

1. This task gives students an opportunity to recall learning experiences or refer to images and text in the book, and to recall or research the process of photosynthesis. They should be able to explain that green plants use carbon dioxide and water to make glucose and oxygen with energy tranferred from light. This checks that they understand the process and are not getting confused with respiration or 'plant food'.

2. This involves recalling that temperature is an important factor when considering plant growth. The greenhouse will ensure that plants are warmer and are protected from the cold (and frost). The Sun will heat up the air in the greenhouse, and the walls and roof keep the warm air inside.

3. This involves recalling and explaining the factors that affect the rate of photosynthesis in plants. The students should recall at least that the amount of carbon dioxide and the amount of available water will affect the rate by using the word equation for the reaction. From their class investigations, they should recall that temperature and the amount of light also affect the rate of photosynthesis. They may need prompting to remember that the amount of chlorophyll in the leaves will also have an effect.

4. To complete this task, students need to apply what they have learned about plant nutrients. Plants use minerals from the soil to be healthy. Minerals are needed for healthy growth. If plants are grown in the same place every year, they will use up all the minerals that they need. Ben digs in well-rotted manure every spring. As this breaks down, it releases minerals back into the soil. There is no mention of Joe adding manure, and he grows his plants in the same place every year. Ben moves his vegetable plots every two years. Higher-attaining students may explain the use of different minerals in the plant.

5. The students need to explain the process of transpiration, and possibly the adaptations of xylem cells and the role of diffusion in the transport of water and minerals. Transpiration is important for the flow of water (from the soil through to the leaves) and minerals through the plant.

6. This task involves the students thinking across the key ideas that they have explored and then selecting relevant ideas that will help plants to grow well. Possible ideas include:

   - using manure (or fertilisers) to increase available nutrients
   - moving individual vegetables to different areas of the allotment every year or so as nutrients are used up in any area
   - buying a greenhouse to extend growing periods
   - leaving a light on in the greenhouse all night (if possible) so that photosynthesis occurs 24 hours a day
   - increasing the amount of available carbon dioxide in the greenhouse to increase the amount of photosynthesis – for example, leaving a fossil-fuel heater in the greenhouse to increase the amount of carbon dioxide
   - planting crops so that they all get the maximum amount of light to increase the extent of photosynthesis
   - watering the plants on a regular basis to increase the rate of transpiration (and the uptake of nutrients) and photosynthesis
   - using polytunnels to keep young plants warmer and to restrict the movement of carbon dioxide released from the plants by respiration.

Chapter 2: Looking at Plants and Ecosystems

2.11 Understanding food webs

Lesson overview

Learning objectives

- Describe how food webs are made up of a number of food chains.
- Make predictions about factors affecting plant and animal populations.
- Analyse and evaluate changes in a food web.

Learning outcomes

- Describe food webs as a number of interrelated food chains. [O1]
- Predict the effects of different environmental factors on plant and animal populations – e.g. disease and drought. [O2]
- Analyse and evaluate the impact of changes in a food web. [O3]

Skills development

- Thinking scientifically: analyse data
- Working scientifically: develop explanations
- Learner development: communicate effectively

Resources needed sticky labels; polystyrene packing pellets /dry leaves /ping pong balls; Worksheet 2.2.11a; Worksheet 2.2.11b copied on to card and cut up; Worksheet (teacher) 2.2.11c; Worksheet (teacher) 2.2.11d

Digital resources Quick starter; Interactive activity: Organise organisms into a food chain

Common misconceptions The arrows in a food chain go from consumer to consumed.

Key vocabulary food chain, food web, primary consumer, secondary consumer, tertiary consumer, trophic level

Teaching and learning

Engage

- **Pairs to fours** Identify the students' prior knowledge by asking them to work in pairs to **construct** three food chains with at least three links. The groups then merge to form fours and the new groups **select** their 'best' food chain. Take feedback from each group about their food chain and why they selected it. [O1]

    Higher-attaining students can link their food chains to make a food web.

- The students **discuss** and **explain** what the arrows mean in the food chains in their groups. Take feedback and discuss this as a class. Ensure that they understand that the arrows represent the energy flow through the food chain. [O1]

- Working in their original pairs, the students read and **discuss** 'The ups and downs of food chains' section in the Student Book and answer questions 1–3. [O1]

Challenge and develop

- **Think, pair share** The students read the 'Food webs and trophic levels' section in the Student Book individually and **think about** the answers to questions 4–6 in silence. They then pair up and **share** with their partner to agree on answers. Take feedback the class and reach a consensus. [O1]

- Ask the students to look at the examples of food chains they noted earlier and **identify** the different trophic levels (producer, primary consumers etc.). On the whiteboard write the words 'herbivore' and 'carnivore' and ask the students what these terms mean and how they relate to the different trophic levels. [O1]

- The students work in groups to **discuss** and complete task 1 of Worksheet 2.2.11a. [O1]

Explain

- Ask the students to **discuss** in pairs 'What happens to plants and animals when they die?'. Take feedback and elicit that they are broken down by decomposers. Ask 'Where will decomposers be in the food chain?', 'Why are they important?'. (They recycle nutrients.) [O1]

Key Stage 3 Science Teacher Pack 2

Chapter 2: Looking at Plants and Ecosystems

- Remind the students that food chains and webs show the energy flow through an ecosystem. Ask 'What happens to the energy?'. Discuss their responses. Arrange the students to **carry out** the 'Modelling energy flow' activity – see Worksheet (teacher) 2.2.11c for instructions. [O1&2]
- The students can then complete the 'Food web' activity (task 2 of Worksheet 2.2.11a). [O1&2]

Consolidate and apply

- The students work in groups to **construct** a food web, using the cards from Worksheet 2.2.11b, on a large sheet of paper by drawing connecting arrows. Ask 'What is the producer?', 'Which are the primary consumers?', 'Which are the decomposers?', etc. The groups leave their web to return to later. [O2]
- They **make predictions** about the impact of different factors affecting the organisms in one food chain from their food web – e.g. if the acacia trees die; if the dingo population increases; if the rains fail. [O2]
- **Pair talk** The students read the 'Knock-on effects' section in the Student Book and **discuss** the answers to questions 7 and 8. Take feedback. [O3]

Extend

Ask students able to progress further to:

- complete task 3 of Worksheet 2.2.11a, **analysing** the impact of different factors on a food web. [O3]
- carry out the 'How much food is needed?' activity described on Worksheet (teacher) 2.2.11d. [O3]

Plenary suggestions

Learning triangle The students draw a large triangle with a smaller inverted triangle inside it. In the three outer triangles they write something they've seen, something they've done and something they've discussed. In the central triangle they write something they've learned. [O1, 2&3]

Answers to Student Book questions

1. the numbers would decrease   2. the grass biomass would increase; the fox numbers would decrease
3. if an animal is reliant on one food source and it fails, the animal will die, so it is better to have different food sources
4. a ranking within a food web; for example a producer, primary consumer etc
5. *producers*: leaf litter, grass seed; *primary consumers*: worm, mouse, rabbit; *secondary consumers*: shrew, owl, fox; *tertiary consumer*: owl
6. rabbit numbers would increase; because more grass seed becomes available
7. The numbers of capelin and Arctic cod would increase initially and more cod would be available for the harbour seal. Less food would be available for polar bears so they would eat more cod and harbour seals. Orca would have less food so would eat more harbour seal and humpback whales. The numbers of amphipod and Arctic char would increase.
8. The copepod photosynthesises using light to make glucose. When Arctic char eat the copepods, some energy is transferred from the copepod to the Arctic char. The capelin eat the Arctic char. Energy in the Arctic char is transferred to the capelin. Energy in the capelin is transferred to the Arctic tern when it is eaten.

Answers to Worksheet 2.2.11a

1. a) i) phytoplankton ii) krill iii) Arctic cod iv) seal b) i) Arctic cod & seal ii) phytoplankton iii) Arctic cod iv) the Sun
2. a) any correct food chain – e.g. bladderwrack → grey mullet → common seal; algae → sea urchin → herring gull; bladderwrack → winkle → crab → herring gull; algae → limpet → lobster → common seal

   b) common seals eat more lobsters (or die) so limpets increase in number; bladderwrack seaweeds will increase

   c) i) increase ii) decrease iii) decrease d) i) increase ii) decrease iii) decrease (because algae take over their habitat) iv) decrease
3. a) bladderwrack increase; grey mullet increase; seal stays same (because there are fewer lobsters); winkle, crab and herring gull numbers all decrease too

   b) i) shrimp, water fleas and eels all increase, so cyclops, algae and caddis fly larvae decrease; only eels are left as food for humans. ii) algae increase dramatically; primary consumers increase etc. (students do not know about eutrophication so this answer will suffice) iii) water levels reduced, so less oxygen available, and larger fish die; invertebrates decrease iv) young fish/shrimp decrease; more algae grow, increasing caddis fly and cyclops; shrimp and young fish then start to increase slowly v) fish gills block, so the fish cannot get the oxygen needed for respiration and die; less oxygen will diffuse into the water at the surface; invertebrates may survive better because they have a short life-span and reproduce quickly

   c) it will decrease rapidly, because roach eat the same food as carp, meaning less food is available for the carp

Chapter 2: Looking at Plants and Ecosystems

2.12 Exploring the importance of insects

Lesson overview

Learning objectives

- Describe the impact of low pollination on fruit production.
- Explain why artificial pollination is used for some crops.
- Evaluate the risks of monoculture on world food security.

Learning outcomes

- Describe the impact of low pollination on crop yield and how this could potentially be avoided. [O1]
- Explain why hand-pollination is cost effective for some crops. [O2]
- Analyse and evaluate the risks involved with monoculture – particularly with regard to food security in poorer countries. [O3]

Skills development

- Thinking scientifically: analyse data
- Working scientifically: develop explanations
- Learner development: communicate effectively

Resources needed at least four types of flowers (e.g. lily, antirrhinum, hydrangea, rose); Worksheet 2.2.12; Practical sheet 2.2.12; Technician's notes 2.2.12

Digital resources Quick starter; Slideshow: A description of how bees pollinate plants and how honey is made; Interactive activity: Define the conditions required for enhancing bee populations; Video

Common misconceptions Food security is guaranteed.

Key vocabulary food security, yield, pesticide, monoculture

Teaching and learning

Engage

- The students work in groups to **discuss** what pollination is, why it is important and how animals, especially insects, help in the process of pollination. [O1]
- Alternatively ask the students to work in pairs and **brainstorm** on a sheet of paper what they know about how plants and insects help each other to survive. [O1]

Challenge and develop

- **Think, pair, share** Ask the students to **think about** the question 'Why are some apples on the same tree small and some large?' They then **discuss** this in pairs. Take feedback. [O1]
- Ask the students to read the 'Fruit production and bees' section in the Student Book and to answer question 1. [O1]
- The students work in pairs to complete task 1 of Worksheet 2.2.12. Ask the groups to **present** their work to the class and to **peer assess** the work of other groups using 'three stars and a wish' (the 'stars' are things they have done well, learned, understood or enjoyed, while the 'wish' is something they could improve on, need to complete or need help with). Discuss how wild bees can increase successful pollination and summarise the key points for each part of the worksheet task on the whiteboard. [O1]
- The students **examine** closely the four types of flowers provided to **identify** adaptations for pollination (bright colour, pollen guides, scent etc.) and **complete the observation record** on Practical sheet 2.2.12. [O1]

Explain

- **Pairs to fours** Explain to the students that some of our foods come from plants that have both male and female flowers (e.g. cucumber) and that many farmers hand-pollinate the female flowers by collecting pollen

Chapter 2: Looking at Plants and Ecosystems

from the male flowers and 'painting' it on female flowers. Ask the students to **discuss** with a partner why some farmers do this and take feedback from the class. The students then form groups of four to **develop** a cartoon strip to **explain** the process of hand-pollination. [O2]

- Working in their groups, the students read the 'Ensuring pollination' section in the Student Book. They **discuss** this and answer questions 3 and 4. Take feedback from the class. Ensure that they **understand** that artificial pollination is more reliable, but that insect pollination can result in larger crops. [O2]

Consolidate and apply

- Ask the students to complete task 2 of Worksheet 2.2.12 – their task is to **assess** and **agree** the advantages and disadvantages of artificial pollination and **summarise** their ideas on flipchart paper. Display the flipcharts around the room and encourage the students to read them and to **feedback** their final ideas. [O2]
- To apply their knowledge, the students work in groups to **research** and **make a presentation** about date farming. [O2]

Extend

Ask students able to progress further to:

- work in small groups to complete task 3 of Worksheet 2.2.12 – they are to **analyse** and **evaluate** the practice of monoculture in agriculture and **explain** how farmers ensure the pollination of these crops (questions 5 and 6 in the Student Book). [O3]
- **research** robotic bees and **prepare** a slideshow to share with the class (two slides maximum). [O2]

Plenary suggestions

Achievements and goals The students **discuss** and **identify** three things they have learned in this lesson along with one thing they want to know more about and one target for future learning. [O1, 2,&3]

The big ideas The students write down the most important ideas from the lesson. They share their facts in groups and compile a prioritised master list of facts. Take feedback and find out which other group(s) agreed with the prioritised points. [O1, 2,&3]

Answers to Student Book questions

1. to ensure that there are plenty of bees to pollinate the fruit tree flowers; resulting in higher fruit yield
2. by leaving areas of land unfarmed, and encouraging the planting of wild and cultivated flowers that bees like to feed on – e.g. clover, buddleia, lilac
3. there are no bees to pollinate flowers, so without artificial pollination they would get no fruit from their trees
4. artificial pollination ensures that flowers are pollinated; but it takes a lot of time; may not be cost effective and often reduces the size of fruits
5. *Disadvantages* include: single crop has a short flowering period, so bees have short feeding period and then no food; flowering may not coincide with when bees are active; cash crops are grown at expense of food crops; if the crop fails, there is no back-up. *Advantages*: can be very profitable; easy to farm very large fields and to look after just one crop
6. rent bee hives to place around a crop; hand-pollinate (e.g. dates); plant strips of wild flowers that are left untended in and around the cash crop to attract bees

Answers to Worksheet 2.2.12

1. b) i) poster to show the importance of bees pollinating crops and wild flowers etc

    ii) vast areas of monoculture have destroyed hedgerows; pollen from a monoculture is restricted to a short season (and bees may not be active then); outside that short season the bees have no food

    iii) leave ares of land unfarmed; encourage planting of wild and cultivated flowers that bees like to feed on – e.g. clover, buddleia, lilac

2. a) bright colours; scent; pollen guides; nectar for them to feed on   b) to attract insects; increase chance of pollination

    c) Simple description of at least three of: wings, e.g. sycamore; parachutes, e.g. dandelion; thick shell for water dispersal, e.g coconut, sea bean (drift seeds); bright sugary fleshy fruits, e.g. peach; burrs or hooks, e.g. thistle; exploding, e.g. laburnum

    d) *Advantages*: ensures pollination; can use pollen from plant with features wanted; *Disadvantages*: time taken; labour intensive; fruits often smaller.

3. See answers to Student Book questions 5 and 6. Also: cash crops grown at the exense of food crops, so whilst landowners can make money, the small farmers and workers often have very little food for themselves or their livestock; if the crop fails, thare is no money.

Chapter 2: Looking at Plants and Ecosystems

2.13 Looking at other examples of interdependence

Lesson overview

Learning objectives
- Describe examples of the interdependence of organisms.
- Explain how organisms help other organisms to survive.
- Explain ideas about habitat destruction.

Learning outcomes
- Describe a range of examples of interdependence. [O1]
- Explain how organisms help or depend on each other for survival. [O2]
- Communicate, in a creative way, the impact of rainforest destruction on biodiversity. [O3]

Skills development
- Thinking scientifically: evaluate risks
- Working scientifically: develop explanations
- Learner development: communicate effectively

Resources needed Worksheet 2.2.13a; Worksheet 2.2.13b copied on to card and cut up

Digital resources Quick starter; Slideshow: Some examples of interdependence; Interactive activity: Match the key interdependence terms to their definition; Hangman: Key vocabulary game

Key vocabulary niche, symbiosis, commensalism, mutualism, parasitism, competition

Teaching and learning

Engage
- The students work in groups of eight to **brainstorm** examples of interdependence between organisms that they have already met – e.g. animals dependent on plants for homes, food and oxygen; predator–prey relationships; bacteria and tubeworms in deep-sea environments. [O1]

Challenge and develop
- **Home and away** The students read and **discuss** the 'Niches and relationships' section in the Student Book. They complete the 'What does it mean?' group activity (task 1 of Worksheet 2.2.13a). Each home group member (numbered 1–8) goes to a different 'Information station' (numbered 1–8), where they read the information on the cards from Worksheet 2.2.13b. They **summarise** the information with examples. On returning to their home groups, the students **teach** the others what they have found out. [O1&2]

- Students use the information from this group activity to answer questions 1–3 in the Student Book. If they need help, they should ask a member of their group first. If no one knows the answer they can look at the information stations. If they are still having problems they can then come to the teacher. Ensure that all students **understand** the concept of a 'niche'. [O1&2]

Explain
- Working with a partner, the students read the 'Competition' section in the Student Book. They **discuss** and answer question 4. Take feedback from the class and reach a consensus. [O1&2]

- Using the examples of the relationships identified earlier in task 1, 'What does it mean?', ask the students to work with a partner to complete part a) of 'Explaining relationships' (task 2 of Worksheet 2.2.13a) using books or the internet to carry out their **research**. [O2]

Consolidate and apply
- Working in their pairs, the students complete part b) of 'Explaining relationships' (task 2 of Worksheet 2.2.13a). The activity involves **explaining** how adaptations in wading birds allow them to co-exist on the seashore without competing for the same food source. [O1&2]

Chapter 2: Looking at Plants and Ecosystems

- Still in their pairs, ask the students to **produce a presentation**, **explaining** a range of examples of interdependence in organisms – it must be suitable for a Year 6 class. [O1&2]

Extend
Ask students able to progress further to:

- read the 'Problems in the rainforest' section in the Student Book. They work in pairs to **discuss** and **answer** questions 5 and 6. Take feedback and discuss their different ideas. [O3]
- to **research** the impact of rainforest destruction on other organisms and to **communicate** their ideas using a medium of their choice. Encourage them to be **creative**! Assign each group the work of another group to **peer-assess** during presentations. [O3]

Plenary suggestions
Mind map Students work in pairs to **make a mind map** of what they have learned from the lesson. [O1, 2&3]

Answers to Student Book questions

1. as a minimum – descriptions of examples of symbiosis; commensalism; mutualism and parasitism
2. *oxpecker* benefits by having a source of food (bugs) and protection from possible predators
   rhinoceros benefits from having irritating bugs removed
3. the role of an organism within a particular ecosystem – its predators, its prey, its habitat etc
4. any correct example from the lesson (see the cards on Worksheet 2.2.13b)
5. over 50% of the world's animal species live in rainforests; many of which are now endangered; rainforests provide resources such as wood; they provide oxygen from photosynthesis; they are homes to indigenous tribes
6. *Advantages*: the land can be used for another purpose – e.g. build a dam, provide a wild life reserve. *Disadvantages*: if the remaining species cannot adapt to the new conditions, they may become extinct; animals may not find a mate; traditional trails may be splintered.

Answers to Worksheet 2.2.13a

1.

Relationship	Explanation	Examples
Predator and prey	One animal eats another	Bear and salmon; cheetah and antelope; lion and zebra; polar bear and seal; fox and rabbit
Symbiosis	Two different animals live together; relationship may be beneficial, detrimental or neutral	Crocodile and plover; chemosynthetic bacteria and tubeworms
Commensalism	One organism gains; the other is not hurt	Ferns and mosses growing up tree trunk; barnacles on a whale's tail; egrets on cattle
Mutualism	Both organisms gain	Bee and flower; sea anemone and clown fish; moray eel and cleaner fish
Parasitism	One animal gains and may hurt the other	Acacia trees and ants; tapeworms and humans; ticks and dogs
Decomposition	Breakdown of dead and decaying matter	Worms; fungi (e.g. on tree stump); bacteria
Competition	Two different animals want the same resource at the same time	Plants competing for space and sunlight; male fish fighting over a female fish; wolves competing with eagles for the remains of a fox kill
Niche	Where an organism lives and its relationship to other organisms	Different warblers feeding in different parts of the same tree

2. a) depends on the organisms selected
   b) birds have beaks of different sizes and shapes; to reach different types of food at different depths in the sand
3. ideas presented should include: loss of habitat; breeding areas and food; habitat divided up by roads etc.; species become endangered and may become extinct

Chapter 2: Looking at Plants and Ecosystems

2.14 Understanding interactions in the environment

Lesson overview

Learning objectives
- Describe some effects of human activity on the environment.
- Explain why many species are endangered.
- Analyse and evaluate secondary data and recommend solutions for species survival.

Learning outcomes
- Describe some effects of human activity on the environment. [O1]
- Explain why a range of species are endangered. [O2]
- Critically analyse and evaluate secondary data, and recommend possible solutions to help each species to survive. [O3]

Skills development
- Thinking scientifically: analyse data
- Working scientifically: interpret evidence
- Learner development: communicate effectively

Resources needed photo of a waterside environment; large sheets of paper; Worksheet 2.2.14

Digital resources Quick starter; Slideshow: A look at some British species which are endangered; Interactive activity: Order the level of risk scientists assign to a species, from most to least threatened; Video

Key vocabulary endangered, biodiversity, extinct, vulnerable, captive breeding

Teaching and learning

Engage
- Show the students a picture of a waterside environment. Ask them 'What living organisms might be found here?' (plants, fish, insects, bacteria etc.) and 'What might humans do to harm an environment like this?' (pollution, building, litter etc.) [O1]

Challenge and develop
- **Pair work** The students work in pairs to **devise** a questionnaire that **investigates** human impact on their local environment. Ask 'What do you think are the four most important environmental questions for your area?'. Take feedback. The students could give their questionnaire to 20 people to complete and then **discuss** the findings. [O1]

- **Optional task** The pairs **research** the effects of the following factors: deforestation, habitat loss, overfishing, hunting/poaching, introduction of invasive species, the pet trade, building roads (fragmentation of habitats), dredging (e.g. in the United Arab Emirates), water pollution, litter and air pollution. The students then work together to make a 'Big Book' (see Worksheet 2.2.14) **describing** some of the ways in which humans have an impact on the environment and **suggesting** ways in which we can help to make it better. If time is short, students could be given a pack of pre-printed resource materials (some more relevant than others), and the time could be limited to 15 minutes. [O1]

- Working in pairs, the students read and **discuss** the 'How humans affect the environment' section in the Student Book and answer questions 1–3.

Explain
- Start a discussion with the class about endangered species, asking if anyone can **explain** what such a species is. Take feedback and reach an **agreed** definition. **Brainstorm** with the class why a species may become endangered and record their ideas. [O2]

Key Stage 3 Science Teacher Pack 2 © HarperCollins*Publishers* Limited 2014

Chapter 2: Looking at Plants and Ecosystems

- Using the recorded list of reasons why an organism may become endangered, and information from previous discussions, the students work in groups of four to **explain** what can be done to help prevent these scenarios. Take feedback from each group and encourage the students to **ask each other questions** about the ideas. [O2]

Consolidate and apply

- Working in pairs, the students use books and the internet to **research** why the following species are endangered: orang-utan, cheetah, dugong, polar bear, turtles and one other animal of the students' choice. Take feedback from the class and discuss the students' ideas (task 2a of Worksheet 2.2.14). [O1&2]
- Using their research, the students work collaboratively to **make a presentation**, such as a slideshow, **explaining** why many different animals are endangered. The presentation must be suitable for a Year 7 class (task 2b of Worksheet 2.2.14). [O1&2]

Extend

Ask students able to progress further to:

- work with a partner to extend their previous work by **analysing** and **evaluating** steps taken to help protect the animals. They should **recommend** solutions for the survival of species (task 3 of Worksheet 2.2.14). [O3]
- **research** how environmentalists work to assess, measure and minimise damage to the environment using books and the internet. They should **explain** how the actions they **suggest** are scientifically based on the measurements they have made. [O3]

Plenary suggestions

- **Summarise** Ask the students tob their learning in no more than 30 words. Take feedback from the class. [O1, 2&3]

Answers to Student Book questions

1. for example: hunting animals for food, sport, medicines and to keep as pets; using fur, skin, horns and tusks for making clothing, bags, shoes and ornaments; constructing buildings, roads and other structures such as dams and reservoirs that destroy the habitats needed by plants and animals
2. suitable answers: pollution; deforestation; acid rain; habitat loss; overfishing; poaching; hunting; war; mining; building
3. suitable answers: recycle waste; don't buy food unless it will be eaten; don't buy unneeded clothes that aren't essential; don't throw litter; re-use plastic bags
4. a species with so few of its kind alive that it is in danger of dying out
5. factors include: habitat loss; hunting and poaching; change in habitat due to dredging; global warming caused by carbon emissions; plastic bags
6. investigating and protecting the environment and biodiversity
7. to provide breeding grounds with expert veterinary care in order to increase populations that cannot be hunted, poached or killed for sport etc

Answers to Worksheet 2.2.14

1. Ideas may include any or all of the factors listed earlier: deforestation, habitat loss, overfishing, hunting/poaching, introduction of invasive species, the pet trade, building towns/roads, making large fields to grow monocultures, draining land dredging, water pollution, litter, air pollution.
2. *Orang-utan* – habitat destruction for biofuel growth; illegal trading of young; killed for food or for being an agricultural pest

   Cheetah – hunting and poaching; killed for being an agricultural pest; through lack of food

   Dugong – habitat destruction due to dredging and building; entanglement in fishing gear

   Polar bear – global warming; loss of food supply

   Turtle – pollution; entanglement in fishing gear; poaching and illegal trading of eggs, meat and shells; coastal development; plastic and other marine debris; global warming; ocean pollution
3. Ideas include: game reserves; captive breeding and re-release to natural habitat; international protection from hunting/poaching; replanting tree habitats. Suggestions will depend on the factors identified for task 2:

   Orang-utan – replant forests; game wardens patrolling areas; pay farmers subsidies to keep land as it is

   Cheetah – game reserves patrolled by wardens; breed natural food herds

   Dugong – stop coastal development and dredging; plant sea grass beds; fine fishing trade for entanglement

   Polar bear – manage their food supply   *Turtle* – stop coastal development pollution; fine fishing trade for entanglement; patrol breeding sites; stop production of plastic bags

Chapter 2: Looking at Plants and Ecosystems

2.15 Learning about ecological balance

Lesson overview

Learning objectives

- Describe ways in which organisms affect their environment.
- Explain why prey populations affect predator populations.
- Evaluate a model of predator–prey populations and explain the importance of predators.

Learning outcomes

- Describe some ways in which organisms affect their environment. [O1]
- Explain why prey populations affect predator populations. [O2]
- Evaluate a model of predator–prey populations and explain the importance of predators. [O3]

Skills development

- Thinking scientifically: analyse data
- Working scientifically: make predictions
- Learner development: act responsibly

Resources needed graph paper; lion and antelope cards for the modelling activity (at least 20 lions and 50 antelope cards per group); Worksheet 2.2.15a; Worksheet 2.2.15b

Digital resources Quick starter; Slideshow: A look at the predator-prey relationship between a Canadian lynx and a Snowshoe hare; Interactive activity: Sort the statements into those which refer to predators and those which refer to prey organisms

Key vocabulary ecology, predator, prey, equilibrium

Teaching and learning

Engage

- Ask the students to work in groups of four to **brainstorm** examples of organisms that affect the environment around them in a positive way or a negative way. Take feedback from the class and encourage the groups to add to their list. [O1]

Challenge and develop

- The students work in pairs to read and **discuss** the 'How organisms affect the environment' section in the Student Book and answer questions 1 and 2. Take feedback and encourage the students to add any new interactions to their list. [O1]

- Returning to the initial groups of four, the students **explore** how organisms affect their environment using task 1 of Worksheet 2.2.15a to complete fact files about animals chosen from crown-of-thorns starfish, locusts, cane toads, decomposers, worms and kangaroos (and/or the organisms they identified during the initial brainstorm). [O1]

Explain

- Distribute Worksheet 2.2.15b and discuss scenario 1 with the class: 'What would happen to prey numbers if there were no predators?'. Explain that a population with no predators and plenty of food will increase. [O2]

- **Pairs to fours** In pairs, the students **discuss** the question 'Will it keep increasing forever?'. The pairs then merge to form fours. Take feedback – ensuring that the students understand that eventually food and space will limit the size of the population. This is the 'carrying capacity', shown in the second graph on Worksheet 2.2.15b. Watch a web-based animation to model this – e.g. from BBC Bitesize. [O1&2]

- Move on to discuss scenario 2: 'What would happen to predator numbers if there were no prey?'. Then 'What will be the environmental impact from these two scenarios?'. The students then **study** the lynx and snowshoe hare example on Worksheet 2.2.15b. [O1&2]

Chapter 2: Looking at Plants and Ecosystems

Consolidate and apply

- Working in groups of four, the students do task 2 of Worksheet 2.2.15a, the 'Lion hunt' activity, **modelling** population growth in predator–prey populations. [O1&2]
- Ask the students to **summarise** the relationship between the population sizes of lions and antelope. They should use the words 'if' and 'then' to show a cause-and-effect relationship. [O1&2]

Extend

Ask students able to progress further to:

- work in pairs to **evaluate** the task 2 model of predator–prey populations (task 3 of Worksheet 2.2.15a) [O3]
- work in groups of four to **design** a poster **explaining** the importance of top predators in an environment and **explaining** how, over time, our treatment of top predators has helped to make them endangered. [O3]

Plenary suggestions

'3–2–1' activity Ask the students to **reflect on** their learning by responding to three statements: 'Three things I learned are...'; 'Two things I found interesting were...'; 'One thing I am going to tell someone else is...' [O1, 2&3]

Self-assessment Alternatively they **reflect on** their own achievements and goals by completing these statements: 'Things I did well today...'; 'Things I need to remember...', 'Things I need to improve...'. [O1, 2&3]

Answers to Student Book questions

1. the study of interactions between organisms and their enviornments
2. for example: locust swarms decimate crops; worms aerate soil and breakdown decaying leaf litter into smaller pieces so that microbes can break it down further
3. relative numbers of predators and prey; the carrying capacity of the environment for both predator and prey
4. Low prey population means low predator population; when the prey increases, predator numbers also increase.
5. More predators can be introduced into the environment; to eat the prey population; to control pests.
6. Predators keep the balance of other organisms in the environment.

Answers to Worksheet 2.2.15a

1. *Name*: crown-of-thorns starfish. *Habitat*: coral reefs. *Facts*: fertilisers and pesticides are thought to have caused a population explosion. *Interactions*: destruction of coral reefs. *Impact*: negative.

   Name: locusts. *Habitat*: Africa, Middle East and Asia. *Facts*: swarm in millions. *Interactions*: destroy vast amounts of crops. *Impact*: negative.

   Name: cane toads. *Habitat*: South America. *Facts*: successful as an invasive species in Australia, the Caribbean and the United States. *Interactions*: kill native wildlife. *Impact*: negative.

   Name: decomposers. *Habitat*: worldwide. *Facts*: they are mainly bacteria and fungi. *Interactions*: break down dead and decaying matter to release nutrients back into the soil. *Impact*: positive.

   Name: worms. *Habitat*: soil and sand. *Facts*: worm casts give a crumb like structure to the soil. *Interactions*: create burrows to allow gas exchange in soil or sand; break up large leaves etc. into smaller pieces for bacteria and fungi to breakdown. *Impact*: positive.

   Name: kangaroos. *Habitat*: Australasia. *Facts*: may harass humans. *Interactions*: compete with farm animals for food and water; trample crops; eat crop roots. *Impact*: negative.

2. When lion numbers are low, the antelope can breed and increase; as lion numbers increase, the antelope population will maintain itself up to a certain point; if there are too many lions, the antelope population will decrease until it dies out; the lions will die or move elsewhere until the antelope migrate to the area again and populations increase, and so on.

3. a) As prey increase, the predators increase; as prey decrease, predators decrease.

   b) Most animals eat more than one type of food; there was no disease; there was no hunting or poaching; the model assumes that there is plenty of water and habitats etc.

   c) By introducing any of the factors listed in b) into the model

Answers to Worksheet 2.2.15b

1. because there is an abundant supply of resources, and low interaction with predators
2. because of competition for food and other resources; influenced by other organisms in the environment and environmental conditions
3. there are fewer and fewer animals competing for remaining food
4. Lynx usually have large populations at the same time or just after hares do; lynx populations are always smaller than hare populations.

Chapter 2: Looking at Plants and Ecosystems

2.16 Understanding the effects of toxins in the environment

Lesson overview

Learning objectives
- Describe how toxins pass along the food chain.
- Explain how toxins enter and accumulate in food chains.
- Evaluate the advantages and disadvantages of using pesticides.

Learning outcomes
- Describe how toxins pass along the food chain. [O1]
- Explain the process of bioaccumulation. [O2]
- Critically evaluate the use of pesticides. [O3]

Skills development
- Thinking scientifically: analyse data
- Working scientifically: develop explanations
- Learner development: ask questions

Resources needed brightly coloured counters/coloured squares; a clear plastic bag for every student; food web predator/prey name tags (the number will depend on the number of students – in a group of 35 students have at least five levels within the food web, e.g. 12 zooplankton/shrimp/clams/worms or crab, 9 small fish, 7 large fish, 5 seals, 2 sharks; print each food web level on different coloured paper or have students colour them); Worksheet 2.2.16

Digital resources Quick starter; Interactive activity: Match the farming chemical to its use; Slideshow: A look at bioaccumulation of mercury

Key vocabulary fertiliser, insecticide, toxin, bioaccumulation

Teaching and learning

Engage
- Working in groups of four, the students **brainstorm** why chemicals are used in agriculture. Take feedback from the class and encourage the students to add new ideas to their list. [O1]
- Alternatively ask the groups to **discuss** man-made pollution that affects the natural environment – e.g. acid rain, radiation poisoning and chemicals in rivers. Ask 'What causes these types of pollution?', 'What effects does it have on human and animal populations?' and 'What can be done to reduce or eliminate it?' Create a class chart outlining these points. [O1]

Challenge and develop
- Working in pairs the students **read** and **discuss** the 'Why are chemicals used in agriculture?' section in the Student Book and answer questions 1–2. Take feedback from the class and encourage the students to add any new points to their list. [O1]
- **Group work** Working in groups of four, the students read and **discuss** the 'Chemicals entering the food chain' section in the Student Book and answer question 3. [O1]
- The students **discuss** and answer the following questions: 'How do poisons get into the ocean and wetlands? How do the poisons get into an animal? Do you think that the poisons stay in the body of the animal or do they leave? What do you think happens to the poisons when the small animal is eaten by a bigger animal?' (task 1 of Worksheet 2.2.16). [O1]

Key Stage 3 Science Teacher Pack 2 © HarperCollins*Publishers* Limited 2014

Chapter 2: Looking at Plants and Ecosystems

Explain

- The students work as a class to **model** how DDT accumulates in a marine food chain and then answer the questions in task 2 of Worksheet 2.2.16. In a group of 35 students have at least five levels within the food web – e.g. 12 zooplankton/shrimp/clams/worms or crab; 9 small fish; 7 large fish; 5 seals; 2 sharks. [O1&2]
- Working in pairs, the students read the 'Accumulation of toxins in the food chain' section in the Student Book and answer questions 5 and 6. [O1&2]

Consolidate and apply

- Back in groups of four, the students **design a poster** using pictures, numbers, acronyms and up to 20 words to explain 'bioaccumulation'. [O1&2]

Extend

Ask students able to progress further to:

- work with a partner to **brainstorm** ways of keeping toxins out of the waterways. [O3]
- work collaboratively in groups of four to complete task 3 of Worksheet 2.2.16 and **evaluate** the advantages and disadvantages of using pesticides on crops, **giving a presentation** to the class outlining their research and conclusions. [O3]

Plenary suggestions

Question setting Working in groups of four, the students **develop questions** starting 'How, where, when, why and what' on the topic, and link these to their answers. Students **peer-assess** another group's work. Take feedback. [O1, 2&3]

Answers to Student Book questions

1. farmers need to produce more crops in the same, or less, space and as quickly as possible; they usually specialise in either crops or livestock; if they grow crops continually, the soil is deprived of nutrients; artificial fertilisers dissolve quickly in soil water; pesticide use means more crop
2. If farmers have no livestock; they have no manure.
3. *primary consumer*: for example sheep, cow, bird, (named) insect, rabbits

   secondary consumer: for example humans, birds of prey, insect-eating birds and animals, foxes
4. run-off from fields; blown in wind to waterways; fall from the air; urban street run-off; pests and other insects are covered in the toxins; absorbed by plant roots; eaten by other animals
5. some DDT was absorbed by waterweeds; fish ate a number of waterweed that each contained DDT; so the fish had the total DDT from each plant; large fish ate some small fish and had the total DDT from each small fish; the otter had the total DDT from every large fish it ate; which either killed it or meant the babies were too ill to survive
6. more large fish would survive to eat more smaller fish; then less water weed would be eaten and it would grow more

Answers to Worksheet 2.2.16

1. a) i) fertilisers and/or pesticides from fields; loss of cargo from ships; ships sinking with cargo; from rivers entering oceans and wetlands   ii) from food eaten or water drunk

   iii) they stay in the body; absorbed from digestive system   iv) poisons in small animal absorbed into bigger animal
2. a) the shark; may survive but would be very ill, and offspring would not be healthy

   b) the population will be destroyed

   c) it ate lots of animals that each contained some DDT; the shark absorbed the DDT from each animal

   d) Humans use/produce the toxins that enter the water or land on plants; the primary consumer has a small amount of toxin; the secondary consumer eats many primary consumers and absorbs the toxin from each organism; this happens all the way up the food chain until the top predator has accumulated a large amount of toxin.
3. a) *Advantages*: more food produced; diseases eradicated or controlled, e.g. malaria. *Disadvantages*: could cause CCD in bees; accumulates in food chains; causes death.

Chapter 2: Looking at Plants and Ecosystems

2.17 Exploring how organisms co-exist

Lesson overview

Learning objectives
- Describe the role of niches.
- Explain the concept of resource partitioning.
- Analyse and evaluate the role of variation in enabling organisms to co-exist.

Learning outcomes
- Describe the role of niches. [O1]
- Explain the concept of resource partitioning. [O2]
- Analyse and evaluate how beak adaptations in seashore birds allow them to survive in the same ecosystem. [O3]

Skills development
- Thinking scientifically: analyse data
- Working scientifically: interpret evidence
- Learner development: act responsibly

Resources needed images of an elephant and a hyena; equipment and materials as detailed in the Technician's notes; Worksheet 2.2.17; Practical sheet 2.2.17; Technician's notes 2.2.17

Digital resources Quick starter; Interactive activity: Define four key ecological terms; Hangman: Key vocabulary game

Key vocabulary specialist, generalist, resource partitioning, co-exist, variation

Teaching and learning

Engage
- Working in groups of four, the students **discuss** and recall what a niche is from Topic 2.13. Take feedback from the class, and encourage the students to **question** each other. [O1]
- Alternatively display images of an elephant and hyena on the board and ask the students to work in pairs to **identify** as many adaptations as they can that make each animal a successful competitor and say why. [O1]

Challenge and develop
- The students work in pairs to read and **discuss** the 'Exploring niches' section in the Student Book and answer questions 1–3. Take feedback from the class and ensure that the students **understand** that niches allow organisms to undertake different roles in a habitat and that competition arises when niches overlap. [O1]
- Ask the students to work in pairs to complete task 1 of Worksheet 2.2.17. [O1]

Explain
- Read the 'Competition in detail' section in the Student Book with the students. Ask them to **explain** in their own words what the different types of competition are. They then complete task 2 of Worksheet 2.2.17. [O1&2]
- Working with a partner, the students **discuss** and answer questions 4 and 5 in the Student Book. [O1&2]

Consolidate and apply
- Working in groups of four, the students **design** an information leaflet for another class explaining about competition and the concept of resource partitioning. Encourage them to be creative. For lower-attaining students it may be better to model how this should be done. [O1&2]

Key Stage 3 Science Teacher Pack 2 © HarperCollins*Publishers* Limited 2014

Chapter 2: Looking at Plants and Ecosystems

- Students work in pairs to complete task 3 of Worksheet 2.2.17, **investigating** how different barnacles are adapted for their particular niches. [O2]

Extend

- Ask students able to progress further to work in groups of four to **investigate** different types of bird beaks using the **modelling** task in Practical sheet 2.2.17. After the task, discuss as a class and evaluate how different beaks help wading birds to get food in different estuary habitats. [O2&3]

Plenary suggestions

Summary Ask the students to work in pairs to **summarise** the lesson in 30 words or less. Take feedback and ask the students to **peer-assess** the statements. [O1, 2&3]

The big ideas The students write down three ideas they learned during the lesson. They **share** their facts in groups and compile a prioritised master list of facts. Take feedback and find out which other group(s) agreed. [O1, 2&3]

Answers to Student Book questions

1. for example: dugong; giraffe; koala bear; beaver; otter; polar bear; orchid; hummingbird
2. for example: fox; eagle; lion; shark; rat; cockroach
3. when niches overlap and organisms compete for resources
4. correct explanation to include: organisms eat the same food; live in the same place; but use this same resource in a slightly different way; or a correct description of an example of partitioning
5. they live in different zones of the same tree and feed on different insects at different times
6. different warblers feed on insects but in different parts of the tree at different times and with different preferences
7. cows eat the majority of the taller grass plants, but the rabbits nibble on the stubs of grass blades left behind by the cows

Answers to Worksheet 2.2.17

1. a) *orca*: ocean; top predator
   b) *macaw parrot*: rainforest; herbivore
   c) *dugong*: shallow coastal sea areas in Middle East; herbivore; *sea grass*: shallow coastal sea areas; producer
   d) *hyena*: African savannah; predator/scavenger; *lion*: African savannah; top predator; *antelope*: African savannah; herbivore

2.

Animal	What is it competing for?	Competition between the same species or different species	Adaptations that make it a successful competitor
polar bears	territory; a mate; food	same species	size; big teeth; big claws; camouflaged
hyena and cheetah	food	different species	*hyena*: agility; sharp teeth *cheetah*: speed; agility; sharp teeth; large claws
koi carp	food	same species	size; strength
trees and bushes	light; space; nutrients; water	different species	height; number and size of roots; number of leaves

3. a) A *specialist* has a narrow niche; it may only be able to survive in very specific environmental conditions and has a very limited diet – e.g. panda
   A *generalist* has a broad niche; it can live in a wide range of environmental conditions and eat many different types of food – e.g. human
   b) *Orca* – some are generalists and some are specialists; *macaw* – mostly generalists; *dugong* – specialist; *hyena and lion* – generalists; *antelope* – generalist
   c) Different species of barnacles have different niches; *Balanus* lives nearer to low-tide level; *Chthamalus* lives nearer to high-tide level.

2.18 Checking students' progress

The 'Checking your progress' section in the Student Book indicates the key ideas developed in this chapter and shows how students progress to more complex levels. It is provided to support students in:

- identifying those ideas
- developing a sense of their current level of understanding
- developing a sense of what the next steps in their learning are.

It is designed either to be used at the end of a chapter to support an overall view of the progress, or alternatively during the teaching of the unit. Students can self assess or peer assess using this as a basis.

It would be helpful if students can be encouraged to provide evidence from their understanding or their notes to support their judgements. In some cases it may be useful to explore the difference in the descriptors for a particular idea so that students can see what makes for a 'higher outcome'.

It may be useful with some descriptors to provide examples from the specific work done, such as an experiment undertaken or an explanation developed and recorded. If marking and feedback use similar ideas and phrases this will enable students to relate specific marking to a more general sense of progress.

Chapter 2: Looking at Plants and Ecosystems

To make good progress in understanding science students need to focus on these ideas and skills:

Students who are making modest progress will be able to:	Students who are making good progress will be able to:	Students who are making excellent progress will be able to:
State that green plants need sunlight to grow and to make food.	Identify water and carbon dioxide as the raw materials for photosynthesis, and glucose and oxygen as the products.	Explain the chemical changes involved in photosynthesis and the roles of light and chlorophyll.
Describe how gases enter and leave a leaf and how light energy for photosynthesis is captured.	Describe how cells in the leaf and root are adapted for their functions.	Relate and explain how the structure of palisade, mesophyll and guard cells allows them to perform their function.
Describe how levels of light, temperature and carbon dioxide affect the rate of photosynthesis.	Explain how levels of light, temperature and carbon dioxide affect the rate of photosynthesis.	Apply learning about the factors affecting photosynthesis to solve problems.
Name some of the nutrients needed by plants and supplied by fertilisers; state how they enter the plant dissolved in soil water.	Explain why nutrients are needed by plants, how spreading manure adds them to the soil and how water passes through the plant.	Explain how mineral deficiencies affect plants and how different factors affect the rate of transpiration.
Describe how some bacteria produce food by chemosynthesis.	Compare chemosynthesis with photosynthesis.	Explain why some bacteria use chemosynthesis and how they support food chains.
Describe an example of a simple food web.	Explain how energy flows through a food web and explain factors that can affect food webs, such as loss of a species or toxin accumulation.	Explain the importance of predators in an environment and evaluate changes in a food web.
Describe an example of interdependence of organisms in an ecosystem – for example as the pollination of crops by insects.	Explain examples of interdependence of organisms in an ecosystem – for example through symbiosis, commensalism and parasitism.	Analyse an example of interdependence of organisms in an ecosystem – for example, the effects of the destruction of rainforests.
Identify some ways in which organisms affect, and are affected by, their environment – for example through pollution or destruction of habitats.	Explain some ways in which organisms affect, and are affected by, their environment – for example, predator–prey relationships.	Analyse and evaluate the factors affecting endangered species and recommend solutions.

2.19 Answers to Student Book questions

This table provides answers to the Questions section at the end of Chapter 2 of the Student Book. It also shows how different questions assess attainment in terms of the focus and style of a question as well as the context. Question level analysis can indicate students' proficiency in approaching different aspects of scientific understanding and different types of answer.

Q	Answer	Marks available	Focus: Knowledge & understanding	Focus: Application	Focus: Evaluation of evidence	Style: Objective test question	Style: Short written answer	Style: Longer written answer	Context: Photosynthesis and chemosynthesis	Context: Transpiration and plant nutrients	Context: Interdependence of organisms	Context: Organisms and the environment
1	c	1	x			x			x			
2	d	1	x			x			x			
3	b	1	x			x					x	
4	b	1	x			x			x			
5	Any two from: • They are long and narrow • They contain many chloroplasts • The chloroplasts are concentrated at the top of the cell	2	x				x		x			
6	Any two from: • pollution • poaching/hunting • deforestation • overfishing • introducing invasive species • building • litter • war • breeding programmes • tree planting • creating nature and game reserves	2	x				x					x
7	*Similarities* Both processes involve: • conversion of carbon compounds to sugars • an energy source *Differences* • Light is used in photosynthesis; hydrogen sulfide is used in chemosynthesis • Photosynthesis is in green plants; chemosynthesis is in bacteria (and some other organisms)	1 1 1 1	x x x x					x x x x	x x x x			
8	b	1		x		x			x			
9	c	1		x		x					x	
10	• Top predator • Living on the jungle floor (and in trees)	1 1	x x				x x				x x	

Chapter 2: Looking at Plants and Ecosystems

Q	Answer	Marks available	Focus: Knowledge & understanding	Focus: Application	Focus: Evaluation of evidence	Style: Objective test question	Style: Short written answer	Style: Longer written answer	Context: Photosynthesis and chemosynthesis	Context: Transpiration and plant nutrients	Context: Interdependence of organisms	Context: Organisms and the environment
11	• The macaw, chimpanzee and red-eyed tree frog populations would rise uncontrollably	1	x					x			x	
	• Insects populations would decrease very rapidly due to predation by the red-eyed tree frog	1	x					x			x	
	• The orchids and banana trees would be destroyed by the large populations of herbivores	1	x					x			x	
	• The ecosystem would collapse	1	x					x			x	
12	c	1	x			x				x		
13	Each oyster will retain some of the HAB in its body; the person will have the total amount in each oyster's body	1	x				x					x
14	• Photosynthesis	1	x				x		x			
	• It has chloroplasts to absorb the light energy needed	1	x				x		x			
15	• The thick waxy cuticle makes it more waterproof and impermeable to water	1		x			x			x		
	• Sunken stomata and rolled leaf increase humidity and reduce exposure to wind, thereby preventing excess transpiration	1		x			x			x		
16	• Lynx populations go up when there are planty of hares to eat	1		x				x				x
	• Hare populations rise when lynx populations drop due to less predation	1		x				x				x
	• Peaks and troughs in lynx populations are always just behind those in hare populations OR there are generally more hares than lynx as each lynx needs to eat a number of hares to survive	1		x				x				x
	• Yes; population sizes will vary, but as long as there are lynx and hares, the general pattern will be the same as lynx eat hares OR the data covers a 75-year period so should be reliable	1		x				x				x
	Total possible:	30	12	12	6	7	11	12	12	4	7	7

Chapter 3: Explaining Physical Changes

3.1 Introduction

When and how to use these pages

The Introduction in the Student Book indicates some of the ideas and skills in this topic area that students will already have met from KS2 or from previous KS3 work, and provides an indication of what they will be studying in this chapter. *Ideas you have met before* is not intended to comprehensively summarise of all the prior ideas, but rather to point out a few of the key ones and to support the view that scientific understanding is progressive. Even though students might be meeting contexts that are new to them, they can often use existing ideas to start to make sense of them.

In this chapter you will find out indicates some of the new ideas that the chapter will introduce. Again, it isn't a detailed summary of content or even an index page. Its purpose is more to act as a 'trailer' and generate some interest.

The outcomes, then, will be recognition of prior learning that can be built on, and interest in finding out more.

There are a number of ways this can be used. You might, for example:

- Use *Ideas you have met before* as the basis for a revision lesson as you start the first new topic.
- Use *Ideas you have met before* as the centre of spider diagrams, to which students can add examples, experiments they might have done previously or what they found interesting
- Make a note of any unfamiliar/difficult terms and return to these in the relevant lessons.
- Use ideas from *In this chapter you will find out* to ask students questions such as:
  - Why is this important?
  - How could it be used?
  - What might we be doing in this topic?

Overview of the chapter

In this chapter the students will learn about the particle model and its ability to explain different physical processes. They will learn to apply the standard model to explain particular phenomena, such as changes of state, thermal expansion, diffusion, density, concentration and pressure. They will learn to evaluate the strengths and weaknesses of the model in terms of what it can and can't explain, adapting it to suit a particular purpose. The discovery of Brownian motion will be explored as a focus for how scientists work. The students will also learn about different colloids, such as simple gels, foams, emulsions and aerosols, and how the particle model can be used to explain what these are and how they behave. In terms of analytical skills, the students will use graphs to explore the idea of latent heat, how melting and boiling points are affected by solubility and how temperature affects the solubility of solids and gases – the particle model will be applied to each of these cases. Finally ideas about the conservation of mass will be further developed to explain physical processes, linking it to the calculation of efficiency of separation processes.

Obstacles to learning

Students may need extra guidance with the following terms and concepts:

- **Particle model** Students should be clear about accurate representation of particles in solids, liquids and gases. For the same substance being represented, its particles should all be the same shape and size. In a solid, there should be no gaps between the particles and the arrangement should show clear uniformity. In liquids, all particles should be touching another liquid particle.
- **Gases** Students often think there is air in between gas particles – there is nothing between gas particles.
- **Changing state** There is no temperature change at the melting point and boiling point. Latent heat energy goes into changing the particle arrangement and internal energy from one state into another. Evaporation and boiling are not the same thing – evaporation takes place at all temperatures between the melting point and the boiling point; only part of the liquid changes into a gas. Boiling only occurs at the boiling point, when all the liquid changes into a gas.

Chapter 3: Explaining Physical Changes

- **Thermal expansion** Particles themselves do not expand when heated – they simply gain kinetic energy and take up more room as they vibrate more vigorously. Over the whole length of a solid, the solid is seen to expand.
- **Density** This depends on the mass and the volume. Not all big objects sink (e.g. timber) and not all small object float (e.g. stone). Gases have different densities – some, like carbon dioxide, will sink in air.
- **Dissolving** When making up solutions, the volumes do not just add up. The solute particles fit into the spaces between the solvent particles, resulting in a lower total volume compared to the sum of the individual volumes.
- **Solubility** Solubility of gases decreases with temperature because the particles gain in energy, overcoming the solute-solvent forces and coming out of solution.

	Topic title:	Overarching objectives:
2	Using particles to explain matter	The properties of different states of matter (solid, liquid and gas) in terms of the particle model, including gas pressure
3	Understanding solids	
4	Exploring Brownian motion	Brownian motion in gases
5	Understanding liquids and gases	The properties of different states of matter (solid, liquid and gas) in terms of the particle model, including gas pressure
6	Changing state	Changes of state in terms of the particle model
7	Understanding evaporation	Changes of state in terms of the particle model Energy changes on changes of state (qualitative)
8	Exploring thermal expansion	Changes with temperature in motion and spacing of particles
9	Making sense of models	A simple Dalton atomic model
11	Explaining the density of solids and liquids	The differences in arrangements, in motion and in closeness of particles explaining changes of state, shape and density, the anomaly of ice–water transition
12	Explaining the density of gases	Similarities and differences, including density differences, between solids, liquids and gases
13	Explaining concentration and pressure	The properties of different states of matter (solid, liquid and gas) in terms of the particle model, including gas pressure
14	Exploring diffusion	Diffusion in liquids and gases driven by differences in concentration Diffusion in terms of the particle model
15	Conserving mass	Conservation of mass changes of state Conservation of material and mass, and reversibility, in melting, freezing, evaporation, sublimation, condensation, dissolving
16	Deciding between physical and chemical changes	Mixtures, including dissolving The difference between chemical and physical changes
17	Explaining the properties of mixtures	Mixtures, including dissolving The properties of different states of matter (solid, liquid and gas) in terms of the particle model, including gas pressure
18	Using particle models	The differences in arrangements, in motion and in closeness of particles explaining changes of state, shape and density, the anomaly of ice–water transition

Chapter 3: Explaining Physical Changes

3.2 Using particles to explain matter

Lesson overview

Learning objectives
- Recognise differences between solids, liquids and gases.
- Describe solids, liquids and gases in terms of the particle model.

Learning outcomes
- Use accurate observations to draw inferences about the properties of solids, liquids and gases. [O1]
- Draw circle diagrams and other models to demonstrate the differences between the arrangement of particles in solids, liquids and gases. [O2]
- Use particle diagrams to explain the differences in energy and the forces on the particles in different states of matter. [O3]

Skills development
- Thinking scientifically: use models
- Working scientifically: record evidence
- Learner development: ask questions

Resources needed sticky labels; equipment and materials as detailed in the Technician's notes; Worksheet 2.3.2; Practical sheet 2.3.2 (the last page copied onto card); Technician's notes 2.3.2

Digital resources Quick starter; Interactive activity: Drag the solid, liquid or gas to the correct group when at 25°C and at atmospheric pressure; Interactive activity: Place the elements in order, from strongest to weakest forces between the elements

Common misconceptions Particles in a solid do not move. Particles in a liquid do not touch. In particle diagrams, the particles do not have to be the same size/shape. There is air between the particles of a gas.

Key vocabulary particles, energy, intermolecular forces

Teaching and learning

Engage
- Review the idea that all matter is made up of particles. Ask the students what they understand by the term 'model' and how models might be important in science.
- Demonstrate the three states of matter in water, using a beaker of ice, a beaker of water and a beaker of boiling water. Ask the students to **devise questions** about their observations and to write these on a sticky label in 30 seconds. Collate these into common areas and review and answer them at the end of the lesson. [O1]
- Ask the students to **infer** one common thing all the states have and one thing that is different about them. [O1]

Challenge and develop
- **Group activity** Each group member should have a role – a chairperson, two recorders of observations and two organisers of equipment and materials. Ask them to follow the instructions on Practical sheet 2.3.2 – they are going to **investigate** and **record** observations about solids, liquids and gases. [O1]

  Lower-attaining students can use the cards from page 3 of Practical sheet 2.3.2 to help them with their explanations.

- Ask the groups to answer the questions on Practical sheet 2.3.2 and **think about** how the particles are behaving to account for their observations and to summarise their inferences. Each group should **develop** their own particle model for the three states. Each chairperson should **present** their group's model. [O1&2]

  Higher-attaining students could **think about** what other observations they would need to carry out to **confirm** their ideas.

Chapter 3: Explaining Physical Changes

Explain

- Show the students the accepted version of the particle model in the Student Book and/or use a simulation. Ask them to **identify** any differences between their models and the accepted model. Ask the students how the accepted particle model is different to theirs. What could account for the differences? What further investigations are needed to prove the accepted model? [O2&3]

Consolidate and apply

- Working in groups of eight, the students **role-play** being particles in solids, in liquids and in gases, **explaining** their actions. [O2&3]

    Alternatively, for higher-attaining students, provide pairs of students with polystyrene balls, cocktail sticks and a large sheet of paper. Ask them to **make models** of solids, liquids and gases showing the energy and the forces between the particles.

- Ask all the students to **draw** their own particle diagrams for a solid, a liquid and a gas on a poster with annotations to **explain** their arrangement, energy and forces. They should **link** one piece of evidence from their practical work to each. They should attempt all the tasks of Worksheet 2.3.2 and answer the questions in the Student Book. [O2]

Extend

- Ask students able to progress further to **explain** how the particle model might change for a solid at −50 °C compared with one at 20 °C, and why at 20 °C metals are solids, water is a liquid and oxygen is a gas. [O3]

Plenary suggestions

Scientists Ask the students to **reflect** in pairs on how they have worked as real scientists. What skills have they shown? Why was it important to develop a model from their observations? Why did they need to compare their model with the accepted model?

Question time Read out at least five of the questions devised at the start of the lesson on sticky labels. Select different students to provide answers. Save any questions that cannot be answered for the appropriate lesson.

Answers to Student Book questions

1. any three solids – e.g. metal, plastic and wood; any three liquids – e.g. oil, water and petrol; any three gases – e.g. air, oxygen, carbon dioxide
2. The particles in *solids* are very close together in a regular arrangement; in *liquids* they are still touching but have no regular arrangement; in *gases* they are very far apart in a random order.
3. any suitable cartoon that correctly reflects the energy of the particles in different states
4. steam
5. The particles in *air* are far apart; so your hand can easily pass through the air; very little resistance. The particles in a *solid* are close together; with very strong forces; preventing your hand from going between the wood particles.
6. It is easier to pull jelly apart; the forces between jelly particles must be weaker than between metal particles.
7. As the energy of the particles increases, the forces between them decrease; gas particles have a lot of energy and very weak forces between them.
8. nothing

Answers to Worksheet 2.3.2

1. *Solid* – all the particles should be the same size; and touching each other; in a regular arrangement.
   Liquid – all the particles should be the same size; and touching each other; there is no regular arrangement.
   Gas – all the particles should be the same size; not touching; with no regular arrangement.
2. a) the particles can vibrate; but they cannot move about b) the particles can move around; but they are still in contact with each other c) The particles move quickly; in all directions
3. a) i) particles have the least energy; and move slowly ii) particles have more energy; and move slowly
   iii) particles have the most energy; and move very quickly; in a random motion
   b) i) very strong intermolecular forces; holding the particles in position
   ii) less strong than in solids; forces hold the particles together; but they are not strong enough to keep them moving from their positions iii) very weak intermolecular forces
   c) *solid* – strong forces; so a hand cannot push through; *liquid* – forces are not strong enough; to stop a hand; *gas* – weak forces; so a hand passes through easily

Chapter 3: Explaining Physical Changes

3.3 Understanding solids

Lesson overview

Learning objectives
- Describe the properties of solids.
- Relate the properties and behaviour of solids to the particle model.

Learning outcomes
- Describe how the properties of solids vary. [O1]
- Explain some properties of solids using the particle model. [O2]
- Adapt the particle model to explain differences in the properties of different solids. [O3]

Skills development
- Thinking scientifically: use models
- Working scientifically: record observations
- Learner development: ask questions

Resources needed mini-whiteboards; sticky notes; A3 paper; equipment and materials as detailed in the Technician's notes; card sort; Worksheet 2.3.3; Practical sheet 2.3.3 (second page copied onto card); Technician's notes 2.3.3

Digital resources Quick starter; Slideshow: Explaining properties of gases, liquids and solids

Common misconceptions Particles in all solids are the same.

Key vocabulary malleable, strength, hardness, soluble, conduct, alloy

Teaching and learning

Engage
- **Show and tell** Provide the students with mini-whiteboards. Ask them to **draw** the particle model for a solid and **show** their drawings. Identify and challenge any mistakes – for example particles of different sizes and incorrect structure.
- Show the students a candle and a block of metal. Ask them to feel them and to **describe** as many differences in their properties they can think of. Make a list and come back to this at the end of the lesson. [O1]

Challenge and develop
- **Group work** Working in groups of three, the students work through Practical sheet 2.3.3. Ensure that they wear safety goggles throughout, if they are using metal filings. Ask the students to **investigate** the different properties of solids and to **record** their observations. [O1&2]
- Using the Student Book to help, they answer the questions on Practical sheet 2.3.3, and to **make predictions** about what the particle models for the different solids must be like. They can sort the cards from page 2 of the Practical sheet to help them further. Ask them to work in their groups to **draw annotated** particle posters for at least three of the solids they have investigated. [O1, 2&3]
- Ask each group to display their posters around the room. Provide each group with sticky notes and ask them to **peer-review** each poster, saying two positive things and one area where they could be improved. Allow time for them to address any comments and make necessary improvements. [O2&3]

Explain
- Demonstrate the properties of sodium. Show how sodium can be easily cut with a scalpel, how it floats on water, how it reacts with water and how it can conduct electricity. [O1&2]

Key Stage 3 Science Teacher Pack 2 © HarperCollins*Publishers* Limited 2014

Chapter 3: Explaining Physical Changes

- Ask the students to **plan** and **carry out** a role-play, modelling the particles in sodium, where possible, to explain all the properties they can identify through this demonstration. [O1, 2&3]

    Lower-attaining students should **identify** all the properties.

    Middle-attaining students should **draw/act out** a particle model for sodium, **explaining** how the model accounts for the properties

    Higher-attaining students should **produce/act out** different particle models, accounting for each property shown.

Consolidate and apply

- Ask the students to attempt the tasks of Worksheet 2.3.3 and answer the Student Book questions. [O1, 2&3]
- **Pair work** Provide the students with the descriptions of different solids with the particle models to match up from the card sort. Ask them to **match** the cards and **suggest** an example of the solid described. [O1&2]

Extend

- Ask students able to progress further to carry out some **research** into less familiar solids – e.g. titanium, potassium and brass. They should **produce** their own card sort game, which matches cards showing the particle models with cards showing their properties and uses. [O3]

Plenary suggestions

Properties Return to the list of properties compiled at the start of the lesson. Ask the students to add to the list. [O1]

'Top trumps' The students could **produce** their own 'top trump' cards of the different solids they investigated using the results from their investigation. [O1]

What we have learned Ask the students to **reflect on** three things they have learned about solids and the particle model. [O1, 2&O3]

Answers to Student Book questions

1. ductility
2. diamond is the hardest material; and will be able to drill through any material
3. The particle model should show that most of the particles are small; with only a few much larger particles.
4. The arrangement of the particles in an alloy does not allow for smooth layers; this makes it much harder to pull the metal into thin wires.
5. use thicker springs; to show strong intermolecular forces; and thinner ones for weaker forces
6. Copper is very hard and strong; wax can break easily and is soft. The particle model should show that copper has much stronger intermolecular forces than wax; copper is ductile.

Answers to Worksheet 2.3.3

1. hardness; strength; ductility; solubility; conduction of heat; and electricity
2. a) sodium and iron are metals; both will conduct heat; and electricity

    b) sodium is soft but iron is hard; sodium reacts with water very quickly but iron reacts very slowly; iron is ductile but sodium is not very ductile
3. a) The particle model should show that copper is hard with strong intermolecular forces – e.g. Figure 2.2.3c in the Student Book.

    b) The particle model should show that copper conducts electricity – e.g. Figure 2.3.3c in the Student Book.

Answers to Practical sheet 2.3.3

A–3
B–1
C–2

Chapter 3: Explaining Physical Changes

3.4 Exploring Brownian motion

Lesson overview

Learning objectives
- Describe how theories develop.
- Describe and explain Brownian motion in terms of particles.

Learning outcomes
- Identify the steps in developing theories, including Brownian motion. [O1]
- Use observations to develop hypotheses. [O2]
- Change hypotheses in the light of new evidence and use this to develop theories. [O3]

Skills development
- Thinking scientifically: understand how theories develop
- Working scientifically: develop explanations
- Learner development: ask questions

Resources needed equipment and materials as detailed in the Technician's notes; Worksheet 2.3.4; Practical sheet 2.3.4; Technician's notes 2.3.4

Digital resources Quick starter; Interactive activity: Re-order the statements about the movement of a drop of red dye in water

Common misconceptions Once made, a theory cannot be changed.

Key vocabulary hypothesis, Brownian motion, kinetic theory, evidence

Teaching and learning

Engage
- **Pair talk** Ask the students to **match** the terms 'hypothesis', 'theory', 'evidence', 'evaluate', 'prediction' and 'refute' to their definitions on the interactive whiteboard or as a card sort using task 1 of Worksheet 2.3.4. [O1]
- Remind them about developing theories using evidence. Discuss the idea that theories are supported by evidence. Present different ideas related to particles as follows: (a) particles in a liquid can move; (b) particles in a solid do not move away from their positions. [O1]
- Ask the students to work in pairs to **consider** what evidence might be given to support each idea. They may come up with the idea that when ink is dropped in water, the ink particles spread through the water; this is evidence that the particles of a liquid move. A pen mark may be made on a piece of wax. Applying different tests to the wax will show that the pen mark does not move, inferring that particles in a solid do not move. [O1]

Challenge and develop
- **Group work** In small groups, students should follow the stages of the **scientific process** as follows: **making** predictions, **developing** a hypothesis, **testing** a hypothesis, **making** observations and **reformulating** a hypothesis based on new evidence. Practical sheet 2.3.4 provides full instructions for how this can be achieved. The students will use five cups of cola and add different solutes to it to discover how cola behaves. [O1, 2&3]
- Students should **use the evidence**, and scientific knowledge and understanding, to turn their hypothesis into a theory. Explore how their hypotheses have changed with different observations, and how these may lead to the development of a theory. [O2&3]

Chapter 3: Explaining Physical Changes

- Discuss the experiments of Robert Brown using the Student Book. If possible, either demonstrate Brownian motion (see Technician's notes 2.3.4) or show a video of it. Discuss the different hypotheses that Brown developed and the different types of experiments he did to test his hypotheses. [O1, 2&3]

Explain

- Divide the students into groups of three and ask them to **draw a flow chart** on a poster to describe each step of the scientific process carried out in their investigation. They should **explain** how they carried out each step in their investigation, providing examples of each. [O1, 2&3]
- Ask them to use the Student Book to **apply** the flowchart to Robert Brown's observations and hypotheses, as shown in task 2 of Worksheet 2.3.4. [O2&3]

  Higher-attaining students should **explain** how they have changed their original hypothesis in light of new evidence, as set out in task 3 of Worksheet 2.3.4. [O3]

Consolidate and apply

- Ask the students to use their posters and **prepare** a short presentation to **explain** the processes involved in how scientists work, using Robert Brown as an example. Select different groups to deliver their presentations. [O1&2]

  Higher-attaining students should also **include an explanation** of the link between hypotheses and theories and the need for peer review. [O3]

- The students should answer all the Student Book questions. [O1, 2&3]

Extend

- Ask students able to progress further to use the Student Book and other resources, to **explain** how Einstein was able to use models and analogies to support and develop the theory to explain Brownian motion. [O3]

Plenary suggestions

What we have learned Ask the students to **reflect on** three things they have learned about the scientific process.

Investigative skills Ask them to **write a target** for how they might improve their own investigative skills based on their learning in this lesson.

Answers to Student Book questions

1. a scientific explanation based on experimental evidence; it is possible to make testable predictions from a hypothesis
2. others can confirm that your evidence is reliable and without bias
3. only living things caused Brownian motion to occur
4. he carried out many investigations using non-living objects
5. If observations do not agree with an established theory, this means the theory might be wrong.
6. These are useful tools that help scientists to explain what can't be seen, felt or heard; they can help in understanding what is happening.
7. It is better to find evidence to refute it, rather than support, to be sure of its validity. We cannot prove that a theory stands with only evidence that supports it, only if you can find no evidence against it.

Answers to Worksheet 2.3.4

1. 1 with e; 2 with c; 3 with a; 4 with b; 5 with f; 6 with d
2. a) he predicted that non-living organisms would not show Brownian motion
   b) he observed a range of living and non-living organisms exhibiting Brownian motion
   c) he hypothesised that pollen grains moved because they were living
   d) he tested non-living organisms to prove his hypothesis
   e) non-living organisms behaved in the same way as living organisms, so he had to change his ideas
3. a) He was not able to turn his hypothesis into a theory because the evidence refuted his earlier hypothesis. He was unable to develop a new hypothesis to support the evidence of his many investigations.
   b) He could have made observations of liquids at different temperatures; Brownian motion increases at higher temperatures.

Chapter 3: Explaining Physical Changes

3.5 Understanding liquids and gases

Lesson overview

Learning objectives
- Compare different properties of liquids and gases.
- Relate the properties and behaviour of liquids and gases to the particle model.

Learning outcomes
- Describe some properties of liquids and gases. [O1]
- Design and carry out an investigation to compare the viscosity of different liquids. [O2]
- Use the particle model to explain experimental data and applications of liquids and gases. [O3]

Skills development
- Thinking scientifically: use models
- Working scientifically: design investigations
- Learner development: communicate effectively

Resources needed images or examples of liquids and gases in different applications; equipment and apparatus as detailed in the Technician's notes; Worksheet 2.3.5; Practical sheet 2.3.5; Technician's notes 2.3.5

Digital resources Quick starter; Interactive activity: Place the fluids in order of most to least viscous at room temperature; Slideshow: Volume and compression - How much air is in a scuba tank?; Hangman: Key vocabulary game

Common misconceptions All liquids behave in the same way. Gases don't dissolve in water, they just make bubbles.

Key vocabulary viscosity, compressed, solubility

Teaching and learning

Engage
- Show some images or examples of liquids and gases in different applications. Ask the students to **identify** the properties which are helpful in each application. [O1]

Challenge and develop
- Ask the students to **summarise** all the properties of liquids and gases and write them on the board. Question them about the evidence for these properties. They may struggle with evidence for the properties of gases.

    a) Demonstrate the ability of carbon dioxide to flow (see the instructions in Technician's notes 2.3.5). Ask the students to **explain** their observations.

    b) Demonstrate the compression of gases using a gas syringe and a balloon. Ask the students to **explain** why liquids cannot be compressed but gases can.

    c) Show the bubbles in a fizzy drink. Ask questions about what this shows about the solubility of carbon dioxide. Ask 'How could we prove that some of the carbon dioxide dissolves in the water?'. [O1]

- Arrange the students in mixed ability groups. Ask them to **design an investigation**, using Practical sheet 2.3.5 for guidance, of the effect of temperature on the flow of liquids. They should **plan** to collect valid and reliable evidence. Recap the meanings of the terms 'valid' and 'reliable' and discuss how these apply to their design. Check through the each group's plans and then ask them to **carry out** their investigation and **record** their observations. A suggested procedure is:
    - Place a beaker of oil in water baths at five different temperatures, e.g. 5, 20, 25, 30 and 40 °C.
    - Check with a thermometer that the oil has reached the required temperature.

Chapter 3: Explaining Physical Changes

- Place the viscometer in the clamp stand and position a small beaker under the viscometer.
- Fill the viscometer with oil and time how long it takes to empty.
- Repeat this three times at each temperature and calculate averages. [O1&2]
- The students should produce graphs of their results. [O1&2]
- Using the Student Book to help, the students should **write an explanation** of their findings. Select different groups to **share** their results and analysis. [O3]

Explain

- Explore further ideas of compression using the Student Book, and some of the applications relating to this, such as a real example of the bicycle pump. The students should answer the questions in the Student Book about a bicycle pump works. [O1&3]
- Show the students the graph of how different gases dissolve in water in the Student Book (Figure 2.3.5d). Ask them to **devise a role-play** to explain the data in the graph. [O1&3]

Consolidate and apply

- Ask the students to work in pairs to produce two annotated posters about liquids and gases. They should **explain** all the properties they have come across, using adapted versions of the particle model. [O1&3]
- Ask the students to attempt the tasks of Worksheet 2.3.5 and answer any questions in the Student Book not yet attempted. [O1, 2&3]

Extend

- Tell students able to progress further that gases increase in viscosity with increasing temperature, but that the viscosity of liquids is reduced as their temperature increases. Ask them to **develop** their own hypothesis and attempt to develop the particle model to explain this. [O3]

Plenary suggestions

Evidence Return to the list of properties of liquids and gases compiled earlier. Ask the students to add any further evidence from their learning this lesson.

Venn diagram Ask the students to **draw** a Venn diagram to summarise the properties of liquids and gases, putting common properties in the centre.

Answers to Student Book questions

1. for example flushing toilets; putting liquids in moulds; 'dry ice' on stage
2. a) the temperature; the amount of liquid used; the time to allow the liquids to flow
   b) a temperature below 10 °C; about 20 cm^3 of oil; about 5 minutes
3. more of the gas can be carried in a container if it is compressed to a liquid
4. When the piston lifts up, there is more space inside for the air particles to flow in; the piston becomes full of air. When the piston is pushed down, the air particles can be compressed; and are forced into the tyre.
5. Carbon dioxide is more soluble in water than oxygen; this is because the intermolecular forces between the particles of water and carbon dioxide are stronger; than the forces between the carbon dioxide molecules. (Conversely for oxygen.)
6. When it gets hotter the gas particles have more kinetic energy; they are able to escape the intermolecular forces between themselves and the water particles more easily; and less gas remains in the solution.
7. The waste output from a factory may have a different temperature from the water in the river; which would alter the oxygen and carbon dioxide levels in the water; this would affect the fish.

Answers to Worksheet 2.3.5

1. a) ability to flow b) ability to flow and take the shape of the container c) ability to flow and be compressed
   d) ability to take the shape of the container and be compressed e) ability to take the shape of the container and be compressed f) ability to take the shape of the container and be compressed
2. a) use the same amount of liquid; allow the liquids to flow in the same type of tube; use the same temperature
   b) 20 seconds c) i) a bar graph ii) data for independent variable is discrete
   iii) the scale of the graph would be awkward because it needs to have a range from 1 to 10 000
3. Diagrams should show the honey–honey particles having much stronger forces than the water–water particles; the honey particles are likely to be much larger than the water particles.

Chapter 3: Explaining Physical Changes

3.6 Changing state

Lesson overview

Learning objectives

- Recognise changes of state as being reversible changes.
- Use scientific terminology to describe changes of state.
- Explain changes of state using the particle model and ideas about energy transfer.

Learning outcomes

- Describe and recognise changes of state, using correct terminology and the particle model. [O1]
- Interpret and explain data relating to melting and boiling points. [O2]
- Use the particle model to explain latent heat. [O3]

Skills development

- Thinking scientifically: analyse data
- Working scientifically: interpret evidence
- Learner development: ask questions

Resources poster paper; graph paper; paper glue; equipment and materials as detailed in the Technician's notes; Worksheet 2.3.6; Practical sheet 2.3.6; Technician's notes 2.3.6

Digital resources Quick starter; Interactive activity: Drag the examples of change in state to the correct group – melting, condensing or sublimation; Video

Common misconceptions Temperature increases during changes of state. All solids have the same melting point.

Key vocabulary sublimation, melting point, boiling point, latent heat

Teaching and learning

Engage

- Recap ideas about changes of state using ideas from the Student Book. Ask the students to complete the cloze activity in task 1 of Worksheet 2.3.6. [O1]

Challenge and develop

- Demonstrate the melting of salol and the boiling of water. While doing so, select a group of eight students to **model** being the salol particles as the solid is heated. Alternatively, or additionally, show a simulation of a solid being melted and a liquid being heated to boiling. Ask the students to **record** all the changes they **observe** as the solid and liquid change state. Introduce and define the terms 'melting point' and 'boiling point' and apply these to the role-play. Challenge any misconceptions during this. [O1&2]

- Demonstrate, or show a video of, carbon dioxide (dry ice) or iodine subliming (see Technician's notes 2.3.6). Ask the students to **compare** the melting of wax to the heating of carbon dioxide or iodine. They should notice there is no liquid phase for carbon dioxide or iodine. Introduce the term 'sublimation'. [O1]

- Ask the students to **follow the instructions** on Practical sheet 2.3.6 and **record** the temperature as the stearic acid is heated – if time allows they should do the same for ice. They should **collect** reliable data and **work out** mean temperatures. Ask them to draw graphs of their findings. [O1&2]

- Discuss their graphs. Encourage the students to **explain** what is happening at each part of their graph, and ask them to **compare** these for the two substances investigated. Use the Student Book to support this. [O1, 2&3].

Chapter 3: Explaining Physical Changes

Explain

- Working in pairs, ask the students to **make posters** of their graphs, including annotations to explain what is happening to the particles at each step. [O&3]

    Lower-attaining students should be able to **identify** the parts where changes of state are taking place. They should also be able to **describe** how the arrangement and movement of the particles are changing, and how these might be different for the two substances.

    Middle-attaining students should be able to **describe** how the energy and forces between the particles are changing. They should **identify** the melting and boiling points.

    Higher-attaining students should be able to **explain** why the temperature does not change during the changes of state. They should be able to **explain** differences between the two substances.

Consolidate and apply

- Ask the students, working in their pairs, to do task 2 of Worksheet 2.3.6. They use the cards to position the melting points and boiling points on the thermometer scale as appropriate, and then answer the questions, and also question a) of task 3. [O2]

Extend

- Provide students able to progress further with data and questions about latent heat, melting points and boiling points of different substances – question b) of task 3 of Worksheet 2.3.6. Question c) then asks them to **predict** what the change-of-state graphs would look like for each, if the solid was be heated for some time. [O3]

Plenary suggestions

True/false quiz Ask the students to use the graph of ice melting (Figure 2.3.6c) in the Student Book. Play 'true' or 'false' using statements such as:

- Ice melts at 0 °C.
- The temperature changes as ice melts.
- Once the ice has melted, the temperature of the water remains constant.
- The boiling point of water is not fixed.
- The energy needed to boil water is less than the energy needed to melt ice.

What I have learned Ask each student to **share** with their partner all the new ideas learned in the lesson.

Answers to Student Book questions

1. freeze some water to make ice; then heat the ice to make water
2. a) changing a solid to a liquid   b) changing a gas to a liquid   c) changing a liquid to a gas
   d) changing a liquid to a solid   e) changing a solid to a gas
3. the intermolecular forces between copper particles are much higher; than those between aluminium particles
4. hydrogen has weaker intermolecular forces than mercury; the strongest intermolecular forces are in ice
5. a) solid and liquid   c) liquid   d) liquid and gas   e) gas
6. all the energy is being used to overcome the intermolecular forces; to enable the water to boil and change state
7. No; different substances have different strengths of intermolecular force; some will require much more energy than others to overcome these forces. In carbon dioxide and ice, the intermolecular forces between the carbon dioxide particles are much weaker than in ice; and need much less energy to change state – this why it sublimes.

Answers to Worksheet 2.3.6

1. close together; vibrate; kinetic energy; intermolecular forces; melting; liquid; quickly; intermolecular forces; boiling; gas
2. Check that the cards are correctly placed on the thermometer.
   a) i) gas   ii) liquid   b) i) liquid   ii) gas
3. a) i) oxygen; nitrogen; water; mercury   ii) magnesium; water; mercury   iii) water; mercury
   b) i) true   ii) false   iii) true
   c) Graph for aluminium should show a much higher melting temperature and a very much higher boiling point; with a much longer flat part where the liquid is boiling.

Chapter 3: Explaining Physical Changes

3.7 Understanding evaporation

Lesson overview

Learning objectives

- Investigate factors affecting evaporation.
- Explain the differences between boiling and evaporation using the particle model.

Learning outcomes

- Investigate and describe factors affecting evaporation. [O1]
- Describe the processes occurring in evaporation and boiling using the particle model. [O2]
- Use the particle model to explain how different factors affect evaporation. [O3]

Skills development

- Thinking scientifically: ask questions
- Working scientifically: design investigations
- Learner development: collaborate effectively

Resources needed equipment and materials as detailed in the Technician's notes; Worksheet 2.3.7; Practical sheet 2.3.7; Technician's notes 2.3.7

Digital resources Quick starter; Interactive activity: Drag the items to the correct group – boiling point less or greater than water; Slideshow: Factors affecting evaporation - Why does nail varnish remover dry more quickly than water?

Common misconceptions Evaporation and boiling are the same thing.

Key vocabulary evaporation, boiling, surface area

Teaching and learning

Engage

- Place a few cm^3 of alcohol in an evaporating dish and the same amount of oil in another. Use a hairdryer and blow over each to the same extent. Ask pairs of students to **devise** three questions about what they see. [O1]
- Select different students to **share** their questions and write them on the board. Ask pairs of students to select any question that can be investigated experimentally. Explore what it is that makes an 'effective' question – ascertain that it should address the independent and the dependent variables. Ask the students to change the question they selected into an effective question that can be investigated and take feedback. [O1]
- Ask the students to look at the images on Worksheet 2.3.7 and **explain** whether they show evaporation or boiling. Ask them to give three key differences between evaporation and boiling. [O1&2]

Challenge and develop

- Explore what has happened in each of the dishes – where have all the particles of alcohol gone? Why are the oil particles still there? Use the Student Book to discuss the differences between evaporation and boiling. [O2]
- Either show a simulation or use role-play by a small group of students to **explain** what is happening when a liquid evaporates and how this differs from when it boils. Select different pupils to **summarise** how evaporation and boiling are different. [O2&3]
- Divide the students into pairs and ask each to **devise** their own question to find out about one (different) factor that can affect evaporation. The images of evaporation in the worksheet should act as a stimulus. They should use their question to **plan** an investigation using Practical sheet 2.3.7. [O1]

Chapter 3: Explaining Physical Changes

- Check through their plans first, including safety, then ask them to carry out their investigations and **record** their findings. They should **plot** an appropriate graph of their results. Discuss the terms 'repeatable' and 'reproducible'. Ask students to reflect on these two terms and how they apply to their investigation. [O1]

Explain

- Ask students to develop their own models/or use role-play to explain their findings. They should be prepared to **present** their findings and explanations to the class. [O2&3]

Consolidate and apply

- Ask the students to attempt tasks 2 and 3 of Worksheet 2.3.7. [O2&3]
- Ask them to **make a list of applications** in which evaporation might be needed to take place quickly, and situations where evaporation must be prevented. [O2]

Extend

- Ask students able to progress further to **research** and use the particle model to **explain** the strategies that two different animals and two different plants use to reduce unwanted evaporation. [O3]

Plenary suggestions

Acrostic Ask the students to make an acrostic of the word 'evaporation'.

Summarising They could summarise the key similarities and differences between evaporation and boiling.

Answers to Student Book questions

1. Clouds are made from the evaporation of water.
2. it comes from your body (respiration)
3. it will take place near the boiling point; the temperature is higher; so there is more heat transferred to the liquid particles; so more will evaporate
4. *Boiling* is where the whole of the liquid changes to a gas at a fixed temperature. *Evaporation* is where some of the particles escape to become a gas; at temperatures between the melting point and the boiling point.
5. The more heat transferred by the Sun; the higher the rate of evaporation. The larger the surface area; the higher the rate of evaporation. The stronger the surface wind; the higher the rate of evaporation.
6. The effect of temperature; the energy transferred by heat will directly affect the kinetic energy of more surface particles; changing the state from liquid to gas more quickly.

Answers to Worksheet 2.3.7

1. a) evaporation b) boiling c) boiling d) evaporation e) evaporation
2. In *boiling* the whole liquid changes into a gas; bubbles can be seen throughout the liquid; this happens at a fixed temperature. In *evaporation* only the surface of the liquid changes into a gas; this happens at any temperature between the melting point and boiling point.
3. a) Evaporation happens only at the surface; so more particles will evaporate from a large surface area than a smaller surface area.

   b) The higher the temperature the more energy the particles in a liquid have; so more of them will get enough energy to escape and form a gas.

   c) The greater the wind speed, the higher the energy the air particles have; they transfer this energy to the surface particles of the liquid; so the more energy transferred the higher the rate of evaporation. In addition the wind will also remove particles from near the liquid's surface, allowing space for other particles to escape.

   d) The intermolecular forces between, for example, alcohol particles are weaker than those of water; so less energy is needed for these particles to escape as a gas; so alcohol will evaporate much faster than water.

Chapter 3: Explaining Physical Changes

3.8 Exploring thermal expansion

Lesson overview

Learning objectives
- Identify how heat affects the arrangement and movement of particles.
- Use the particle model to explain the effects of heat on expansion.

Learning outcomes
- Describe how solids, liquids and gases behave when heat is applied to them. [O1]
- Compare the thermal expansion of different solids and liquids. [O2]
- Use the particle model to explain expansion in solids, liquids and gases. [O3]

Skills development
- Thinking scientifically: use models
- Working scientifically: develop explanations
- Learner development: communicate effectively

Resources needed masking tape; poster paper; equipment and materials as detailed in the Technician's notes; Worksheet 2.3.8; Practical sheet 2.3.8; Technician's notes 2.3.8

Digital resources Quick starter; Video

Common misconceptions Particles themselves get bigger when they are heated. Heat is made of 'heat molecules'.

Key vocabulary thermal expansion

Teaching and learning

Engage
- Demonstrate a metal ball passing through a ring. Now heat the ball with a Bunsen burner. The students should **observe** that the metal ball can no longer fit through the ring. Ask them to work in pairs and **develop a hypothesis** for this observation. Discuss ways it can be tested further. [O1]
- Demonstrate the 'dancing coin' experiment described in Technician's notes 2.3.8. Encourage the students to again develop a hypothesis for their observations and to think of other ways to test these. [O1]
- Demonstrate heating a crushed ping pong ball in boiling water. The students should notice that the ping pong ball regains its shape. What hypothesis can they come up with about the expansion of gases? [O1]

Challenge and develop
- Discuss the term 'thermal expansion' using the Student Book and answering questions 1 and 2. Select a group of students to **role-play** being particles in a solid. Use masking tape to mark the area they stand in. Ask them to show what happens when they are heated. The observers should **identify** what happens to the overall volume of the solid. Emphasise the fact that the particles themselves do not expand, just the volume they occupy as they are heated. Repeat with liquids and gases, comparing the expansion between solids, liquids and gases. [O1&2]
- Working in groups of three, the students **carry out** the two investigations outlined on Practical sheet 2.3.8. They will make 'thermometers' using water and alcohol, and **observe** the expansion of gases at different temperatures. The amount of expansion in a solid is small and difficult to measure accurately. [O1&2]
- Ask the students to **draw** appropriate graphs of their observations. Explore their conclusions from their investigations. [O1&2]

Chapter 3: Explaining Physical Changes

Explain

- The students work in groups of three to **create** annotated posters of particle diagrams to **explain** the observations from each investigation. [O1, 2&3]

Consolidate and apply

- The students should do tasks 1 and 2 of Worksheet 2.3.8, **explaining** comparisons in the expansion of solids, liquids and gases. [O1, 2&3]
- Show the students a bimetallic strip as drawn in task 3 of Worksheet 2.3.8. Ask them to **write an explanation** about how it might work. [O3]

Extend

- Ask students able to progress further to look again at the graph of the expansion of ice on Worksheet 2.3.8. Ask them to suggest some explanations for this anomalous behaviour. [O3]

Plenary suggestions

Applications Ask the students to think of as many examples of thermal expansion in action as they can.

Problem solving Can they also think of problems that are caused by thermal expansion? How might some of these be solved?

Answers to Student Book questions

1. the lid will expand on heating; making it fit more loosely; and so be easier to remove
2. The air inside the balloon will expand; taking up more space; this may cause the balloon to pop.
3. lead; aluminium; copper; steel; glass
4. Copper will expand on heating; long lengths should not be used; and room for expansion allowed for.
5. If filled with a *solid*, the expansion may be too small to detect and measure. With a *gas*, the expansion will be large; meaning that a large container will be needed; this is not practical.
6. The sea will get warmer with increased global warming; this will cause the seawater to expand taking up more room and sea levels will rise; causing flooding.

Answers to Worksheet 2.3.8

1. a) The gas inside the aerosol expands on heating; because it is inside a closed container, the pressure increases; to such an extent that the can will explode.

   b) The railway line has buckled; this is because the iron has warmed up and expanded; because there is nowhere else for it to move to, it changes shape and buckles.

   c) As the seawater warms, it expands; this means that the volume increases; and the sea level will rise.

2. a) As water cools from 4 °C to 0 °C, the volume of water increases; it will take up more space; this can cause the pipes to burst.

   b) Water does not expand uniformly on heating; so it is not suitable for use in a thermometer.

   c) Mercury is a liquid in this range of temperature; and it expands uniformly.

3. Check that the diagram shows that brass curves more than iron; the particles in brass are further apart than the particles in iron.

Chapter 3: Explaining Physical Changes

3.9 Making sense of models

Lesson overview

Learning objectives

- Describe the concept of a 'good enough' model.
- Link the particle model to elements and compounds.
- Evaluate the strengths and weaknesses of the particle model.

Learning outcomes

- Describe different models that can be used to represent particles. [O1]
- Apply and adapt models to make them more suitable for use. [O2]
- Evaluate the strengths and limitations of particle models. [O3]

Skills development

- Thinking scientifically: use models
- Working scientifically: develop explanations
- Learner development: ask questions

Resources needed equipment and materials as detailed in the Technician's notes; Worksheet 2.3.9; Technician's notes 2.3.9

Digital resources Quick starter; Hangman: Key vocabulary game

Common misconceptions There is only one particle model.

Key vocabulary atom, element, compound, particle model

Teaching and learning

Engage

- Show the students one or two demonstrations (see Technician's notes 2.3.9):
  - a jar with a layer of carbon dioxide in the bottom – if a lighted splint is held in the air it stays lit, but it goes out when held in the bottom of the jar
  - using corn flour and water showing its unusual properties when it is hit.
- Ask the students to **draw** a particle model for solids, liquids and gases. Ask them to **apply** the model to the materials in the demonstration(s). Ask the students to **consider** if the particle model can account for all the observations. [O1&2]

Challenge and develop

- Discuss the idea that John Dalton was the first chemist known to propose the idea that particles are made up of atoms, and that since then our idea of what atoms are like has changed considerably in the light of new evidence. Lead the students to the understanding that the particle model is one that can explain some but not all things – use the Student Book to help. [O1&2]

- Using popcorn, demonstrate an alternative model for looking at particles during a change of state. Ask them to **apply** this model for explaining changes of state. Ask them to use **role-play** and polystyrene balls (see Technician's notes 2.3.9) as two alternative models for explaining changes of state, and to **consider** their strengths and limitations. [O1, 2&3]

- Now demonstrate how ice floats on water. Ask the students to **select** a model that can explain why ice floats. What would each of the models predict should happen? Help them to understand that a new model is needed to explain this phenomenon. Use the Student Book to 'see' the forces between the particles in ice and in

Chapter 3: Explaining Physical Changes

water. Ask the students to **construct** their own three-dimensional model to explain how this phenomenon works. [O2&3]

- Provide the students with coloured paper clips, coloured modelling clay and building bricks. Give them with the list of compounds and elements in the second section of Worksheet 2.3.9 and ask them to **make models** using the different materials. [O1, 2&3]

Explain

- Working in pairs, ask the students to compare all the models used so far for explaining changes of state and **rank** them in order of most useful to least useful. They should **explain** their reasons. [O2&3]
- Ask them to do the same for the element and compound models. [O2&3]

Consolidate and apply

- Ask the students to complete the tasks of Worksheet 2.3.9, using appropriate models to **explain** the situations given in task 3 of Worksheet 2.3.9. [O1, 2&3]

Extend

- Ask students able to progress further to **consider** the question 'Is there a perfect particle model?' Ask them to use evidence and observations to **justify** their answer. [O3]

Plenary suggestions

Models Return to the 'standard' particle model and ask the students to **summarise** its limitations. Ask them to give three reasons why scientists need to use and adapt models.

Answers to Student Book questions

1. Liquids and gases can flow but solids cannot; solids have a fixed shape; solids are stronger than liquids and gases.
2. When the solid popcorn kernels get hot they move around more; just like the particles of a solid when it changes into a liquid. As more energy is transferred to the popcorn, the particles move more and more. When they finally pop, they move like the particles of a gas; in a random way flying all over the place. One problem is that the 'gas' popcorn particles are unlike the 'solid' particles; in reality the particles remain the same no matter what the state of the substance.
3. H_2O should have one oxygen atom and two smaller hydrogen atoms; HCl should have one large chlorine atom and one small hydrogen atom; ideally of the same size as in the water molecule.
4. it shows the types of atoms present; and the approximate scale of their sizes
5. both models can explain why steam diffuses faster than liquid water; because both show that the particles in a gas move faster than those in a liquid
6. the standard particle model does not show the shape of the ice crystals; and so cannot explain this

Answers to Worksheet 2.3.9

1. a) any of the three can be chosen; with a suitable reason – they all have strengths and limitations
   b) in the gas state the particles themselves change form; which does not occur with real particles. In the 'liquid' state the particles of popcorn do not stay close together
   c) the gas particles are free to move in any direction
   d) any answer; with a suitable reason
2. suitable models built with the correct numbers and types of atoms in different colours; ideally the solid particles should be made in 3-D matrix
3. a) building bricks or molecular modelling kits can be used; the sizes and types of particles can be represented
   b) popcorn, role-play and paperclips would not be suitable; they cannot adequately show different sizes and types of particles
   c) role-play could be used; it can show that aluminium has stronger intermolecular forces than water
   d) popcorn and polystyrene balls; cannot show the forces between the particles
   e) modelling clay is probably the most adaptable; any shape or sized particles can be represented

Chapter 3: Explaining Physical Changes

3.10 Applying key ideas

Explaining heat packs

Objectives

- Extract ideas about changes of state, expansion and energy changes from the text, including earlier sections of the topic.
- Apply ideas about the particle model to explain some physical processes.
- Use ideas and information about particles to explain the properties of different states of matter and how changes of state can be applied.

Outcome

- Making clear and effective responses to questions, indicating understanding and the next steps in learning.

The purpose of this activity is to provide an opportunity to see how successfully students are grasping the key ideas so far. It is not designed to be used as a formal test – it might be that students work on the questions collectively. It does provide an opportunity for you to look at written work, engage students in discussions and form ideas about progress being made.

The tasks are progressive. Lower-attaining students should be able to tackle the first task, middle-attaining students should be able to work through the next two and the more challenging final task is most suitable for the higher-attaining students.

Resources needed sodium acetate heat packs; self-heating cups; Worksheet 2.3.10; Technician's notes 2.3.10

Teaching and learning

Engage

- Quiz the students in relation to the key terminology used in previous lessons. Provide them with the key words and ask them to come up with their own definitions.
- Demonstrate how quickly a supersaturated solution of sodium acetate crystallises by making a sculpture using the directions in Technician's notes 2.3.10. Use a thermometer to show that there is a temperature change during the crystallisation process. Explore reasons for the transfer of heat using ideas about changes of state.

Challenge and develop

- Discuss changes of state, emphasising the energy transfers that take place. Focus on the fact that as liquids change to solids heat needs to be transferred from the liquid to the surroundings. This is a useful energy transfer used in hand warmers. Discuss also the need for heat to be transferred to a liquid for it to turn into a gas.
- Working in pairs, give the students sodium acetate hand warmers and self-heating cups based on phase-change materials. Ask them to **discuss** the heat transfers involved and to **think about** what is happening to the particles. In the case of the self-heating cups, one model uses an oil-type solid in a sealed unit within the cup. When the coffee is hot, energy is transferred from the coffee to a suitable temperature for drinking. The solid oil melts to form a liquid. When the coffee cools, the liquid changes state to become a solid. Energy is transferred back to the coffee in the process, heating it up. There are other types of heat packs available – some rely on chemical reactions.
- Ask the students to think about in what other ways changes of state may be useful in energy transfers.

Explain

- Ask the students to read the text about *Explaining heat packs* in the Student Book. Depending on their ability to assimilate text, you may need to adopt the following strategies.
- Have students working in pairs, with Worksheet 2.3.10 and highlighters. One student highlights key ideas and the other (using a different colour) any words they don't understand.
- Using the text as a source of ideas, they draw a spider chart with 'changes of state' at the centre, surrounded by aspects relating to it. They could include the names of changes, how they come about and applications.

Key Stage 3 Science Teacher Pack 2 © HarperCollins*Publishers* Limited 2014

Chapter 3: Explaining Physical Changes

- Work with groups of students who have difficulty with reading to support them in decoding the text and accessing the ideas.

Consolidate and apply

- Now ask the students to attempt the tasks in the Student Book. They might do this individually or collaboratively – in either case, encourage them to **identify** and **record** their ideas.
- Ask them to present their responses to various tasks, either orally or by displaying their work.

Extend

- For students able to progress further, the later tasks give opportunities for extension work.

Plenary

How did you do? Ask the students the following questions to **reflect on** how well they responded to the tasks: What did they find easy to do? What was hard? What do they still not understand about the particle model and changes of state? Provide the students with some overall feedback, indicating ideas that they have grasped effectively and those that may need developing further.

Likely responses and next steps in learning

1. This task gives the students an opportunity to recall information about liquids and solids. They should include ideas about the particles' arrangements, energy and forces, and how these affect the properties. The hand warmer is hard when it is solid and strong, but very flexible when it is a liquid. The differences in energy between the particles should be compared, and the comparative strength of the intermolecular forces.

2. This task involves describing what happens when a liquid becomes a solid and vice versa. Accurate particle diagrams should be drawn – all the particles the same size, and all particles in the liquid touching. The students should discuss the energy transfers taking place – when a liquid changes to a solid, energy is transferred by heat to the surroundings. This heat transfer is how the hand warmer works – useful heat energy is transferred.

3. a) This task requires students to engage with the text. They need to explain that as the sodium acetate changes from liquid to solid, energy must be transferred by heat because particles in a liquid have more energy than particles in a solid. So energy must be transferred away to the surroundings for a change in state to occur.

   b) The students should also appreciate that once a hand warmer has become solid, there is no more transfer of heat. It needs to be 'turned' back into a liquid. For this energy is required, so the solid's particles can gain energy to be turned into a liquid again.

4. a) Here the students need to appreciate that in an *iron–oxygen* hand warmer a chemical change takes place to make iron oxide – this reaction transfers heat to the surroundings. This is an irreversible change, with new bonds being formed between oxygen and iron. This should be shown in the particle diagrams.

   With *calcium chloride* and *water*, energy is transferred by heat to the surroundings as the calcium chloride dissolves. This is a reversible change – the particle diagram needs to reflect this.

   b) *Iron–oxygen disadvantages*: the students may realise that this is a slow reaction and that not a great deal of heat is transferred. The iron and oxygen must be kept separate until heat is required. Once the iron has reacted, it has 'gone' and there is no more and it must be discarded. Heat transfer ceases when the reaction stops.

   Iron–oxygen advantages: there are no problems activating the reaction – heat is transferred as soon as the reactants come into contact with each other.

   Calcium chloride and water disadvantages: separate containers are needed for the calcium chloride and water. Once the calcium chloride has dissolved it must be discarded and no further heat transfer is possible.

   Calcium chloride and water advantages: a lot of heat energy can be transferred by this change, making it suitable for keeping drinks hot.

   Sodium acetate disadvantages: a metal disc is needed to activate the change; eventually this will run out. The change will only transfer energy over an hour or so.

   Sodium acetate advantages: the pack can be re-heated to form a liquid and reused several times.

Chapter 3: Explaining Physical Changes

3.11 Explaining the density of solids and liquids

Lesson overview

Learning objectives

- Use the particle model to explain density differences between solids and liquids.
- Use the particle model to explain anomalies between ice and water.

Learning outcomes

- Make predictions about floating and sinking using ideas about density. [O1]
- Calculate the densities of solids and liquids. [O2]
- Use the particle model to explain factors relating to density. [O3]

Skills development

- Thinking scientifically: use equations
- Working scientifically: record evidence
- Learner development: collaborate effectively

Resources needed equipment and materials as detailed in the Technician's notes; Worksheet 2.3.11; Technician's notes 2.3.11

Digital resources Quick starter; Slideshow: What is density?; Interactive activity: Drag the items to the correct group – density less or greater than water?

Common misconceptions Density is the same as mass. A big object will sink, but a small object will float.

Key vocabulary density, mass, volume, float

Teaching and learning

Engage

- Tell the students you are going to put two identically sized cans of cola into containers of water – one is normal cola, the other is diet cola. What do they **predict** will happen? Note the predictions of selected students. In the demonstration the diet cola is found to float, and the normal cola sinks. Ask the students to **discuss** in pairs what is happening and to propose a hypothesis. [O1]
- Show the students a range of objects in task 1 of Worksheet 2.3.11. Recap ideas about floating and sinking from other chapters. Ask the students to **make predictions** about what will sink and float and to explain why. Review the idea that density depends on mass and volume. Demonstrate whether the objects float or sink. [O1]

Challenge and develop

- Use the Student Book to define the term density and find out how it can be calculated. [O2]
- Ask the students to use task 2 of Worksheet 2.3.11 to **calculate** the density of solid and molten iron and to compare them. Can they explain the difference in density of the solid state and the liquid state? Students should **identify** that the density of water is anomalous. [O1&2]
- Show the students the setup for putting an ice cube into ice cold water at about 4 °C and a chocolate square into melted chocolate. Working in pairs, ask the students to **predict** what will happen and to use the particle model to **explain** this. Do the demonstrations at the same time – the ice floats and the chocolate sinks. Ask the students to **suggest** a possible explanation. [O1&3]
- Discuss the particle model for ice and water from the Student Book. Explore the structure of ice compared with that of most solids. The particles have a regular structure, but there are spaces between the molecules of ice. Use the Student Book to help the students to **identify** that the ice molecules have special

Key Stage 3 Science Teacher Pack 2 © HarperCollins*Publishers* Limited 2014

Chapter 3: Explaining Physical Changes

intermolecular forces between them which keep them in this arrangement. (There is no need to discuss hydrogen bonding in any depth at this stage.) [O1&3]

Explain

- Working in pairs, ask the students to **make 3D models** of ice crystals and gold. They should **explain** how they are different, why the density of liquid gold is less than that of solid gold, and why ice is less dense than cold water but more dense than hot water. [O1&3]

Consolidate and apply

- Ask the students to **show** their models and **share** their explanations. [O1&3]
- Ask them to look at the graph (Figure 2.3.11c in the Student Book) showing how the density of ice changes with temperature. Ask them to **draw particle models** for each of the points where the shape of the graph changes in the worksheet. They should sketch what the graph will look like for a solid like gold. [O3]
- They should answer the questions in task 3 of Worksheet 2.3.11 and also the Student Book questions. [O1, 2&3]

Extend

- Ask students able to progress further to **find out** about hydrogen bonding and how it accounts for the anomalous behaviour of ice and water. [O3]

Plenary suggestions

Life on Earth Ask the students to think of ways that this anomalous behaviour of ice and water affects life on Earth, and other physical processes such as freeze–thaw action.

Spread the word Ask them to **share** two things they have **learned** with three other people.

Answers to Student Book questions

1. a) the paper floats on top of the syrup
   b) the iron sinks in the alcohol
   c) the brick will float within the liquid; and not on top; they have the same density
   d) the baby oil floats on top of the water; they are immiscible liquids
2. there are fewer particles dissolved using sweeteners; so it is less dense
3. The particles of the hot liquid have more energy; and so move further apart. This means the particles are less closely packed; and the hot liquid is less dense than the colder liquid; causing the hotter liquid to rise.
4. There are more dissolved salts in the Dead Sea water; so it is more dense than a human body; so the body floats.
5. a) 4 °C b) 0 °C
6. Ice is less dense than cold water; and so floats on top. This slows down the freezing process for the water at the bottom; and it remains liquid until it is so cold that the whole body of water freezes. Fish can therefore survive at the bottom of the lake while the water remains as a liquid.

Answers to Worksheet 2.3.11

1. a) *Float* – wood, plastic, oil; *Sink* – brick, metal (most), glass, marble, honey (and then dissolve)
   b) They have a density higher than 1.0 g/cm^3. c) They have a density lower than 1.0 g/cm^3.
   d) mass; volume
2. a) 7.9 g/cm^3 b) 7.0 g/cm^3
   c) the liquid has a bigger volume; because its particles have more energy; and move more freely taking up more space; the mass stays the same
   d) Ice is a solid but it is less dense than liquid water at a higher temperature of 4 °C; normal solids are more dense than their liquids.
3. a) Appropriate particle diagrams showing at A the particles of solid ice taking up more space than the particles at B, which will take up the smallest space. Particles at C will take up the largest space for the same number of particles.
   b) Sketch should show that gold has a much higher density than water (about 20 times more dense) and that the density decreases slightly with increased temperature. The density changes in a solid are much less marked than in a liquid.

Chapter 3: Explaining Physical Changes

3.12 Explaining the density of gases

Lesson overview

Learning objectives
- Use the particle model to explain differences in the densities of gases.
- Evaluate a method of measuring density.

Learning outcomes
- Link the density of a gas with its uses – e.g. helium, carbon dioxide, argon. [O1]
- Use the particle model to explain differences in the densities of gases. [O2]
- Use the Periodic Table and an investigation to calculate the densities of gases. [O3]

Skills development
- Thinking scientifically: use equations
- Working scientifically: evaluate methods
- Learner development: collaborate effectively

Resources needed equipment and materials as detailed in the Technician's notes; Worksheet 2.3.12a; Worksheet 2.3.12b; Practical sheet 2.3.12; Technician's notes 2.3.12

Digital resources Quick starter; Interactive activity: Place the gases in order, from highest to lowest density at standard room temperature; Video

Common misconceptions All gases float. All gases are less dense than air. There is no difference in the density of gases.

Key vocabulary density, mass, volume

Teaching and learning

Engage
- Show a video that illustrates the differences in the densities of different gases – for example that found at the RSC website www.rsc.org/learn-chemistry when you search in the resources for 'bubbles that float and sink'.
- Use three different balloons – one filled with helium, another with air and the third with carbon dioxide – to explore differences in the densities of these gases. Consider the chemical formula of the gases, in conjunction with the Periodic table. Using task 1 of Worksheet 2.3.12a, ask the students to **work out** the molecular mass of each. Ask them to **relate** the molecular mass to their observations and the data about density. [O1, 2&3]
- Discuss how the different densities of gases are used in different applications. [O1]

Challenge and develop
- Demonstrate the diving raisins experiment using Technician's notes 2.3.12. The students should **write an explanation** using a particle model. Question them about the processes in terms of density and mass. What would they expect to happen to the mass of the lemonade bottle over time? Would this mass change occur more or less quickly without the raisins? [O2]
- The students can now **measure** the density of carbon dioxide using the procedure on Practical sheet 2.3.12. There are a number of potential areas for error in the investigation – the students should focus on **identifying** these. They should try to **minimise the errors** as far as they can and aim to obtain a reliable value for the density of carbon dioxide. [O2&3]
- Take feedback from across the class and write down all the obtained values for the density of carbon dioxide. Provide them with the accepted value of 2 g/l. Examine the experimental setup together and **identify** and **discuss** all the possible sources of error. Explore how the students attempted to minimise their errors. Ask

them to **write an explanation** of how they would change their investigation to **improve the accuracy** of their measurements. [O3]

Explain

- Discuss the applications of gases in different situations such as air balloons and fire extinguishers, and the use of chlorine in war – use the second section of the topic in the Student Book. Ask the students to **draw** particle diagrams to **explain** how the property of density is being applied in each case. [O1&2]

Consolidate and apply

- Use the Student Book to introduce the observation that if the mass of a sample of a gas is the same as its molecular mass in grams, the gas will occupy a volume of 22.4 l, regardless of which gas it is. This observation can be used to calculate the density of gases. Select some higher-attaining students to **calculate** the density of different gases – e.g. ammonia (NH_3), hydrogen chloride (HCl), nitrogen (N_2) and bromine (Br_2), as suggested in task 3 of Worksheet 2.3.12a. [O3]

Extend

- Ask students able to progress further to consider how they would **plan** to measure the densities of other gases, using a chamber of fixed volume, a vacuum pump and precise scales. [O3]

Plenary suggestions

Density Ask the students to write down at least one difference between the densities of gases and those of solids and liquids.

Unknown gas Tell them that a previously unknown gas called phloaton has a molecular mass of 52. Ask them how they would find the density of the gas. Ask them why they could not determine the density of phloaton as a solid or liquid in this way.

Answers to Student Book questions

1. correctly drawn bar graph; names of gases on *x*-axis; density on *y*-axis; appropriate scale
2. carbon dioxide; chlorine
3. helium is lighter than air; does not need to be heated to make it less dense
4. chlorine is denser than air; it filled the trenches instead of floating away
5. a) 32 ÷ 22.4 = 1.4 g/l   b) 44 ÷ 22.4 = 2.0 mg/l   c) 64 ÷ 22.4 = 2.9 mg/l   d) 58 ÷ 22.4 = 2.6 mg/l

Answers to Worksheet 2.3.12a

1. a) *hydrogen* 2; *helium* 4; *carbon dioxide* 44; *ammonia* 17; *chlorine* 71
   b) the bigger the mass, the higher the density
   c) i) chlorine   ii) helium   iii) carbon dioxide
2. The sketch should show the airship balloon filled with much smaller particles of helium; which are much more spread out than the surrounding air particles. The helium particles are much smaller than the nitrogen and oxygen particles in the air. The helium is much less dense than air; so the airship floats.
3. a) i) 17 ÷ 22.4 = 0.76 g/l   ii) 36.5 ÷ 22.4 = 1.63 g/l   iii) 160 ÷ 22.4 = 7.14 g/l
   iv) 16 ÷ 22.4 = 0.71 g/l   v) 48 ÷ 22.4 = 2.14 g/l
   b) In this theoretical calculation of density, it is assumed that the gas particles have no intermolecular forces between them. This is not true; these can play a small part in causing gases to have a slightly lower volume than expected.

Chapter 3: Explaining Physical Changes

3.13 Explaining concentration and pressure

Lesson overview

Learning objectives
- Describe what is meant by concentration and pressure.
- Use the particle model to explain differences in concentration and pressure.

Learning outcomes
- Make liquids of known concentrations. [O1]
- Apply ideas of pressure and concentration to explain different applications. [O2]
- Use ideas about particles to explain differences in concentration and in pressure. [O3]

Skills development
- Thinking scientifically: use equations and models
- Working scientifically: develop explanations
- Learner development: collaborate effectively

Resources needed mini-whiteboards; equipment and materials as detailed in the Technician's notes; Worksheet 2.3.13; Practical sheet 2.3.13; Technician's notes 2.3.13

Digital resources Quick starter; Slideshow: Working out concentration - A fizzy drink example

Common misconceptions Pressure is a force. Liquids are either concentrated or dilute.

Key vocabulary concentration, concentrated, dilute, pressure, kilopascal

Teaching and learning

Engage
- Show the students diluted cordial drinks of different strengths. Give them mini-whiteboards and ask them to draw the particles of water and the particles of cordial in different colours. Discuss the differences between them and introduce the term 'concentration' using the 'What is concentration?' section in the Student Book. [O2&3]

Challenge and develop
- Working in pairs, the students follow the instructions on Practical sheet 2.3.13. They will be making solid–liquid and liquid–liquid solutions of different concentrations. [O1&2]
- Demonstrate how the reaction of a concentrated solution compares with that of a dilute solution (see Technician's notes 2.3.13). Show the reaction of hydrochloric acid and magnesium ribbon using 2 M HCl and 0.5 M HCl. Ask the students to **develop an explanation** of their observations. [O2&3]
- Discuss the idea of pressure in gases using the 'Explaining pressure in liquids and gases' section in the Student Book. You can use a balloon to show the students that gases exert a pressure. Blow up a balloon and allow them to feel the balloon at different stages. They should **establish** that the more particles of air there are, the higher the pressure they exert. [O2]

Explain
- Demonstrate the collapsing can experiment, using the instructions in Technician's notes 2.3.13. Ask the students to work in pairs to **draw** particle diagrams, **explaining** what they have observed. [O2&3]

Consolidate and apply
- Ask the students to **compare** and **contrast** ideas relating to concentration and then to pressure. How are they different and how are they similar? [O1, 2&3]

Chapter 3: Explaining Physical Changes

- Ask them to answer the questions in the Student Book and on Worksheet 2.3.13. [O1, 2&3]

Extend

- Ask students able to progress further to **research** deep sea creatures and find out how they are adapted to withstand such high pressures without imploding. [O3]

Plenary suggestions

Learning triangle Ask the students to draw a learning triangle to **reflect on** their learning – a large triangle with a smaller inverted triangle that just fits inside it (so they have four triangles). In the outer three they write:

- something they've seen
- something they've done
- something they've discussed.

Then they add to the central triangle something they've learned.

Applications Ask the students to think of everyday examples where ideas about concentration and pressure are applied.

Answers to Student Book questions

1. a; c; b
2. you would add more water; drawings should show more water molecules to cordial molecules after dilution
3. $25 \div 100 = 0.25$ g/cm^3
4. $10 \div (10 + 90) \times 100\% = 10\%$ volume
5. there are fewer particles so there is less pressure
6. graphs should have the correct axes, and an increasing line, starting from 0

Answers to Worksheet 2.3.13

1. a) the more concentrated acid is reacting more vigorously; producing more bubbles
   b) diagrams should show molecules of acid; and water; fewer of water in the dilute solution
2. a) $5 \div 20 = 0.25$ g/cm^3
   b) $15 \div 25 = 0.6$ g/cm^3
   c) $10 \div (10 + 200) = 0.05$ g/cm^3
   d) $5 \div (5 + 5) = 0.5$ g/cm^3
3. drawing to show that there are more air particles outside the can, producing a higher pressure as they collide with the sides of the can

Chapter 3: Explaining Physical Changes

3.14 Exploring diffusion

Lesson overview

Learning objectives
- Use the particle model to explain observations involving diffusion.

Learning outcomes
- Describe how diffusion occurs in liquids and gases. [O1]
- Explain observations relating to diffusion in terms of particles. [O2]
- Make predictions, using ideas about particles, relating to factors affecting the rate of diffusion. [O3]

Skills development
- Thinking scientifically: use models
- Working scientifically: develop explanations
- Learner development: communicate effectively

Resources needed equipment and resources as detailed in the Technician's notes; Worksheet 2.3.14; Practical sheet 2.3.14; Technician's notes 2.3.14

Digital resources Quick starter; Slideshow: Observing diffusion with bromine gas; Interactive activity: Drag the items to the correct group – speeds up or slows down diffusion of particles; Hangman: Key vocabulary game

Common misconceptions Diffusion occurs in solids.

Key vocabulary diffusion, equilibrium, concentration gradient

Teaching and learning

Engage
- **Pair talk** The students should **discuss** and **write down** three things they can remember about diffusion. Use the Student Book to recap ideas about diffusion. [O1&2]
- Show the students three containers each with a different concentration of cordial. Ask them to **predict** what would happen if the solution with the highest concentration was put into the container with the lowest concentration, so the solutions could mix. [O2&3]

Challenge and develop
- Set up a circus of three different investigations for students to **make observations** from. Ask the students to **follow the procedures** given on Practical sheet 2.3.14 and to **record** their observations. In Experiment 2, only allow the students to add the chemicals to the Petri dish if you have given then specific permission – lead nitrate is TOXIC. If you have any doubts at all about the students using this themselves, add the chemicals to the Petri dishes yourself. See Technician's notes 2.3.1.4. When the students have completed one investigation, they should move on to the next. [O1&2]
- Explore their findings. Ask selected students from different groups to **role-play** what is happening to the particles in each of the investigations. [O1&2]
- Discuss different ways in which the rate of diffusion could be increased in each case. [O2&3].

Explain
- **Pair work** Ask the students to **draw** annotated particle diagrams to **explain** the observations in each investigation. Task 2 of Worksheet 2.3.14 may be used for support here. [O1, 2&3]

Chapter 3: Explaining Physical Changes

Consolidate and apply

- Use the 'Explaining diffusion' section in the Student Book to discuss the reaction between concentrated ammonia and hydrochloric acid in a long glass tube. Explore the way the reaction occurs and the part that diffusion has to play. Discuss why the product is not formed in the centre of the tube. [O1, 2&3]

- **Pair talk** Ask the students to **consider** all the different factors affecting the rate of diffusion – task 3 of Worksheet 2.3.14 will help. Ask them to **develop an explanation**, using particle diagrams, for why one particular factor is likely to have the greatest impact on the rate of diffusion. They should explain why the other factors are likely to have less effect. [O2&3]

Extend

- Tell students able to progress further that chromatography is an example of diffusion. Show them the chromatogram from their practical investigation. Ask them to **draw a particle model** of the chromatogram to **explain** how diffusion makes this process possible. They can **carry out some research** to help them. [O3]

Plenary suggestions

Diffusion speeds Ask the students to consider all the investigations and demonstrations they have seen in the lesson. Ask them to **rank** the investigations/demonstrations in order of where diffusion occurred fastest to where it occurred slowest. [O2&3]

Answers to Student Book questions

1. making a drink using cordial; the particles diffuse throughout the water; stirring just helps this process
2. there are fewer particles the further away you are from the source; they have spread out
3. the one with the ink in pure water; as it has biggest concentration gradient
4. Coffee in hot water will reach equilibrium first; the water is hot so its particles have more kinetic energy; and will be able to move faster; compared to the cold water.
5. diffusion would occur much more slowly
6. heat the tube; the particles will gain energy; and move more quickly
7. Ammonia particles are smaller; and will move faster than the hydrochloric acid particles; so they will meet the hydrochloric acid particles closer to where the latter have diffused from.

Answers to Worksheet 2.3.14

1. a) the red food colouring in the hot water diffused further and faster; than the blue colouring in the cold water
   b) a yellow solid would form in the water between the two crystals
2. a) The particles in the hot water move faster; and will carry the dissolved food colouring faster; so the red food colouring will spread further and faster.
   b) The crystals dissolve in the water; and diffuse away from the source; because these areas are at a high concentration. They form closer to the lead nitrate crystal; because its particles are heavier; and will not diffuse as fast as the potassium iodide particles.
3. a) An increase in temperature increases the rate of diffusion; the particles have more energy and so can be carried further and faster.
   b) The bigger the particles, the harder it is to diffuse; and so will not be carried as far. Lead nitrate particles and HCl particles are the heavier particles; so the initial reactions occurred nearer to them; because they did not diffuse as far.
   c) The steeper the concentration gradient, the faster the rate of diffusion; a dilute solution of cordial will not diffuse as fast; as a concentrated solution when put in a beaker of water.

Chapter 3: Explaining Physical Changes

3.15 Conserving mass

Lesson overview

Learning objectives
- Use the particle model to explain the Law of Conservation of Mass.

Learning outcomes
- Recognise that mass is conserved in all physical processes and chemical reactions. [O1]
- Use mass to find the efficiency of separating sand from salt. [O2]
- Explain what happens to unexpected changes in mass using the particle model. [O3]

Skills development
- Thinking scientifically: consider the quality of evidence
- Working scientifically: record evidence
- Learner development: collaborate effectively

Resources needed equipment and materials as detailed in the Technician's notes; Worksheet 2.3.15; Practical sheet 2.3.15a; Practical sheet 2.3.15b; Technician's notes 2.3.15

Digital resources Quick starter; Interactive activity: Which of the statements about chemical reactions are true, and which are false?

Common misconceptions When solutions are made, the volumes can just be added to get the total volume.

Key vocabulary Law of Conservation of Mass, chemical reaction, physical change, efficiency

Teaching and learning

Engage
- Demonstrate mass conservation during changes of state using some ice and wax. Put them in separate conical flasks with a balloon covering the opening – weigh each flask and record the masses. Heat the flasks – when all solids are melted, weigh each flask and record its mass. Continue to heat the flasks, until much of the liquid has evaporated – now weigh the flasks again. Ask the students to **draw a conclusion** from this demonstration. [O1]

Challenge and develop
- **Group work** Ask the students to **carry out** the experiment on Practical sheet 2.3.15a. They will first make up different solid–liquid and liquid–liquid solutions, **recording** the mass and the volume and **accounting** for unexpected differences. [O1&3]

- Explore their findings and ask them to account for their observations. Select a small group of students to **role-play** their explanations. [O3]

- Now ask students to do the follow-on activity described on Practical sheet 2.3.15b. They are given a mixture of known mass of sand and salt to separate. They have to **plan** the separation as carefully as possible and **work out** the efficiency of the separation process. [O1&2]

Explain
- Show the students another demonstration. Weigh an effervescent antacid tablet and a conical flask with some water in it. Add the tablet to the flask, leave to react and then record the mass at the end. Working in pairs, the students **devise an explanation** to account for the apparent anomaly. Can they **predict** the mass of gas that should have escaped? [O1, O3]

Key Stage 3 Science Teacher Pack 2

Chapter 3: Explaining Physical Changes

Consolidate and apply

- **Pair work** Working in pairs, the students **design** a poster to show a way of carrying out the antacid investigation to show that mass is conserved. If time allows, give them the opportunity to **carry this out**. [O1&3]
- Ask the students to attempt the tasks on Worksheet 2.3.15 and answer the Student Book questions. [O1, 2&3]

Extend

- Ask students able to progress further to **evaluate** their salt separation investigation and **make improvements** to the design to make it more efficient. [O3]

Plenary suggestions

Describing conservation of mass Ask the students to **write a description** of the meaning of 'conservation of mass' for some students who have not yet heard of it. They should include some examples in their description. [O1&3]

Answers to Student Book questions

1. 100 g
2. steam particles will escape into the air; causing the mass to decrease
3. less than 100 cm^3 but more than 80 cm^3; some sugar particles will occupy the gaps between the water particles
4. 94 g; mass must be conserved; the total mass is the mass of the sugar + the mass of the water.
5. five per cent of the original amount of gold; was not recovered by the process. It could be stuck in the machinery; still dissolved in the cyanide; or in the sodium hydroxide
6. 10 × 50 ÷ 100 = 5 kg

Answers to Worksheet 2.3.15

1. a) 25 g
   b) 20 g
   c) i) 58 g   ii) no; there will be less
   iii) some of the water will evaporate into the air; or condense on the sides of the container
2. a) decanter
   b) There are fewer places where oil particles or water particles can be 'lost'; in the filtration system, water is lost in the filter; and on the sides of the container; and solids are left on the filter; and cannot be collected easily.
   c) 27 ÷ 30 × 100 = 90%
3. Suitable particle diagrams: the *decanter* showing water particles at its base; the *filtration system* showing water particles in the filter paper and on the funnel; solid particles will be on the filter paper and the sides of the funnel.

Chapter 3: Explaining Physical Changes

3.16 Deciding between physical and chemical changes

Lesson overview

Learning objectives
- Use the particle model to explain the differences between physical and chemical changes.
- Recognise that mass is conserved in all changes.

Learning outcomes
- Describe the features of physical changes and chemical changes. [O1]
- Explain how mass is conserved in all changes. [O2]
- Use the particle model to explain physical changes and chemical changes. [O3]

Skills development
- Thinking scientifically: ask questions
- Working scientifically: interpret evidence
- Learner development: collaborate effectively

Resources needed equipment and materials as detailed in the Technician's notes; Worksheet 2.3.16; Practical sheet 2.3.16; Technician's notes 2.3.16

Digital resources Quick starter; Slideshow: Changes that are easily reversed and changes that are not easily reversed; Interactive activity: Drag the change into the correct group – physical or chemical change?

Common misconceptions All chemical changes give off gases.

Key vocabulary physical change, reversible, chemical change, exothermic, endothermic

Teaching and learning

Engage
- Demonstrate the three changes outlined in Technician's notes 2.3.16:
  - burning a hydrogen balloon, or showing a video of this
  - the 'elephant toothpaste' demonstration using hydrogen peroxide
  - heating a small amount of iodine in a flask and watching it sublime.
- Ask the students to **observe** closely and **make a list** of all their observations. Remind them of the terms 'physical change' and 'chemical change'. Ask them to **decide** which are physical changes and which are chemical changes and **explain** their reasoning. [O1]
- Use the Student Book to recap all the signs of physical changes and of chemical changes. Make the students aware that some of these signs, like temperature changes, are not definitive in themselves – it is the changes to the particles themselves which matter the most. [O1]

Challenge and develop
- Working in pairs, ask the students to **carry out** the different investigations given on Practical sheet 2.3.16. They should **make full observations**, stating if changes are physical or chemical. [O1, 2&3]

  Higher-attaining students are expected to weigh the chemicals before and after the change to **establish** that mass is conserved in all changes.

- Encourage the students to **explore** their findings and to **identify** any changes that caused them difficulty. Select different students to **share** the particle diagrams they have developed and **discuss** any misconceptions. [O3]

Chapter 3: Explaining Physical Changes

Explain

- Demonstrate burning steel wool, measuring the mass of the wool before and after the reaction – instructions are given in Technician's notes 2.3.16. Ask the students to **write an explanation** to show why in some combustion reactions the mass increases after burning. [O2&3]

    Higher-attaining students should **draw** particle diagrams to **explain** what changes are taking place in the chemical reactions they have observed. For balanced particle diagrams, provide students with the balanced symbol equations for the reactions, so they can draw the particle diagrams.

    Ask higher-attaining students to also **consider** why, in the case of solubility, there may be temperature changes involved. They should use their previous understanding of solubility and forces. [O3]

Consolidate and apply

- **Pairs to fours** Working in pairs, ask the students to **draw a poster** about physical and chemical changes, using particle diagrams to make the differences clear. Ask two pairs to swap posters and use the Student Book to **peer-assess** them, identifying two good things and one thing for improvement. [O1, 2&3]
- The students should attempt all the tasks of Worksheet 2.3.16. [O1, 2&3]

Extend

- Ask students able to progress further to **investigate** the heating of hydrated copper sulphate, and adding of water to the white product. Can they determine if this is a chemical change or a physical change and **explain** what is happening?

Plenary suggestions

Changes at home Ask the students to think of everyday changes they observe at home. Ask them to **classify** them as being physical or chemical and to **justify** their decisions.

Physical or chemical? Ask the students to work in pairs and **discuss** why is it important to be able to classify changes as being physical or chemical.

Answers to Student Book questions

1. *physical processes* – e.g. dissolving; changes of state; making mixtures
   chemical changes – e.g. frying an egg; baking a cake; making toast
2. chemical; there is a colour change
3. *heating iodine* physical; *sodium left in air* chemical; *decomposition of copper carbonate* chemical ; *melting of water* physical; *magnesium reacting with chlorine* chemical
4. physical change – no change in the atoms or molecules; chemical change – clear change in the atoms and molecules; correct word equation
5. physical; the rubber is still rubber; there is no change in the atoms and molecules
6. the sodium chloride can be 'brought back' by evaporating the water

Answers to Worksheet 2.3.16

1. a) no; no; yes; no; no; chemical
   b) yes, it is being heated; no; no; no; no; physical
   c) yes; yes; yes; no; no; chemical
   d) yes, it is being burned; yes; yes; yes; yes; chemical
   e) no; no; no; no; no; physical
   f) yes, it glows; yes; yes; no; no; chemical
   g) a little; no; yes; yes; no; chemical
   h) a little; yes; yes; no; no; chemical
   i) a little; yes; no; no; no; no; physical
2. a) magnesium + oxygen → magnesium oxide; iron + oxygen → iron oxide
   b) the product should be heavier than the metal
3. Appropriate particle diagrams; with the same atoms in the reactants as in the products; clearly showing that different products have been made.

Chapter 3: Explaining Physical Changes

3.17 Explaining the properties of mixtures

Lesson overview

Learning objectives
- Use the particle model to explain the properties of mixtures.

Learning outcomes
- Describe different types of colloids. [O1]
- Explain the properties of different colloids using the particle model. [O2]
- Use the particle model to explain the properties of colloids, and how solutions affect melting and boiling points. [O3]

Skills development
- Thinking scientifically: ask questions
- Working scientifically: design investigations
- Learner development: communicate effectively

Resources needed equipment and materials as detailed in the Technician's notes; Worksheet 2.3.17; Practical sheet 2.3.17; Technician's notes 2.3.17

Digital resources Quick starter; Interactive activity: Match the terms about mixtures and changing states to their correct definition; Video

Common misconceptions Materials are classified as being solids, liquids or gases.

Key vocabulary emulsion, colloid, foam, gel

Teaching and learning

Engage
- Show the students a range of different substances that are hard to classify as solids, liquids or gases – e.g. toothpaste, jelly, shaving foam, hair gel, mayonnaise, aerosol, fizzy drink, paint, milk and whipped cream. Ask the students to **identify** which states of matter are clearly evident in each substance. [O1]
- Introduce the term 'colloid', in which one state of matter is dispersed in another. Ask the students to use the Student Book to **identify** particular types of colloid in the materials demonstrated. [O1]

Challenge and develop
- Using Practical sheet 2.3.17, and working in pairs, the students will **plan an investigation** to work out how to **produce** the tallest foam using *Mentos* and diet cola. It would be best to carry out this investigation outside because the foam produced will shoot upwards creating a mess. With permission, the students could use a camera or video recorder to measure the height of their foam more accurately. If this investigation is not possible, effervescent antacid tablets and water could be used as an alternative suitable for the classroom, carrying out the investigation in a bucket. When their plans have been approved, ask the students to **carry out** their investigation. They should **identify** reasons why some conditions might produce more foam than others. [O1&2]
- Discuss the term 'emulsion'. Show the students what happens when washing-up liquid is added to oil and water that have been separated. Ask them to use the particle diagram (Figure 2.3.17c) in the Student Book to **explain** what is happening. [O2&3]

Explain
- Explore what happens to ice when salt is added to it. Show the students different concentrations of salt solution that have been kept overnight in a freezer and the graph (Figure 2.3.17a) in the Student Book. Ask the students to **discuss** their observations and the graph and **explain** what is happening. [O3]

Chapter 3: Explaining Physical Changes

Higher-attaining students should use the particle model to **develop an explanation**, using ideas from the Student Book. [O3]

Consolidate and apply

- For each of the materials used at the start of the lesson, ask the students to **draw particle models** to best represent each of them. [O2&3]

Extend

- Students able to progress further could **investigate** the properties of hydrogels. They could **find out** what the particle model is like in order to explain hydrogel behaviour. [O3]

Plenary suggestions

Properties Ask the students to **summarise** what properties the particle models for a foam, a gel and an aerosol can and cannot explain.

Key words Ask them to **write definitions** of the key words for the lesson.

Answers to Student Book questions

1. −11 °C
2. Adding 15% salt to water means the water will not freeze until it cools to −11 °C; at temperatures lower than −11 °C it will become ice. This is safer for traffic; because the roads will not be as slippery.
3. the mixture will separate; into two or more layers
4. adding an emulsifier means that all the ingredients will be perfectly mixed throughout; and not end up as layers
5. *foams* – shaving foam; cleaning foam; *gels* – toothpaste, hand cleanser; *aerosols* – inhaler for asthmatics; deodorant
6. A *foam* should show liquid particles; with gas particles trapped in between. An *aerosol* should show gas particles, with liquid or solid particles, in between. A *gel* should show solid particles; surrounding liquid particles.

Answers to Worksheet 2.3.17

1. These will depend on the investigation chosen – one example is given here:
   a) type of liquid
   b) sparkling water, lemonade, tonic water
   c) height of foam
   d) use a strip of card marked with measurements attached to a wall by the experiment
   e) the number of *Mentos*; the amount of liquid; the temperature of the liquid
   f) This will depend on the investigation chosen – ensure that the control variables are not the same as the independent or the dependent variables; sensible values have been chosen.
   g) foam shooting into eyes; and onto clothes; slipping on the liquid
   h) wear eye protection; wear clothing protection; mop up all spillages
2. a) Make the marks on the card as close as possible. Take a photo of the foam at its maximum height so you can measure the height.
   b) Repeat each investigation at least three times. Omit anomalous readings; use the mean height.
3. a) Ask another group to carry out our investigation; see if they obtain the same results.
   b) if the results fit a pattern; if the results from the repeat investigations are very similar
   c) Any suitable answer – such as use a height sensor to measure the height accurately.

Chapter 3: Explaining Physical Changes

3.18 Using particle models

Lesson overview

Learning objectives
- Use 'good enough' particle models to explain different observations.

Learning outcomes
- Use particle models to explain separation processes. [O1]
- Use particle models to explain how the solubilities of solids and gases change with temperature. [O2]
- Explain the effectiveness of different models in explaining chemical changes. [O3]

Skills development
- Thinking scientifically: use models
- Working scientifically: develop explanations
- Learner development: ask questions

Resources needed graph paper; equipment and materials as detailed in the Technician's notes; Worksheet 2.3.18; Practical sheet 2.3.18a; Practical sheet 2.3.18b; Technician's notes 2.3.18

Digital resources Quick starter; Slideshow: A look at how sugar dissolves in water; Interactive activity: Place the events in order of how sugar dissolves in tea; Hangman: Key vocabulary game

Common misconceptions Solids and gases increase in solubility with temperature.

Key vocabulary particle model

Teaching and learning

Engage
- Use the 'Explaining separation processes' section in the Student Book to recap the limitations of the standard particle model.
- Ask the students to **reflect on** what they have learned in recent lessons and to **identify** how they have adapted the particle model in different situations, so that it can be applied to explain a range of phenomena.

Challenge and develop
- Ask the students to **look at** task 1 of Worksheet 2.3.18a. They will **use** and **adapt** the particle model to explain what is happening in chromatography. [O1]
- Working in pairs, ask them to **investigate** how the solubilities of ammonium chloride and sodium chloride change with temperature. They are to **draw graphs** of their results and **compare** their findings. They should follow the instructions in Practical sheet 2.3.18a. [O1&2]
- Working in pairs, the students **carry out** two chemical changes as described in Practical sheet 2.3.18b. These are between iron(II) sulfate and sodium hydroxide, and between iron(III) chloride and sodium hydroxide. They should use the particle model to show what is happening in each reaction. [O3]

Explain
- Working in pairs, the students **adapt** the particle model to **explain** the solubility graphs they have obtained from their investigation. Ask them to **share** their adapted models and their explanation with the class. [O1&2]

Consolidate and apply
- Ask the students to attempt tasks 2 and 3 of Worksheet 2.3.18 and the questions in the Student Book. [O1, 2&3]

Chapter 3: Explaining Physical Changes

- Ask them to **compare** the particle models they have used in their different investigations. Explore the idea of whether one model could be better or worse than another. [O2&3]

Extend

- Ask students able to progress further to **consider** the strengths and drawbacks of always using particular symbols to represent particles, instead of just using circles. [O3]

Plenary suggestions

Concept map The students could draw a concept map using the particle model to **explain** all the properties about particles they have learnt over the course of the unit.

What do I know? Ask them to **write definitions** for all the key words used in the lesson.

Answers to Student Book questions

1. The alcohol particles have been given a different colour; so they can be distinguished from the water particles; to see what is happening to the alcohol particles.
2. Particles of the liquid should be smaller than the particles of the solid. The explanation should show that the particles of the liquid go through the gaps in the filter paper, but the particles of the insoluble solid are too big to pass through.
3. Diagram should show stronger solute–solute forces between less soluble solutes; and stronger solute–solvent forces for more soluble solutes.
4. Diagram should show more spaces at higher temperatures; so more solute particles can fill the spaces. *Strengths* – shows why more solute can be dissolved; at a higher temperature. *Limitations* – does not show that the particles have more energy at a higher temperature.
5. magnesium + hydrochloric acid → magnesium chloride + hydrogen; Mg + 2HCl → MgCl$_2$ + H$_2$

    Particle diagram should show the correct colours for particles of magnesium; hydrogen and chlorine; hydrogen particles should be much smaller than magnesium and chlorine; particle diagram should represent the symbol equation given above.
6. lead nitrate + potassium iodide → lead iodide + potassium nitrate; Pb(NO$_3$)$_2$ + 2KI → PbI$_2$ + 2KNO$_3$

    Particle diagram should show the correct colours for the atoms involved; correct particle model to match the symbol equation above.

Answers to Worksheet 2.3.18

1. A simple way to describe chromatography is to think of the particles as having different sizes. Those that move least could be the heaviest. This is not strictly true because there are many complicated factors involved. It is, however, a 'good enough' model at this stage.
2. a) Check graphs to ensure the data is correctly plotted; temperature on *x*-axis and solubility on *y*-axis; appropriate scale.

    b) There is a steep curved line for the ammonium chloride; compared with sodium chloride.

    c) Ammonium chloride is much more soluble than the sodium chloride; as temperature increases; ammonium chloride solubility is affected more by increased temperature; sodium chloride solubility is hardly affected at all.

    d) Ammonium chloride is more soluble because the forces between the ammonium chloride particles and water particles are much stronger than the forces between the sodium chloride particles and water particles. Also the forces between sodium chloride particles are stronger than the forces between the ammonium chloride particles. As the temperature increases, the forces between the ammonium chloride particles and water particles become stronger and between other ammonium chloride particles they become weaker.

    e) Any acceptable model to show the above explanation.
3. Relevant colours indicated in the Student Book used; with the correct numbers of atoms represented in the formula and the symbol equations; should have the same numbers of atoms in the reactants as in the products.

Chapter 3: Explaining Physical Changes

3.19 Checking students' progress

The 'Checking your progress' section in the Student Book indicates the key ideas developed in this chapter and shows how students progress to more complex levels. It is provided to support students in:

- identifying those ideas
- developing a sense of their current level of understanding
- developing a sense of what the next steps in their learning are.

It is designed to be used either at the end of a chapter to support an overall view of the progress, or alternatively during the teaching of the chapter. Students can self assess or peer assess using this as a basis.

It would be helpful if students can be encouraged to provide evidence from their understanding or their notes to support their judgements. In some cases it may be useful to explore the difference in the descriptors for a particular idea so that students can see what makes for a 'higher outcome'.

It may be useful with some descriptors to provide examples from the specific work done, such as an experiment undertaken or an explanation developed and recorded. If marking and feedback use similar ideas and phrases this will enable students to relate specific marking to a more general sense of progress.

Chapter 3: Explaining Physical Changes

To make good progress in understanding science students need to focus on these ideas and skills:

Students who are making modest progress will be able to:	Students who are making good progress will be able to:	Students who are making excellent progress will be able to:
Compare the properties of solids, liquids and gases.	Draw circle diagrams to demonstrate the differences between the arrangement of particles in solids, liquids and gases, and describe their different properties.	Use particle diagrams to explain the differences in energy and forces between the particles in different states of matter, accounting for differences in their properties.
Recognise how theories are developed.	Use observations to develop hypotheses.	Change hypotheses in the light of new evidence and use this evidence to develop theories.
Use correct terminology and the particle model to describe changes of state, including evaporation.	Interpret and explain data relating to melting and boiling points.	Use the particle model to explain latent heat and how impurities affect melting and boiling points.
Describe how solids, liquids and gases behave when heat is applied to them.	Describe applications and problems caused by thermal expansion.	Use the particle model to explain expansion in solids, liquids and gases.
Describe a model that can be used to represent particles.	Apply and adapt models to make them more suitable for use.	Evaluate the strengths and limitations of particle models.
Make predictions about floating and sinking using ideas about density.	Use the particle model to explain the density differences between gases and calculate density of solids.	Use the particle model to explain factors relating to density.
Describe what is meant by the terms 'concentration' and 'pressure'.	Calculate concentrations of solutions.	Use ideas about particles to explain the effects of pressure.
Describe how diffusion occurs in liquids and gases.	Explain observations relating to diffusion in terms of particles.	Make predictions, using ideas about particles, about factors affecting the rate of diffusion.
Describe features of physical and chemical changes, recognising how mass is conserved.	Use ideas about particles to describe separation processes.	Apply the particle model to explain physical and chemical changes, taking conservation of mass into account.
Describe different types of colloids.	Explain the properties of different colloids using the particle model.	Evaluate the particle model in its ability to explain colloids and their properties.
Use particle models to describe different separation processes.	Use particle models to explain how the solubility of solids and gases changes with temperature.	Evaluate the effectiveness of the particle model in explaining physical changes.

Chapter 3: Explaining Physical Changes

3.20 Answers to Student Book Questions

This table provides answers to the Questions section at the end of Chapter 3 of the Student Book. It also shows how different questions assess attainment in terms of the focus and style of a question as well as the context. Question level analysis can indicate students' proficiency in approaching different aspects of scientific understanding and different types of answer.

Q	Answer	Marks available	Focus: Knowledge & understanding	Focus: Application	Focus: Evaluation of evidence	Style: Objective test question	Style: Short written answer	Style: Longer written answer	Context: Solids, liquids gases and changing state	Context: Properties of solids, liquids and gases	Context: Diffusion, pressure and concentration	Context: Physical and chemical changes, mixtures
1	b	1	x			x			x			
2	c	1	x			x					x	
3	a	1	x			x						x
4	d	1	x			x						x
5	• Movement of pollen grains in water under a microscope	1	x				x		x			
	• Movement of many non-living substances such as talc, when suspended in a liquid	1	x				x		x			
6	• Particles gain in kinetic energy and move further apart	1	x				x			x		
	• Viscosity decreases because the particles have more energy to overcome forces	1	x				x			x		
7	• Ice floats on water	1	x					x		x		
	• Ice is less dense than water	1	x					x		x		
	• Particles in ice have spaces between them	1	x					x		x		
	• This is due to strong intermolecular forces	1	x					x		x		
8	d	1		x		x			x			
9	c	1		x		x					x	
10	(i)	1		x		x						x
11	c	1		x		x					x	

Key Stage 3 Science Teacher Pack 2 © HarperCollins*Publishers* Limited 2014

Chapter 3: Explaining Physical Changes

Q	Answer	Marks available	Focus: Knowledge & understanding	Focus: Application	Focus: Evaluation of evidence	Style: Objective test question	Style: Short written answer	Style: Longer written answer	Context: Solids, liquids gases and changing state	Context: Properties of solids, liquids and gases	Context: Diffusion, pressure and concentration	Context: Physical and chemical changes, mixtures
12	• See if the change was reversible	1		x			x					x
	• Evaporate off the water and see if calcium chloride crystals were left	1		x			x					x
13	Any two from:	2	x				x				x	
	• concentration = mass ÷ volume											
	• In 1 litre you need 20 mg of fertiliser											
	• In 250 cm^3 you need 20 ÷ 4 = 5 mg of fertiliser											
14	• Aerosols are liquids or solids suspended in a gas	1	x					x			x	
	• When heated, the gas expands and the particles move further apart with more energy	1	x					x			x	
	• The expansion means there is more pressure from the gas on the sides of the container	1	x					x			x	
	• Eventually the aerosol will heat enough to blow the can apart	1	x					x			x	
15	Any two from:	2			x		x				x	
	• Butane is easier to change into a liquid											
	• Butane has a higher boiling point, so it will change with less pressure											
	• Less energy needs to be transferred from the butane to change it into a liquid											
	Accept converse statements relating to hydrogen											
16	a) Xmenium has a melting point of just over 80 °C and a boiling point of just over 140 °C	2			x			x	x			
	b) The melting point is too high to be useful	1			x			x	x			
	A salt can be added to lower the melting point	1			x			x	x			
	Total possible:	30	12	12	6	8	10	12	8	7	10	5

Chapter 4: Explaining Chemical Changes

4.1 Introduction

When and how to use these pages

The Introduction in the Student Book indicates some of the ideas and skills in this topic area that students will already have met from KS2 or from previous KS3 work, and provides an indication of what they will be studying in this chapter. *Ideas you have met before* is not intended to comprehensively summarise of all the prior ideas, but rather to point out a few of the key ones and to support the view that scientific understanding is progressive. Even though students might be meeting contexts that are new to them, they can often use existing ideas to start to make sense of them.

In this chapter you will find out indicates some of the new ideas that the chapter will introduce. Again, it isn't a detailed summary of content or even an index page. Its purpose is more to act as a 'trailer' and generate some interest.

The outcomes, then, will be recognition of prior learning that can be built on, and interest in finding out more.

There are a number of ways this can be used. You might, for example:

- Use *Ideas you have met before* as the basis for a revision lesson as you start the first new topic.
- Use *Ideas you have met before* as the centre of spider diagrams, to which students can add examples, experiments they might have done previously or what they found interesting.
- Make a note of any unfamiliar/difficult terms and return to these in the relevant lessons.
- Use *In this chapter you will find out* to ask students questions such as:
  - Why is this important?
  - How could it be used?
  - What might we be doing in this topic?

Overview of the chapter

In this chapter, the students will learn about the characteristics of chemical change. They will consider many examples of chemical changes and use these to explore the new products that are formed. The students will use models to reinforce the rearrangement of atoms during reactions. They will practice representing atoms and molecules as formulas and will write word equations for many reactions. The students study reactions in the context of acids and alkalis, considering their reactions together as well as the reactions of acids with metals and carbonates. The relevance of acids and alkalis to our everyday lives is considered as well as the applications of neutralisation reactions. The students learn about the pH scale and compare the uses of different indicators. Combustion is considered as an example of a chemical change. The students study the effects of the products of combustion on the atmosphere and the wider community of plants and animals.

This chapter offers a number of opportunities for students to investigate chemical changes at first hand. They study reactions to identify evidence for a chemical change and then explain the changes using equations. The students have the opportunity to use models to explore how the atoms are rearranged during reactions to make new products and to work collaboratively.

Obstacles to learning

Students may need extra guidance with the following concepts:

- **Acids and alkalis** Not all acids are dangerous – we use, and even consume, many acids. However, many acids in a laboratory need to be handled with care. Conversely, not all alkalis are safe.
- **Salts** There are many salts, not only table salt (sodium chloride).
- **Reactions** Reactions can create new products, but these depend on the atoms present in the reactants – new substances do not just 'appear', and reactants do not 'disappear'. Students may have the misconception that when carbonates react with acids, carbon dioxide is released from the carbonate. Another misconception is that all neutralisation reactions result in a solution of pH 7.
- **Combustion** Heating and burning are not the same, and things do not 'disappear' when they burn.

Chapter 4: Explaining Chemical Changes

	Topic title:	Overarching objectives:
2	Exploring acids	Defining acids and alkalis
3	Exploring alkalis	
4	Using indicators	The pH scale for measuring acidity/alkalinity; and indicators
5	Using universal indicator	
6	Exploring neutralisation	Defining acids and alkalis in terms of neutralisation reactions The pH scale for measuring acidity/alkalinity; and indicators
7	Explaining neutralisation	Defining acids and alkalis in terms of neutralisation reactions Chemical reactions as the rearrangement of atoms Representing chemical reactions using formulas and using equations Reactions of acids with alkalis to produce a salt plus water
8	Understanding salts	Chemical reactions as the rearrangement of atoms Representing chemical reactions using formulas and using equations Reactions of acids with alkalis to produce a salt plus water
9	Exploring the reactions of acids with metals	Reactions of acids with metals to produce a salt plus hydrogen
10	Exploring the reactions of acids with carbonates	Chemical reactions as the rearrangement of atoms Representing chemical reactions using formulas and using equations
12	Investigating the effectiveness of antacids	Reactions of acids with alkalis to produce a salt plus water
13	Understanding the importance of acids and alkalis	Defining acids and alkalis in terms of neutralisation reactions Reactions of acids with alkalis to produce a salt plus water
14	Exploring combustion	Combustion Fuels and energy resources
15	Understanding combustion and the use of fuels	
16	Exploring the effects of burning	Combustion Chemical reactions as the rearrangement of atoms Representing chemical reactions using formulas and using equations The production of carbon dioxide by human activity
17	Understanding acid rain	Combustion The composition of the atmosphere

Chapter 4: Explaining Chemical Changes

4.2 Exploring acids

Lesson overview

Learning objectives

- Recognise acids used in everyday life.
- Describe what all acids have in common.
- Evaluate the hazards that acids pose.

Learning outcomes

- Identify everyday substances that contain acids. [O1]
- Explain the similarities between all acids. [O2]
- Evaluate the hazards posed by a number of acids and how they may be reduced. [O3]

Skills development

- Thinking scientifically: evaluate risks
- Working scientifically: n/a
- Learner development: ask questions

Resources needed lemon juice; vinegar; black tea; small disposable cups; disposable spoons; drinking water; images or packaging of common acids (e.g. sulfuric, hydrochloric, nitric, ethanoic, citric) *or* packaging or objects linked to acid use (e.g. pickled foods, fruit juices, cordials, tea, paint, explosives, fertilisers, car batteries, ink); Worksheet 2.4.2

Digital resources Quick starter; Interactive activity: Match the foods to the main acid(s) they contain; Interactive activity: Match the hazard to the symbol; Slideshow: What do acids have in common?; Video

Common misconceptions All acids are harmful.

Key vocabulary acid, corrosive, irritant, hydrogen

Teaching and learning

Engage

- Ask the students to taste a small amount of lemon juice, vinegar and black tea. They should use disposable spoons for each liquid and water should be provided to rinse the mouth after each sample. In pairs, ask students to **describe** the taste of the liquids. [O1&2]
- Lead a class discussion to share descriptions. Establish that these liquids taste sour because they all contain an acid. [O1&2]

Challenge and develop

- Show images or packaging of common acids. You should include sulfuric acid, hydrochloric acid and nitric acid used in the laboratory, and some of those from the 'engage' activity – ethanoic acid (vinegar), citric acid (lemon juice). Ask the students to **record** the name of each acid but do not explain other uses for acids at this stage. [O1]
- Show images of uses of common acids. Ask the students to work in pairs to **suggest** what each image is showing. Then reveal the name of each acid involved. Alternatively you could show packaging or objects linked to each use of acids – pickled foods (in vinegar which contains ethanoic acid), fruit juices (citric acid), cordials (citric acid), tea (tartaric acid), paint (nitric acid), explosives (nitric acid), fertilisers (nitric acid or sulfuric acid), car batteries (sulfuric acid), ink (tannic acid). [O1]

Explain

- Ask the students to **read** the 'What do acids have in common?' section in the Student Book as a class. [O2]

Chapter 4: Explaining Chemical Changes

- The students work individually to answer the questions. [O2]
- The students work in pairs to **compare** and **agree** on answers. They should then **amend** their work as appropriate. [O2]
- Ask each student to **design** another question about what acids are and what they have in common. They then join with their partner and try to answer each other's question. [O2]
- Ask pairs to **share** some questions across the class. [O2]

Consolidate and apply

- Ask the students to look at the images or packaging of common acids again. Ask them to **find** and **draw** any hazard symbols. [O3]
- Lead a class discussion asking the students to **explain** what each symbol means. [O3]
- Ask the students to **rank** each of the acids and products that they have seen in terms of how dangerous they are. Ask the pairs to form fours to **compare** and **agree** the rank order. Worksheet 2.4.2 could be attempted here. [O3]

Extend

- Ask students able to progress further to evaluate each of the products and a danger associated with working with it. Students should **develop** a list of precautions to take when handling any of the products. [O3]

Plenary suggestions

Loop card game Arrange the students in groups of about eight. Each student writes an example of an acid on a piece of coloured card and writes a use on a piece of different-coloured card. The cards are mixed up and then each student chooses one 'acid' card and one 'use' card. The students then play a loop card game, with one student reading out an acid and the student who has the correct use identifying themselves. This student then reads out their acid and so on. [O1&2]

Answers to Student Book questions

1. lemons, oranges, vinegar, fizzy drinks, tea etc.
2. sulfuric acid and nitric acid
3. sour
4. universal language; the user doesn't need to be able to read
5. dilute acids are not as dangerous; irritant is not corrosive
6. wear gloves; wear eye protection; take care not to spill
7. they are corrosive (destroy skin, attack metals)
8. hydrogen; nitrogen; oxygen
9. it is likely to be an acid because it tastes sour and contains hydrogen

Answers to Worksheet 2.4.2

1. a) nitric b) ethanoic c) citric d) sulfuric e) lactic
2. *sulfuric* – fertilisers and car batteries; *nitric* – fertilisers, paints and explosives; *ethanoic* – vinegar; *citric* – citrus fruits and preservatives; *tartaric* – tea
3. a), b) A: irritant/caution – care not to spill on skin, use eye protection; B: corrosive – great care, wear gloves and eye protection

Chapter 4: Explaining Chemical Changes

4.3 Exploring alkalis

Lesson overview

Learning objectives

- Recognise alkalis used in everyday life.
- Describe what all alkalis have in common.
- Identify the hazards that alkalis pose.

Learning outcomes

- Identify everyday substances that contain alkalis. [O1]
- Recognise what alkalis have in common and the hazards associated with some. [O2]
- Evaluate the hazards posed by a number of alkalis and how they may be reduced. [O3]

Skills development

- Thinking scientifically: evaluate risks
- Working scientifically: n/a
- Learner development: communicate effectively

Resources needed bars of soap; water; paper towels; packaging from everyday alkalis (e.g. bleach, washing powder, washing up liquid, shampoo, toothpaste, indigestion remedy, lime for soil, hair bleach, oven cleaner, disinfectant, baking powder); concentrated ammonium hydroxide (caustic soda) (optional); large sheets of paper; pens; Periodic Table; Worksheet 2.4.3

Digital resources Quick starter; Interactive activity: Drag the products to the correct group - acidic or alkaline?; Slideshow: What do alkalis have in common?

Common misconceptions Alkalis are not dangerous.

Key vocabulary soapy, hydroxide

Teaching and learning

Engage

- Ask the students to wet their hands slightly and apply some soap – they should not wash the soap off straight away. Ask them to rub their hands together and to **describe** what they see and feel. Take some feedback and write some of the descriptive words on the whiteboard. [O1&2]
- Explain that soap is an example of a substance that contains an alkali. Explain that other alkalis also feel soapy, although some are too harmful to feel in this way. [O2]

Challenge and develop

- Ask the students to look at packaging from everyday alkalis. [O1]
- **Pairs to fours** Ask the students to work in pairs to **sort** these products into those that they think are harmful and those that they think are not harmful. [O1&2]

    You could support lower-attaining students by providing simple pictures on cards, rather than packaging, to be sorted.

- The pairs merge to form fours to **compare** their sorting. Encourage the students to look at packaging and to **ask questions** if they cannot **agree** on any product. [O1&2]
- Discuss how harmful some of these substances can be using caustic soda as an example. [O2]

Explain

- Ask the students to **recall** the meanings of the hazard symbols on the packaging. In pairs, the students **discuss** the precautions that should be taken with both an irritant and a corrosive alkali. [O2&3]

Key Stage 3 Science Teacher Pack 2 © HarperCollins*Publishers* Limited 2014

Chapter 4: Explaining Chemical Changes

- Ask some pairs to **share** their ideas about the precautions to take. Ask other students to **comment** on the ideas, **suggesting** any changes. Tasks 1 and 2 of Worksheet 2.4.3 could be used here. [O2&3]

Consolidate and apply

- As a class, read the 'Useful acids' section in the Student Book. Answer the questions verbally as a class. [O1, 2&3]
- Ask pairs of students to **consider** what life would be like without alkalis. [O1]
- The pairs **plan** and **produce** a poster highlighting the importance of alkalis and the consequences of not having alkalis. [O1, 2&3]
- Merge the pairs to form fours and each group **peer assesses** the two posters, **recording** feedback as 'two stars and a wish'. As the students work, you could share some good examples of feedback from groups to model the process for others. [O1, 2&3]

Extend

- Show students able to progress further some chemical formulas for other alkalis. Ask them to **suggest** which elements each alkali contains. Then ask them to **locate** the elements on the Periodic Table and **suggest** what their position tells us. Task 3 of Worksheet 2.4.3 can be used here.

Plenary suggestions

What have I learned? Ask the students to work in pairs to **suggest** three things that they have learned today. Pairs then form fours and each group **agrees** a list of three things. [O1, 2&3]

Sharing knowledge Ask, one at a time, groups to **share** something that they learned. Work around the class asking groups to **share** a new suggestion until there are no new ideas. [O1, 2&3]

Answers to Student Book questions

1. bleach; oven cleaner; soap; disinfectant; washing powder
2. s*afe* – toothpaste and baking powder; *not safe* – bleach and oven cleaner
3. sensible suggestions such as unable to wash; clean our teeth; clean our houses as we do now
4. they contain hydroxide 'particles'
5. a) calcium, hydrogen, oxygen; b) sodium, hydrogen, oxygen
6. $Mg(OH)_2$ (MgOH is a reasonable suggestion)
7. to allow blind people to know that the bottle contains a dangerous chemical
8. see Figure 2.4.2c in the Student Book
9. Caustic soda is a strong alkali and is corrosive; bleach is a weaker alkali and is an irritant.

Answers to Worksheet 2.4.3

1. washing-up liquid; soap; toothpaste
2. a) toothpaste; soap; shampoo
   b) i) caution   ii) corrosive   iii) corrosive   iv) caution
3. a) i) sodium, oxygen, hydrogen   ii) calcium, oxygen, hydrogen   iii) magnesium, oxygen, hydrogen
   b) a sentence stating that alkalis contain hydroxide 'particles'

Chapter 4: Explaining Chemical Changes

4.4 Using indicators

Lesson overview

Learning objectives

- Use indicators to identify acids and alkalis.
- Analyse data from different indicators.
- Compare the effectiveness of different indicators.

Learning outcomes

- Exemplify an indicator and describe why indicators are useful. [O1]
- Explain how an indicator may be produced and analyse the data generated. [O2]
- Compare the effectiveness of different indicators. [O3]

Skills development

- Thinking scientifically: consider the quality of evidence
- Working scientifically: interpret evidence
- Learner development: act responsibly

Resources needed equipment and materials as detailed in the Technician's notes; Worksheet 2.4.4; Practical sheet 2.4.4; Technician's notes 2.4.4

Digital resources Quick starter; Slideshow: What are indicators? A look at different types of indicator; Interactive activity: Drag the acids to the correct group – strong or weak

Common misconceptions Indicators turn only red or blue.

Key vocabulary indicator, acid, alkali, litmus, neutral

Teaching and learning

Engage

- Ask the students to observe as you perform a 'magic trick'. Pour some acid into a beaker with tiny amount of litmus solution previously wiped around bottom (so that it appears empty), without explaining what the liquid is. Ask the students to **describe** their observations. [O1]
- Next pour in some alkali (see Technician's notes 2.4.4), without explaining what the liquid is. Ask them to **describe** their observations. [O1]
- Ask the students to **share** any ideas to **explain** the colour changes. [O1]
- Define an indicator as a substance that has different colours in acids and alkalis. Ask the students to try to **explain** the colour changes using the extra information. Take some feedback. [O1&2]
- Ask the students to **describe** what an indicator is in their own words to a partner. They could **write** this definition down. [O1]

Challenge and develop

- Arrange the students in groups of four. Ask them to **consider** the uses of indicators. [O1]
- After a few minutes of discussion, each group chooses a spy to find ideas from another group. The spy also **shares** their own group's ideas. The spy then returns to their original group. [O1]
- Ask groups to **share** ideas across the class– you could refer to the Student Book to reinforce ideas and fill any gaps in knowledge. [O1]

Chapter 4: Explaining Chemical Changes

Explain

- Arrange the students in pairs. Direct half of the groups to **make** an indicator from red cabbage, and the other half to **make** an indicator from beetroot (alternatively you could use blackberries, raspberries or onion skins). [O2]

  You could differentiate this task by allowing lower-attaining students to use grape juice as an indicator without the need to prepare the material.

- Ask the students to follow the instructions on Practical sheet 2.4.3. [O2]
- As the indicator solutions are cooling (or at any other convenient time), you could discuss the background to the experiment with the students. This could include explaining where indicators are found in nature. [O1&2]

Consolidate and apply

- Ask the students to use their indicators to **test** a known acid, a known alkali, solution X and solution Y. They should **record** their observations in a table. [O2]
- Ask them to **analyse** the results to decide whether solutions X and Y are acids or alkalis. [O2]
- Pairs merge to make groups that made different indicators. Ask them to **compare** the results of the two indicators. [O2&3]
- Ask the students to work individually to **write** a paragraph to **summarise** the effectiveness of the two indicators. You could differentiate this task by providing key words to be included – e.g. 'alkali', 'colour change'. Worksheet 2.4.4 could be used here. [O2&3]

Extend

- Ask students able to progress further for **suggestions** of substances that are neutral. They should predict their observations when their indicator is added to this substance. If time allows, students should test this substance and try to find other neutral substances.

Plenary suggestions

Learning triangle The students work individually to **construct** a learning triangle. They should draw a large triangle with a smaller inverted triangle that just fits inside (so that they have four triangles). In the outer triangles, the students write:

- something they've seen
- something they've done
- something they've discussed.

Then in the central triangle, they write something that they've learned. [O1, 2&3]

Answers to Student Book questions

1. it is a substance that has different colours in an acid and an alkali   2. red in acid; blue in alkali
3. a table showing *red litmus paper*: red in acid; blue in alkali; red in neutral
   blue litmus paper: red in acid; blue in alkali; blue in neutral
4. test soils; test swimming pool water; test waste from industries
5. these flowers contain anthocyanins that change colour in different acids and alkalis
6. the tested liquid is an alkali
7. it could be acid or neutral
8. Red cabbage is the most useful; because it has a different colour in acid, alkali and neutral. Both beetroot and cherries have the same colour in acid as in neutral.

Answers to Worksheet 2.4.4

1. indicator; colour; litmus; red; blue   2. A alkali, B alkali, C acid
3. two sensible examples such as detecting water pollution, testing pool water, testing soils with an explanation of how or why it is used

Chapter 4: Explaining Chemical Changes

4.5 Using universal indicator

Lesson overview

Learning objectives

- Describe what the pH scale measures.
- Measure and record pH values.
- Identify the advantages of universal indicator.

Learning outcomes

- Describe pH as a measure of strength of acid or alkali. [O1]
- Interpret measurements of pH made using universal indicator. [O2]
- Explain clearly and fluently the advantages of universal indicator over other indicators. [O3]

Skills development

- Thinking scientifically: use units and nomenclature
- Working scientifically: record evidence
- Learner development: act responsibly

Resources needed equipment and materials as detailed in the Technician's notes; Worksheet 2.4.5; Practical sheet 2.4.5; Technician's notes 2.4.5

Digital resources Quick starter; Interactive activity: Match the colour given from universal indicator paper to the correct product; Hangman: Key vocabulary game

Key vocabulary strong/weak alkali, strong/weak acid, universal indicator; pH number

Teaching and learning

Engage

- Ask the students to **observe** as you add universal indicator (just identified as 'an indicator' at this stage) to sulfuric acid. (Keeping all these the test tubes to refer to later will be helpful). They **describe** the colour change. [O1]
- Add universal indicator (stress that this is the same indicator) to a weak acid, such as ethanoic acid. Again, ask the students to **describe** the colour change. [O1]
- Ask them to **discuss** in small groups how the same indicator could give different colour changes in two acids. Ask the students to **share** ideas across the class. [O1]

Challenge and develop

- Explain that some acids are stronger than others. Ask the students to suggest which is stronger – sulfuric acid or ethanoic acid. You could refer back to hazard labels and to the fact that vinegar contains ethanoic acid if the students need more information. [O1]
- Arrange the students in pairs. Ask them to **explore** and **record** the colour changes of universal indicator when it is added to a strong alkali (sodium hydroxide) and a weak alkali (sodium hydrogencarbonate (baking powder) solution. [O1&2]
- Ask the students to **share** their observations across the class about the differences between strong and weak alkalis.

Explain

- Ask the students to look at Figure 2.4.5c, the pH colour chart, in the Student Book. Ask them to **describe** the position of each of the chemicals observed so far on the scale. [O1&2]

Chapter 4: Explaining Chemical Changes

- Ask them to **suggest** what else the pH scale shows, apart from whether a substance is an acid or an alkali. [O1&2]
- The students work in pairs to **test** a range of substances with universal indicator using Practical sheet 2.4.5. They should **record** their observations in a table they have **designed** themselves. [O2]
- Ask the students to **analyse** their observations and **record** the pH of each substance and whether it is a strong acid, a weak acid, neutral, a weak alkali or a strong alkali. Encourage them to reflect on the way that they recorded the results – could this be improved? Worksheet 2.4.5 could be used here. [O1&2]

Consolidate and apply

- **Pairs to fours** Ask the students to work in pairs to **discuss** the advantages of universal indicator over other indicators used in previous lesson. [O3]
- The pairs merge to form fours to **share** ideas. [O3]
- They then work individually to **produce** a creative piece of writing. They should **imagine** that they work for a company selling universal indicator. They must **write** the text for a poster to advertise universal indicator, **highlighting** its advantages over other indicators. [O3]

Extend

- Provide students able to progress further with a coloured liquid, such as cola, and ask them why it would be difficult to test this liquid with universal indicator. Ask them how they could **test** this liquid. They should then **explain** their solution to the problem using the words 'concentrated' and 'dilute'.

Plenary suggestions

Narratives Ask groups of four to **share** their narratives. Each group then chooses one narrative to read out. Encourage the students to **justify** why they chose this piece of work to share. [O3]

Answers to Student Book questions

1. a) sulfuric acid   b) ethanoic acid   c) oven cleaner   d) soap
2. vinegar and orange juice contain a weak acid; sulfuric acid is a strong acid
3. pH 5
4. increases
5. increases
6. a) red   b) red
7. Universal indicator gives a full range of colours; so it can tell us about the strength of an acid or alkali.

Answers to Worksheet 2.4.5

1. a) correctly coloured pH chart
   b) labels: A strong acids (pH 1–4); B weak acids (pH 5 and 6); C neutral (pH 7); D weak alkali (pH 8 and 9); E strong alkali (pH 10–14)
2. a) A: pH in range 11–14, strong alkali; B: pH in range 1–2, strong acid; C: pH 6, weak acid
   b) green (pH 7)
3. the paragraph should include the idea that universal indicator has a range of colours; linked to the strength of the acid or alkali; litmus does not indicate the strength

Chapter 4: Explaining Chemical Changes

4.6 Exploring neutralisation

Lesson overview

Learning objectives

- Describe examples of neutralisation.
- Use indicators to identify chemical reactions.
- Explain colour changes in terms of pH and neutralisation.

Learning outcomes

- Describe some examples of neutralisation. [O1]
- Describe the changes to indicators when acids and alkalis are mixed. [O2]
- Explain the changes to an indicator when acids and alkalis are mixed. [O3]

Skills development

- Thinking scientifically: consider the quality of evidence
- Working scientifically: develop explanations
- Learner development: collaborate effectively

Resources needed equipment and materials as detailed in the Technician's notes; Worksheet 2.4.6; Practical sheet 2.4.6; Technician's notes 2.4.6

Digital resources Quick starter; Interactive activity: Match the everyday neutralisation reactions together; Video

Common misconceptions Mixing an acid and an alkali always results in a neutral solution.

Key vocabulary neutralisation, titration

Teaching and learning

Engage

- If possible show a video clip, without sound, of real-life examples of neutralisation. Alternatively show some images of examples of neutralisation without an explanation. [O1]
- The students should note down what they observe. [O1]
- Ask them to **suggest** links between what they have seen and take feedback. Tasks 1 and 2 of Worksheet 2.4.6 could be attempted here. [O1]

Challenge and develop

- Arrange the students in pairs. Ask them to add some universal indicator to hydrochloric acid in a conical flask. They should **record** their observations. Next, ask them to add sodium hydroxide using a dropping pipette – again, they record their observations. Do not give too much guidance at this point. [O2]
- Ask the students to **describe** their observations. Ask them to **explain** the pH of the various solutions they produced during this activity. [O2]
- Use the feedback to show that different groups made different observations and elicit that this depended on the amount of alkali added. [O2&3]

Explain

- Set the groups the challenge of producing a neutral solution. The students follow the instructions on Practical sheet 2.4.6 and then answer the questions. Stress that they should work carefully to **produce** a solution of pH 7. [O2]

Chapter 4: Explaining Chemical Changes

- Demonstrate a titration (see Technician's notes 2.4.6) and ask the students to **observe** the end point of the neutralisation. [O2]
- Ask them to **discuss** the two methods of neutralisation and to **compare** the accuracy. Take feedback. [O2&3]
- Ask the students to **note** the volumes of acid and alkali used. Take **comments** about the relationship between the two volumes, stressing that the acid and alkali are of equal concentration. [O3]

Consolidate and apply

- Ask the students to work individually to **write a conclusion** about titration using key words – for example 'neutralisation', 'acid', 'alkali'. Task 3 of Worksheet 2.4.6 could be used to add structure to this task. [O2&3]

  You could differentiate by asking higher-attaining students to also include 'hydroxide' and 'hydrogen'.

Extend

- Ask students able to progress further to **comment** on the volumes of acid and alkali used. Stress that the acid and alkali had equal concentration. Ask them to suggest how the volume of each used would change with given changes in concentration. [O3]

Plenary suggestions

Freeze frame The students work in pairs to **display** a freeze-frame of an example of neutralisation. Other members of the class **guess** what is being represented. [O1]

Answers to Student Book questions

1. the reaction between acids and alkalis; in which acids and alkalis cancel each other out
2. the pH increases; as the solution becomes less acidic
3. the pH decreases; as the solution becomes less alkaline
4. if the water became too alkaline, it would kill the plants and animals living there
5. students should draw a suitable table summarising examples such as toothpaste neutralises acid in the mouth and antacids neutralise acid from the stomach
6. purple; to blue; to green
7. The solution could change from green to yellow, orange or red. This is because the solution is becoming more acidic.
8. the acid can be added more gradually/more precisely; it is easier to reach the end point

Answers to Worksheet 2.4.6

1.

When alkali is added to an acid...	...the solution becomes less acidic.
As acid is added to an alkali...	...the pH of the alkali decreases.
When a solution is neutral...	...it is pH7
One way that acids and alkalis can be mixed carefully...	...is by titration

2. a) alkali toothpaste; neutralises acid; from bacteria in the mouth
   b) antacids neutralise stomach acid
   c) acidic bee sting neutralised by alkaline bicarbonate
   d) acidic nettle sting neutralised by alkaline substance from dock leaf
3. a) red; orange; yellow; green
   b) to mix the acid and alkali
   c) pH 7
   d) i) turn blue (and then purple if more added) ii) solution would become alkaline if more alkali is added after neutral

Chapter 4: Explaining Chemical Changes

4.7 Explaining neutralisation

Lesson overview

Learning objectives

- Recall the equation for a neutralisation reaction.
- Explain how water is made during a neutralisation reaction.
- Apply a model to explain neutralisation

Learning outcomes

- Recognise water as a product of neutralisation. [O1]
- Explain the formation of a salt and water during neutralisation. [O2]
- Explain and evaluate a model of neutralisation. [O3]

Skills development

- Thinking scientifically: use equations
- Working scientifically: n/a
- Learner development: communicate effectively

Resources needed building bricks in four colours; modelling clay; video cameras (optional); mini-whiteboards; Worksheet 2.4.7

Digital resources Quick starter; Interactive activity: Drag the chemicals to the correct group – product or reactant; Slideshow: A model for neutralisation

Common misconceptions A reaction can create something completely new, not related to the reactants.

Key vocabulary water, neutral, salt, equation

Teaching and learning

Engage

- Give out some building bricks of different colours. Ask the students to **suggest** why these might be useful when they are **learning** about acids and alkalis reacting. [O3]
- Give the students a key to a colour that represents H and a colour that represents O. Ask the students to work in pairs to make water and 'hydroxide'. [O1&3]

Challenge and develop

- Ask the students to **recall** what all acids contain and what all alkalis contain.
- Demonstrate a model of acids and alkalis using the building bricks. Use one colour to represent the main body of the acid, and another colour to represent the main body of the alkali. Choose different colours to represent H and O – add a brick to the acid to represent H and add bricks to the alkali to represent O and H. Ask the students to **explain** what each shows to check their understanding. [O1&2]
- Demonstrate neutralisation, explaining that H and OH react. Remove the H and OH and ask the students to **predict** what these will form. [O1]
- Demonstrate the joining of H and OH to form water. Tell the students that the other parts of the 'molecules' join to form a salt. Ask the students to **describe** which parts of the model represent the salt. [O2]

Explain

- Read 'The neutralisation equation' section of the Student Book as a class. Ask the students to **explain** in their own words what the equation for neutralisation shows. They should **record** the equations and their **explanation**. [O1&2]

Chapter 4: Explaining Chemical Changes

- The students answer the questions from the Student Book. Worksheet 2.4.7 could also be used here. [O1&2]
- Read out a pH number. Ask the students to **identify** a substance in the neutralisation word equation that the pH matches. They could use mini whiteboards for this activity. [O1&2]

Consolidate and apply

- **Group work** Arrange the students in groups of three. Ask the groups to **make** a visualisation of neutralisation. Encourage them to do this in any way they choose – for example using modelling clay, building bricks, students acting etc. Ask them to film the visualisations if possible. [O3]
- Ask the groups to **present** their work to the rest of the class. The audience could be invited to give feedback. [O3]
- Ask the students to **consider** how effective the model is. They should **consider** whether the model helps in understanding neutralisation and **evaluate** if anything is not represented by the model (for example, the change in pH). [O3]

Extend

- Ask students able to progress further to **make** a card-sorting activity about neutralisation – this could be for a specific reaction or the general reaction. They can choose to make cards to sequence or to match. [O1&2]

Plenary suggestions

Designing for remembering Ask the students to work in pairs to **design** a way of remembering the equation for neutralisation. [O1, 2&3]

Sharing ideas Ask the pairs to **share** their ideas across the class. Take feedback as to any of the ideas that students will adopt. [O1, 2&3]

Answers to Student Book questions

1. water; salt
2. hydrogen; hydroxide
3. pH 7
4. acid + alkali → salt + water
5. a) water   b) the salt
6. water; sodium chloride
7. Models help us to visualise things that we cannot see.
8. suitable drawings linked to the model
9. check the drawings are linked to Figure 2.4.7d; to show circle diagrams of water and sodium chloride

Answers to Worksheet 2.4.7

1. a) water   b) hydroxide   c) decreases   d) 7
2. a) acid + alkali → salt + water
   b) i) sodium hydroxide + hydrochloric acid → sodium chloride + water
      ii) sodium hydroxide + nitric acid → sodium nitrate + water
      iii) sodium hydroxide + sulfuric acid → sodium sulfate + water
3. a) a diagram showing some representation of H and OH being lost from acids and alkalis, respectively; combining to form water
   b) questions should relate to information in the cartoon/ comic strip; the students must be able to answer their own questions

Chapter 4: Explaining Chemical Changes

4.8 Understanding salts

Lesson overview

Learning objectives

- Name examples of salts.
- Describes the uses of common salts.
- Predict the reactants used in and the salts made by different neutralisation reactions.

Learning outcomes

- Identify some common salts. [O1]
- Describe the uses of some common salts. [O2]
- Predict the reactants and salts made in different neutralisation reactions. [O3]

Skills development

- Thinking scientifically: use equations
- Working scientifically: n/a
- Learner development: collaborate effectively

Resources needed table salt; information about sodium chloride, magnesium chloride, iron sulfate and calcium sulfate to include the neutralisation reaction that each can produce and their uses; large sheets of paper; pens; Worksheet 2.4.8

Digital resources Quick starter; Interactive activity: Match the salts to their uses

Common misconceptions All salts are the same as table salt (sodium chloride).

Key vocabulary salt, base

Teaching and learning

Engage

- Show the students some table salt. Ask them to work in pairs to **list** as many uses as possible of salt. [O2]
- Ask the pairs to **share** their ideas, one a time. Record a list of the ideas. [O2]

Challenge and develop

- Ask the students to **recall** the neutralisation equation and display it. Then ask them to **think about** which acid and alkali would have been used to make sodium chloride. After a few minutes, ask them to **discuss** their ideas with a partner. [O3]
- Then ask them to **share** their ideas across the class. Ask those who make sensible suggestions to **explain** their reasoning to others. [O3]
- Ask the students to **read** the 'Making predictions' section in the Student Book. [O1&3]
- Give some examples of acids and alkalis and ask the students to **suggest** the name of the salt produced. [O1&3]
- Give the names of some other salts, such as magnesium chloride, iron sulfate and calcium sulphate, and ask them to **predict** the names of the acid and alkali that would produce them. [O1&3]

Explain

- **Jigsaw activity** Arrange the students in groups of four for a jigsaw activity to **learn** about different salts. Assign each student in a group to 'sodium chloride', 'magnesium chloride', 'iron sulfate' or 'calcium sulfate'. [O1&2]

Chapter 4: Explaining Chemical Changes

Assign higher-attaining students sodium chloride because there will be more information to study and collate.

- The groups then split to form new 'expert groups' made using others assigned the same salt. Give each group relevant information (see 'Resources needed'); you could also provide a sample of the salt that they are studying for students to **examine**. Allow 10 minutes for groups to **assimilate** the information and **write notes** using only 10 words, supported by diagrams. Ask the students to **learn** about how the salt can be made and what its uses are. [O1, 2&3]

- The students return to their original groups of four and spend a few minutes **teaching** the rest of the group what they have learned. The rest of the group should **complete** Worksheet 2.4.8 as a summary of the work. [O1, 2&3]

Consolidate and apply

- Read the 'Bases and neutralisation' section in the Student's Book as a class. Ask the students to **explain** to a partner, in their own words, the difference between a base and an alkali. Take some feedback and ask others to **comment** on the accuracy of the statements. [O3]

- Ask the students to return to their notes made during the jigsaw activity and **amend** them to include bases. [O3]

- Ask them to continue working in groups of four to **produce** a concept map of the work done so far on acids and alkalis. Encourage the students to look at their own work as well as the Student Book. Display the concept maps. [O1, 2&3]

Extend

- Ask students able to progress further to consider the formulas of some common acids and alkalis (such as hydrochloric acid and nitric acid, and sodium hydroxide and potassium hydroxide). Ask them to try to **write symbol equations** for the neutralisation reactions.

Plenary suggestions

Concept mapping Ask the students to look at the concept maps of other groups. Encourage them to **amend** their own maps if they pick up other ideas. Keep the concept maps because they will be revisited and added to in later lessons. [O1, 2&3]

Answers to Student Book questions

1. in food; on icy roads; producing chlorine, hydrogen and sodium hydroxide
2. for example: magnesium chloride – cement; iron sulfate – killing moss; calcium sulfate – plaster of Paris
3. a product of a neutralisation reaction
4. calcium...
5. sodium chloride
6. hydrochloric acid + magnesium oxide → magnesium chloride + water
7. an alkali is a base that dissolves in water; both neutralise an acid to produce a salt and water
8. Copper oxide doesn't dissolve in water; sodium hydroxide does dissolve in water; they both neutralise an acid.
9. acid + base → salt + water; the products of both reactions are the same/both react in a similar way

Answers to Worksheet 2.4.8

1. relevant summary based on the information provided
2. a) magnesium chloride b) sodium chloride c) calcium sulfate d) sodium sulfate e) calcium nitrate
3. suitable explanation using a scientific vocabulary; including that a base is a substance that will neutralise an acid; and that soluble bases are called alkalis

Chapter 4: Explaining Chemical Changes

4.9 Exploring the reactions of acids with metals

Lesson overview

Learning objectives

- Describe the reaction between acids and metals.
- Explain the reaction between acids and metals.
- Compare the reactivities of different metals.

Learning outcomes

- Describe the observations made when acids react with metals. [O1]
- Explain the reaction between acids and metals. [O2]
- Compare the reactivities of different metals. [O3]

Skills development

- Thinking scientifically: use equations
- Working scientifically: make predictions
- Learner development: act responsibly

Resources needed equipment and materials as detailed in the Technician's notes; Worksheet 2.4.9; Practical sheet 2.4.9; Technician's notes 2.4.9

Digital resources Quick starter; Interactive activity: Drag the metal to the correct group, depending on how it reacts with acid

Common misconceptions When a metal reacts with an acid, it vanishes.

Key vocabulary chemical reaction, salt, hydrogen, reactivity

Teaching and learning

Engage

- Show a web-based video of a reaction between calcium and an acid. [O1]
- Ask the students to **suggest** how they can tell that a chemical reaction has taken place. [O1&2]
- Ask them to **explain** what the bubbles in the reaction show (a gas is produced). Tell them as well that the reaction causes an increase in temperature. [O1&2]
- Ask the students to work in pairs to **list** some clues that a chemical reaction is taking place. Ask them to **share** their ideas as a class and to **construct** a list. If necessary, refer students to the 'Reacting acids with metals' section in the Student Book. [O1]

Challenge and develop

- Ask the students to **recap** what new products are made during the reactions – you could display this in equation form. Ask them to **suggest** how the reaction of acids with metals is different from the reaction between acids and alkalis (you can see a gas formed in a metal/acid reaction). [O2]

Explain

- **Pair work** Pairs **carry out** a practical to explore the reactions of acids with metals (using Practical sheet 2.4.9). [O1]
- The students **record** their observations. [O1]
- If time allows, ask them to **observe** reactions of other metals for evidence of hydrogen gas.
- The students could attempt tasks 1 and 2 of Worksheet 2.4.9. [O1]

Chapter 4: Explaining Chemical Changes

- If time allows, demonstrate the reaction of copper with concentrated nitric acid. You could ask the students to **predict** the outcome before you carry out the demonstration. [O1]

Consolidate and apply

- Ask the students to **share** their findings across the class. [O1&2]
- Share the general equation for the reaction of acids with metals with students. Ask them to work individually to answer the questions on Practical sheet 2.4.9. [O1, 2&3]

Extend

- Ask students able to progress further to **plan** an investigation into a factor that could affect the rate of the reaction between acids and metals. Ask them to **consider** the variables that they will change, measure and control – they could also make a prediction. Section 3 of Worksheet 2.4.9 could also be used here.

Plenary suggestions

Describing and applying ideas Show a web-based video of sodium reacting with hydrochloric acid. Ask the students to **describe** what they see. Then ask them to **suggest** what products are made. Students should be able to **describe** the equation. Point out that the solution turns cloudy as sodium chloride forms. [O1&2]

Then show a video of potassium reacting with hydrochloric acid. Ask the students to **rank** sodium and potassium in order of reactivity. [O3]

Answers to Student Book questions

1. bubbles of gas; change of temperature; colour change; change in mass
2. bubbles of gas; change of temperature (increase)
3. a gas is produced
4. nitric acid + copper → copper nitrate + hydrogen
5. hydrochloric acid + magnesium → magnesium chloride + hydrogen
6. Hydrogen burns in air; large amount of hydrogen gas could cause a big explosion.
7. magnesium; zinc; iron; copper
8. a lot of bubbling; steam
9. hydrochloric acid + magnesium → magnesium chloride + hydrogen
   hydrochloric acid + zinc → zinc chloride + hydrogen
   hydrochloric acid + iron → iron chloride + hydrogen
   hydrochloric acid + copper → no reaction

Answers to Worksheet 2.4.9

1. bubbles of gas; colour change; tube feels warmer
2. a) from most to least reactive – magnesium; iron; copper
   b) more bubbles; more vigorous reaction (could see a flame)
   c) between magnesium and iron
3. a) more bubbles; faster reaction because more acid molecules in concentrated acid
   b) fewer bubbles, slower reaction; reaction will stop sooner because there is less magnesium to react
   c) more bubbles; faster reaction because the magnesium powder has a bigger surface area

Chapter 4: Explaining Chemical Changes

4.10 Exploring the reactions of acids with carbonates

Lesson overview

Learning objectives

- Describe the reaction between acids and carbonates.
- Explain the reaction between acids and carbonates.
- Write word equations for the reactions between acids and carbonates.

Learning outcomes

- Describe the observations made in reactions between acids and carbonates. [O1]
- Explain the reactions between acids and carbonates. [O2]
- Summarise the reactions using word equations. [O3]

Skills development

- Thinking scientifically: use units and correct nomenclature
- Working scientifically: interpret evidence
- Learner development: act responsibly

Resources needed coloured card; graph paper; equipment and materials as detailed in the Technician's notes; Worksheet 2.4.10; Practical sheet 2.4.10; Technician's notes 2.4.10

Digital resources Quick starter; Slideshow: Summarising the reactions of acids with carbonates; Hangman: Key vocabulary game

Common misconceptions Carbon dioxide is 'released' from carbonates when they react with acids.

Key vocabulary carbonate, carbon dioxide, limewater

Teaching and learning

Engage

- Ask the students to **make observations** as you react hydrochloric acid with magnesium ribbon, and hydrochloric acid with copper carbonate. It would be useful to carry out these reactions at the same time (for example in Petri dishes on an overhead projector). Ask the students to **compare** the reactions. [O1]
- Ask them to **share** their observations across the class and to **predict** what causes the bubbles in each reaction. If students suggest that both gases are hydrogen, since they know that acids and metals produce hydrogen, use this as a way to discuss the need for testing gases to be sure of what they are. [O1]

Challenge and develop

- Tell the students that the gas produced by the reactions of acids and metal carbonates is different from that produced by the reactions of acids and metals. Ask them to use the name of the reactants to **predict** the name of the gas produced. [O1&2]
- Ask the students to **discuss** in pairs what they know about carbon dioxide. After a few minutes, ask them to **share** their ideas across the class. Lead the discussion to the fact that we breathe out more carbon dioxide than we breathe in and that we can use this to show the effect of carbon dioxide on limewater. [O2]
- Ask a volunteer to breathe out into limewater. Ask other students to **observe** the change to the limewater. Ask them to **describe** the test for carbon dioxide in their own words to a partner. [O2]

Key Stage 3 Science Teacher Pack 2

Chapter 4: Explaining Chemical Changes

Explain

- **Pair work** The students **investigate** the reaction of hydrochloric acid with carbonates, using Practical sheet 2.4.10. You should demonstrate how to collect the gas produced and bubble it into limewater prior to beginning the practical work. [O1]
- The students **record** their observations, including the effect of the gas on limewater (table provided on the practical sheet). [O1]
- Ask them to use their observations to answer the questions on Practical sheet 2.4.10. Tasks 1 and 2 of Worksheet 2.4.10 could also be attempted here. [O2&3]

Consolidate and apply

- Show the students samples of limestone rocks and shells. Ask them to **comment** on their relevance to this lesson. Explain that both limestone and shells contain a high proportion of calcium carbonate. Ask the students to **discuss** in pairs the effect of an acid spill in the sea. Ask them to **share** their ideas. Task 3 of Worksheet 2.4.10 could be used here. [O1&2]
- Demonstrate an egg being left in a large beaker of vinegar. Ask them to **recap** what type of acid is found in vinegar (ethanoic). Ask them to **predict** what will happen to the shell – incubate overnight and allow the students to observe the changes. [O1&2]

Extend

- Ask students able to progress further to **write a word equation** for the reaction between ethanoic acid and calcium carbonate. They could also be given the formulas for hydrochloric acid and calcium carbonate and asked to **work out the formulas** of the products. [O3]

Plenary suggestions

Loop game Arrange the students in groups of eight. Ask them to write the reactants of a reaction used in the last few lessons on a piece of coloured card. Ask them to write the products of the same reaction on a piece of different-coloured card. Shuffle the cards and then redistribute one card of each colour to every student in the group. Ask them to **play** a loop card game with one student reading out the products on their card. The student with the related reactants on one of their cards identifies themselves. They then read out the reactants on their other card and so on. [O3]

Answers to Student Book questions

1. calcium carbonate   2. carbon dioxide gas is produced
3. bubble the gas through limewater; carbon dioxide turns limewater milky
4. hydrochloric acid + calcium carbonate → calcium chloride + carbon dioxide + water
5. sulfuric acid + copper carbonate → copper sulfate + water + carbon dioxide
6. the reaction would be faster; because of the increased surface area   7. at the start of the experiment
8. the acid; or the carbonate; has eventually all reacted
9. there would be a steep upward curve that levels off; if a graph is drawn the x-axis should be labelled 'Time' and the y-axis 'Volume of gas'

Answers to Worksheet 2.4.10

1. carbon dioxide; limewater; salt; limestone; calcium; fizzing
2. a) → magnesium chloride + carbon dioxide + water   b) → magnesium sulfate + carbon dioxide + water
   c) → copper sulfate + carbon dioxide + water   d) → calcium nitrate + carbon dioxide + water
3. a) check that graphs are suitably drawn; with a line of best fit
   b) mass decreases over time; because carbon dioxide gas is given off; slows down gradually
      acid + carbonate → salt + carbon dioxide + water
   c) mass read from graph; approximately 165 g
   d) use limestone chips with distilled water (or on their own)
   e) If the acid had the same volume; the mass would decrease by more; and more quickly

Chapter 4: Explaining Chemical Changes

4.11 Applying key ideas

Ever-changing urine

Objectives

- Identify some factors that affect the pH of urine.
- Explain how knowledge of the pH of urine can be used by medical practitioners.
- Apply knowledge about acids and alkalis to reactions in the body.

Outcome

- Clear and effective responses to questions, indicating understanding and the next steps in learning.

The purpose of this activity is to provide an opportunity to see how successfully students are grasping the key ideas so far. It isn't designed to be used as a formal test – it might be that students work on the questions collectively. It does provide an opportunity for you to look at written work, engage students in discussions and form ideas about progress being made.

The tasks are progressive. Lower-attaining students should be able to tackle the first two or three tasks and higher-attaining students will find the later ones more challenging.

Resources needed equipment and materials as detailed in the Technician's notes; highlighters; Worksheet 2.4.11; Technician's notes 2.4.11

Teaching and learning

Engage

- Show the students a beaker containing a clear liquid – ask them to suggest what the liquid is. Ask the groups to **suggest** ways of working out what the liquid is, steering the discussion to the use of indicators and pH to identify acids and alkalis.

- Challenge the students to **think back** over the last few lessons. Ask them to **discuss** some of the ideas they have met. Take feedback and say that it is important as learners that they develop a sense of their own progress.

Challenge and develop

- If possible, show a web-based video clip of *Friends*, Season 4, Episode 1 'The one about the jellyfish'. View it beforehand to locate the section required and to check suitability. Alternatively show photos or a web-based clip of 'box' jellyfish. Ask the students to **discuss** why jellyfish are so dangerous and why they think that it has been suggested that urinating on a jellyfish sting may help. Elicit the idea that a neutralisation reaction may be helpful.

- Arrange the students in pairs and ask each pair to **determine** the acidity or alkalinity of both 'urine' (made from tea) and 'jellyfish venom' (see Technician's notes 2.4.11). Give little other guidance and allow the students to **decide** for themselves that using universal indicator might be a good idea.

- Ask each pair to **decide** if the urine would be useful to treat a jellyfish sting and take a class vote. (Because both solutions are slightly alkaline, the sting would not be neutralised.) Explain that it is most likely to be a myth that urine would be useful (however, vinegar appears to be more successful).

Explain

Ask the students to read the 'Ever-changing urine' passage in the Student Book. Depending on their ability to **assimilate** text you may need to adopt strategies such as:

- Have students working in pairs, with copies of the Student Book text (provided as Worksheet 2.4.11) and highlighters. One student highlights key ideas and the other (using a different colour) any words they don't understand.

Key Stage 3 Science Teacher Pack 2

Chapter 4: Explaining Chemical Changes

- Have students working in pairs to **summarise** each paragraph using no more than 10 words but supported with diagrams.
- Work with groups of students who have difficulty with reading to support them in **decoding** the text and **accessing** the ideas.

Consolidate and apply

- Now ask the students to attempt the tasks – they might do this individually or collaboratively. In either case, encourage them to **identify** and **record** their ideas.
- Ask them to **present** their responses to the different tasks, either orally or by displaying their work.

Extend

- For students able to progress further, the later tasks give opportunities for extension work.

Plenary

Ask the students for responses to questions such as:

- How well was I able to approach those tasks?
- Did I manage to present some high quality responses?
- Are there some ideas that I need to strengthen in the later part of this topic?

If there are, make a note.

Provide the class with some overall feedback, indicating ideas that they have grasped effectively and those that may need developing further.

Likely responses and next steps in learning

1. This task gives students an opportunity to revisit the pH scale and the colours that they have observed using universal indicator. This task requires them to take information from the text and present it in a different format – it will demonstrate understanding of what the pH scale shows.

2. This task involves the students identifying information from the text about the effect of some medicines on the pH of urine. It also requires them to think more widely about the consequences of stopping any medication and to appreciate that a time lag would be needed for the drugs to be out of the body system.

3. This task gives the students the opportunity to summarise much of the information in the text and to display it in a different format. They will need to consider how to display information because they are asked to consider how examples of three factors affect the pH.

4. This task requires the students to deduce the acidity or alkalinity of different foods and then to explain an application. They will need to identify that acids and alkalis react in a neutralisation reaction, cancelling each other out. For this activity, it is not expected that students need to consider the relative sizes of the effects of different foods.

5. The students are required to consider the strength and concentration of different acids and alkalis in this task. It is sufficient here for students to recognise that some acids and alkalis are stronger than others; and that some foods contain a more concentrated form of the acid or alkali. They should use the examples given in the task box to exemplify their answer. Students may also mention variation in portion size as a factor.

6. This task requires the students to write an equation for a reaction between an acid that has not been used before with a carbonate. They should be encouraged to predict the name of the salt (calcium citrate) and to research the name if necessary – they could be encouraged to research the formula of the acid. The students are required to consider the reasons why this reaction may not reduce the kidney stone size – such as the calcium carbonate is a solid mass, rather than a powder which would increase the rate of reaction; citric acid is a weak acid; the acid is very dilute in wine.

Chapter 4: Explaining Chemical Changes

4.12 Investigating the effectiveness of antacids

Lesson overview

Learning objectives

- Design an investigation to compare the effectiveness of indigestion remedies.
- Analyse data to identify a suitable indigestion remedy.

Learning outcomes

- Describe indigestion remedies and the way that they work. [O1]
- Design a suitable investigation to compare indigestion remedies fairly. [O2]
- Analyse data to make a justified decision about the best remedy. [O3]

Skills development

- Thinking scientifically: analyse data
- Working scientifically: design investigations
- Learner development: collaborate effectively

Resources needed equipment and materials as detailed in the Technician's notes; Worksheet 2.4.12; Practical sheet 2.4.12; Technician's notes 2.4.12

Digital resources Quick starter; Interactive activity: Place the steps of the antacid experiment into the correct order

Common misconceptions Antacids neutralise stomach acid to form a neutral solution (pH 7).

Key vocabulary indigestion, heartburn, antacid, base, neutralisation

Teaching and learning

Engage

- Show some adverts for indigestion remedies and, if possible, video clips. [O1]
- Ask the students to work in pairs to **discuss** and **write down** anything that they know about indigestion or its remedies. [O1]
- If necessary, remind them that we always have acid in our stomach (approximately pH 1–2). If the sphincter at the top of the stomach opens, this acid can move up towards the throat. This causes heartburn or indigestion. Ask the students to **suggest** what indigestion remedies are. Ask them to **suggest** what the reaction between the stomach acid and the remedy is. [O1]

Challenge and develop

- **Group work** Ask the students to work in groups of four to **brainstorm** how they could **investigate** which is the most effective remedy. Encourage students to be as creative as possible at this stage and to **generate** as many ideas as possible. Allow them access to packaging during this activity (or to copies of ingredient and dosage information). [O1&2]
- Ask the groups to **share** some of their ideas across the class. [O1&2]

Explain

- Ask groups of four to split into pairs. The new pairs should **plan** an investigation to find the most effective remedy for indigestion. Encourage students to use the information and **discussion** from the previous activity to help them. Practical sheet 2.4.12 can be used to support planning. [O2]

Chapter 4: Explaining Chemical Changes

- Check each group's plan for suitability and safety before allowing them to **carry out** the investigation. You will need to be flexible in terms of equipment needed. It will be useful to set up some beakers of distilled water with universal indicator added, to remind the students what neutral pH looks like. [O2]
- If the students need support, give them some ideas about how to carry out the investigation. For example:
  - Use the recommended dose of remedy and, if it is in tablet form, crush it in a pestle and mortar.
  - Set up two beakers of hydrochloric acid and add universal indicator to each – keep one for comparison and add the remedy to the other.
  - Observe the colour change of the indicator and record this along with any other observations.
  - Repeat with at least one more remedy for comparison.

  You could ask higher-attaining students to use a pH meter to generate data about changes in pH over time.

Consolidate and apply

- Ask students to **analyse** their data to decide which indigestion remedy is the most effective (Practical sheet 2.4.12 supports this analysis). [O3]
- Encourage those students without a full set of results to **collaborate** with another group carrying out the investigation in a similar way. Worksheet 2.4.12 could be used to give practice in interpreting data. [O3]

Extend

- Ask students able to progress further to **evaluate** the investigation, **suggesting** improvements and the next steps.

Plenary suggestions

Adverts The students create an advert to promote the remedy that they have found to be the most effective. Encourage them to **consider** the adverts that were seen at the start of the lesson. Remind them of the need to educate as well as entertain an audience. [O1, 2&3]

Answers to Student Book questions

1. hydrochloric acid; strong (pH 1)
2. digestion of proteins; prevention of the survival of some bacteria
3. a burning sensation in the chest and throat; caused by stomach acid moving up the oesophagus
4. calcium carbonate; magnesium hydroxide
5. an alkali (or base) neutralises the stomach acid; making the solution less acidic
6. increase the pH
7. stomach acid is approximately pH 1–2
8. 'Acid-ease' liquid; it changes the pH from 1 to 6; takes only 3 minutes
9. the time may decrease; because of increased surface area of 'Acid-ban' tablets

Answers to Worksheet 2.4.12

1. C; B; A; D
2. a) saliva is alkaline; helps to neutralise any acid that leaves the stomach
   b) limestone contains calcium carbonate; that neutralises acid
   c) bicarbonate of soda is alkali; so it neutralises acid
   d) this prevents acid from moving up the oesophagus easily
3. a) A pH 4; B pH 6; C pH 5
   b) B; it neutralises the acid to a pH nearest to neutral
   c) C takes longer; but neutralises the acid to pH7; so this could be better
   d) look for sensible suggestions such as cost, availability and taste

Chapter 4: Explaining Chemical Changes

4.13 Understanding the importance of acids and alkalis

Lesson overview

Learning objectives

- Classify common useful chemicals as acids or alkalis.
- Explain the importance of acids and alkalis in everyday life.
- Explore common misconceptions about acids and alkalis.

Learning outcomes

- Identify two uses of acids and two of alkalis in everyday life. [O1]
- Describe several examples of uses of acids and alkalis. [O2]
- Explain some common misconceptions about acids and alkalis. [O3]

Skills development

- Thinking scientifically: ask questions
- Working scientifically: n/a
- Learner development: ask questions

Resources needed packaging and/or pictures of uses of acids and alkalis; concept maps started in Topic 4.8; pens; Worksheet 2.4.13 (with the second page copied onto card)

Digital resources Quick starter; Slideshow: Acids and alkalis in industry - The chloralkali industry; Interactive activity: Are the statements about acids and alkalis fact or fiction?; Video; Video

Key vocabulary fertiliser, misconception

Teaching and learning

Engage

- Provide the students with packaging and/or pictures to represent uses of acids and alkalis. Ask the students to work in pairs to sort the packaging and pictures into groups to show those linked with acids and those linked with alkalis. [O1&2]
- Ask the pairs to merge with another group and **compare** their sorting. Ask the new groups to **discuss** any items sorted differently to reach a consensus. Higher-attaining students could be asked to add examples of their own onto extra cards. [O1&2]

Challenge and develop

- Choose some packaging or pictures that generate cognitive conflict. For example, show toothpaste packaging and ask the students to **describe** how they grouped it. Generate some discussion and ask the students to **suggest** reasons why it could be grouped under either acid (because it neutralises acid produced by bacteria in the mouth) or alkali (because toothpaste is alkaline). Task 1 of Worksheet 2.4.13 could also be considered during this activity. [O1&2]
- Ask the students to **discuss** other examples that could be placed in either group. After a short discussion in groups, ask students to **share** ideas across the class. [O1&2]

Explain

- Ask the students to **explain** what is meant by a 'misconception'. Ask some students to **share** their ideas across the class. [O3]
- **Group talk** Arrange the students in groups of four. Ask the groups to read the common misconceptions on the cards from Worksheet 2.4.13. Ask them to **discuss** each statement to **decide** whether they think it is

Chapter 4: Explaining Chemical Changes

accurate or inaccurate. Explain that the idea is not just to **classify** each statement, but to **justify** the decision. [O3]

- **Envoys** After the groups have discussed most of the statements, ask each to send a spy/envoy to a different group. The spy/envoy **listens** to other group's ideas and also **shares** ideas of their own group. They then return to their original group of four and **share** what they learned from the group that they visited. The groups could use the Student Book for support. [O3]

Consolidate and apply

- Arrange the students in groups of four that worked together on the concept map in Topic 4.8. Ask them to **refresh** their memories of the work completed so far. [O1&2]
- Ask the groups to **add to**, or **amend** their maps, based on recent work. Encourage them to **consider** the common misconceptions highlighted in the previous activity. [O1, 2&3]

Extend

- Ask students able to progress further to **research** the use of acids or alkalis in industry. This could be an example already mentioned or a different application. Task 2 of Worksheet 2.4.13 could act as a starting point for this activity. [O2]

Plenary suggestions

Question time Ask each group to design a question related to the work on acids and alkalis – they should also develop a mark scheme. Encourage the students to construct questions worth several marks, rather than a single mark. Groups swap questions and attempt to answer them. [O1, 2&3]

Answers to Student Book questions

1. in medicines (taste nicer); in making cigarette papers (burn more slowly)
2. it dissolves the glass; without changing its colour
3. neutralisation
4. making fertilisers
5. paper manufacture
6. fertilisers increase plant growth; these plants are needed for food
7. an idea from which we can't actually see what is going on; we have to use our imagination
8. a gas is not always produced; e.g. neutralisation reactions produce just a salt and water
9. they can help us to visualise things that we cannot see or touch

Answers to Worksheet 2.4.13

1. *uses of acids* – b, c, f, g, j, l; *uses of alkalis* – a, d, e, h, i, k
2. a) sulfuric acid; sulfur dioxide; sulfur trioxide; hydrochloric acid; nitric acid
   b) making fertilisers and other acids; removing impurities from metals
   c) clear, colourless liquid; corrosive; can burn skin (even in dilute form)
3. a) inaccurate; e.g. copper does not react with dilute sulfuric acid
   b) inaccurate; weak acids are not corrosive
   c) inaccurate; carbon dioxide is formed during the reaction
   d) inaccurate; e.g. acid + alkali produces no gas
   e) inaccurate; new products formed
   f) accurate

Chapter 4: Explaining Chemical Changes

4.14 Exploring combustion

Lesson overview

Learning objectives

- Explain the terms fuel and combustion.
- Recall what is needed for combustion.
- Analyse the fire triangle and apply it to putting out fires.

Learning outcomes

- Describe the terms fuel and combustion. [O1]
- Describe what is needed for combustion using the fire triangle. [O2]
- Apply the fire triangle to putting out fires. [O3]

Skills development

- Thinking scientifically: consider the quality of evidence
- Working scientifically: make predictions
- Learner development: communicate effectively

Resources needed equipment and materials as detailed in the Technician's notes; pens; poster paper; Worksheet 2.4.14; Technician's notes 2.4.14

Digital resources Quick starter; Interactive activity: Match the method of putting out a fire to what it removes from the fire triangle; Hangman: Key vocabulary game

Common misconceptions Electricity is a fuel.

Key vocabulary chemical reaction, fuel, combustion, fire triangle

Teaching and learning

Engage

- Show a video clip of a fire being started. Alternatively light a small fire using a fire stick. Ask the students to **watch** the video first. Then ask them to **describe** what they have seen with a partner. [O1]
- Show the video for a second time and ask the students to **discuss** with a partner how to explain what was happening. This would be a good opportunity to emphasise the difference between 'describe' and 'explain' to students. [O1]

  'Explain' could be scaffolded for lower-attaining students with the use of 'because' in an explanation.

- Define 'combustion' as the scientific name for burning. [O1]

Challenge and develop

- Now light a Bunsen burner using a match – then light a candle with a burning splint. Ask the students to **consider** the similarities between the fire, the lit Bunsen and the burning candle. Ask pairs to **identify** three things that are essential for each of the fires. Pairs form fours and **share** their ideas. [O1&2]
- Ask the groups of to **share** their ideas across the class, with each group **identifying** one of the essential factors for burning. Take feedback, asking those with three factors to share their ideas first. Encourage the other students to contribute in terms of **agreeing** or **disagreeing**. [O1&2]
- Ask the students to read about the fire triangle in the Student Book. Ask them to **explain** the fire triangle to a partner in their own words. The students should then answer questions 1–5. Worksheet 2.4.14 could also be attempted here. [O2]

Chapter 4: Explaining Chemical Changes

Explain

- Set up a demonstration of a candle burning in a jar under water. Ask the students to **predict** what will happen to the candle and the water. They watch the demonstration and then **reflect on** whether or not their prediction was correct. [O2&3]
- Show the students a bigger bell jar and ask them to **predict** how the demonstration will differ from that using the smaller jar. The students watch the demonstration and **reflect on** whether their prediction was correct. (Although there is the additional effect of expansion and contraction of gases inside the bell jar, it is best to focus on any difference due to reaction with oxygen at this stage.) Use questions and answers to check understanding and dispel any misunderstandings. [O2&3]

Consolidate and apply

- Ask the students to work individually to **design** a safety poster to educate campers about the use of barbeques and campfires, and how to put fires out. [O1, 2&3]

Extend

- Ask students able to progress further to **research** the effect on the water level of the changing temperature inside the bell jar when the candle is lit and then goes out.

Plenary suggestions

Hot seat Each student **plans** a question linked to the lesson. One student is selected to be in the hot seat and the others take turns to ask their question. If a question is answered incorrectly, the student asking the question takes over in the hot seat. [O1, 2&3]

Answers to Student Book questions

1. new products are formed; it is irreversible
2. a) burning b) a material that can be burned to release energy
3. this provides more oxygen for the reaction
4. a) friction between the flint and steel b) wood
5. a) removes the fuel b) takes away some of the heat
6. candle wax
7. water rises inside the jar; and the level drops outside the bell jar; because of the oxygen used up (also the effect of hot air cooling inside the jar)
8. it will burn for longer in a larger jar; because more oxygen is available

Answers to Worksheet 2.4.14

1. a) labels to show fuel; heat; oxygen
   b) i) e.g. coal, oil, gas, wood ii) using a flame; friction iii) fanning
2. a) heat is removed b) oxygen is reduced c) no fuel d) oxygen is reduced
3. description of combustion; and an explanation of how to remove some/each of factors of fire triangle

Chapter 4: Explaining Chemical Changes

4.15 Understanding combustion and the use of fuels

Lesson overview

Learning objectives

- Identify applications of combustion reactions.
- Identify fuels used in different applications.
- Compare the energy content of different fuels.

Learning outcomes

- Describe some applications of combustion reactions. [O1]
- Identify the source of fuels in different combustion reactions. [O2]
- Analyse data to compare the energy of different fuels. [O3]

Skills development

- Thinking scientifically: analyse data
- Working scientifically: interpret evidence
- Learner development: act responsibly

Resources needed pictures of examples of combustion; mini-whiteboards (optional); equipment and materials as detailed in the Technician's notes; Worksheet 2.4.15; Practical sheet 2.4.15; Technician's notes 2.4.15

Digital resources Quick starter; Interactive activity: Exothermic or endothermic? Drag the phrases to the type of reaction they're associated with; Slideshow: So many fuels - Fossil fuels and plants; Interactive activity: Place, in order, the fuels that you think hold the most to the least energy (in Joules/Kg)

Key vocabulary exothermic, energy, alcohol

Teaching and learning

Engage

- Show the students some pictures of examples of combustion and ask them to **identify** the fuels. Mini whiteboards could be used for this activity. [O2]

Challenge and develop

- **Group work** Arrange the students in pairs and ask them to **brainstorm** as many applications of burning as possible. As a class, compile a list. [O1]

Explain

- Ask the groups to **consider** and **discuss** how we can compare the efficiency of different fuels in these situations. Take feedback from across the class. [O2&3]
- Show the students the spirit burners containing different alcohols and ask them to **discuss** in pairs how we could compare the efficiency of the fuels. [O3]
- They then use Practical sheet 2.4.15 to **investigate** one alcohol. The pairs **pool** their results so that all have data for each alcohol – they then **calculate** the energy transferred by each. [O3]

    For lower-attaining students, the maximum temperature reached could be measured for a fixed mass of alcohol contained in the burners.

Key Stage 3 Science Teacher Pack 2 © HarperCollins*Publishers* Limited 2014

Chapter 4: Explaining Chemical Changes

Consolidate and apply

- The students work individually to **write a conclusion** for the investigation. [O3]
- Ask them to use a show of hands about which fuel they would buy. Introduce some other factors – such as the comparative costs of fuels or their availability, and ask the students to **reconsider** their choice. [O3]

Extend

- Ask students able to progress further to **evaluate** the experiment to improve repeatability and reproducibility.

Plenary suggestions

Learning triangle The students work individually to construct a learning triangle. They should draw a large triangle with a smaller inverted triangle that just fits inside (so that they have four triangles). In the outer triangles, they write:

- something they've seen
- something they've done
- something they've discussed
- then, in the central triangle, something they've learned. [O1, 2&3]

Answers to Student Book questions

1. one that releases energy
2. a suitable table displaying uses such as transportation, fireworks, generating electricity
3. a fuel is burned; and energy is released. This is used, for example, to boil water. The steam produced drives a turbine, which can generate electricity
4. a) e.g. coal b) wood
5. one that can power a power-generation plant – e.g. coal, gas, renewable fuels such as wind, solar
6. one part of ethanol; for every nine parts of petrol
7. sensible suggestions such as: the temperature increase; maximum temperature reached; mass of alcohol used
8. alcohols are highly flammable
9. cost; availability; cleanliness

Answers to Worksheet 2.4.15

1. cooking; fireworks; transportation; trucks; electricity
2. a) coal b) crude oil (diesel) c) wood d) wax e) gas
3. check the students' information; make sure they have supplied referenced sources

Chapter 4: Explaining Chemical Changes

4.16 Exploring the effects of burning

Lesson overview

Learning objectives

- Summarise combustion using an equation.
- Compare complete and incomplete combustion.
- Explain what is meant by the conservation of mass.

Learning outcomes

- Summarise and explain the complete combustion equation. [O1]
- Compare the reactants and products of complete and incomplete combustion. [O2]
- Explain the Law of Conservation of Mass and how it can be proved. [O3]

Skills development

- Thinking scientifically: analyse data
- Working scientifically: develop explanations
- Learner development: plan progress

Resources needed equipment and materials as detailed in the Technician's notes; building bricks such as Lego; Worksheet 2.4.16 (second page copied onto card); Practical sheet 2.4.16; Technician's notes 2.4.16

Digital resources Quick starter; Interactive activity: Drag the substances to the correct group - hydrocarbon or not

Common misconceptions Mass is lost when we burn things. The material being burned is 'lost'.

Key vocabulary hydrocarbon, complete combustion, oxidation, incomplete combustion

Teaching and learning

Engage

- Set up a demonstration of burning as described in Technician's notes 2.4.16. Ask the students to **observe** what happens carefully. First ask them what the demonstration shows. If necessary, remind them about the limewater test for carbon dioxide, and tell them that anhydrous copper sulfate tests for water. [O1]
- Ask the students to **describe** what they have seen – then ask them to **explain** their observations. Ask them to **suggest** a word equation for this reaction and try to build up an equation as a class. [O1]

Challenge and develop

- Use the Student Book to **explore** the equation for complete combustion. [O1]
- Use building bricks to **explore** the equation further and show that same atoms are present in the reactants and products – but they have been rearranged. The students can do the task 1 of Worksheet 2.4.16. [O1]
- Ask the students to **read** the 'Incomplete combustion' section in the Student Book, and then complete tasks 2 and 3 of Worksheet 2.4.16. [O2]
- The students can then answer questions 1–6 in the Student Book verbally so that you can assess their understanding. [O1&2]

Explain

- **Pair work** Ask pairs of students to **consider** and then **discuss** what will happen to a mass of steel wool when it is burned. [O2]
- Ask each pair to **read the instructions** on Practical sheet 2.4.16. They can then **carry out** the experiment and **record** the masses of the crucible and steel wool before and after burning. [O2]

Chapter 4: Explaining Chemical Changes

- The students answer the questions on Practical sheet 2.4.16 and state whether or not their results support the theory of the conservation of mass. [O3]

Consolidate and apply

- Tell the students that the theory has been proved and ask them to **suggest** why the results may not have supported it. [O3]
- Ask the students to read the 'Conservation of mass' section in the Student Book. Allow time for them to **discuss** in small groups and then take feedback about whether or not the data supports the conservation of mass theory. [O1]
- Ask the students to write two sentences to compare the experiments and **explain** the different findings. [O1]

Extend

- Ask students able to progress further to **evaluate** the experiment in more detail and **identify** potential sources of error. They should **suggest** how these could be minimised. [O3]

Plenary suggestions

Equations Provide the students with all of the cards from page 2 of Worksheet 2.4.16, showing all the reactants and products for complete and for incomplete combustion. Ask them to work in pairs to arrange both of the equations as quickly as possible. [O1&2]

How have I worked? Ask the students to **reflect on** the way that they worked in this task and to consider if they could have worked more effectively. Share some ideas across the class. [O1&2]

Answers to Student Book questions

1. sufficient oxygen 2. the fuel reacts with/gains oxygen 3. the greenhouse effect 4. water
5. complete combustion releases more energy; it does not release poisonous carbon monoxide unlike incomplete combustion; it does not release carbon (which can irritate the lungs) unlike incomplete combustion
6.

Complete combustion	Incomplete combustion
water	water
carbon dioxide	carbon monoxide (allow also 'some carbon dioxide')
	carbon

7. yes; the increase in mass was not significant
8. repeat the experiment; to check that the results are similar
9. the mass increases slightly as magnesium is oxidised to magnesium oxide

Answers to Worksheet 2.4.16

1. a) hydrocarbon + oxygen (either order) → carbon dioxide + water (either order)
   b) carbon; hydrogen   c) coal, oil, gas
2. a) there is insufficient oxygen for complete combustion
   b) hydrocarbon + oxygen → carbon monoxide + carbon + water (and some carbon dioxide)
   c) Hydrocarbon, oxygen (less in incomplete) and water are involved in both *complete* and *incomplete combustion*. Carbon and carbon monoxide are only involved in *incomplete* combustion. (Carbon dioxide is mainly involved in *complete* combustion; could be grouped in both.)
3. a) i) Carbon dioxide and water are produced.   ii) *Anhydrous copper sulfate* turns blue; water produced; *limewater* stays clear; no significant amount of carbon dioxide is produced.
   b) carbon (soot) harmful to lungs; carbon monoxide toxic (attached to red blood cells)

Chapter 4: Explaining Chemical Changes

4.17 Understanding acid rain

Lesson overview

Learning objectives

- Describe how combustion can cause acid rain.
- Describe the effects of acid rain.
- Explain the effects of acid rain.

Learning outcomes

- Describe how combustion contributes to acid rain. [O1]
- Describe the effects of acid rain. [O2]
- Explain the effects of acid rain. [O3]

Skills development

- Thinking scientifically: ask questions
- Working scientifically: n/a
- Learner development: communicate effectively

Resources needed large sheets of paper and pens; cress seeds grown in weak acid, strong acid and distilled water; research materials such as textbooks, newspaper articles, access to the internet (optional); Worksheet 2.4.17

Digital resources Quick starter; Slideshow: How does burning affect rain?; Interactive activity: Re-order the process of acid rain formation from sulfur dioxide; Hangman: Key vocabulary game

Common misconceptions Acid rain is a strong enough acid to burn your skin.

Key vocabulary sulfur dioxide, acid rain

Teaching and learning

Engage

- Show the students three samples of cress and explain that one sample was grown using distilled water, one was grown using weak acid and one was grown using strong acid. Ask the students to **identify** each sample. [O2]
- Ask them to **suggest** what the lesson is about. Bounce ideas around the students, eliciting a link between combustion from previous lessons, acid and plants.

Challenge and develop

- **Group work** Arrange the students in threes. Describe a scenario about acid rain damaging plants in Scandinavia, when the pollution causing it was produced in the UK. [O1]
- The groups **produce** an annotated poster to **explain** how the acid rain was formed and how it caused acid rain in another country. Give the groups clues as they need them. For example, 'fossil fuels contain sulfur', 'sulfur combines with oxygen when its burned to form sulfur dioxide', 'sulfur dioxide dissolves in water to form sulfuric acid'. Once the groups have attempted all that they can, give them the Student Book and ask them to read the 'How does burning affect rain?' section and **add information** to their poster. [O1]
- The students can complete tasks 1 and 2 of Worksheet 2.4.17 as reinforcement. [O1]

Chapter 4: Explaining Chemical Changes

Explain

- Ask the students to **carry out** research into:
  - the effects of acid rain
  - treatment of acid rain
  - prevention of acid rain.
- Encourage groups to **collaborate** and **share** the workload. This research could be done using textbooks, newspaper articles or the internet, for example [O2&3]
- The students return to their groups and **teach** each other what they **learned**. Other students in the group should take notes. [O2&3]

Consolidate and apply

- Ask the students to **write** a newspaper article to educate people about how acid rain could be prevented. Encourage them to write in a newspaper style while keeping the article factual. This is outlined in task 3 of Worksheet 2.4.17. [O1, 2&3]

Extend

- Ask students able to progress further to **consider** whether fossil fuels should have their costs increased to try to dissuade people from using them. They should **back up** their opinion with evidence.

Plenary suggestions

Hot seat Ask each student to develop a question based on acid rain. Choose one student to be in the hot seat to answer questions. Each student takes a turn to ask a question. If a question is answered incorrectly, the questioner becomes the new person in the hot seat. [O1, 2&3]

Answers to Student Book questions

1. carbon dioxide; sulfur dioxide; nitrogen oxides
2. gases rise into the atmosphere; and dissolve in water
3. clouds can travel huge distances; before acid rain falls
4. a) damages leaves; removes nutrients from the soils; adds harmful chemicals to the soil
   b) can cause respiratory diseases
   c) can wear away stone
5. Damaged leaves mean that photosynthesis cannot happen efficiently; and plants slowly die (nutrients are washed away slowly, harmful chemicals added slowly).
6. fossil fuels are used to generate electricity; we would need to use less electricity
7. suggestions such as: expensive to set up; don't generate as much electricity; strong wind and sunshine not always available
8. sensible suggestion such as adding calcium oxide to a sample of acid rain; and measuring the pH change

Answers to Worksheet 2.4.17

1. a) C; A; D; E; B
   b) nitric acid
   c) clouds containing the acid; are carried long distances by prevailing winds
2. a) statues and structures are damaged
   b) the plants cannot photosynthesise; and so they die
   c) plants absorb aluminium; which poisons them
3. a) article to include ideas such as reduce amount of fossil fuels burned by cars, power stations etc
   b) letter to include ideas about being difficult to reduce the amount of transport, explanation of why we need power stations etc

Chapter 4: Explaining Chemical Changes

4.18 Checking students' progress

The 'Checking your progress' section in the Student Book indicates the key ideas developed in this chapter and shows how students progress to more complex levels. It is provided to support students in:

- identifying those ideas
- developing a sense of their current level of understanding
- developing a sense what the next steps in their learning are.

It is designed either to be used at the end of a chapter to support an overall view of the progress, or alternatively during the teaching of the unit. Students can self assess or peer assess using this as a basis.

It would be helpful if students can be encouraged to provide evidence from their understanding or their notes to support their judgements. In some cases it may be useful to explore the difference in the descriptors for a particular idea so that students can see what makes for a 'higher outcome'.

It may be useful with some descriptors to provide examples from the specific work done, such as an experiment undertaken or an explanation developed and recorded. If marking and feedback use similar ideas and phrases this will enable students to relate specific marking to a more general sense of progress.

Chapter 4: Explaining Chemical Changes

To make good progress in understanding science students need to focus on these ideas and skills:

Students who are making modest progress will be able to:	Students who are making good progress will be able to:	Students who are making excellent progress will be able to:
Identify some everyday substances that contain acids and alkalis.	Explain what all acids have in common and what all alkalis have in common.	Evaluate the hazards posed by some acids and alkalis and how these risks may be reduced.
Give an example of an indicator and state why indicators are useful.	Explain what an indicator is and analyse results when using an indicator.	Compare the effectiveness of different indicators.
Describe some examples of neutralisation.	Describe the changes to indicators when acids and alkalis are mixed.	Explain the changes to indicators in terms of pH when acids and alkalis are mixed.
Recognise that water is one product of neutralisation.	Explain the formation of salt and water during neutralisation, giving some examples of common salts.	Predict the reactants or products of different neutralisation reactions.
Describe the observations of reactions between acids and metal, and acids and carbonate, that tell us that a chemical change is taking place.	Explain the general reaction between an acid and a metal, and between an acid and a carbonate, using generic equations.	Summarise specific reactions between acids and metals and between acids and carbonates using word equations and particle drawings.
Describe what indigestion remedies are and explain how they work.	Design an investigation to compare the effectiveness of indigestion remedies.	Analyse data about indigestion remedies to decide which remedy is the most effective.
Summarise the reactants and products of complete combustion.	Compare the reactants and products of complete and incomplete combustion.	Explain the Law of Conservation of Mass and how it can be proven.
Describe how combustion contributes to acid rain.	Describe the effects of acid rain.	Explain, using an equation, the effects of acid rain.

Chapter 4: Explaining Chemical Changes

4.19 Answers to Student Book Questions

This table provides answers to the Questions section at the end of Chapter 4 of the Student Book. It also shows how different questions assess attainment in terms of the focus and style of a question as well as its context. Question level analysis can indicate students' proficiency in approaching different aspects of scientific understanding and different types of answer.

Q	Answer	Marks available	Focus: Knowledge & understanding	Focus: Application	Focus: Evaluation of evidence	Style: Objective test question	Style: Short written answer	Style: Longer written answer	Context: Acids and alkalis	Context: Indicators and pH	Context: Reactions of acids	Context: Combustion
1	d	1	x			x			x			
2	a	1	x			x			x			
3	c	1	x			x				x		
4	a	1	x			x					x	
5	acid + alkali → salt + water	2	x				x				x	
6	Heartburn is caused by (stomach) acid (moving up from the stomach)	1	x				x				x	
	the alkali neutralises the acid	1	x				x				x	
7	Any four from: • fossil fuels are burned • sulfur in the fuels reacts with oxygen in the air to form sulfur dioxide • sulfur dioxide reacts with water in clouds • to form sulfuric acid • this falls as acid rain Or similar using nitrogen oxides and nitric acid as examples	4	x					x				x
8	b	1		x		x					x	
9	c	1		x		x					x	
10	b	1		x		x						x
11	limewater (turns milky)	1		x		x					x	

Chapter 4: Explaining Chemical Changes

Q	Answer	Marks available	Focus: Knowledge & understanding	Focus: Application	Focus: Evaluation of evidence	Style: Objective test question	Style: Short written answer	Style: Longer written answer	Context: Acids and alkalis	Context: Indicators and pH	Context: Reactions of acids	Context: Combustion
12	Alkali	1		x			x		x			
	it has a pH higher than 7 / many alkalis feel soapy	1		x			x		x			
13	Concentrated acid contains more acid particels/dilute acid contains fewer acid particles (dilute contains more water)	1		x			x		x			
	so more acid particles to react	1		x			x		x			
14	Any four from: • correctly labelled fire trangle • add no more fuel and wait until fire goes out • cover the fire (e.g. with sand) to stop oxygen getting in • reduce heat by pouring on water • any other sensible suggestion linked to fire triangle	4	x					x				x
15	Unknown metalis more reactive than zinc but less reactive than calcium	1			x		x				x	
	reaction is more vigorous than with zinc but less vigorous than with calcium	1			x		x				x	
16	B, A, C	1			x			x		x		
	B has different colours in acid, alkali and neutral	1			x			x		x		
	A is different in acid and alkali, but not alkali and neutral	1			x			x		x		
	C is the same in all so can't distinguish acids and alkalis	1			x			x		x		
	Total possible:	30	12	12	6	8	10	12	6	5	10	9

Chapter 5: Exploring Contact and Non-Contact Forces

5.1 Introduction

When and how to use these pages

The Introduction in the Student Book indicates some of the ideas and skills in this topic area that students will already have met from KS2 or from previous KS3 work, and provides an indication of what they will be studying in this chapter. *Ideas you have met before* is not intended to comprehensively summarise of all the prior ideas, but rather to point out a few of the key ones and to support the view that scientific understanding is progressive. Even though students might be meeting contexts that are new to them, they can often use existing ideas to start to make sense of them.

In this chapter you will find out indicates some of the new ideas that the chapter will introduce. Again, it isn't a detailed summary of content or even an index page. Its purpose is more to act as a 'trailer' and generate some interest.

The outcomes, then, will be recognition of prior learning that can be built on, and interest in finding out more.

There are a number of ways this can be used. You might, for example:

- Use *Ideas you have met before* as the basis for a revision lesson as you start the first new topic.
- Use *Ideas you have met before* as the centre of spider diagrams, to which students can add examples, experiments they might have done previously or what they found interesting.
- Make a note of any unfamiliar/difficult terms and return to these in the relevant lessons.
- Use *In this chapter you will find out* to ask students questions such as:
  - Why is this important?
  - How could it be used?
  - What might we be doing in this topic?

Overview of the chapter

In this chapter, the students learn about the fields that exist due to magnetism, electrostatic charge and gravity.

By using the ideas of particles and positive/negative charge, the students learn about the causes of electrostatic effects. They study applications such as photocopying and dangers such as lightning.

The students learn how to calculate pressure using the size of a force and the area over which it acts. They learn about the effect of depth on pressure in liquids and some of the consequences of this. They learn about variations in pressure and its effect on weather. The students begin to interpret weather charts with high/ low pressure systems and isobars.

The effect of density on floating and sinking is explained, and the students compare upthrust forces when objects are lowered into water. They learn about the significance of the displacement of water.

Obstacles to learning

The students may need extra guidance with the following difficult concepts:

- **Magnetism** Many metals are not magnetic. The Earth's North Pole is actually a magnetic south-seeking (S) pole. Gravity and magnetism are fundamentally different.
- **Gravity** Many students have difficulty explaining why heavy and light objects fall at the same rate, even though more massive objects have a bigger force acting on them.
- **Electrostatic charge** An electrostatically charged object can attract uncharged objects by inducing charge.
- **Pressure** Although force and pressure are linked, they are not the same thing. Air is made of particles that have mass and weight, and these contribute to atmospheric pressure. Pressure has a variety of different units – the students will calculate in N/m^2 where $1\ N/m^2 = 1$ pascal (Pa). They are also likely to encounter kilopascals, bars, millibars and pounds per square inch (psi). On a global scale, wind circulates in pressure systems rather than flowing from high pressure to low pressure.

Chapter 5: Exploring Contact and Non-Contact Forces

	Topic title	Overarching objectives
2	Exploring magnets	Non-contact forces: forces between magnets Magnetic poles, attraction and repulsion
3	Understanding magnetic fields	Magnetic poles, attraction and repulsion Magnetic fields by plotting with compass, representation by field lines Earth's magnetism
4	Investigating static charge	Non-contact forces: forces due to static electricity Separation of positive or negative charges when objects are rubbed together: transfer of electrons, forces between charged objects
5	Explaining static charge	
6	Understanding electrostatic fields	Non-contact forces: forces due to static electricity Separation of positive or negative charges when objects are rubbed together: transfer of electrons, forces between charged objects The idea of electric field, forces acting across the space between objects not in contact
7	Applying what we know about electrostatics	
8	Exploring gravity on Earth	Non-contact forces: gravity forces acting at a distance on Earth and in space
9	Applying our understanding of gravity to space travel	
11	Exploring pressure on a solid surface	Pressure measured by ratio of force over area – acting normal to any surface
12	Calculating pressure	
13	Exploring pressure in a liquid	Pressure in liquids, increasing with depth; upthrust effects, floating and sinking
14	Explaining floating and sinking	
15	Exploring gas pressure	Atmospheric pressure; decreases with increase of height as weight of air above decreases with height
16	Working with pressure	

Chapter 5: Exploring Contact and Non-Contact Forces

5.2 Exploring magnets

Lesson overview

Learning objectives

- Explain magnetic attraction and repulsion.
- Apply the concept of poles and the laws of attraction and repulsion.
- Predict the effects of arrangements of magnetic poles.

Learning outcomes

- Describe the effects of attraction and repulsion in relation to magnetic poles. [O1]
- Explain how magnetic poles cause attraction and repulsion and why this is a non-contact force. [O2]
- Apply the concepts of poles and magnetic forces to various contexts as examples of non-contact forces. [O3]

Skills development

- Thinking scientifically: ask questions
- Working scientifically: make predictions
- Learner development: ask questions

Resources needed equipment and materials as detailed in the Technician's notes; Worksheet 2.5.2; Practical sheet 2.5.2; Technician's notes 2.5.2

Digital resources Quick starter; Slideshow: Magnetic levitation - A look at the use of magnetic repulsion and attraction in the operation of Maglev trains; Interactive activity: Drag the statements about magnets into the correct true or false groups

Common misconceptions All metals are magnetic.

Key vocabulary non-contact force, attract, pole, repel

Teaching and learning

Engage

- Demonstrate a few examples of forces – e.g. a push, a pull, the friction of a book on a slope, an object falling, a magnet deflecting a compass. Identify the students' ideas by asking them to **sort** the forces into two groups – contact and non-contact. [O2]

- Show the students a suspended magnet being affected by a second magnet. Ask them to **record** and **share** any facts about this that they are sure about and anything they would like to ask questions about. [O1&2]

Challenge and develop

- Allow the students to test some of their ideas from the starter activity by **exploring** the behaviour of a suspended magnet when a second magnet is brought towards it. They can then make any desired changes to their recorded ideas.

  Ensure that they consider the following questions:
    - From what distance can a magnetic force have an effect?
    - What are the rules of attraction and repulsion between the two poles on separate magnets and between a magnet and magnetic materials? [O1&2]

  Higher-attaining students could **devise** a means of detecting tiny magnetic effects.

- Students can then fully **investigate** how the force of attraction between two magnets varies with distance, and also **compare** how different materials allow magnetic force to pass through them. They can use Practical sheet 2.5.2. [O3]

Chapter 5: Exploring Contact and Non-Contact Forces

Explain

- The students **explain** the difference between magnets attracting and repelling. [O1&2]
- They **explain** how their observations support the idea that magnetism is a non-contact force. [O2&3]

Consolidate and apply

- The students can do tasks 1 and 2 on Worksheet 2.5.2. [O1&2]
- Ask the students to **explain** how they can identify the poles on an unlabelled magnet. [O1]

    You could ask higher-attaining students to **suggest** a method of **comparing** the strength of different magnets (task 3 of Worksheet 2.5.2). This need not be carried out at this stage because this topic will be revisited in Chapter 6. [O3]

Extend

- Ask students able to progress further to **predict**, **test** and then **explain** how they could distinguish two apparently identical steel bars, when one is a magnet, without using additional equipment. (They would need to test magnet ends to middles.) [O2&3]

Plenary suggestions

Whole class review Ask the students to **review** and finalise statements from the starter activity and add some new statements. [O1, 2&3]

Pair talk/pairs to fours Demonstrate the force from a supermagnet and its ability to work at distance. Ask the students to produce brief **explanations** of the effect. [O2&3]

Answers to Student Book questions

1. non-contact, pushing or pulling   2. iron, nickel, cobalt, steel   3. north-seeking (N); south-seeking (S)
4. like poles repel; opposite poles attract   5. a) attract (not 'stick')   b) attract   c) no effect
6. A hanging magnet experiences less friction than one on a bench.
7. Contact forces act only when objects are touching e.g. a hand pushing a door, air touching a moving object.

    Non-contact forces can act over a distance even when there is no direct contact e.g. gravity pulling on an unsupported object.
8. Two opposite magnet poles attract one another; two like magnet poles repel one another. ('Attract' is more appropriate than 'stick' because it is a non-contact force. The orientation of the poles affects whether or not they attract.)
9. *similarities*: both are non-contact forces

    differences: gravitational forces only attract, they cannot repel; gravitational forces act on all objects with mass, but magnetic forces only affect magnetic materials

Answers to Worksheet 2.5.2

1. a) true for metals such as iron, nickel, cobalt, steel; false for others
    b) false; both poles attract unmagnetised magnetic materials
    c) true, but not because everything is turning   d) true   e) false; it is a non-contact force
2. a) two pulling arrows in opposite directions; between the magnets
    b) two pushing arrows between the magnets; equal and opposite   c) as for (a); but shorter arrows
    d) four small pushing arrows; two equal and opposite pushing arrows between each pair of like poles
    e) four small pulling arrows; two equal and opposite pulling arrows between each pair of unlike poles
3. there are many potential responses, students should devise fair tests

Answers to Practical sheet 2.5.2

1. N and N repel; S and S repel; N and S attract; magnet poles attract magnetic materials.
2. Other materials between the magnets generally have no apparent effect. A few materials, such as steel, do reduce the force because they redirect the field over a larger area so it becomes weaker. The thickness of a material placed between magnets does affect the force because the field weakens with distance.
3. for example, put a magnet on a sensitive top pan balance, bring a magnetic material incrementally towards the magnet and note the effect on the reading on the balance

Chapter 5: Exploring Contact and Non-Contact Forces

5.3 Understanding magnetic fields

Lesson overview

Learning objectives
- Describe magnetic fields.
- Explore the field around a magnet.
- Explain the shape, size and direction of magnetic fields.

Learning outcomes
- Record and display ideas about magnetic fields. [O1]
- Explain the presence of a magnetic field and indicate how it varies with regard to field lines, direction and strength. [O2]
- Evaluate the concept of magnetic field and force lines. [O3]

Skills development
- Thinking scientifically: understand how theories develop
- Working scientifically: develop explanations
- Learner development: collaborate effectively

Resources needed iron filings in a pepper pot; bar magnets; horseshoe and/or circular magnets; plotting compasses; pencils; A4 card or paper; Worksheet 2.5.3; Practical sheet 2.5.3; Technician's notes 2.5.3

Digital resources Quick starter; Interactive activity: Complete the sentences about magnetic fields

Common misconceptions The Earth's gravity and magnetism are the same.

Key vocabulary magnetic field, strength, field lines, core

Teaching and learning

Engage
- Ask the students to **predict**, **record** and **explain** what happens if iron filings are sprinkled over a piece of card with a bar magnet underneath. After watching a demonstration, they decide which predictions were accurate. *Safety note*: iron filings must be kept way from the eyes; hands should be washed immediately after handling. [O1]
- Encourage the students to **consider** how theories develop by identifying new ideas or questions – for example:
  - What do the lines in the pattern show? (Forces are present which arranged the filings.)
  - Why are there more iron filings closer to the poles of the magnet? (The magnetism is stronger at the poles.) [O1&2]
- Introduce the term 'magnetic field' (an area where a magnetic force exists). [O1&2]

Challenge and develop
- In pairs, the students use plotting compasses to **explore** the magnetic field around a bar magnet. See Practical sheet 2.5.3 for details. [O1&2]

  Higher-attaining students should be able to identify where the field is weaker independently.

- Ask the students to **explain** how they could decide if a magnetic field is flat or three-dimensional. [O2]
- **Pairs to fours** Forming groups of four, the students **develop** explanations and **develop** collaboration, the students **discuss** what they think about the Earth's magnetic field. After this, refer them to Figure 2.5.3c in the Student Book showing the Earth's magnetic field. They **identify** where the two pairs agreed and disagreed. [O2&3]

Chapter 5: Exploring Contact and Non-Contact Forces

Higher-attaining students should be able to take on different collaborative roles.

Explain

- Ask the original pairs of students to **describe** the magnetic field model of the Earth's magnetism shown in Figure 2.5.3c and **explain** its strengths and weaknesses (question 8 in the Student Book). For example, it can show the strength and extent of the magnetic field; direction arrows of force lines can be misleading because N and S poles both attract magnetic materials; gaps between force lines suggest there is no magnetic force there; the Earth's core is a moving fluid, rather than a fixed magnet; the magnetic and geographic poles are not at exactly the same positions. [O3]

Consolidate and apply

- Ask pairs of students to **explore** the magnetic field around a horseshoe magnet or a circular magnet using a plotting compass. [O2&3]
- Ask them to **predict** the field pattern around pairs of magnets N to N and N to S (task 2 of Worksheet 2.5.3). They could use a plotting compass to **test** their ideas. [O1&2]

Extend

- Ask students able to progress further to attempt the more challenging questions in task 3 of Worksheet 2.5.3. [O2&3]

Plenary suggestions

Learning triangle At the end of the lesson ask the students to draw a large triangle with a smaller inverted triangle that just fits inside it (so they have four triangles). Ask them to **think back** over the lesson and identify in the outer three triangles something they've seen, something they've done and something they've discussed. They then add in the central triangle something they've learned. [O1, 2&3]

Answers to Student Book questions

1. the shape and the relative strength of the magnetic field; they do not show the direction of the magnetic force
2. The magnetic field is stronger near the poles.
3. steel; nickel
4. The outer core contains liquid iron-rich materials which flow; electric currents are created and produce a magnetic field.
5. both magnetism and gravity produce a force; which declines in strength with distance. Gravity is stronger; acts over a greater distance; is always an attractive force; and it acts on all objects
6. observe the behaviour of a compass on space probes that fly near to other planets
7. Models make it easier to visualise and understand things. For example: the particle model for states of matter; a scale model of the Solar System; various models for the behaviour of electric currents.
8. see the 'Explain' section above

Answers to Worksheet 2.5.3

1. a) arrowed curved lines from N to S; field lines closer together at the poles
   b) i) close to the S pole ii) close to the N pole iii) equidistant from each pole iv) far away from the magnet
2. a) *first pair*: lines running between the poles; arrowed N to S; *second pair*: opposing lines bending back round towards the S pole of each magnet
   b) anywhere with a high density of field lines
   c) exactly in between the two N poles of the second pair (opposing magnets)
   d) find the place where a small iron/steel object experiences no force; where there is no effect on a plotting compass
3. a) it is unmagnetised steel; the effects of N and S balance. Evidence: the behaviour of a plotting compass or iron filings
   b) the force would be reduced; because the field lines are further apart
   c) Magnetic materials will affect the compass; because they overcome the effect of the Earth's weak magnetic field. Use the compass away from suspect materials; test the compass in a variety of positions and look for consistent readings.

Answers to Practical sheet 2.5.3

1. away from N pole towards S pole
2. the strength of the field; the closer the lines, the stronger the field

Chapter 5: Exploring Contact and Non-Contact Forces

5.4 Investigating static charge

Lesson overview

Learning objectives

- Recognise the effects of static charge.
- Explain how static charge can be generated.
- Use evidence to develop ideas about static charge.

Learning outcomes

- Describe how static charge can be produced and detected. [O1]
- Explain the charge mechanism at work in various contexts. [O2]
- Compare static charge to magnetism in terms of non-contact forces and fields. [O3]

Skills development

- Thinking scientifically: understand how theories develop
- Working scientifically: record evidence
- Learner development: ask questions

Resources needed equipment and materials as detailed in the Technician's notes; Worksheet 2.5.4; Practical sheet 2.5.4; Technician's notes 2.5.4

Digital resources Quick starter; Interactive activity: Drag the materials to classify them as conductors or insulators

Common misconceptions

Key vocabulary charge, static electricity, field, attract, repel

Teaching and learning

Engage

- Stimulate the students' **thinking** with a simple demonstration of an effect of static electricity – e.g. rubbing a balloon on a jumper and sticking it to a wall. From prior knowledge they should be able to **identify** this as static electricity and also give other examples such as charging from a carpet and discharging through a door handle. [O1]

Challenge and develop

- The students **experiment** with rubbing balloons to **collect evidence** to decide if contact or non-contact forces are involved and if attraction, repulsion or both can occur. They can use Practical sheet 2.5.4. [O1, 2&3]
- They then **test** a variety of materials to find out which can be charged by rubbing and attempting to pick up small scraps of paper. [O1&2]
- They **observe** that static electricity can also involve repulsion by suspending a changed nylon rod in a paper cradle/thread so that it can rotate freely and then bringing another charged nylon rod towards it. [O2&3]
- Ask the students to **compare** different situations in which there is a static electric charge and identify what creates the charge (rubbing, friction). [O2]

  Higher-attaining students may be able to **suggest** ideas about charged particles being transferred.

Explain

- The students work in groups of three to **discuss** and **explain** the ideas they have discovered about static electricity, and then **present** them to the class, possibly as a slideshow. [O1, 2&3]

Key Stage 3 Science Teacher Pack 2

Chapter 5: Exploring Contact and Non-Contact Forces

Consolidate and apply
- The students can do tasks 1 and 2 of Worksheet 2.5.4. [O1&2]
- Ask them to **suggest** how they could find out if surfaces (walls, screens, benches) around the room are statically charged or not. (Test if scraps of paper/dust are attracted.) [O1&2]
- **Pair talk** Ask the students to **discuss** and **compare** the effects of static charge with magnetism in task 3 of Worksheet 2.5.4 and be prepared to **feed back** their ideas. [O3]

    Higher-attaining students may be able to **compare** and **contrast** fields due to static charge, magnetism and gravity.

Extend
- Ask students able to progress further to **suggest** or **find out** how static electricity could be removed from a charged item. [O2]

Plenary suggestions
'I think that is…because…' Ask the students to **summarise the evidence** in relation to the following statements, and to accept or reject the statements as appropriate: [O1, 2&3]
- Static electricity exerts a non-contact force.
- Objects can be charged by rubbing.
- Some charged objects repel each other, some attract.
- When an object is charged it has a force field around it.

Answers to Student Book questions

1. metals; carbon
2. still or stationary
3. it must not be in contact with another conductor
4. an electrostatic field; a force of attraction
5. the force can act from a distance; for example when scraps of paper jump to a charged comb
6. suspend one comb on a thread (non-conducting) and bring the other close to it
7. both create a field that can exert a non-contact force; which can be attractive or repulsive
8. Compare how much deflection results when an opposing object is brought close to a similar suspended one; some adjustments for weight may be necessary to make the comparison fair.
9. TV screens become charged when the TV is switched on; because it is insulated from the rest of the TV; and the surroundings; the charge attracts dust particles. Walls do not become statically charged; because they lose any charge through the building.

Answers to Worksheet 2.5.4

1. a) and c) are true
2. a) the charge leaks away through the wall or air; no force of attraction remains
   b) there is more rubbing on a carpeted floor; and so more static charge builds up
3. students should only partially agree, they should describe the similarities and differences outlined above to justify

Answers to Practical sheet 2.5.4

3. non-contact force
4. positive and positive repel; negative and negative repel; positive and negative attract

Chapter 5: Exploring Contact and Non-Contact Forces

5.5 Explaining static charge

Lesson overview

Learning objectives

- Explain static charge in terms of electron transfer.
- Apply this explanation to various examples.

Learning outcomes

- Describe how electrons may be transferred from one object to another. [O1]
- Relate the concept of electron transfer to observed effects. [O2]
- Use the concept of electron transfer to explain the effectiveness of charging and discharging. [O3]

Skills development

- Thinking scientifically: understand how theories develop
- Working scientifically: interpret evidence
- Learner development: communicate effectively

Resources needed equipment and materials as detailed in the Technician's notes; Worksheet 2.5.5; Practical sheet 2.5.4; Technician's notes 2.5.5

Digital resources Quick starter; Slideshow: Atoms and ions - How electron transfer between atoms forms ions, which assemble into alternating lattices due to electrostatic attractions; Interactive activity: Arrange the sentences on static charge into the correct order; Hangman: Key vocabulary game

Key vocabulary electron, positive charge, proton, negative charge, neutral

Teaching and learning

Engage

- Use a van de Graaff generator (see Technician's notes 2.5.5) to demonstrate a static electricity effect so that the students can **recall** the main points from the previous lesson. Invite them to **make suggestions** about why rubbed objects may become charged. [O1]

    Higher-attaining students may be able to use ideas about particles and electricity to **suggest** the idea of charged particles.

- Refer the students to a simple atomic model – negative electrons orbiting a nucleus containing neutrons and positive protons (for example Figure 2.5.5a in the Student Book) and ask them to **decide** if this supports their suggestions. [O1]

Challenge and develop

- Explain that electrons can transfer easily from some substances during rubbing. The students can answer questions 5 and 6 in the Student Book – for question 6 they need to realise that some materials lose electrons more easily than others. [O1&2]

- If students did not compare the attraction or repulsion of combinations of rods in the previous lesson (see Practical sheet 2.5.4) they should do that now – nylon/nylon; nylon/polythene; polythene/polythene. Ask them to **describe** and **draw** the distribution of electrons on the rods and to **identify the rules** (like charges repel; unlike charges attract). [O1&2]

- Students **observe** more electrostatic effects with the van de Graaff generator. For example:
    - charge the globe and discharge with the earthing sphere held a few centimetres away
    - charge a volunteer student by asking them to stand on a rubber mat and to hold the globe when the generator is started
    - use accessories such as the a cluster of threads, a perspex container containing polythene balls, or a stack of aluminium foil tart cases

Chapter 5: Exploring Contact and Non-Contact Forces

- light an LED from the top of the globe.

  Ask the class to **interpret the evidence** and relate it to the movement and distribution of electrons. [O1, 2&3]

  Higher-attaining students should be able to think in terms of relative numbers of electrons when **considering** the size of charge.

Explain

- **Pair work** Allocate different electrostatic effects to pairs of students. Each pair produces a poster for display to **explain** their effect. Ensure that all effects are covered across the class. [O1, 2&3]

  Higher-attaining students should be able to use their posters to **explain** more challenging ideas in greater depth.

- Envoys could **communicate** their effect to other groups. [O1, 2&3]

Consolidate and apply

- Ask the students to **compare** how noticeable the attraction is between two recently charged rods and then between ones that have been left for some time. They explain the difference in terms of loss of electrons to the surroundings. [O1, 2&3]

- As reinforcement, ask the students to complete task 3 of Worksheet 2.5.5. [O1, 2&3]

  Task 3 of the worksheet provides extra challenge for higher-attaining students,

Extend

- Ask students able to progress further to **find out** how the theory of static electricity developed.

Plenary suggestions

The big ideas Ask the students to write down, individually, three things they have learned during the lesson. Then ask them to **share** their facts in groups and to **compile** a master list of facts, with the most important at the top. Take feedback. [O1, 2&3]

Answers to Student Book questions

1. protons; neutrons; electrons
2. there are equal numbers of protons (positive charge) and electrons (negative charge) so the charge is balanced / neutralised
3. by gaining electrons
4. by losing electrons
5. electrons are transferred from the rod to the cloth; so the cloth becomes negatively charged
6. Some materials give up electrons more easily than others; in some cases electrons may be transferred to the rod from the cloth.
7. in damp weather the static charge can become neutralised; as electrons are transported by the water in the air
8. a) the globe is positive so it attracts electrons from the person
   b) all the strands of the person's hair have become positively charged; because they have lost electrons; the hairs repel each other
   c) electrons flow onto the globe; so the positive charge is neutralised

Answers to Worksheet 2.5.5

1. a) diagram should show charges as well as protons, electrons and neutrons
   b) when it is rubbed, it loses electrons
2. a) attraction happens when positive is brought towards negative; repulsion occurs between positive–positive or negative–negative
   b) A: one rod with + signs, one with − signs; B and C: both rods + or both rods −
   c) diagrams and labels should show charges and attraction/repulsion
3. a) atoms contain positive particles in the nucleus; which are surrounded by negative particles; some of which are free to move. When positive and negative particles no longer balance; an object is statically charged
   b) LED being lit; electrical sparks; insulators and conductors behave differently

Chapter 5: Exploring Contact and Non-Contact Forces

5.6 Understanding electrostatic fields

Lesson overview

Learning objectives
- Explain static electricity in terms of fields.
- Explain how charged objects affect other objects.

Learning outcomes
- Describe the electric field around a charged object. [O1]
- Explain how we can use the idea of a field in relation to static charge. [O2]
- Use the idea of induced charge to explain field effects and compare this with magnetism. [O3]

Skills development
- Thinking scientifically: ask questions
- Working scientifically: develop explanations
- Learner development: communicate effectively

Resources needed nylon and polythene rods; woollen sock or cloth; gold leaf electroscope; tin can; balloon; digital coulombmeter (optional); Worksheet 2.5.6; Technician's notes 2.5.6

Digital resources Quick starter; Interactive activity: Drag the sentences into the correct order, to explain why a statically charged balloon sticks to a wall

Key vocabulary electrostatic field, induced

Teaching and learning

Engage
- Demonstrate the deflection of a fine stream of water by a charged rod (or refer to Figure 2.5.6a in the Student Book). Tell the students that the water has no charge and in this lesson they will try to solve the problem of how uncharged materials can be attracted or repelled. [O1, 2&3]
- The students **devise questions** about what they need to know to **solve** the problem of water being deflected. [O1, 2&3]

Higher-attaining students may make links to magnets attracting some unmagnetised materials.

Challenge and develop
- The Students **identify evidence** that a wall is not normally charged (dust does not stick or no reading on a coulombmeter). They then **observe** the failure of an uncharged balloon to stick to a wall and the sticking of a charged balloon. [O1&2]
- Present the students with four possible models of charge distribution on the surface of a normal wall – no charges; even distribution of positive and negative charges; all negative charges; all positive charges. The students **use evidence** from previous lessons to choose the best model (even distribution of positive and negative charges). [O1&2]
- **Pairs to fours** The students **suggest** ideas about the effect of bringing a negatively charged balloon towards a wall. (The field from the balloon repels electrons in the wall, leaving the surface positive. Refer to Figure 2.5.6b in the Student Book.) [O1, 2&3]

Higher-attaining students may be able to **suggest** how their ideas could be tested (e.g. using a coulombmeter to see if the change in charge distribution can be detected).

Chapter 5: Exploring Contact and Non-Contact Forces

Explain

- Demonstrate a gold leaf electroscope. Challenge the students to **explain** how the charge is distributed during the charging and discharging. Ask them to **draw diagrams**. [O1&2]

  Higher-attaining students could be challenged to **describe** this without the use of diagrams to **develop** their skills in written explanations.

Consolidate and apply

- The students **observe** how a gold leaf electroscope can be charged using a cloth and rod in a tin can, so that the leaf remains deflected because the charge is conserved. See Technician's notes 2.5.6 for more details about the procedure. [O1&2]
- The students complete the appropriate tasks in Worksheet 2.5.6. [O1&2]
- They **compare** the effects they have seen in the lesson to magnetic field effects. [O3]

Extend

- Students able to progress further can **observe** and **explain** the effect of the electrostatic field round a charged object as it is brought towards the electroscope. [O3]

Plenary suggestions

Revisit starter The students revisit the questions they devised at the start of the lesson and provide answers. [O1, 2&3]

What we have learned The students **write a summary** of the main learning points on large sheets of paper. The papers are circulated so that ideas are **shared**. Different groups **clarify** any doubts or contradictions and finalise their learning points. [O1, 2&3]

Answers to Student Book questions

1. an electrostatic field
2. the water is attracted; even though it is not touching the rod
3. Equal numbers of positive and negative charges; balance each other.
4. A positive field attracts negative particles; and repels positive particles; and vice versa.
5. Diagram should show an even distribution of + and – charges in unaffected water; and uneven distribution in the affected water; showing attraction of negative particles towards the positive charges on the rod.
6. The metal is a good conductor; so the charge can flow away.
7. The insulation stops the particles moving in or out; so that the charge can stay on the working part of the electroscope.
8. a) The overall charge is neutral; there is no force on the gold leaf.

   b) Charge is induced in the copper strip; and gold leaf. The negatively charged rod repels electrons from the cap; into the strip and leaf. Both become negative so repel each other.

   c) Electrons would gradually spread out from the surface of the strip and leaf; and so they would become neutral again. The leaf would no longer be repelled; and would return to resting against the copper strip.

Answers to Worksheet 2.5.6

1. a) + and − charges should be drawn evenly distributed

   b) both balloons are negatively charged; and repel each other

   c) diagram should show the balloon hanging down; at an angle; because it is attracted towards the rod

   d) the balloon should be hanging at an angle; away from the rod; or be moving away

2. a) A: insulator; B: copper strip; C: gold leaf

   b) when the electroscope is charged; the gold leaf is repelled from the copper strip; because they have the same charge

   c) there is an induced negative charge on the gold, and the lower part of the copper strip; causing repulsion

   d) Charge a rod on a cloth, so that electrons are transferred to the rod. Bring the rod towards the cap of the electroscope so that the leaf deflects. Touch the cap so that electrons can flow away from the electroscope. Remove the rod, which leaves the electroscope positively charged.

3. a) Give an electroscope a known charge. Bring the object with unknown charge towards the electroscope. If the leaf drops, the unknown charge is the opposite to the charge on the electroscope.

   b) compare the degree of deflection of the gold leaf, when the objects are held at a set distance from the disc

Chapter 5: Exploring Contact and Non-Contact Forces

5.7 Applying what we know about electrostatics

Lesson overview

Learning objectives
- Apply an understanding of static electricity to various situations.
- Explain how static electricity can be useful and can be dangerous.

Learning outcomes
- Describe some examples and applications of static electricity. [O1]
- Explain various examples of applications of static electricity in terms of charge mechanism. [O2]
- Compare and contrast useful and dangerous instances of static charge in terms of charge mechanism. [O3]

Skills development
- Thinking scientifically: evaluate risks
- Working scientifically: present evidence
- Learner development: plan progress

Resources needed selection of resources and/or internet access for information about applications of electrostatics; card; scissors; Worksheet 2.5.7

Digital resources Quick starter; Slideshow: Antistatic devices - Problems (as opposed to applications) of electrostatic attraction, and practical solutions to such problems; Interactive activity: Drag the sentences into the correct order, to explain electrostatic paint spraying; Video

Key vocabulary electrostatic attraction, lightning

Teaching and learning

Engage
- Show some video clips of lightning strikes. The students help to **plan progress** by collecting ideas about what mechanisms are at work and identifying what they need to find out more about. [O1, 2&3]

Challenge and develop
- Ask the students to form groups of three and to use a variety of resources (including the Student Book) to **research** how static electricity plays a part in various applications such as paint spraying, powder coating, photocopying, ink-jet printing and electrostatic precipitation of smoke particles. You could allocate one application to each group and then ask them to **share** what they found out. [O1&2]
- The groups could additionally **present evidence** of the benefits of using static charge in their various applications. [O1&2]
- Ask the students to do tasks 1 and 2 of Worksheet 2.5.7. [O1&2]
- Read the 'Lightning' section of the Student Book as a class. Discuss this and ask the students to **compare** lightning with other static charge effects. [O2&3]
- The students **evaluate risks** posed to planes by static charge. (In a lightning strike the plane's electronics are shielded; during refuelling the plane is connected to Earth.) [O2&3]

Explain
- Ask the students to write a piece **comparing** and **contrasting** lightning in nature with the van de Graaff generator. [O2&3]

    Higher-attaining students may be able **consider** in more detail how the charge is generated in each case.

Chapter 5: Exploring Contact and Non-Contact Forces

Consolidate and apply

- Ask the students to produce a table giving a summary of applications of static electricity including charge mechanism, what is attracted and alternatives to the use of static charge. [O1&2]

Extend

- Ask students able to progress further to **find out** about the Faraday cage and to explain how the body of a car or plane protects the occupants using task 3 of Worksheet 2.5.7. [O3]

Plenary suggestions

Pairs to fours card sort The students work in pairs to write some 'statement' cards, along with corresponding 'explanation' cards, about topics covered in the lesson. The cards are then jumbled and the pairs swap cards with another pair and attempt to sort each other's cards. [O2&3]

Answers to Student Book questions

1. It is easier to spray difficult shapes than to brush them; paint goes on evenly; less paint is wasted.
2. The paint droplets in the spray are positively charged; and are attracted to the negatively charged object.
3. negative; so that it is attracted towards areas of the positively charged plate.
4. An area of plate with a weaker positive charge; would attract less toner; this would give a lighter shade of grey.
5. The working parts are insulated from the outer casing; the outer casing is earthed; the outer casing is not a conductor.
6. A sharp image is projected onto the plate. The charged and uncharged areas correspond accurately to the image. The attraction of toner is controlled by the location and size of charge.
7. The strong negative field from the cloud induces a positive charge in the ground; by repelling electrons (or attracting positively charged particles).
8. There are big differences in charge; between different parts of the clouds.

Answers to Worksheet 2.5.7

1. a) by gaining electrons from the negatively charged grid as they pass it
   b) they are attracted to the metal grid; which is connected to Earth
   c) the cost of fitting the equipment to the chimney; may not remove all harmful products from the smoke
2. a) i) dust is attracted   ii) 3; inconvenient but not harmful
   b) i) the paint is attracted to the object being sprayed   ii) 4 or 5; better quality finish / less paint wasted
   c) i) a discharge (spark) could affect the plane's electronics or ignite the fuel   ii) 1 or 2; lack of control or major fire could result
   d) i) there could be lightning   ii) 1 or 2; a huge, damaging current could result; could be fatal to humans

Chapter 5: Exploring Contact and Non-Contact Forces

5.8 Exploring gravity on Earth

Lesson overview

Learning objectives
- Explain the effects of gravity.
- Compare gravity to other non-contact forces.
- Use the concept of a gravitational field.

Learning outcomes
- Explain the effects of gravity and how they vary around the Earth. [O1]
- Apply the concept of a gravitational field to describe the causes and effects of gravity. [O2]
- Evaluate the concept of a gravitational field as a means of explaining the effects, including acceleration. [O3]

Skills development
- Thinking scientifically: use equations
- Working scientifically: design investigations
- Learner development: develop resilience

Resources needed sticky notes; forcemeters; netting (e.g. from packs of oranges, to hold a ball while its weight is measured with a forcemeter); balls of similar size but different masses, e.g. tennis ball and foam ball (PE departments often have these to teach tennis to beginners); tape measures; stopwatches; calculators; Worksheet 2.5.8; Practical sheet 2.5.8

Digital resources Quick starter; Slideshow: Weightlessness - Creating zero-gravity/weightlessness for astronaut training using a parabolic flight path; Interactive activity: Link the statement about gravitational fields with its correct description

Key vocabulary gravity, weight, gravitational field, accelerate

Teaching and learning

Engage
- **True/false** To explore the students' ideas about gravity on Earth, ask them work in pairs to write a mix of true and false statements on separate sticky notes, attempting to include the key vocabulary words. The statements are passed round so that other pairs can state whether each statement is true or false. Alternatively ask the class to do task 1 of Worksheet 2.5.8. [O1, 2&3]
- Group the statements that:
  - all students agree are correct
  - all students agree are misconceptions
  - cause doubt or disagreement among students. [O1, 2&3]

  Higher-attaining students may be able to **provide explanations** to others in relation to the statements that cause disagreement.

Challenge and develop
- This can be a student activity or a demonstration. Using forcemeters, **compare** the force that balls of different masses are pulled down by (i.e. their weights). Also **compare** the descent of the balls as they fall to Earth. Provide an explanation that, despite the *force* of gravity being higher on the larger mass, the *acceleration* is the same for all masses in a gravitational field. [O3]
- Using the idea of gravitational field, the students attempt to **explain** a range of familiar and unfamiliar phenomena from video clips, pictures and descriptions – for example, free fall, weight is less the further you are from Earth and get far enough from Earth and you have no weight. [O1&2]

Chapter 5: Exploring Contact and Non-Contact Forces

- Remind the students about how lines of magnetic force show the strength and direction of a magnetic field. Ask the students to **draw** field lines to show the gravitational field of the Earth. (Straight lines spearing into the Earth – see Figure 2.5.8b in the Student Book.) Task 2 of Worksheet 2.5.8 can be done here. [O2]
- Students **design an investigation** and carry it out to answer the question 'How does gravity affect the acceleration of falling balls of different weights?' The students need somewhere to drop balls safely from a height and time how long it takes them to hit the ground. The greater the height, the better the results – but safety for the students and passers-by is paramount. The students can use Practical sheet 2.5.8. They are given the equation (derived from the second equation of motion) $a = 2h \div t^2$ to **calculate** acceleration. The students need to show resilience in **comparing** their calculated value to the real value of 10 m/s^2 and **suggest reasons** for discrepancies (timing errors, air resistance). [O3]

Higher-attaining students may be able to work out the units for acceleration.

Explain

- The students sketch and **explain** the motion of the following:
  - an object travelling through space a long way from Earth
  - an object passing close enough to Earth for its path to be deflected
  - an object passing close to Earth such that it changes direction and crashes into Earth.

  The students need to use the idea of field strength being weaker further away from Earth. [O1, 2&3]

Higher-attaining students could add force arrows to their sketches.

Consolidate and apply

- **Listening triads** The students work in groups of three. Each student takes on one role – talker, questioner or recorder. The talker **explains**, **compares** and **contrasts** the Earth's gravitational field with magnetic and electrostatic fields. The questioner **prompts** and **seeks clarification**. The recorder **makes notes** and **gives a report** at the end of the conversation. [O1, 2&3]

Extend

- Students able to progress further can do task 3 of Worksheet 2.5.8 and questions 7 and 8 in the Student Book. [O3]

Plenary suggestions

Revisit starter The students revisit the statements from the starter activity. After time for **discussion**, students **decide** which statements should be moved to a different group or get modified. [O1, 2&3]

Answers to Student Book questions

1. weaker
2. it is further from the Earth; so gravity is weaker
3. it would 'float' like the astronauts; it would be falling at the same rate as the space station and everything in it
4. towards the centre of the Earth
5. The gravitational field is weaker further away from the Earth.
6. The gravitational field lines all point toward the centre of the Earth; whereas the magnetic field lines point to the North Pole.
7. the object is accelerating; because the force of gravity is acting
8. In one second it would accelerate towards the Earth; up to a speed of 10 m/s. It would then continue towards the Earth at 10 m/s. There would be no change in speed or direction; because no force would be acting (assuming no air resistance).

Answers to Worksheet 2.5.8

1. a) T b) F c) T d) F e) T f) F g) F h) T i) F j) F
2. a) Magnetic field lines looping round the Earth from S to N; gravitational field lines radiating inwards from space towards the centre of the Earth
   b) The further apart the field lines, the weaker the field.
   c) Compared to the magnetic field, the gravitational field is stronger; reaches further; and affects all objects.
3. a) the cars should be equally spaced b) the gaps should increase as the object falls, as in Figure 2.5.8c in the Student Book c) i) 10 m/s after 1 s ii) 20 m/s after 2 s

Chapter 5: Exploring Contact and Non-Contact Forces

5.9 Applying our understanding of gravity to space travel

Lesson overview

Learning objectives

- Apply ideas about gravity on Earth to other places.
- Explore how gravitational fields vary.
- Consider the effects of these changes.

Learning outcomes

- Describe how gravity varies at different places in space. [O1]
- Explain how gravitational fields vary in space and describe the effects. [O2]
- Analyse the implications of changing gravitational fields on space travel. [O3]

Skills development

- Thinking scientifically: ask questions
- Working scientifically: interpret evidence
- Learner development: collaborate effectively

Resources needed large sheets of paper; Worksheet 2.5.9

Digital resources Quick starter; Interactive activity: Are the statements about space travel true or false?; Interactive activity: Complete the sentences about exploring the Earth's atmosphere; Hangman: Key vocabulary game; Video

Common misconceptions There is no gravity deep in the Solar System.

Key vocabulary air resistance

Teaching and learning

Engage

- Show a video clip of a space rocket launch. Explore the students' thinking by asking them to react to and **ask questions** about information concerning space travel. The Saturn-V rocket used for missions to the Moon carried over 1.3 million litres of fuel. Even at its closest, Mars is more than 100 times further than the Moon, so how is it possible to have enough fuel to travel there? [O1]

Challenge and develop

- The students draw two dots at the opposite edges of a blank page to represent two planets. They add arrows and labels to **describe** the gravitational forces acting on a spacecraft at various points between them. (Gravity pulling close to either planet; no gravity at some point in between.) [O1]
- They add field lines to their diagram to show the extent of fields corresponding to the forces. [O2]
- They **interpret evidence** that exists, or could be gathered, to find out if gravitational fields exist throughout the Solar System (e.g. planets are held in orbit, observed paths of debris in space, spacecraft motion). [O2]
- The students **apply** their knowledge of forces and motion to **explain** what propulsion a rocket would need in order to fly from one planet to the other. [O3]

Explain

- **Pair talk** Ask the students to read the 'Voyager spacecraft' section in the Student Book. Students **collaborate** to **explain** what energy such a spacecraft would need. Focus on propulsion but also mention systems needs. [O2&3]

    Higher-attaining students may be able to **speculate** on some of the challenges that long-distance manned space travel would present.

Chapter 5: Exploring Contact and Non-Contact Forces

- Ask the students to answer questions 1–3. [O1, 2&3]

Consolidate and apply

- The students use ideas from this and the previous lesson to **illustrate** the relative sizes and directions of forces needed for a spacecraft as it is launched, departs from Earth's gravitational field and passes through the gravitational fields of other bodies during a journey to a distant destination. Tasks 1 and 2 of Worksheet 2.5.9 can be used to support this. [O1, 2&3]

    Higher-attaining students should be challenged to **explain** more fully the wider range of forces at work – e.g. air resistance decreasing when leaving Earth's atmosphere; reaction forces; balanced and unbalanced forces.

Extend

- Students able to progress further could use the internet or other resources to **find out** about black holes, why their gravity is so strong and what its effects are. They could answer the questions in task 3 of Worksheet 2.5.9. [O2&3]

Plenary suggestions

Hot seat Ask each student to **think up a question**. Select someone to put in the 'hot seat' and the other students ask their questions and say at the end whether the answer was correct or incorrect. [O1, 2&3]

Answers to Student Book questions

1. gravity (getting smaller with height); air resistance (getting smaller with height); thrust from the rocket (possibly being reduced with height)
2. the rocket has massive engines and the large fuel capacity needed; Voyager is protected from the effects of air resistance
3. In space there is no air; so there is no air resistance to overcome.
4. With increased distance from the Earth: the gravitational field reduces in strength; the air becomes less dense (fewer particles) so friction decreases.
5. it would continue in a straight line; at the same speed; until another force affected it
6. They are so far from planets and stars; that any gravitational forces pulling Voyager off course are extremely weak.
7. Their path would be uncontrollable; they would deviate as they passed planets; they could be pulled into orbit or onto the surface of planets.
8. Propellers push against the particles of the air or water; there is nothing in space for a propeller to push against; rocket/jet engines push against their own exhaust gases.

Answers to Worksheet 2.5.9

1. a) arrows showing pulling force towards Earth; getting smaller as the rocket gets further away; tiny or no arrow on the furthest one
   b) air resistance: decreases with distance as atmosphere becomes less dense; no air resistance outside the atmosphere
2. a) they have strong gravity; which would extend well away from the planet; it would affect the course of Voyager
   b) 10 m/s
   c) the Sun; it has the biggest acceleration due to gravity; and so has the strongest field
3. a) they are extremely massive/dense
   b) it is made of gas; so has no solid surface to land on
   c) mass/density and radius

Chapter 5: Exploring Contact and Non-Contact Forces

5.10 Applying key ideas

Exploring Earth's atmosphere and beyond

Objectives

- To extract ideas about magnetism, electrostatic charge and gravity from the text, including earlier sections of the topic.
- To apply ideas about magnetism, electrostatics and gravity.
- To evaluate ideas in relation to magnetism, electrostatics and gravity.

Outcome

- Clear and effective responses to questions, indicating understanding and the next steps in learning.

The purpose of this activity is to provide an opportunity to see how successfully students are grasping the key ideas so far. It isn't designed to be used as a formal test – it might be that students work on the questions collectively. It does provide an opportunity for you to look at written work, engage students in discussions and form ideas about progress being made.

The tasks are progressive. Lower-attaining students should be able to tackle the first two or three tasks and higher-attaining students will find the later ones more challenging.

Resources needed van de Graaff generator and pinwheel; Worksheet 2.5.10; Technician's notes 2.5.10

Teaching & learning

Engage

- Challenge the students to think back over the last few lessons and identify some of the key ideas they've met. Draw out some responses about these ideas and say that it's important, as learners, that they develop a sense of their own progress.
- Tell the story some of epic balloon flights such as the first non-stop circumnavigation by Breitling Orbiter 3. Ask the students to **suggest** some of the forces/fields, challenges and dangers involved.

Challenge and develop

- **Pair talk** Using the van de Graaff generator, demonstrate an electrostatic effect that the students have not seen before – e.g. the rotation of a pinwheel or the repulsion of a bunch of terylene threads (see Technician's notes 2.5.10). The students **discuss** the charge mechanism and the possible explanation of the effect.

Explain

Ask the students to read the 'Exploring Earth's atmosphere and beyond' passage in the Student Book. Depending on their ability to assimilate text, you may need to adopt strategies such as:

- Have students working in pairs, with copies of the text (provided as Worksheet 2.5.10) and highlighters. One student highlights key ideas, and the other (with a different colour) any words not understood.
- Work with a group of students who have difficulty with reading to support them in decoding the text and accessing the ideas.

Consolidate and apply

- Now ask the students to attempt the tasks – they might do this individually or collaboratively. In either case, encourage them to **identify** and **record** their ideas.
- Ask them to **present** their responses to various tasks, either orally or by displaying their work.

Extend

- For students able to progress further, the later tasks give opportunities for extension work.

Plenary

Ask the students for responses to questions such as:

- How well was I able to approach those tasks?
- What ideas from the chapter was I able to use?
- What ideas from other areas of science was I able to use?
- Are there some ideas that I need to strengthen in the later part of this topic?

If there are, make a note.

Provide the class with some overall feedback, indicating ideas that they have grasped effectively and those that may need developing further.

Likely responses and next steps in learning

1. The students should draw lines of magnetic force that loop round the Earth from South Pole to North Pole. The lines are closer together near the poles, suggesting a stronger field. The stronger field near the poles would attract more particles and so the surface there would be hit more frequently than other parts of the world. This helps to check that the students can distinguish between the different types of field.
2. The balloon would largely be affected by the Earth's gravitational field. Force arrows should show the upwards force due to balloon's buoyancy to be larger than downwards force of the weight. The students may indicate the action of other forces such as the updrafts and downdrafts associated with clouds and the horizontal push due to wind. This checks understanding of how to represent force sizes and directions with arrows drawn to scale.
3. The students should refer to charge building up due to the removal/addition of charged particles (electrons). They may suggest that charge could be induced on the balloon by the presence of charges on nearby clouds. They may also suggest that friction of air currents could cause the necessary transfer of charged particles. A better response would include diagrams and refer to electrons. The charge on an object can be determined by bringing a known charge towards it – like charges repel; unlike charges attract.
4. Lightning involves large quantities of energy and very high temperatures. A conductor made of a highly conductive metal like copper allows the charge in the base of a cloud to equalise with respect to the Earth rather than it happening through a person, building, tree etc.
5. The metal cage would provide best protection by acting as a Faraday cage. The foam would give protection from physical knocks, but would provide little protection from lightning – especially if it became wet. The plastic insulator may give some protection, but lightning has so much energy that that the insulation could be overcome. A combination of all three may be best, provided it doesn't prevent the instruments collecting data and transmitting it back to Earth.
6. Challenges include: overcoming the Earth's gravity at launch; lack of atmosphere in space; extreme cold; large distances involved. Balloons are unsuitable because they can only operate where there is an atmosphere. Planes cannot fly where there is no air for the wings to work. The difficulties are overcome by space rockets. They have massive engines and fuel tanks so that they can carry spacecraft beyond the limits of Earth's gravity. The spacecraft and instruments are protected until they have left the atmosphere. Spacecraft have thrusters that can keep the spacecraft travelling in the right direction. The best responses are likely to bring in aspects of scientific knowledge from earlier in KS3.
7. Copper dust may help in stopping charges building up within a cloud because copper is a conductor. However, the strong air movements could carry the tiny charged copper particles to any part of the cloud, so it may not help. More creatively minded students may suggest other ideas for equalising the charge within a storm cloud – for example spraying charged particles (as happens with paint spraying) or suspending lightning conductors within clouds.

Chapter 5: Exploring Contact and Non-Contact Forces

5.11 Exploring pressure on a solid surface

Lesson overview

Learning objectives

- Explain how pressure can be applied on a solid surface.
- Describe some effects of varying pressure.

Learning outcomes

- Describe the effects of varying pressure on a solid surface and suggest factors that affect this. [O1]
- Explain how the pressure on a solid surface may vary and the effects this has. [O2]
- Analyse situations in which factors have been changed to alter the pressure applied. [O3]

Skills development

- Thinking scientifically: consider the quality of evidence
- Working scientifically: make predictions
- Learner development: act responsibly

Resources needed wine bottle corks; steel pins; drawing pins; coloured strips of paper (two colours, one of each per student); Worksheet 2.5.11a (copied onto card); Worksheet 2.5.11b

Digital resources Quick starter; Slideshow: Pressure, ice and snow - Effects of increasing and decreasing pressure on ice and snow - Applications to winter activities; Interactive activity: Drag the descriptions which represent high or low pressure; Video

Common misconceptions Force and pressure are the same.

Key vocabulary pressure, area

Teaching and learning

Engage

- Ask the students to **make predictions** about pressure – for example 'Will an elephant do more or less damage to a wooden floor than a woman in stiletto heels?'. (An elephant weighs about 5000 kg and a woman about 50 kg. An elephant's foot is about 40 cm in diameter, area about 1200 cm^2; the area of a stiletto heel is less than 1 cm^2.) [O1&2]

  Higher-attaining students should be able to bring in the quantitative idea of surface area.

Challenge and develop

- Ask the students to **imagine** the forces needed to cut modelling clay first using a ruler and then using a knife. Relate 'sharpness' to the degree of pressure. [O1&2]
- Students **analyse** the effect of pressing a drawing pin into a wine bottle cork (or similar) compared with an ordinary steel pin – make it clear that you expect sensible behaviour here. Elicit that with the drawing pin the force at both ends is the same, but the pressure is very much different. [O1&2]
- Present the students with a range of situations in which high pressure is desirable or low pressure is desirable – the students **sort** them by pressure value. For example:
  - ice skates, nails, scissor blades, hole punch (high pressure desirable)
  - skis, caterpillar tracks on a digger, multiple broad pillars on a bridge (low pressure desirable). [O1&2]
- Based on the previous activity, the students **discuss** the reasons why and how pressure is either reduced or increased. The students can answer questions 1 to 6 in the Student Book. Worksheet 2.5.11b also supports the students' learning here. [O3]

  Higher-attaining students may be able to **suggest** and **explain** their own examples of reducing and increasing pressure.

Chapter 5: Exploring Contact and Non-Contact Forces

Explain

- **Pairs to fours** The students **explain** how pressure varies between a sledge with runners compared to one with a large flat base and how well each works on different textures of snow. Students **consider** the quality of evidence that they would need to test their explanations. [O1, 2&3]

Higher-attaining students may be able to **appreciate** that pressure causes ice or snow to melt under a sledge runner, which provides lubrication and reduces friction.

Consolidate and apply

- Give pairs of students a shuffled set of the cards from Worksheet 2.5.11a and ask them to **match up** the stems and ends of sentences about high and low pressure. [O1&2]

Higher-attaining students may be able to produce their own sentence ends and also their own statements about pressure without scaffolding.

Extend

- The students can answer questions 7–9 in the Student Book. [O3]

Plenary suggestions

Heads and tails Each student writes a question about pressure on a coloured-paper strip and the answer on a different-coloured strip. In groups of six to eight, each student gets a question and an answer at random. One student reads out their question – the student holding the answer then reads it out, followed by reading out their question. [O1, 2&3]

Answers to Student Book questions

1. newton (N)
2. ... smaller the pressure
3. there is very high pressure at the point of the pin
4. The feet have a large surface area; so the pressure due to the camel's weight is reduced; this helps stop the camel sinking in the sand.
5. A sharp blade directs the force through a smaller area than a blunt one; the higher pressure cuts more easily.
6. Wheels have a larger contact area than a blade; and so exert less pressure; there would be very low friction; so the roller skates would slip; and steering and stopping would be difficult.
7. Narrow racing skis exert a higher pressure and would sink into soft snow; the wider powder skis would exert a low pressure on hard icy snow and would be hard to control.
8. Longer handles, acting as levers, would produce a bigger force; a narrower cutting blade would concentrate the force onto a smaller area; and the higher pressure would cut the tin lid more easily.
9. Annotated diagrams should show wide padded straps; and a waist belt to spread the weight further; and reduce the pressure on the shoulders.

Answers to Worksheet 2.5.11a

a with i; b with v; c with i; d with iii; e with iv

Answers to Worksheet 2.5.11b

1. a) true b) true c) false d) true e) false
2. E, B, C, A, D
3. a) The large area reduces the pressure on the ground; and also of the reaction force on the foot; this is needed because of the huge weight (force).

   b) The large number of small teeth provides high pressure at the point of each tooth; this helps the saw cut through the material.

   c) The pointed teeth create high pressure; which helps the teeth to penetrate the prey.

   d) The caterpillar tracks cover a much larger area than wheels; and so the pressure on the ground of the large weight of the vehicle is reduced; this helps to stop the tank sinking into the ground and getting stuck.

Chapter 5: Exploring Contact and Non-Contact Forces

5.12 Calculating pressure

Lesson overview

Learning objectives

- Identify the factors that determine the size of pressure on a solid.
- Calculate the size of pressure exerted.

Learning outcomes

- Describe the factors that affect the pressure applied to a solid. [O1]
- Calculate the pressure applied from the force and the area. [O2]
- Explain how the force and area can be varied to alter the pressure applied. [O3]

Skills development

- Thinking scientifically: use units and nomenclature
- Working scientifically: evaluate data
- Learner development: collaborate effectively

Resources needed equipment and materials as detailed in the Technician's notes; calculators; Worksheet 2.5.12; Practical sheet 2.5.12; Technician's notes 2.5.12

Digital resources Quick starter; Interactive activity: Order the pressures, from highest to lowest

Key vocabulary formula, pascal (Pa)

Teaching and learning

Engage

- Ask pairs of students to **compare** the pressure exerted on modelling clay by two wooden blocks with masses on top – one block should have twice the surface area of the other. The students should see that when the force on the larger block is twice that on the smaller block, the depth of the indent is the same in each case. They should attempt to **explain** this. [O1]

    Higher-attaining students may make quantitative links between force, area and pressure.

Challenge and develop

- Ask the students to **complete** the statements:
    - As force increases, pressure..... (increases)
    - As area increases, pressure ..... (decreases)

    Then ask them to **suggest** which of these formulas is correct:

    pressure = force ÷ area   or   pressure = force × area

    Then ask them to **suggest** the units that pressure is measured in, given that force is in N and area is m^2. (1 N/m^2 = 1 pascal, Pa) [O1, 2&3]

    Higher-attaining students may be aware of other commonly used units for pressure – bars, psi.

- The students should **calculate** pressures in a range of examples such as those in the 'Example calculations' section of the Student Book and task 1 of Worksheet 2.5.12. [O2]

- The Students **collaborate** in pairs to **investigate** how pressure affects how far a block sinks into sand when different forces are applied (Practical sheet 2.5.12). [O2]

Explain

- The students **analyse** their data and use it to **describe** and **explain** the relationship between force, area and pressure and how far the block sinks into sand. [O1, 2&3]

Chapter 5: Exploring Contact and Non-Contact Forces

Consolidate and apply

- **Pair work** The students work in pairs to **write questions** that require pressure calculations. After **working out** the answer to their own questions, they **share** questions with other pairs. [O2]

   Higher-attaining pairs could be grouped together so that they can challenge one another more effectively.

- The students could **calculate** the pressure they exert on the floor. The area of a foot can be estimated by drawing round it on squared paper. [O2]

- They can then do tasks 2 and 3 of Worksheet 2.5.12. [O2&3]

Extend

- Students able to progress further should **explain**, using their own estimates for force and area in pressure calculations, how the pressure exerted by an army tank caterpillar track compares to that of the tyres of a family car (a typical caterpillar track is 5 m long and 0.5 m wide, and a tank weighs about 500 000 N; a typical contact area for a car tyre is 0.3 m^2, a typical weight of a car is 15 000 N). [O2&3]

Plenary suggestions

The big ideas The students write down three ideas they have learned about pressure. They then **share** their facts in groups and **compile** a master list with the most important at the top. Ask for ideas to be shared and find out which group(s) agreed. [O1, 2&3]

Answers to Student Book questions

1. pascal (Pa); N/m^2
2. $P = F \div A$
3. N/cm^2
4. 10 Pa
5. 125 Pa
6. pressures are 20 Pa and 40 Pa respectively; the second crate exerts the greater pressure
7. 0.5 m^2
8. a) The pressure is higher when the person is standing; the area of the feet is smaller than the area of the bottom and legs when sitting. (Higher-attaining students may realise that the force is not applied equally over the contact area, so the situation is actually more complex.)

   b) estimate the contact area in both cases; by drawing the outline on squared paper; measure weight of the person in newtons; use the pressure formula

   c) the force is higher when you bounce; so the pressure increases

Answers to Worksheet 2.5.12

1. a) A: 12 m^2; B: 8 m^2; C: 6 m^2

   b) i) 1.25 Pa   ii) 1.67 Pa (to 3 s.f.)   iii) 0.83 Pa
2. a) 20 000 Pa; 25 000 Pa

   b) 1200 N; 200 N
3. a) any reasonable ideas; minimum of four contact points

   b) need to know the combined weight of the rack and load; measure the total contact area of the mounting points for the rack; use the formula $P = F \div A$

   c) fit more contact points; or ones with a larger combined area

   d) i) the pressure the roof can withstand; the maximum total force the car body can support without damage; a sensible safety margin to allow for bumpy roads and misuse of the rack

   ii) people may overload the rack; the rack may weaken with age; bumpy roads will lead to greater force and pressure

Answers to Practical sheet 2.5.12

1-3. Students' own answers.
4. Pressure causes objects to sink in sand. When the pressure becomes too large the sand might not support the object.
5. choose more solid ground / build wide strong foundations to reduce the pressure

Chapter 5: Exploring Contact and Non-Contact Forces

5.13 Exploring pressure in a liquid

Lesson overview

Learning objectives
- Describe how pressure in a liquid alters with depth.
- Explain pressure increases in relation to particles and gravity.

Learning outcomes
- Describe how pressure increases with depth in a liquid and some effects of this. [O1]
- Explain why pressure increases with depth in a liquid. [O2]
- Identify the causes and implications of pressure increase with depth in a liquid. [O3]

Skills development
- Thinking scientifically: use equations
- Working scientifically: present evidence
- Learner development: collaborate effectively

Resources needed equipment and materials as detailed in the Technician's notes; Worksheet 2.5.13; Technician's notes 2.5.13

Digital resources Quick starter; Interactive activity: Complete the sentences about pressure in liquids

Key vocabulary pressure, depth, decompression

Teaching and learning

Engage
- Show the students a can with three holes in its side at different heights. Before they see the Student Book, ask them to **predict** the outcome of filling the can with water. [O1&2]
- Ask the students to attempt to **explain** why the water squirts furthest from the lowest hole. [O1&2]

   Higher-attaining students may realise that it has to do with water pressure varying with depth.

Challenge and develop
- The students **predict** what will happen when a plastic bag full of water is punctured in several places with a knitting needle – demonstrate this. (The water flows from all the holes showing that pressure does not depend on direction.) [O2]
- The students **predict** and **explain** what would happen if a beaker covered in an elastic membrane was submerged in deep water – demonstrate this. (Regardless of orientation, the membrane will bulge inwards due to the water pressure). [O2]
- The students can do tasks 1 and 2 of Worksheet 2.5.13. In task 2 they **present evidence** in the form of a graph showing how pressure varies with depth. [O1&2]
- Ask the students to **suggest** how the graph could inform the design of a submarine. [O3]

Explain
- Use the 'Explaining pressure in liquids' section of the Student Book to explain liquid pressure in terms of particles. [O1&2]
- Show the students a U-tube partially filled with water. They compare the levels in the two sides and try to **explain** what they see in terms of particles and gravity. Ask them further to **explain** why, when water is poured into one arm, the levels equalise again. [O2&3]

Chapter 5: Exploring Contact and Non-Contact Forces

Higher-attaining students may be able to appreciate that atmospheric pressure is also acting but is the same on both sides.

- **Pair talk** Students **collaborate** to **discuss** the pressure that a diver experiences in a tall, narrow tank of water compared to a swimming pool of the same depth. (Pressure is the same in both cases because the number of particles of water in a column above the diver is the same.) [O2&3]

Consolidate and apply

- The students can do questions 1–5 in the Student Book. [O1, 2&3]
- They could **suggest** an explanation for the fact that divers experience pain in their ears when descending (increased pressure presses on the ear drum).

Extend

Ask students able to progress further to:

- read the 'Working at pressure' section of the Student Book and answer the questions. [O3]
- do task 3 of Worksheet 2.5.13. [O3]
- **explain** why a syringe with a narrow opening will squirt further than one with a wide opening. (The force is acting through a smaller area when the opening is narrow, therefore the pressure is higher.). [O3]

Plenary suggestions

'I think that is...because...' challenge students to **provide explanations** for why:

- a dam wall is wider at the base than at the top
- a sealed pop bottle full of air will gradually collapse when it is taken down into deep water, and then will expand to its original size when it is brought back up again. [O1, 2&3]

Answers to Student Book questions

1. there is more water above you pressing down
2. a) the pressure could crush their bodies and damage lungs, bones etc
   b) a whale's body is flexible; the ribs are joined by very flexible cartilage; and so can be compressed without damage
3. there are more particles above B compared to A
4. The particles in a liquid behave in a similar way to the marbles; they are both closely packed, touching and cannot be compressed; when pressure is applied to either, it is transferred throughout the particles/marbles.
5. The marbles do not move/flow as freely as water particles; pressure is not distributed so evenly.
6. It has thick walls of a strong material such as steel; the spherical shape has fewer weak points than other shapes; special tough, transparent material for the windows.
7. The internal pressure of deep-sea creatures is balanced by the outside pressure; they experience no crushing effect.
8. More gases (especially nitrogen) dissolve in the blood when the pressure is higher; when pressure is reduced rapidly the gas comes out of solution as bubbles, as when a fizzy drink is opened; the bubbles cause pain, illness and possibly death.

Answers to Worksheet 2.5.13

1. a) lower b) squash/compress c) withstand high pressure d) the pressure drops and their bodies expand and rupture
2. a) check for appropriate scales, labels, accurate points, straight line b) 1000
   c) it makes the numbers easier to manage d) pressure is proportional to depth
   e) Cannot confidently agree; the student may be correct; but it is a much higher pressure than the data we have; so there is a chance that the relationship does not remain the same.
3. Good points are bold; suggested additions/alterations are italicised.

The pressure in a liquid depends on how deep it is. The closer to the surface you are, the *lower* the pressure. **When you are in deep water the column of water above you presses down to create pressure.** Divers can*not* avoid the pressure of the column of water on their ear drums by ensuring their ears do not point towards the surface. *The pressure in a liquid acts in all directions.*

Pressure has a variety of different effects. If a dam in a reservoir leaks near its base the water will flow out much more *quickly* than if the leak is near the surface. **Submarines have to be very strong to withstand the pressure in the deep oceans. The huge weight of water particles above the submarine cause very high pressure, which presses on the submarine from all directions.**

Chapter 5: Exploring Contact and Non-Contact Forces

5.14 Explaining floating and sinking

Lesson overview

Learning objectives

- Explain why some objects float and others sink.
- Relate floating and sinking to density, displacement and upthrust.
- Explain the implications of these ideas.

Learning outcomes

- Suggest why some objects float and others sink. [O1]
- Explain why some objects float and others sink using concepts of density, displacement and upthrust. [O2]
- Apply ideas of density and displacement to predict the outcome of various situations. [O3]

Skills development

- Thinking scientifically: analyse data
- Working scientifically: make predictions
- Learner development: act responsibly

Resources needed equipment and materials as detailed in the Technician's notes; Worksheet 2.5.14; Practical sheet 2.5.14; Technician's notes 2.5.14

Digital resources Quick starter; Slideshow: Balloons - Hot-air, hydrogen and helium balloons – to emphasise that buoyancy isn't limited to water; Interactive activity: Define the key terms about floating and sinking; Hangman: Key vocabulary game

Key vocabulary density, buoyancy, upthrust, displaced

Teaching and learning

Engage

- Check the students' understanding of density from earlier work by asking them to **explain** why steel and wooden blocks of equal volume have different weights, and why wood floats but steel sinks. [O1&2]
- Suspend a piece of wood from a forcemeter and note its weight. Identify the students' prior knowledge by asking them to **predict** how the forcemeter reading will change when the wood is lowered slowly into water. Repeat with an object that sinks. [O2]

  Higher-attaining students may notice that water is displaced.

Challenge and develop

- Ask the students to push a tennis ball or a block of wood into a bowl of water to feel the upwards pushing force (upthrust). Then ask them to **explore** the existence of upthrust on objects that sink by repeating with a block of aluminium. [O2]

- The students can then **investigate** the readings on newtonmeter and top pan balance as they lower blocks of different materials into water. They can use Practical sheet 2.5.14 to guide their method and subsequent data analysis. They will be required to **act responsibly** for this activity to be successful. [O2]

- The students should also **measure** the volume of water displaced when a block is lowered in. They then **relate** the weight of water displaced to the size of the upthrust measured. [O2]

- Return to the discussion of why wood floats and aluminium sinks, asking the students to **suggest explanations** using the terms 'density', 'displacement' and 'upthrust'. [O1&2]

- Ask the students to **explain the evidence** that the upthrust is the same for steel and aluminium blocks (of the same size) when submerged in water. (Archimedes' principle: upthrust = weight of fluid displaced) [O2]

Chapter 5: Exploring Contact and Non-Contact Forces

Explain

- Ask the students, working individually, to **explain** floating and sinking in relation to density, using diagrams and text. [O1&2]
- **Pairs to fours** Working in pairs they **produce** an explanation of how a boat made of steel floats. Then they join with another pair to check agreement and **refine** their explanation. Take feedback. [O3]

Consolidate and apply

- Use the Student Book questions for consolidation. [O1, 2&3]
- Students **suggest** why a can of diet cola floats in water whereas as standard cola sinks. (The density of standard cola is higher because of dissolved sugar.) [O1, 2&3]

  Higher-attaining students could draw particle diagrams to **explain** the difference between the two types of cola.

- Ask the students to **apply** the idea of average density to **explain** why the shape and the total mass of a steel ship are important. [O3]

Extend

- Ask students able to progress further to **predict**, **investigate** and **explain** the effect of upthrust with a more dense liquid such as strong saline. [O3]

Plenary suggestions

'I think that is...because...' Show the students four boiling tubes, sealed with bungs – one is full of water; one is half full of water; one is full of strong saline; one is half full of water with some lead shot added. The students **predict** whether each will float or sink, and **explain** why. Alternatively task 3 of Worksheet 2.5.14 may be used. [O1, 2&3]

Answers to Student Book questions

1. for example: stone, copper and pottery sink; wood, cork and expanded polystyrene float
2. they are no longer supported by the upthrust of the water
3. the particles are more massive and/or are more tightly packed
4. how large the upthrust force is: 7 – 4 = 3 N
5. a) the wood is less *dense* than water b) the water provides *upthrust* which partially supports the weight of the steel
   c) the object *displaces* water equivalent to its own volume
   d) the boat is *buoyant* because it *displaces* a large volume of water, which gives a large *upthrust*
6. a) equal sized upward and downward arrows b) equal sized upward and downward arrows, bigger than in (a)
   c) two downward-acting arrows (weight and the downward push) balanced by a large upthrust arrow
   d) small downward arrow (weight) and large upthrust arrow
7. The weight of the boat would increase and it would sit lower in the water; the upthrust would increase the lower the boat sat as more water was displaced; eventually the water overflows out of the boat and it sinks.

Answers to Worksheet 2.5.14

2. a) *balance* 10 N; *forcemeter* 7 N   b) *balance* 13 N ; *forcemeter* 4 N
   c) *balance* 11.5 N ; *forcemeter* 5.5 N   d) *balance* 17 N ; *forcemeter* 0 N
3. a) A with ii   B with iv   C with iii   D with i

   D must contain lead because lead is the densest of the materials involved and so will sink

   C must be a tube of water in a beaker of salt solution because it is most buoyant; it is the least dense liquid in the tube and the most dense in the beaker

   B is the opposite case to C

   A is between B and C because the tube and beaker contain liquids of equal densities (water).

   b) the glass and bung of the boiling tube must be more dense than water

Answers to Practical sheet 2.5.14

1. always the same   2. much lower
3. the difference between the forcemeter reading in air and that when submerged in water

Chapter 5: Exploring Contact and Non-Contact Forces

5.15 Exploring gas pressure

Lesson overview

Learning objectives
- Explore how the pressure in a gas varies with height above the Earth.
- Explain the implications of this changing pressure.

Learning outcomes
- Describe how atmospheric pressure changes according to height. [O1]
- Explain why atmospheric pressure changes according to height. [O2]
- Identify implications of differing atmospheric pressure at different heights and across the world. [O3]

Skills development
- Thinking scientifically: use units and nomenclature
- Working scientifically: develop explanations
- Learner development: plan progress

Resources needed equipment and materials as detailed in the Technician's notes; Worksheet 2.5.15; Technician's notes 2.5.15

Digital resources Quick starter; Interactive activity: Drag the descriptions which represent high or low atmospheric pressure

Common misconceptions Wind flows from high to low pressure systems.

Key vocabulary atmospheric pressure, weather front, altitude

Teaching and learning

Engage
- Identify the students' prior knowledge about atmospheric pressure by holding an upturned tube of water with its neck submerged in a beaker of water. Why does the water not run out? The students work in pairs to **produce** and then **share explanations**. Display the best explanation. [O1]
- Explore the idea of atmospheric pressure further by inviting students to attempt to separate Magdeburg hemispheres before and after evacuation. [O1]

  Higher-attaining students may be able to draw particle diagrams to **explain** the Magdeburg hemisphere behaviour.

Challenge and develop
- Ask the students to read the section 'Explaining pressure in the atmosphere' in the Student Book and then ask them to **describe** the relationship between height and air pressure. [O1]
- Remind the students of how water pressure varies with depth and ask them to use this to **explain** the variation of air pressure with height. (Air particles have weight because gravity is pulling them. The higher you are, the fewer air particles there are to press down on you.) [O2]
- Display a surface pressure chart, for example from the website of the Meteorological Office. Explain the numbers (the surface pressure is probably shown in hectopascals, hPa (1 hPa = 100 Pa). The students will need to become familiar with different units. Standard atmospheric pressure = 1013 hPa. The lines are isobars – lines of equal atmospheric pressure). Ask the students to find out (using the Student Book or other resources) what type of weather is associated with:
  - high pressure (sinking air is pressing down reducing cloud growth and leading to sunny weather)
  - low pressure (clouds can grow more easily leading to rain)
  - close spacing of isobars (strong winds as air circulates around the pressure systems)
  - wide spacing of isobars (light winds). [O3]

Chapter 5: Exploring Contact and Non-Contact Forces

Explain

- Discuss why mountaineers experience difficulty in breathing. (The higher the altitude, the lower the air pressure and fewer oxygen molecules are available.) [O3]
- Ask the students to **draw** annotated particle diagrams to illustrate how air pressure and oxygen availability vary with height. [O1&2]

  Higher-attaining students may be able to **explain** the body's reduced ability to release energy through respiration at altitude.

Consolidate and apply

- Worksheet 2.5.15 can be used for consolidation. [O1, 2&3]
- **Pair talk/Pairs to fours** The students **explain** (verbally, in writing and using diagrams) what would happen to a balloon partially inflated at sea level and then released to a high altitude. [O1, 2&3]

  Higher-attaining students should be challenged to **explain** what would happen to the balloon if it were taken under water or warmed up in relation to its surroundings.

Extend

- Ask students able to progress further to **find out** about the challenges presented by high-altitude balloon flight. [O3]

Plenary suggestions

'I think that is…because…' The students watch a demonstration of a partially inflated balloon in a bell jar being evacuated using a vacuum pump (see Technician's notes 2.5.15) – they then write their own explanation. [O2&3]

Lower-attaining students could be provided with various explanations to select from.

Applications Ask the students to **identify** potential implications and uses of understanding atmospheric pressure (e.g. better weather predictions to anticipate natural disasters; better training for athletes; improved treatment of people with breathing difficulties). [O1, 2&3]

Answers to Student Book questions

1. the weight of gas particles pulled towards Earth by gravity
2. Gas particles are attracted to massive objects in space because of gravity; so between the massive objects there are few particles.
3. at high altitude the balloon will expand and burst; because the atmospheric pressure is so low
4. There is a lower density of particles of gas in a low pressure area.
5. it may be cloudy and possibly rainy in the west; finer to the east; may be windy in the north and west
6. any location where the pressure is low; and/or there is a weather front – for example over Ireland and Iceland
7. diagrams should show approximately three times as many particles per unit volume at sea level
8. extra weight to carry; expensive; difficulty obtaining supplies
9. more red blood cells might be produced; lung capacity might increase; heart might become bigger/stronger – all linked to increasing ability to deliver oxygen to body cells

Answers to Worksheet 2.5.15

1. a) with ii b) with v c) with iv d) with i e) with vii
2. a) A is a good model; it shows particles and how they are closer together lower down; could be improved by showing more particles

   in B the darker shading correctly represents denser air at low altitude; but it does not show any particles

   C is poor: there are no particles and it incorrectly suggests that there is a dense layer in the middle of the atmosphere
3. Students' accounts could mention: the death zone, wind, low temperature, snow, ice, steep terrain, exhaustion, breathing difficulties, altitude sickness, training, preparation, equipment.

Chapter 5: Exploring Contact and Non-Contact Forces

5.16 Working with pressure

Lesson overview

Learning objectives
- Give examples of how pressure affects our lives.
- Explain how pressure is used and managed.

Learning outcomes
- Identify problems and benefits related to pressure. [O1]
- Describe how the effects of pressure are dealt with or used. [O2]
- Explain how pressure is used and managed in a variety of situations. [O3]

Skills development
- Thinking scientifically: understand how theories develop
- Working scientifically: evaluate data
- Learner development: respect others

Resources needed materials and equipment as detailed in the Technician's notes; Worksheet 2.5.16; Practical sheet 2.5.16; Technician's notes 2.5.16

Digital resources Quick starter; Slideshow: High tides and flooding - Effects of low atmospheric pressure on sea level, and the consequent effects when coupled with high tides; Interactive activity: Barometers are devices used to measure pressure - Order the statements to describe their operation; Hangman: Key vocabulary game

Key vocabulary pressurised, barometer, altimeter, valve

Teaching and learning

Engage
- Drop some raisins into freshly opened, chilled lemonade. Bubbles of carbon dioxide form around the raisins so they become buoyant and rise to the surface. At the surface the bubbles detach and escape, and the raisins sink again. Ask the students to **discuss** this effect and to **suggest** how this might relate to the floating and sinking of a submarine. (A submarine submerges by taking on water; to surface, compressed air is used to pump out the water.) [O2]

   Higher-attaining students may be able to **reason** that compressed air has a high density and so displaces relatively little water. When it is expands it can displace more water.

Challenge and develop
- Demonstrate a barometer in a bell jar attached to a vacuum pump. Discuss and ask the students to **suggest** how a barometer helps in making weather predictions, or how it can be used as an altimeter. (It contains a partially evacuated, sealed, flexible metal box. When the atmospheric pressure decreases it expands, and vice versa; the movements deflect a needle over a scale.) [O2]

- Arrange the students in pairs to **construct** and **test** a Cartesian diver, using Practical sheet 2.5.16. They should then answer the questions on the sheet to show their understanding of how it works. [O2&3]

- Ask the students to **identify** data they would need if they were designing a submarine (ass and volume of the submarine, the size of its tanks). [O3]

- Present the students with applications of high-pressure canisters – for example a soda stream, a self-inflating life jacket, a tyre-repair kit. If possible demonstrate one or more of these in action (see Technician's notes 2.5.16). Ask the students for **explanations**. Discuss how the particle model has helped scientists to develop theories about pressure. [O1, 2&3]

Chapter 5: Exploring Contact and Non-Contact Forces

Explain

- **Snowball activity** Demonstrate a tube siphoning some water from a raised container. Individually, the students try to **explain** how the siphon works and how it is started. Then they **discuss** their ideas with a partner. Pairs form fours and then groups of eight, who should together **agree** on the best explanation. Finally, a spokesperson for each group of eight feeds back ideas to the whole class. The students will need to be respectful of others' ideas that do not match their own. [O1, 2&3]

  Ask higher-attaining students to suggest how the rate of siphoning can be increased (wider tube, bigger height difference).

Consolidate and apply

- The students produce an **explanation** poster about the relevance of air pressure when flying in aeroplanes. They should consider a range of questions – why high-altitude flight requires pressurised cabins and oxygen masks; why aerosols are not allowed in hold luggage; what passengers would experience if the cabin leaked at high altitude. [O1, 2&3]
- The Student Book and Worksheet 2.5.16 provide questions for consolidation. [O1, 2&3]

Extend

- Students able to progress further can **apply** their knowledge of forces to suggest how a submarine could be brought to the surface even if it had run out of compressed air. (Angled fins sticking out horizontally could provide lift when the submarine is propelled forwards.) [O3]

Plenary suggestions

'I think that is…because…' The students **predict** and **explain** what would happen to plastic bottles filled with air and water if they were taken to high altitude. [O1, 2&3]

Exit slips Students write one thing they have learned on a slip of paper and hand it in before leaving. [O1, 2&3]

Answers to Student Book questions

1. because they fly at high altitude; where atmospheric pressure is low; and there is too little oxygen
2. Cabin pressure is equivalent to air pressure at 2000 m; this is different from at ground level.
3. A parent could pass out due to lack of oxygen; and the child may not be able to help them.
4. a) the internal pressure would equalise with the external pressure; the box would not expand/contract; the reading would not change b) a rigid container would not change shape
5. Atmospheric pressure changes with time and location.
6. The pump pressure must be the highest; otherwise no air will enter the tyre.
7. it allows air into the tyre; when the pressure outside is higher than inside; it keeps air in even when the pressure inside is higher
8. Particle-spacing changes should be shown, according to the pressure level. The pump pressure as the plunger is pushed in is higher than the pressure inside the tyre; which is higher than atmospheric pressure; which is higher than the pressure inside pump as the plunger is pulled out.

Answers to Worksheet 2.5.16

1. a) altimeter: an instrument that measures height   b) valve: a device that lets a fluid travel one way only
   c) atmosphere: a mixture of gases around the Earth   d) pressure: force ÷ area
   e) barometer: an instrument for measuring air pressure
2. a) the gas bubbles would escape much more quickly on Everest; the atmospheric pressure there is much lower
   b) the tyre would not inflate; there is no gas for the pump to push into the tyre
   c) the balloon would contract slightly; the air pressure is a little higher at ground level
3. Pushing the syringe piston forces air into the bottle, displacing water, making the bottle more buoyant. To submerge, air is removed by pulling the syringe piston out so that water can enter. It is unrealistic because submarines are not attached to the surface.

Answers to Practical sheet 2.5.16

1. the lid contains air
2. when you squeeze the bottle the pressure increases; when you release the squeeze the pressure decreases
3. When the pressure in the bottle increases, the air in the pen lid contracts and some water enters the pen lid, causing it to sink. When the pressure is lowered, the air expands again, pushing the water out of the pen lid, and the lid rises.
4. If the pressure in the bottle is just right, the weight of the diver can be made to exactly balance the upthrust.

Chapter 5: Exploring Contact and Non-Contact Forces

5.17 Checking students' progress

The 'Checking your progress' section in the Student Book indicates the key ideas developed in this chapter and shows how students progress to more complex levels. It is provided to support students in:

- identifying those ideas
- developing a sense of their current level of understanding
- developing a sense what the next steps in their learning are.

It is designed either to be used at the end of a chapter to support an overall view of the progress, or alternatively during the teaching of the unit. Students can self-assess or peer-assess using this as a basis.

It would be helpful if students can be encouraged to provide evidence from their understanding or their notes to support their judgments. In some cases it may be useful to explore the difference in the descriptors for a particular idea so that students can see what makes for a 'higher outcome'.

It may be useful with some descriptors to provide examples from the specific work done, such as an experiment undertaken or an explanation developed and recorded. If marking and feedback uses similar ideas and phrases this will enable students to relate specific marking to a more general sense of progress.

Chapter 5: Exploring Contact and Non-Contact Forces

To make good progress in understanding science students need to focus on these ideas and skills:

Students who are making modest progress will be able to:	Students who are making good progress will be able to:	Students who are making excellent progress will be able to:
Describe the attraction of unlike poles and repulsion of like poles; show how a magnetic field can be represented.	Identify magnetic attraction and repulsion as non-contact forces; explain how field lines indicate the direction and strength of forces.	Apply and evaluate the concept of magnetic fields in various contexts.
Describe how friction between objects may cause electrostatic charge through the transfer of electrons.	Explain various examples of electrostatic charge; use ideas of election transfer to explain different effects.	Explain why some electrostatic charge mechanisms are more effective than others.
Describe the field around a charged object; describe some applications of static electricity.	Use the idea of fields to explain various examples and applications of static electricity.	Compare and contrast useful and dangerous instances of static charge; compare electrostatic and magnetic fields.
Describe the variation and effects of gravity on Earth and in space.	Apply the concept of gravitational fields to explain the variation and effects of gravity on Earth and in space.	Apply the concept of gravitational fields in explaining gravitational effects on Earth and in space, including acceleration.
Describe the causes and effects of varying pressure on and by solids.	Explain the effects of varying pressure on and by solids; calculate the pressure applied by a solid from the force applied and the contact surface area.	Explain how force and area can be varied to alter the pressure applied.
Describe the variation of pressure in liquids with depth and the effects of this.	Explain the variation of pressure with depth in liquids.	Identify the causes and implications of variation of pressure with depth.
Suggest why some objects float and others sink.	Use the concepts of density, displacement and upthrust in explaining floating and sinking.	Apply ideas about density and upthrust to predict the outcomes of various situations.
Describe how atmospheric pressure varies with height; state some implications of variations in pressure.	Explain why atmospheric pressure varies with height; describe how the effects of pressure used and dealt with.	Identify some implications of pressure variation in situations such as weather patterns and high-altitude activities.

Chapter 5: Exploring Contact and Non-Contact Forces

5.18 Answers to Student Book questions

This table provides answers to the Questions section at the end of Chapter 5 of the Student Book. It also shows how different questions assess attainment in terms of the focus and style of a question as well as its context. Question level analysis can indicate students' proficiency in approaching different aspects of scientific understanding and different types of answer.

Q	Answer	Marks available	Focus: Knowledge & understanding	Focus: Application	Focus: Evaluation of evidence	Style: Objective test question	Style: Short written answer	Style: Longer written answer	Context: Magnetism	Context: Static electricity	Context: Gravity	Context: Pressure	Context: Floating and sinking
1	c	1	x			x				x			
2	d	1	x			x							x
3	a	1	x			x							x
4	d	1	x			x					x		
5	Density of wood < density of water	1	x				x						x
	Density of steel > density of water	1	x				x						x
6	The downward force of each chair leg would be spread over a larger area	1	x				x					x	
	so the pressure on the floor would be reduced	1	x				x					x	
7	Use a plotting compass. Place the compass close to the magnet and mark where its N needle points to	1	x				x	x					
	Move the compass so its S needle points at the previous mark, and mark where its N needle now points. Continue, and draw a line to join the points	1	x				x	x					
	Repeat all around the magnet	1	x				x	x					
	The strength of the field is indicated by how close together the lines are	1	x				x	x					
8	a = b = d (all have load of same mass), c	1		x		x							x
9	c	1		x		x						x	
10	c	1		x		x						x	
11	b	1		x		x						x	

Key Stage 3 Science Teacher Pack 2 © HarperCollins*Publishers* Limited 2014

Chapter 5: Exploring Contact and Non-Contact Forces

Q	Answer	Marks available	Focus: Knowledge & understanding	Focus: Application	Focus: Evaluation of evidence	Style: Objective test question	Style: Short written answer	Style: Longer written answer	Context: Magnetism	Context: Static electricity	Context: Gravity	Context: Pressure	Context: Floating and sinking
12	Test if one rod can pick up more small identical pieces of paper	1		x			x			x			
	from the same distance, than the other rod	1		x			x			x			
13	You could the feel the force of attraction if the field from the magnet was strong enough around the buried metal	1		x			x		x				
	Would only work for magnetic metals such as iron, steel, nickel and cobalt	1		x			x		x				
14	The debris travels in straight lines when a long way from planets, because there is no gravity	1		x				x			x		
	Path is deflected when it enters the gravitational field of a planet	1		x				x			x		
	Larger mass planets have stronger fields and so affect the path more	1		x				x			x		
	It crashes into the third planet because the field is so strong close to it	1		x				x			x		
15	At least two of: less waste, easier to coat awkward shapes, quicker, better coverage	2			x		x			x			
16	Reference to low % of oxygen	1			x		x					x	
	Reference to drop in fitness	1			x		x					x	
	Reference to acclimatisation	1			x		x					x	
	Reference to fitness being never as good as at sea level	1			x		x					x	
	Total possible:	30	12	12	6	8	10	12	6	5	5	11	3

6.1 Introduction

When and how to use these pages

The Introduction in the Student Book indicates some of the ideas and skills in this topic area that students will already have met from KS2 or from previous KS3 work, and provides an indication of what they will be studying in this chapter. *Ideas you have met before* is not intended to comprehensively summarise of all the prior ideas, but rather to point out a few of the key ones and to support the view that scientific understanding is progressive. Even though students might be meeting contexts that are new to them, they can often use existing ideas to start to make sense of them.

In this chapter you will find out indicates some of the new ideas that the chapter will introduce. Again, it isn't a detailed summary of content or even an index page. Its purpose is more to act as a 'trailer' and generate some interest.

The outcomes, then, will be recognition of prior learning that can be built on, and interest in finding out more.

There are a number of ways this introduction can be used. You might, for example:

- Use *Ideas you have met before* as the basis for a revision lesson as you start the first new topic.
- Use ideas on the *Ideas you have met before* as the centre of spider diagrams, to which students can add examples, experiments they might have done previously, or what they found interesting.
- Make a note of any unfamiliar/difficult terms and return to these in the relevant lessons.
- Use ideas from *In this chapter you will find out* to ask students questions, such as:
  - Why is this important?
  - How could it be used?
  - What might we be doing in this topic?

Overview of the chapter

In this chapter, students will learn about magnets and electric circuits. They will learn about early ideas relating to magnetism and recognise changes in the ways that scientists have worked over thousands of years. They will be introduced to the domain theory of magnetism, and use this to explain why some materials are magnetic and why some magnets are stronger than others. The effects of the Earth's magnetic field and its importance to life will be considered. The students will learn about the differences between permanent magnets and electromagnets, and explore various applications of each type – including the D.C. motors and the use of magnets in Maglev trains. They will also learn how electric circuits work and use a range of models and analogies to support their understanding of what is meant by the terms 'current', 'voltage' and 'resistance'. They will apply and evaluate various models to strengthen their understanding. The students will also investigate the different factors that affect the resistance of a conducting wire and how these factors can be exploited for different applications, such as generating heat energy or light energy, or transporting electricity through the National grid system. They will also investigate how current and voltage change in series and parallel circuits, and explore different applications of these circuits and their advantages and disadvantages.

This chapter offers a number of opportunities for students to design, carry out and evaluate investigations that test:

- different methods for making magnets
- the strength of magnets and electromagnets
- the voltage of fruit batteries
- the resistances of different wires.

They will explore the meanings of and differences between the terms 'reproducible' and 'repeatable' experiments, and consider how to make their observations more accurate and valid.

Chapter 6: Magnetism and Electricity

Obstacles to learning

The students may need extra guidance to deal with the following common misconceptions:

- **Magnetism** All metals are magnetic. Magnetism is fixed and cannot be altered within a material. The strength of a magnet is related to its size. Electricity and magnetism are not related. Magnetism is not related to the structure of atoms in a material.
- **Insulators and conductors** All metals conduct electricity equally well.
- **Current** Electric current is used up in a circuit. Charges are produced by a battery and flow all the way around the circuit.
- **Voltage** Voltage and current are interchangeable. The voltage is not related to the battery. Energy in the circuit is used up.
- **Series and parallel circuits** The arrangement of components will have no effect on the voltage and current.

	Topic title:	Overarching objectives:
2	Looking at the history of magnets	Earth's magnetism, compass and navigation
3	Exploring magnetic materials	Magnetic poles, attraction and repulsion
4	Testing the strength of magnets	
5	Describing the Earth's magnetic field	Earth's magnetism, compass and navigation
6	Investigating electromagnetism	The magnetic effect of a current, electromagnets
7	Using electromagnets	Electromagnets
8	Exploring D.C. motors	Other processes that involve energy transfer: completing an electrical circuit
		The magnetic effect of a current, D.C. motors (principles only)
10	Investigating batteries	Other processes that involve energy transfer: completing an electrical circuit
11	Describing electric circuits	Other processes that involve energy transfer: completing an electrical circuit
		Electric current, measured in amperes, in circuits
12	Understanding energy in circuits	Other processes that involve energy transfer: completing an electrical circuit
		Electric current, measured in amperes, in circuits
		Potential difference, measured in volts, battery and bulb ratings
13	Explaining resistance	Potential difference, measured in volts, battery and bulb ratings
		Resistance, measured in ohms, as the ratio of potential difference (p.d.) to current
14	Investigating factors affecting resistance	Resistance, measured in ohms, as the ratio of potential difference (p.d.) to current
		Differences in resistance between conducting and insulating components (quantitative)
15	Explaining circuits using models	Potential difference, measured in volts, battery and bulb ratings
		Resistance, measured in ohms, as the ratio of potential difference (p.d.) to current
16	Describing series and parallel circuits	Series and parallel circuits, currents add where branches meet and current as flow of charge
17	Comparing series and parallel circuits	Electric current, measured in amperes, in circuits
		Series and parallel circuits, currents add where branches meet and current as flow of charge
		Potential difference, measured in volts, battery and bulb ratings
18	Applying circuits	Series and parallel circuits, currents add where branches meet and current as flow of charge

Chapter 6: Magnetism and Electricity

6.2 Looking at the history of magnets

Lesson overview

Learning objectives
- Summarise historical ideas about magnetism.
- Describe how historical ideas about magnetism have changed over time.

Learning outcomes
- Describe early ideas about magnetism. [O1]
- Explain how historical ideas about magnetism were developed. [O2]
- Explain how scientific methods can be used to develop ideas further. [O3]

Skills development
- Thinking scientifically: understand how theories develop
- Working scientifically: develop explanations
- Learner development: ask questions

Resources needed poster paper; marker pens; equipment and materials as detailed in the Technician's notes; Worksheet 2.6.2 (the second page copied onto card); Practical sheet 2.6.2; Technician's notes 2.6.2

Digital resources Quick starter; Slideshow: Developing the compass – From a lodestone on a string to modern binnacle compasses; Interactive activity: Order the discoveries in magnetism, from the oldest to the most recent; Video

Common misconceptions All metals are magnetic.

Key vocabulary magnetism, magnet, peer review

Teaching and learning

Engage
- **Concept map** Ask the students, working in pairs, to write down on poster paper all the key words that they can think of relating to magnets. They should use these words to **produce a concept map** linking all the ideas they have about magnetism, including those from Chapter 5. [O1]
- Ask selected pairs to **show** their work – challenge any misconceptions with further questions.

Challenge and develop
- As a whole class, read through the historical development of magnetism using the 'Early ideas and discoveries' section in the Student Book. Discuss how magnets were first developed from pieces of lodestone and the different ideas that people had about them. Ask the students to answer the first two questions. [O1]
- **Pair work** Ask the students to use Practical sheet 2.6.2 to **construct** their own compass using a ready-magnetised needle to represent a slither of lodestone. Discuss ideas that early scientists had about this effect. [O2]
- Working in small groups, the students **imagine** that they are early scientists and **devise** their own hypothesis about how the compass works. Ask them to **design** an experiment to test this, and to **discuss** their ideas. [O2&3]

Explain
- **Pair work** Arrange the students in ability pairs. Ask them to use the card sort from page 3 of Worksheet 2.6.2. They should develop a timeline of ideas using the cards. [O1&2]

  Middle- and higher-attaining students should **identify any evidence** from the Student Book to support the ideas and annotate their timeline accordingly. [O2&3]

Key Stage 3 Science Teacher Pack 2 © HarperCollins*Publishers* Limited 2014

Chapter 6: Magnetism and Electricity

Consolidate and apply

- Ask the students to complete task 2b of Worksheet 2.6.2 and answer any Student Book questions not yet attempted. [O1, 2&3]

    Higher-attaining students should do task 3 of Worksheet 2.6.2 – they draw up a table to **compare** how scientific information was shared and treated in Gilbert's time with today. What impact do students think peer review has had on scientific developments today? [O3]

- Ask pairs of students to **prepare** a one-minute talk on how ideas about magnetism have changed over time and how scientists work has contributed to this change. [O1, 2&3]

Extend

- Students able to progress further could **research** the development of rare earth magnets. How were these discoveries shared with other scientists? The students could contrast this process with how the findings of Gilbert were shared. [O3]

Plenary suggestions

Concept map development Ask the students to add new ideas to the concept maps started at the beginning of the lesson. [O1, 2&3]

Answers to Student Book questions

1. they attracted the metal tip of Magnes' staff; they point in a north–south direction
2. they could not see how lodestone worked; lodestone moved objects without any visible force being applied
3. Before the 1600s people had not identified a scientific hypothesis about how magnetism worked, and so attributed superstitious ideas to the lodestone. After the 1600s they started to use systematic experiments to test hypotheses about magnetism .
4. Scientific testing led to new discoveries about what magnets could do; and to the discovery of electricity.
5. Scientists publish the findings of investigations; other scientists can validate them using peer review; investigations are much more methodical nowadays, using evidence to support theories. The sharing of information and findings has led to the use of magnets in many new developments.
6. They could have been more systematic in their approach to their experiments; they could have shared their findings with a wider audience, rather than share with than just a few select scientists of the time.

Answers to Worksheet 2.6.2

1. A at 2000 BCE; B at 1000; C at 1600; D at 1600; E at 2000 BCE; F at 1800
2. a) A with none; B with 1; C with 5; D with 3; E with 6; F with 4 and 2

    b) people could not see the force behind the magnetic field; so they treated it superstitiously; no scientific investigations until 1600

3. a) In Gilbert's day there wasn't much peer review of evidence, although there was some use of models and analogies to explain evidence. Using evidence to develop new hypotheses, and using evidence to make developments, was only carried out to a small degree, and there was no global publication of results. Conversely while in Gilbert's day scientific findings were only shared with a few select scientists, today scientists share their findings globally. All the other ways of using and disseminating scientific evidence are used widely today.

    b) More scientists can validate the evidence from an investigation and contribute to the discussions about the evidence and theories linked to it. The data is shared world wide on the internet very quickly, so developments are much faster.

Chapter 6: Magnetism and Electricity

6.3 Exploring magnetic materials

Lesson overview

Learning objectives

- Investigate magnetism in materials.
- Explain magnetism using the domain theory.

Learning outcomes

- Describe the differences between permanent and temporary magnets; describe how to test the strength of a magnet. [O1]
- Describe different methods of making permanent magnets; design an investigation to compare different methods of making magnets. [O2]
- Use the domain theory to explain how materials become magnetised and demagnetised; evaluate experimental designs and make improvements. [O3]

Skills development

- Thinking scientifically: use models
- Working scientifically: design investigations
- Learner development: communicate effectively

Resources needed large arrows cut from card for each student; equipment and materials as detailed in the Technician's notes; Worksheet 2.6.3; Practical sheet 2.6.3; Technician's notes 2.6.3

Digital resources Quick starter; Interactive activity: Classify the statements into those which can magnetise or demagnetise a magnetic material

Common misconceptions An object cannot lose or gain magnetism.

Key vocabulary permanent magnet, temporary magnet, electromagnet, domain

Teaching and learning

Engage

- Demonstrate magnetism using a permanent magnet to pick up paper clips. Show how one paper clip becomes magnetic when attached to the magnet, but is not magnetic when it is removed from the magnet. Ask the students to **discuss** what they think might be happening and to **review** their ideas. [O1]
- Introduce the terms 'temporary' and 'permanent' – use the 'Permanent and temporary magnets' section in the Student Book to help. [O1]

Challenge and develop

- Use the Student Book and Practical sheet 2.6.3 to explore with the students different ways to make magnets. [O2]
- **Group work** Working in pairs, ask the students to **follow at least two methods** from Practical sheet 2.6.3 to make a steel rod magnetic. [O2]
- Ask the students to **plan an investigation** to **compare** how they might test the strength of the magnets they have made. Ask them to focus on how make a simple but standardised test that can be applied to both magnets. Task 2 of Worksheet 2.6.3 can be used for support – the students should **record** their ideas. [O2]
- Ask each pair to **present** their ideas. They will carry out these tests in the next lesson.

Explain

- Use the 'Domain theory' section in the Student Book to explore this theory of magnets. [O3]

Chapter 6: Magnetism and Electricity

- Ask the students to form groups of four or so – give each student a card arrow. Ask them to **role-play** being a magnetic material, with each student representing a particle within the material and their arrow representing their magnetic alignment. [O1&3]

  Middle-attaining students can use the domain theory and **role-play** to **explain** how each method of making a magnet works. [O2&3]

  Higher-attaining students could **role-play** what happens to magnetic material when it is demagnetised by heating or by dropping it. They could also **explain** what happens to the paper clip in the presence and absence of a permanent magnet. [O3]

Consolidate and apply

- Ask the students to answer the Student Book questions and do task 3 of Worksheet 2.6.3. [O1, 2&3]
- Ask them to **make predictions** about which of the methods of making a magnet is most likely to produce the strongest magnet. They should use the domain theory to **explain** why this works. [O1, 2&3]

Extend

- Students able to progress further could **find out** why some materials have much stronger magnetic fields than others, using ideas about domains. They could also find out why some alloys make stronger magnets than pure metals.

Plenary suggestions

Concept map development The students could add to their concept map, produced in the previous lesson, to include ideas they have learned today. [O1, 2&3]

Annotated diagram They could **draw** an annotated diagram to **expain** the difference between temporary and permanent magnets. [O1, 2&3]

Cartoon strip They could draw cartoons for younger students to **explain** how to make magnets using different methods. [O1, 2&3]

Answers to Student Book questions

1. no, only very few; like iron, steel, cobalt and nickel; and alloys containing these metals
2. put it with a very strong permanent magnet; so it is in a strong magentic field
3. their atoms do not line up in domains; in the same way that the atoms of magnetic materials line up
4. The magnetic field causes the atoms in the paper clip to align in a directional magnetic domain. While it is in the magnetic field, the paper clip is also magnetic.
5. When the rod is stroked in the same direction with a magnet, the domains are being lined up; making it a magnet. When it is hit with a hammer the domains are disrupted; and are no longer lined up in the same way.
6. *Heat* – this can cause the domains to change their alignment. When the material is cooled the domains become fixed in position; this has the result of either making a magnetic material non-magnetic, or making a non-magnetic material more magnetic.

   Hammering – this can have different effects. If the material is slightly magnetic it can realign the domains to make it more magnetic; or hammering can change the domain alignment of a strong magnet to remove the magnetism.

   Using a *current* – this can make a non-magnetic material magnetic; by aligning the domains.

Answers to Worksheet 2.6.3

1. a) steel; cobalt; nickel b) bar magnet c) paper clip; nail
2. A standardised test should be written as step-by step instructions; all variables should be given appropriate values; and the procedure must be logical.

   A test is *repeatable* if the same person carries out the test and obtains the same results. A test is *reproducible* if a different person carries out the procedure and obtains the same results.
3. a) Stroking a needle in one direction will align its domains in the same direction; this will cause the material to become magnetic. If the needle is stroked in a random manner, changing directions; it will cause the domains to misalign; and the material is no longer magnetic.

   b) Heating a material causes the atoms to move faster and realign. Heating the iron and cooling it in a magneitc field results in many of the domains becoming fixed in their aligned positions, which makes the iron magnetic. Hitting it with a hammer causes more domains to line up, so the magnetic field is stronger.

Chapter 6: Magnetism and Electricity

6.4 Testing the strength of magnets

Lesson overview

Learning objectives
- Compare different methods of testing magnets.
- Collect data to investigate the strength of magnetism.

Learning outcomes
- Follow a procedure to collect reliable, accurate and valid data. [O1]
- Interpret data using graphs; compare methods of making permanent magnets. [O2]
- Draw and explain conclusions about magnets using the domain theory; use data to evaluate different methods of making magnets and testing magnetic strength. [O3]

Skills development
- Thinking scientifically: consider the quality of evidence
- Working scientifically: record evidence
- Learner development: collaborate effectively

Resources needed poster paper; equipment and materials as detailed in the Technician's notes; Worksheet 2.6.4; Practical sheet 2.6.3 (from previous lesson); Practical sheet 2.6.4; Technician's notes 2.6.4

Digital resources Quick starter; Interactive activity: Order the sentences into a logical sequence, to show how to compare the strength of magnets

Common misconceptions There is only one way to test magnetic strength.

Key vocabulary subjective, reliability, repeatability, reproducibility, accuracy, precision

Teaching and learning

Engage
- Show the students a range of different magnets. Select different students to **investigate** them and ask the students to **identify** some differences between the magnets. Discuss why some magnets are stronger than others using ideas from the previous lesson. [O1]
- **Pair talk** Ask the students to **discuss** and **identify** one or two different ways by which they might test the strength of magnets. [O1]

Challenge and develop
- Use the Student Book to discuss the idea of 'scientific method' and how to make an experiment repeatable and reproducible. Review the students' work from task 2 of the previous lesson's worksheet (Worksheet 2.6.3), and add any new ideas from the Student Book as part of discussions about the different ways that magnetic strength can be tested. Ask the students to form the same groups as in the previous lesson and to **review** and **amend** their plan from that lesson's practical (Practical sheet 2.6.3) so that it is more like a standard procedure. They should **write the plan** up on a poster so that it can be used by another group. [O1&2]
- Ask each group to swap their plan with another group, who will use it and **peer-assess** it. [O1&2]
- Ask the students to **follow the instructions** from the previous lesson's Practical sheet 2.6.3 to make magnets using two different methods, and then to follow the standard procedure given to them by the other group to **test** the strength of the magnets. They can use Practical sheet 2.6.4 for guidance on what to do and how to present their results. [O1&2]
- They should **record** their results and **draw a graph** of their results. [O1&2]
- They should **draw conclusions** from their results. [O3]

Explain

- Ask the students to **peer-review** the procedure given to them by the other group. They should identify at least two strengths and also one area for development. [O2&3]
- Select different groups to **explain** their results using the domain theory. [O3]

Consolidate and apply

- Ask the students to use their data to **decide** which is the most effective method of producing stronger magnets. Rank the methods in order and start a class decision about the methods used. [O2&3]
- Ask the students to **evaluate** each of the different methods they used to test the strength of the magnets. Take feedback and record their findings on the board. A class decision should be made about which is the most effective method for producing reliable and accurate data. [O3]
- Ask the students to answer the Student Book questions. [O1, 2&3]

Extend

- Students able to progress further could use three methods of testing magnetic strength, and **write a detailed report** to evaluate the strengths and weaknesses of all three. They should focus on the accuracy of the methods and make suggestions for improvement, where possible. [O3]

Plenary suggestions

Good procedure Ask the students to write three things that they need to target in order to improve their writing of a procedure, or ask them to summarise what makes an effective standard procedure.

Answers to Student Book questions

1. recording the number of paper clips
2. investigating the magnetic field lines and measuring how close together they are
3. Different people may give different interpretations – for example one person may have better vision than another and therefore make more accurate observations.
4. Distance can be measured to much finer intervals than just counting the number of paperclips held. It is possible to be more accurate with the distance-measurement approach, and give different values for magnets of different strengths; even if each magnet can hold the same number of paper clips.
5. The experiment is not repeatable; because different methods were used to make the magnets. In a repeatable test the same method should be used by the same person.
6. Not necessarily; for an investigation to be reproducible other people have to be able to follow it exactly. This will depend on how well the method for the investigation is written; so exact instructions need to be provided.

Answers to Worksheet 2.6.4

1. a) stronger magnet will hold more paper clips
   b) distance will be greater for stronger magnet
   c) distance will be greater for stronger magnet
2. a) repeatable b) reproducible c) valid d) accurate
3. diagrams should show a greater degree of alignment in a stronger magnet

Answers to Practical sheet 2.6.4

2. Anomalous results should be removed from calculations of mean values. If repeat readings have similar values then the data can be said to be reliable.
5. Explanations should include the understanding that the stronger the magnet, the greater the alignment of domains in the iron.

Chapter 6: Magnetism and Electricity

6.5 Describing the Earth's magnetic field

Lesson overview

Learning objectives
- Explain evidence for the Earth's magnetic field.
- Explain the impact the Earth's magnetic field has on our planet.

Learning outcomes
- Describe some effects of the Earth's magnetic field. [O1]
- Describe the geodynamo theory. [O2]
- Explain evidence for how the Earth's magnetic field works. [O3]

Skills development
- Thinking scientifically: ask questions
- Working scientifically: develop explanations
- Learner development: communicate effectively

Resources needed compasses; resources about the Earth's magnetic field; Worksheet 2.6.5

Digital resources Quick starter; Interactive activity: Complete the sentences about the Earth's magnetic field; Slideshow: Solar wind – The effects on the atmosphere (aurora) and electrical storms

Common misconceptions The strength of a magnet is related to its size. The Earth is a very strong magnet.

Key vocabulary geodynamo theory, magnetosphere, solar wind

Teaching and learning

Engage
- Give the students compasses and ask them to **investigate** which way is north. They could also use information about where the Sun is to help them. [O1]
- **Pair talk** Remind the students that they did some work on magnetic fields in Chapter 5 – working in pairs, ask them to **discuss** and **recall** three facts about magnetic fields. Write a selection of these on the board. [O1]
- Ask the students to **deduce** at least two things about the Earth's magnetic field from the compass and from their knowledge about magnetic fields. If the compass needle is a north-seeking pole, what can they **infer** about the polarity of the Earth's magnetic field if the north end of the compass points in a north direction? [O1]

Challenge and develop
- Use section 2 in the Student Book to introduce the geodynamo theory and to discuss the impact of the magnetic field on the Earth. Videos or other resources could also be used. [O2&3]
- **Small groups** Ask the students to use the information they have gathered, along with other research material and information from Worksheet 2.6.5 and the Student Book, to **prepare a presentation** about the Earth's magnetic field. They should include ideas about how strong the magnetic field is, what impact it has on the Earth and how it works according to the geodynamo theory. Alternatively, or additionally, they can use images from the worksheet and **explain** each one in turn. [O1&2]

    Higher-attaining students should include the evidence for the Earth's magnetic field and evidence of how it works. [O3]

- Select different groups to **present** their ideas.

Chapter 6: Magnetism and Electricity

Explain

- Ask the students to **draw** their own annotated diagram to **explain** to younger students how the Earth is protected from solar winds. [O2&3]
- Ask them to **write an explanation** of what would happen if the magnetic field of the Earth were to disappear. [O1&2]

    Ask higher-attaining students to **summarise** all the evidence for the Earth's magnetic field and how it has behaved over millions of years. [O3]

Consolidate and apply

- The students can complete Worksheet 2.6.5 and answer any Student Book questions not yet attempted. [O1, 2&3]

Extend

- Students able to progress further could **research** how migratory fish, birds and insects use the Earth's magnetic field for navigation – they could **present** their findings to the class.

Plenary suggestions

True/false quiz Provide statements, such as the following, to be answered as 'true or 'false'. [O1, 2&3]
- The geographical north pole of the Earth is the magnetic south pole. (T)
- The geographical north pole of the Earth is in exactly the same place as the magnetic south pole. (F)
- The north pole of a compass has always pointed to geographical north since the Earth was formed. (F)
- The Earth has a magnetic field because it is made of rock. (F)
- Without the magnetosphere life would not exist on this planet. (T)
- The magnetosphere is a uniform field surrounding the Earth. (F)
- The Sun does not affect our magnetosphere. (F)

Challenge Ask the students to **suggest possible reasons** why Venus does not have a magnetic field.

Answers to Student Book questions

1. The north pole of any compass will point in a geographical north direction; no matter where it is on Earth.
2. Lodestone could have become magnetised because it has been in the the Earth's magnetic field for thousands of years; alternatively extreme heat by lightning strikes could have made it magnetic.
3. We cannot travel to the centre of the Earth to take samples or readings.
4. The diagram should show a liquid spinning in the core; with moving charged particles; causing domains within the molten iron to line up.
5. On the night side of the Earth the magnetosphere is furthest away from the Sun; so is not affected by solar winds. It can extend beyond the Earth; because there are no other magnetic or electric fields to interfere with it.
6. Put a compass at different positions on the rock being tested; and observe the direction the compass needle points; map the positions of the compass.

Answers to Worksheet 2.6.5

1. A – migrating animals have special sensors; which detect the Earth's magnetic field

   B – the north pole of a magnetised iron needle is attracted to Earth's magnetic south pole

   C – charged particles from solar winds get trapped inside our magnetosphere

   D – satellites, ships, planes and power grids can be affected by geomagnetic storms; caused by solar winds; weakening the magnetosphere

   E – solar winds are deflected by the magnetosphere; preventing large concentrations of charged particles from harming life on the planet

2. The talk should include the following responses and references: description and explanation of what is happening in all the images from the first task; the north pole of a compass points to Earth's magnetic south pole; changing magnetic fields discovered in rocks; the magnetosphere and its ability to deflect highly charged harmful particles; deflection of the magnetosphere by the solar winds – highly deflected on the day side, hardly deflected and very long on the night side.

   a) 1 with C; 2 with A; 3 with B

   b) We can measure the strength of the magnetosphere and solar winds; and use this data to make daily predictions about whether or not the charged particles are likely to affect satellites, aeroplanes – or even if certain areas need to be evacuated to protect life.

Chapter 6: Magnetism and Electricity

6.6 Investigating electromagnetism

Lesson overview

Learning objectives
- Describe what an electromagnet is.
- Investigate the factors affecting the strength of electromagnets.

Learning outcomes
- Plan to investigate the strength of electromagnets; describe what an electromagnet is. [O1]
- Collect accurate, reliable evidence; describe the factors that affect the strength of electromagnets. [O2]
- Analyse data and draw conclusions; use models and analogies to explain the factors affecting the strengths of electromagnets. [O3]

Skills development
- Thinking scientifically: ask questions
- Working scientifically: design investigations
- Learner development: collaborate effectively

Resources needed poster paper; equipment and materials as detailed in the Technician's notes; Worksheet 2.6.6; Practical sheet 2.6.6; Technician's notes 2.6.6

Digital resources Quick starter; Interactive activity: Classify the statements into those which will increase, or decrease, the strength of an electromagnet; Hangman: Key vocabulary game

Common misconceptions Only other magnets can produce a magnetic effect.

Key vocabulary current, magnetic field, electromagnet, iron core

Teaching and learning

Engage
- Demonstrate the magnetic effect of an electric current. Put a compass needle next to a wire carrying a current (see Technician's notes 2.6.6). Switch the current on and off to show that the magnetic effect can be turned on and off. [O1]
- **Pair talk** Ask the students to **discuss** and **share** some advantages and disadvantages of a magnet that can be switched on and off. [O1]

Challenge and develop
- Remind the students of previous work on magnetic fields and on using plotting compasses to identify the patterns of field lines. They should follow the instructions for Experiment 1 on Practical sheet 2.6.6. Using a plotting compass, the students should identify the magnetic field lines of the wire when the current is switched on and off, and **record** their results on a large sheet of paper. [O1&2]
- Now ask them to use a coil of wire around a nail, as shown in Experiment 2 on Practical sheet 2.6.6. They should **plot** the magnetic field lines using a plotting compass and **compare** the magnetic field with this setup to that of the first method. Use the Student Book (Figure 2.6.6d) to check their pattern of the magnetic field around the nail/coil. [O1&2]
- **Groups** Use the Student Book to discuss the factors that affect the strength of electromagnets. Ask the students to **plan** to investigate one of these factors, using Worksheet 2.6.6 for guidance. [O1&2]
- Check their plans and ask them to **collect data** and **record** the results. [O2]

Explain
- Collect results from each group and ask the students to **explain** them. [O2&3]

Key Stage 3 Science Teacher Pack 2

Higher-attaining students should use their own models and/or analogies to **explain** how different factors affect the strength of their electromagnet. They should **make predictions** about which factor is likely to have the most impact. [O3]

Consolidate and apply

- Gather the results from different groups investigating different factors – discuss which factor has the most impact on magnet strength and suggest why. [O2&3]
- Ask the students to answer the Student Book questions. [O1, 2&3]

Extend

- Ask students who are able to progress further to **draw** the magnetic field lines for electromagnets with more coils, a higher current and a 'stronger' iron core using plotting compasses. They should **compare** the field lines to establish which factor has the biggest effect on electromagnet strength. [O3]

Plenary suggestions

Summary Ask the students to **summarise** their learning about electromagnets. They should then **share** their ideas with a partner. [O1, 2&3]

Answers to Student Book questions

1. It is a temporary magnet; it needs an electric current to produce the magnetic effect; when the current is switched off, there is no longer a magnetic effect.
2. Use a plotting compass to show the deflection in the needle; use iron filings to show the field lines; use paper clips to show the magnetic effect.
3. It enables more of the domains to line up in the same direction.
4. For *lifting paper clips* use an electromagnet with a few coils and a small current passing through it. For *lifting a car*, a large battery will be needed along with several hundred coils.
5. Switch off the current, so there was no longer a magnetic field and the car would no longer be attracted to the electromagnet.
6. they would be closer together
7. To achieve the maximum alignment from the current effect; in an ordered arrangement, one end of the coil behaves like a north pole and the other as a south pole. If the coils were randomly wrapped, this alignment would not be as strong.
8. *Advantages*: With an electromagnet there is more control over the magnetic field; the magnetic field can be switched off when required. The strength of an electromagnet can be changed easily; by increasing or decreasing the current.
   Disadvantages: Electromagnets require an electric current, which costs money; with a permanent magnet there are no extra costs; a permanent magnet can be remagnetised using another strong magnet.

Answers to Worksheet 2.6.6

1.

	Method 1	Method 2
a)	number of coils	size of current
b)	1, 5, 10, 20	1, 2, 4, 6, 8 (A)
c)	number of paper clips attracted	number of paper clips attracted
d)	count	count
e)	type of magnet, current (5 A), time (10 s)	type of magnet, time (10 s), number of coils (10)
f)	overheating the wire	overheating the wire
g)	have current on for only a few seconds	have current on for only a few seconds

2. a) Count all the paper clips precisely; and have someone check.

   b) Repeat each investigation at least three times; remove anomalous data and calculate the mean; if results not consistent repeat until three consistent readings achieved.

3. a) Repeat the experiment yourself and see if the same results are obtained.

   b) Ask someone else to repeat the procedure and see if they get the same results as you.

   c) Use something more lightweight than paper clips, like small pins; so there is a greater degree of accuracy.

   d) Should find that the more coils there are the stronger the electromagnet; and the larger the current the stronger the electromagnet.

Chapter 6: Magnetism and Electricity

6.7 Using electromagnets

Lesson overview

Learning objective
- Describe different applications of electromagnets.

Learning outcomes
- Describe different applications of magnets and electromagnets. [O1]
- Compare and contrast the use of magnets and electromagnets in different applications. [O2]
- Explain the advantages and disadvantages of using electromagnets. [O3]

Skills development
- Thinking scientifically: ask questions
- Working scientifically: develop explanations
- Learner development: communicate effectively

Resources needed a selection of items that use electromagnets or permanent magnets, e.g. anything with a motor; microphone or telephone or loudspeaker; electric bell; recording equipment such as a tape player; computer disk; compass; fridge magnet; magnetic board; magnetic knife holder; Worksheet 2.6.7

Digital resources Quick starter; Slideshow: Electromagnets at work: Magnetic sorting, fire-doors, MRI, Maglev and security tags; Interactive activity: Order the statements to describe the operation of an electric bell; Video

Common misconceptions Permanent magnets and electromagnets can be used in the same applications.

Key vocabulary armature, contact, circuit breaker

Teaching and learning

Engage
- Display a selection of equipment that uses electromagnets and magnets – see 'Resources needed'. If none are available use the images from task 1 of Worksheet 2.6.7. [O1]
- Ask the students to **group** the items according to whether they use magnets or electromagnets. [O1&2]

Challenge and develop
- **Group work** Arrange the students in small groups of similar ability. Provide them with the diagrams from task 2 of Worksheet 2.6.7 – circuits that use electromagnets in useful applications. Ask each group to look at one of the circuits. [O1&2]

  The relay circuit is more suitable for higher-attaining students.

- Ask the students to first try to **work out** what happens when the current is switched on and off – from the circuit diagram and also from the real application if possible. [O1&2]

- They should **write a step-by-step account** of what is happening, and check their work against information from the Student Book, or use the Student Book while writing if they need help. [O1&2]

  The highest-attaining students should be capable of working out what happens in the relay circuit, and could suggest at least three uses for relays.

- Ask one student from each group investigating different devices to form another group of three. They should **share** what they have learned about their device, so that everyone can learn about each one. [O1&2]

Chapter 6: Magnetism and Electricity

Explain

- Ask the students to **explain** what would happen if the electromagnet was replaced by an ordinary magnet in the circuit applications they have investigated. They should **explain** what advantages the electromagnet provides. [O2&3]
- **Pairs** Ask the students to return to some of the items from the starter activity. They should select one and try to **work out** how it operates. [O1&2]

    Higher-attaining students could attempt to **draw a circuit diagram** for further simple applications.

Consolidate and apply

- Ask the students to **consider the advantages and disadvantages** of the electromagnet in each of the circuits in task 2 of Worksheet 2.6.7, as suggested in task 3. [O3]
- They should answer all the questions from the Student Book. [O1, 2&3]

Extend

- Students able to progress further could **devise** their own circuit incorporating an electromagnet to suggest how a crane and an electromagnet work to recycle metals.

Plenary suggestions

Concept map review Ask the students to return to their concept maps from previous lessons and add their learning about electromagnets. [O1, 2&3]

Advertising electromagnets Alternatively they could produce an advert for a company that makes electromagnets, **explaining** how the electromagnets work and what kinds of applications they can be used for. [O1, 2&3]

Answers to Student Book questions

1. they are easy to control because they can be switched off; they can be made in different sizes and their magnetic strength can be controlled so that it is suitable for a particular application
2. it needs a current to make it work
3. the button should not be pressed down; an open switch prevents current flowing
4. the hammer would hit the gong once; but would not move back and forth
5. so that the fault in the circuit can be identified and corrected
6. it works automatically when a large current flows through the circuit; with a switch this has to be done manually and the appliance may already be damaged

Answers to Worksheet 2.6.7

1. magnets – fridge magnet / magnetic boards; magnetic knife holder

    electromagnets – motor in wheelchair; camera
2. Correct step-by-step account of how the electric bell/ circuit breaker work; as given in the Student Book. A relay consists of two circuits. The first contains a simple electromagnet and needs only a small current; this acts as a switch for a second circuit that uses a much larger current. The current flows in the first circuit and attracts the rocker arm to the electromagnet; this pivots and pushes the contacts together; completing the second circuit.
3. Advantages: better control of the circuits; the magnetic effect can be switched off when required; the electromagnet allows these appliances to work, which would not happen if they were replaced with ordinary magnets; if the electromagnet is dropped on the floor, it can be easily remagnetised; the strength of an electromagnet can be increased, whereas for permanent magnets this variability is limited.

    Disadvantages: always needs a current, so always uses energy; large electromagnets are expensive to run; the magnetic effect can be lost after a while and they shouldn't be run for very long periods of time; they need to be set up and maintained in order to operate.

Chapter 6: Magnetism and Electricity

6.8 Exploring D.C. motors

Lesson overview

Learning objective

- Describe the magnetic effect of a current and how this is applied to D.C. motors.

Learning outcomes

- Describe some uses of D.C. motors. [O1]
- Describe the effect of a magnetic field on a wire carrying an electric current. [O2]
- Explain how D.C. motors of different strengths are made. [O3]

Skills development

- Thinking scientifically: ask questions
- Working scientifically: develop explanations
- Learner development: communicate effectively

Resources needed equipment and materials as detailed in the Technician's notes; Worksheet 2.6.8; Practical sheet 2.6.8; Technician's notes 2.6.8

Digital resources Quick starter; Slideshow: Motors large and small: Robots, trains and toothbrushes; Interactive activity: Classify the statements into those which will increase, or decrease the forces produced by an electric motor; Hangman: Key vocabulary game

Common misconceptions An electromagnet and a motor are the same thing. Motors do not need magnets.

Key vocabulary electric motor, motor effect, direct current (D.C.)

Teaching and learning

Engage

- Ask the students to **write down** as many different uses of electric motors in their house as they can think of, as suggested in task 1 of Worksheet 2.6.8. [O1]
- Working in pairs, they **compare** lists and combine them to make a bigger list.
- **Pairs to fours** Ask pairs to join another pair and repeat the process.
- **Pairs to eights** Finally pair again to form groups of eight and write their combined lists on poster paper and see which group has the longest list. [O1]

Challenge and develop

- Demonstrate how a current-carrying wire will move in a magnetic field, using instructions from the Technician's notes. Use the 'Discovering the motor effect' section in the Student Book to support the explanation. Introduce Michael Faraday as the scientist who discovered this effect. [O2]
- **Small groups** Give the students the opportunity to **build** their own motor, as described on Practical sheet 2.6.8. Have one working motor ready-made to show them. [O1&2]
- They could **experiment** to see what factors affect the speed of the motor. [O3]
- They can then do tasks 2 and 3 of Worksheet 2.6.8. [O2&3]

Explain

- **Pairs** Working in pairs, the students imagine that they are Michael Faraday. They should **prepare** a two-minute presentation to their classmates, who will represent distinguished scientists of the time, to **explain** Faraday's discovery and what it may lead to. They could use the Student Book to help them their preparation. [O1, 2&3]

Higher-attaining students should include presentation factors that will increase the speed of the motor.
- Select different pairs to **present** their talks.

Consolidate and apply

- **Pairs** Ask the students to **role-play** at being motor engineers. Ask them to **explain** to each other how their motor works and how to make it work faster. They should listen carefully to each other and **identify** any misconceptions they may have. [O1,2&3]
- Ask them to answer the Student Book questions. [O1,2&3]

Extend

- Students able to progress further could **research** very big motors, identifying particular problems that they may have and how these are resolved. They could **identify** features that limit the size of a motor.

Plenary suggestions

Comparing electromagnets and motors Ask the students to **explain** the similarities and differences between an electromagnet and a motor.

Answers to Student Book questions

1. for example: lawn mower; tumble dryer; dishwasher, hairdryer
2. energy by electric current → energy by movement + energy by heat + energy by sound
3. the wire would move upwards
4. not really; only a small up and down movement is possible
5. the motor would not be able to spin 360°
6. alter the current going through the coils

Answers to Worksheet 2.6.8

1. Items could include washing machine, electric food mixer, tumble dryer, vacuum cleaner, automatic camera, wheelchair, electric drill, hairdryer, lawn mower etc.
2. They need to realise how hard it is to make such measurements. Trying to do this by eye may not be possible. The students may come up with alternative ways of making measurements, perhaps using an electronic counter method.
3. They could increase the number of coils; have a stronger magnet; increase the current.

Chapter 6: Magnetism and Electricity

6.9 Applying key ideas

How can magnets be used to operate trains?

Objectives

- Extract ideas about magnets from the Student Book text, including earlier sections of the chapter.
- Apply ideas about the properties of magnets to explain some of their applications.

Outcome

- Clear and effective responses to questions, indicating understanding and the next steps in learning.

The purpose of this activity is to provide an opportunity to see how successfully students are grasping the key ideas so far. It is not designed to be used as a formal test – it may be that students work on the questions collectively. This activity does provide an opportunity for you to look at written work, engage students in discussions and form ideas about progress being made.

The tasks are progressive. Lower-attaining students should be able to tackle the first two or three tasks and higher-attaining students will find the later ones more challenging.

Resources needed student concept maps about magnets compiled in earlier lessons; permanent magnet; temporary magnet; electromagnet; Worksheet 2.6.9

Teaching and learning

Engage

- Challenge the students to **think back** over the last few lessons and **identify** some of the key concepts. Draw out some responses about these ideas and say it's important that, as learners, we develop a sense of our own progress. Write a list of key words on the whiteboard and revisit the concept maps produced earlier.
- Allow the students a little time to add any further points to their concept maps, gleaned as a result of class discussion.
- Show them a permanent magnet, a temporary magnet and an electromagnet. Invite them to **identify** and **discuss** as many differences and similarities between them as possible, including ideas about domains.

Challenge and develop

- Show video clips of different applications of magnets and electromagnets, including Maglev trains (for example search for 'maglev video' at science.howstuffworks.com) and other uses such as recycling metals. Discuss the benefits of using magnets in these applications.
- **Small group work** Use magazine articles or resources from the internet and ask the students to make a cut-out poster of different applications of magnets. They should **annotate** the posters to **explain** how the magnets are being used in different applications.

Explain

Ask the students to read the 'How can magnets be used to operate trains?' passage in the Student Book. Depending on their ability to assimilate text, you may need to adopt strategies such as:

- Have students working in pairs, with copies of the text (provided as Worksheet 2.6.9) and highlighters. One student highlights key ideas, and the other (with a different colour) any words not understood.
- Work with groups of students who have difficulty with reading, to support them in decoding the text and accessing the ideas.
- Using the Student Book text, they **explain** to each other, in simple terms, how the Maglev train works.

Chapter 6: Magnetism and Electricity

Consolidate and apply

- Now ask the students to attempt the Student Book tasks – they might do this individually or collaboratively. In either case, encourage them to **identify** and **record** their ideas. Ask them to **present** their responses, either orally or by displaying their work.

Extend

- For students able to progress further, the later tasks give opportunities for extension work.

Plenary suggestions

Question time Ask the students for responses to questions such as:

- How well was I able to approach those tasks?
- Did I manage to present some high quality responses?
- Are there some ideas that I need to strengthen in the later part of this topic?

If there are, make a note. Provide the class with some overall feedback, indicating ideas that they have grasped effectively and those that may need developing further.

Likely responses and next steps in learning

1. This task gives the students an opportunity to recall experiences or to refer to images in the book, and to recall or research definitions of the terms. They should be able to describe that electromagnets need an electric current running through a wire to operate, and recognise that when the current is switched off the magnetic effect is no longer present. In their descriptions they should compare this feature of electromagnets to ordinary magnets, which do not need a current and are magnetic all the time.

2. In this task the students apply their ideas about how magnets work in terms of simple attraction and repulsion. They should recognise that large repulsive forces are acting to push the train upwards away from the rail, causing it to levitate. Annotations of the diagram should be made to show this. A more advanced response would include noting that if the current was suddenly switched off, the train would no longer be under the influence of the magnetic field and would drop back on to the rail.

3. This task draws ideas from wider understanding, asking the students to explain how to make an electromagnetic field stronger. They should include and explain ideas relating to increasing the number of coils, using an iron core and increasing the current. They should link these ideas to the domains within the iron core, and how certain factors result in the alignment of more domains. The students should also engage with the text and introduce ideas about using supercooling to generate a higher flow of current, and the use of other materials that may display greater domain alignment resulting in stronger magnets. Linking these factors to the domain theory increases the level of response beyond just recall, giving the opportunity to produce more developed explanations.

4. In this task the students are given an opportunity to evaluate the benefits of using electromagnetism in this less familiar context. For good responses, they should be able to link with other areas of physics, including ideas about energy transfer, and to compare the benefits of a near frictionless track in the Maglev design with the vast amounts of heat and sound energy transferred in a conventional system. They may research around this area further to identify further benefits.

5. In this task, the students link ideas about the effects of the Earth's magnetic field to the electromagnetic system of the Maglev train. They should be able to predict what happens to the Earth during these pole-reversals and explain what impact, if any, they are likely to have on the Maglev train. They should recognise that the magnetosphere is not as strong before and after such reversals, and offers less protection from solar winds. The charged solar wind particles are more likely to affect the weaker magnetic fields in the Maglev trains, but may have less impact on the strong 15 T fields that cause propulsion of the train.

6. In this final task, the students critically evaluate the Maglev train system. They may wish to research around this to add to their arguments. They should recognise clear drawbacks of the system, relating to energy consumption and sound pollution. The risks and hazards to passengers should be highlighted, including the need to have guaranteed back-up electricity generation in the case of failure in the mains electricity supply. All the statements should be accompanied by explanations and, where appropriate, annotated diagrams.

Chapter 6: Magnetism and Electricity

6.10 Investigating batteries

Lesson overview

Learning objectives

- Describe the link between chemical energy and electricity.
- Investigate how fruit batteries work.

Learning outcomes

- Describe different types of battery; design an investigation to control key variables. [O1]
- Describe how to make the most effective fruit batteries; analyse and interpret results. [O2]
- Explain how a fruit battery works using ideas about charge. [O3]

Skills development

- Thinking scientifically: analyse data
- Working scientifically: design investigations
- Learner development: ask questions

Resources needed images of early batteries including the first one produced by Volta; (optional, for the plenary) a plan of an investigation of fruit batteries with deliberate mistakes, possibly as a slideshow; graph paper; equipment and materials as detailed in the Technician's notes; Worksheet 2.6.10; Technician's notes 2.6.10

Digital resources Quick starter; Slideshow: Inside batteries: The similarities and differences between types of cell; Interactive activity: Complete the sentences about batteries; Video

Key vocabulary, battery, electron, electric current, voltage

Teaching and learning

Engage

- Show the students images of early batteries including the first produced by Volta (see Figure 2.6.10a in the Student Book). Discuss how a battery works using ideas presented in the second section in the Student Book. Discuss some examples of applications of batteries. [O1]
- **Pairs** Show the students a range of different batteries. Ask them to **write down** as many differences as they can between the different batteries. Take feedback and write the main differences on the whiteboard. Ensure that they understand that the 'power' of a battery is represented by the voltage it has. Explain that the meaning of the term 'voltage' will be examined in a future lesson. [O1]

Challenge and develop

- Show the students at least one example of a fruit battery connected to a voltmeter (see Technician's notes 2.6.10). Tell them that these batteries work using metal electrodes connected by wire. [O1]
- **Group work** Working in pairs, give the students pieces of fruit and a range of metals to test. Ask them to **plan an investigation** to identify how to make the fruit battery with the highest voltage. They should use Worksheet 2.6.10 to guide their planning. [O1&2]
- Discuss the differences between random and systematic errors in the context of this investigation, and the ways that these might be identified and eliminated. [O1&2]

    Higher-attaining students should **define** all values for control variables and **explain** how to collect accurate, reliable data.

- When their plans have been reviewed, ask the students to **carry out** their investigation, **recording** all their results. [O1&2]
- The students should **plot graphs** to display their results. [O2]

Key Stage 3 Science Teacher Pack 2

Explain

- The students should **explain** the findings of their investigation, using their graphs and results. [O3]
- They could **draw** annotated diagrams of the fruit battery, **explaining** how electrons build up on the plate and how this causes a current to flow in the juice of the fruit. [O3]

Consolidate and apply

- Ask the students to answer the questions in the Student Book. [O1, 2&3]
- They should **consider** why only a small voltage is produced from this setup. They should **compare** their setup with that of Volta and **design** a system to produce more voltage from given fruits and metals. [O3]

Extend

- Students able to progress further could extend their investigation to **find out** which of the variables – for example the metals, the distance between the metals, the depth the metals are inserted into the fruit or the type of fruit – has the most impact on the voltage produced. The students could be given the data from other groups who have investigated these variables and **compare** the results. They should **develop** their own hypothesis first and then use the data to **test** it. [O3]

Plenary suggestions

Spot the mistakes Provide the students with a plan of an investigation into fruit batteries with lots of deliberate mistakes, possibly as a slideshow. Ask them to find and correct the mistakes. [O1, 2&3]

Answers to Student Book questions

1. Chemical energy is being tranferred by electric current and heat; if used for long periods of time, lots of heat is transferred to the surroundings.
2. stored chemical energy → energy transferred by electricity + energy transferred by heating
3. for example:
   - chemical changes occur in the battery
   - electrons move and build up on the negative terminal
   - electrons in the connecting wires move as a result
   - a current flows in the connecting wires
   - energy is transferred by the current to appliances
4. *advantages*: no movement energy or moving parts needed, which can break; a continuous current is produced; smaller batteries can produce more current for the same size of dynamo

   disadvantages: the battery will run out; and will need to be replaced
5. The bigger the difference in reactivities of the metals, the larger the voltage produced.
6. a) Decrease the distance between the metal plates; the charge can be carried more quickly.

   b) Use a fruit with more juice; the bigger the amount of juice, the bigger the flow of charged particles.

Answers to Worksheet 2.6.10

1. a) *Possible variables*: type of metal; type of fruit; distance between metal plates; depth metal plates are inserted into fruit. Any of these many be chosen as an independent variable, with all others as control variables.

   b) For example, if the type of metal is chosen as the independent variable, suitable values would be iron, zinc, copper, magnesium and aluminium.

   c) voltage   d) using a voltmeter   e) whichever of the variables are not chosen as the independent variable

   f) For example, if the type of metal is the independent variable, suitable control variables would be the distance of the plates (10 cm); the depth of the plates (2 cm), the type of fruit (lemon).

   g) acidic juice from the fruits   h) safety glasses would be a good idea

2. a) By making accurate measurements of all control variables; using a mm ruler; using a digital voltmeter to increase the degree of accuracy.

   b) Perform repeats; to see if the investigation is reproducible and repeatable; consistent readings confirms the reliability of the investigation. Produce a suitable graph with the independent variable on the *x*-axis and voltage on the *y*-axis; check the scale to ensure it is suitable.

3. a) Putting the plates at different depths; not accurately putting the plates the same distance apart.

   b) The fact that each fruit is unique and therefore the liquid inside will not be exactly the same as in other fruits; the metal plates may not be brand new and may have some corrosion on them.

   c) For example: make sure the metal plates were thoroughly clean, use a mm ruler to measure distances instead of a cm ruler, ensure the plate had the same surface area, have a large sample size of fruit to ensure reliability.

   d) Appropriate conclusions drawn from the data; the most reactive metal and the least reactive metal plate will produce the greatest voltage.

Chapter 6: Magnetism and Electricity

6.11 Describing electric circuits

Lesson overview

Learning objectives

- Describe and draw circuit diagrams.
- Explain what is meant by current.
- Explain how materials allow current to flow.

Learning outcomes

- Recognise and use symbols to represent components in a circuit; investigate electrical conductors and insulators. [O1]
- Describe what current is, using models and analogies. [O2]
- Explain how electrical conductors work, using models; explain the strengths and weaknesses of different models and analogies that describe how current works. [O3]

Skills development

- Thinking scientifically: using models
- Working scientifically: develop explanations
- Learner development: communicate effectively

Resources needed equipment and materials as detailed in the Technician's notes; Worksheet 2.6.11 (second page printed onto card); Practical sheet 2.6.11; Technician's notes 2.6.11

Digital resources Quick starter; Interactive activity: Match the statements about electric current

Common misconceptions Energy in a circuit is used up because the battery runs out. Current in a circuit is used up.

Key vocabulary component, conductor, insulator, ammeter, ampere

Teaching and learning

Engage

- Ask the students to play 'matching pairs' using the cards cut out from Worksheet 2.6.11. They should **match up** the name of each component with the diagram representing it. [O1]
- Review the success criteria for drawing electric circuits. These criteria include using a ruler to draw straight lines to represent the wires, using the correct circuit symbols to represent different components and ensuring that circuits is closed and have no gaps.

Challenge and develop

- Remind the students of the terms 'conductor' and 'insulator'. Ask them to do task 1b of Worksheet 2.6.11 **predicting** which of the materials are likely to be conductors and which insulators. They can then **build** the circuit shown on Practical sheet 2.6.11 to test their predictions. [O1]
- Discuss the ideas of electric current using ideas in sections 1 and 2 in the Student Book. Use suggested analogies to develop ideas further. [O2]
- Discuss why conductors allow electric currents to pass but insulators do not. [O1&2]

   Ask higher-attaining students to **develop** their own model/ analogy to show how a conductor works. [O3]

- Ask the students to draw their own representations of a simple circuit with a light bulb, with annotations, **explaining** how electric current works to transfer energy to the light bulb. Select different students to **share** their ideas. They should clearly show that current is not used up in the circuit, but enables the transfer of energy. [O1&2]

Chapter 6: Magnetism and Electricity

Higher-attaining students should **discuss** the strengths and weaknesses of the shared analogies. [O3]

Explain

- Demonstrate how to use an ammeter (in a simple series circuit with a battery and a bulb). Connect ammeters at different points in the circuit and ask the students to **measure** the current in each part. Ask them to use their previous ideas to **explain** their findings. [O1&2]

Consolidate and apply

- Ask the students to **consider** the circuits in task 2 of Worksheet 2.6.11. They should **predict** what the ammeter readings are in the given spaces – they could **build** the circuits to test their ideas. [O2]
- Ask the students to answer the Student Book questions. [O1, 2&3]

Extend

- Students able to progress further could **explain** what is happening in the different circuits in task 3 of Worksheet 2.6.11. They should use their own models to **account for** differences in current between the circuits. [O3]

Plenary suggestions

True or false? Play a true/false quiz using questions such as those suggested here:
- Circuits will work if there is a gap in them (F)
- The current is the same all over the circuit (T)
- A voltmeter measures current (F)
- Electrical conductors will not allow current to pass through (F)
- All metals are good conductors of electricity (T)
- The current in a circuit gets used up (F)

Answers to Student Book questions

1. it is a conductor
2. include correct symbols for bulbs and cells; straight lines (drawn using a ruler) for all wires; and no gaps in the circuit
3. so there is a standard way of representing what is in a circuit; this is useful for making circuits from circuit diagrams
4. *water analogy: low current*, slow-moving stream; *high current*, fast-moving stream
   coal truck analogy: low current, few coal trucks moving; *high current*, many coal trucks moving
5. Coal truck analogy; because it conveys the idea of something being transported around the circuit; and being dropped off; the water analogy does not do this in the same way.
6. *Water analogy:* water is flowing all the time; there is no delay; and flow is at a constant rate; so this is a strength of the analogy. Water, however, can be removed from the river or added to it – this is a limitation.
   Coal truck analogy: the trucks do not all move together or at the same rate, so this is a limitation. The number of trucks moving may differ during the circuit – this is another limitation.
7. Because current is the flow of electrons in the conducting wires; electrons are not removed or added when they are connected to a battery. While the battery is on it makes the charges flow, but they cannot escape anywhere and be lost.

Answers to Worksheet 2.6.11

1. a) A – 5; B – 7; C – 2; D – 1; E – 9; F – 3; G – 8; H – 6; I – 4
   b) *conductors*: all the metals and carbon (graphite); *insulators*: plastic and glass
2. a) Diagram shown with straight lines, no breaks. Explanation of how current is the flow of charge in the connecting wires; transferring energy from the battery to the components.
   b) i) both ammeters will read 3 A.   ii) both ammeters will read 5 A   c) 2 A
3. a) A conductor has free charged particles (electrons) that can move; an insulator has very few charged particles that can move.
   b) The second circuit has more batteries; suggesting that increasing the number of batteries produces a larger current.

Chapter 6: Magnetism and Electricity

6.12 Understanding energy in circuits

Lesson overview

Learning objectives
- Describe what the voltage does in a circuit.
- Explain voltage using different analogies.

Learning outcomes
- Recognise the units of voltage; use different models to describe voltage. [O1]
- Relate current and voltage to different models. [O2]
- Compare the strengths and weaknesses of different models. [O3]

Skills development
- Thinking scientifically: use models
- Working scientifically: develop explanations
- Learner development: communicate effectively

Resources needed drinking straw; equipment and materials as detailed in the Technician's notes; Worksheet 2.6.12; Technician's notes 2.6.12

Digital resources Quick starter; Interactive activity: Select the statements which describe current or voltage in an electric circuit; Hangman: Key vocabulary game

Common misconceptions Voltage and current are the same thing. Voltage and current get used up by the circuit.

Key vocabulary voltage, volt, voltmeter, potential difference

Teaching and learning

Engage
- Display a range of electrical appliances, including some that use batteries and others that use mains electricity. Introduce the term 'voltage' and its units. Ask the students look at the appliances and their voltage ratings. **Do not allow** them to switch on the appliances. Ask them to do task 1 of Worksheet 2.6.12 **recording** the voltage used by each appliance and the source of electricity (battery or mains). Can they **identify** any patterns? Can they **give reasons** why some appliance use batteries and others need mains electricity? [O1]

Challenge and develop
- Discuss the meaning of the term 'voltage'; use the analogies in the Student Book. [O1]
- Show the students circuits set up with different numbers of cells and just one light bulb. First show a circuit with one cell and one bulb. Demonstrate how to connect the voltmeter in parallel with the bulb and discuss the reasons for this, using the Student Book. Then show a circuit with two cells and the same bulb – demonstrate the difference in voltage. Finally show a circuit with three cells and the same bulb. Ask the students to **predict** the voltage across the bulb. [O1]
- Demonstrate how to measure the voltage across the cells. The students should **identify** the pattern between the number of cells and the voltage. [O1]
- Select different students to **role-play** how voltage provides a 'push' to drive a current, and also the energy that the current transfers. Discuss the different analogies presented in section 3 in the Student Book, and any others that you may have. [O1&2]

Chapter 6: Magnetism and Electricity

- **Group work** Using a real circuit, ask the students to **consider** each of the models/ analogies in turn. Ask them to **identify the strengths and weaknesses** of each when used to explain what is happening in each of the circuit diagrams in Worksheet 2.6.12. Take feedback from the groups. [O2&3]

Explain

- **Small groups** Ask the students to **develop** their own analogy to explain voltage and how it affects the current. They should **draw a diagram** or **role-play** their idea to explain how it works. [O2]

    Higher-attaining students should **consider the strengths and weaknesses** of their analogies. [O3]

Consolidate and apply

- Ask the students to complete task 2 of Worksheet 2.6.12. Then ask them to **consider** each of the statements in task 3. They should **decide** whether or not their analogy can explain each of the statements, and **refine** their analogy if possible. [O2&3]

- They should answer the Student Book questions. [O1, 2&3]

Extend

- Students able to progress further should **predict** and **explain** what will happen to a circuit when more than one light bulb is added. Is there any change in the voltage or the current? They should use an analogy to **explain**, and also **consider the strengths and weaknesses** of their analogy. [O2&3]

Plenary suggestions

Understanding voltage and current The students should **rank** the circuits in Worksheet 2.6.12 in order of which has the highest voltage, and then which is likely to have the largest current. Then return to the appliances used at the start of the lesson. Can the students now use ideas about voltage to **explain** why different appliances require a different source of electricity? [O1&2]

Answers to Student Book questions

1. There is no 'push' to make the current flow if there is no voltage.   2. 3 V
3. Circuit B; there is more voltage; so a bigger 'push'; which transfers more energy to the circuit.
4. it would have much more energy; and be able to run faster; if it could take the much higher voltage
5. **Straw analogy**: the first circuit will be like blowing very hard through the straw; a high flow of air will come out of the straw; which models lots of energy being transferred to the current. The second circuit will be like blowing gently through the straw; only a small stream of air (the current) will come out. **Waterfall analogy**: first circuit is like a high waterfall resulting in a large flow of water; the second like a small waterfall; so only a trickle flow of water.
6. The air in the straw (the current) comes from the mouth (the battery). In reality the charges in a circuit come from the wires not from the battery; similarly the water in the river comes from the waterfall, which also represents the battery; so this is a limitation.

Answers to Worksheet 2.6.12

1. table correctly completed with appliance, voltage and mains/battery power source

    a) Appliances that use high voltages are likely to use mains electricity.   b) Voltage provides the push to drive the current.

2. **Circuit 1**: Voltage from the cell provides the energy to push the current, which is transferred to the light bulb. **Circuit 2**: One extra cell means there is double the voltage, so a higher push, and more energy is transferred to the bulb; the bulb is twice as bright as the bulb in the first circuit. **Circuit 3**: Two bulbs means the energy from the battery is shared between them, so they are each half as bright as the bulb in first circuit; the same current flows through each bulb as in the first circuit. **Circuit 4**: Double the voltage of circuit 1 is shared between twice as many bulbs, so same brightness as circuit 1. Appropriate analogy applied to each case.

3. a) circuit 1: 1.5 V; circuit 2: 3 V; circuit 3: 0.75 V; circuit 4: 1.5 V

    b) Analogies correctly applied with a clear understanding of how well each is supported. The river analogy is:

    Statement 1 – water (charge) comes from the waterfall (voltage); so this analogy does not support this idea well.

    Statement 2 – water is always moving as a result of the 'push' from the waterfall; so this idea is supported well.

    Statement 3 – water can be removed from the river (evaporation) and added to (rain); so the analogy does not hold here; if the water was in a closed pipe it would work better.

    Statement 4 – if a water wheel was placed in the river, the energy from the water would be transferred to the wheel; without water being used up; so the analogy holds here.

Chapter 6: Magnetism and Electricity

6.13 Explaining resistance

Lesson overview

Learning objectives

- Explain what resistance is and how it affects the circuit.
- Investigate and identify the relationship between voltage and current.

Learning outcomes

- Describe the term 'resistance' and recognise the units; collect reliable data from circuits. [O1]
- Describe the relationship between voltage, current and resistance; present results using appropriate graphs. [O2]
- Derive a mathematical relationship between voltage and current, and make predictions from it. [O3]

Skills development

- Thinking scientifically: analyse data
- Working scientifically: present evidence
- Learner development: communicate effectively

Resources needed graph paper; samples of conductors and insulators; equipment and materials as detailed in Technician's notes; Worksheet 2.6.13; Practical sheet 2.6.13; Technician's notes 2.6.13

Digital resources Quick starter; Slideshow: Measuring electricity – A look at multimeters and measuring V, I and R; Interactive activity: Complete the sentences about resistance in an electric circuit

Key vocabulary resistance, free electron, ohm

Teaching and learning

Engage

- Give the students samples of conductors and insulators. Remind them of prior learning and review the terms 'conductor' and 'insulator'.
- Demonstrate a model of the atoms in a conductor and in an insulator. This could be a transparent tube of fixed polystyrene balls to represent the atomic nuclei and small marbles to represent free charged particles. The conductor should have many, many more charged particles compared to the insulator. The insulator could have larger polystyrene balls, as greater obstacles to the movement of charged particles. Discuss the differences between the two. [O1]

Challenge and develop

- Use the first section in the Student Book to introduce the idea of resistance. Use the analogies provided. Online simulations may also help. [O1]
- Demonstrate different circuits to discuss the effect of resistance. Start with a circuit that has one battery and one light bulb. Connect the bulb in series with the battery, switch and ammeter. Close the switch and note the ammeter reading. Now connect another bulb in series. Explain that this has the effect of increasing the resistance in the circuit. Note the effect on the brightness and the ammeter reading. [O1]
- Discuss how the resistance of the circuits is different. Ask the students to **predict** what would happen, and why, if there were three light bulbs – test their predictions. [O1&2]
- Return to just one bulb in the circuit and add a rheostat. Adjust the rheostat to show how it changes the resistance in the circuit, and the effect this has on the current. [O1&2]
- **Group work** Ask the students to **investigate** the relationship between resistance, current and voltage, following the instructions on Practical sheet 2.6.13 and recording reliable data. Ask them to **present their results** graphically and **analyse** them using the questions on the practical sheet. [O2]

Chapter 6: Magnetism and Electricity

Higher-attaining students should **identify a mathematical link** between current, voltage and resistance. [O3]

Explain

- Ask the students to **write an explanation** of their results. They should use one analogy and show how this can be applied to their results. They could **identify strengths and weaknesses** of the analogy. [O2&3]

Consolidate and apply

- Ask the students to complete Worksheet 2.6.13 and to answer the Student Book questions. [O1, 2&3]
- Ask the students to consider analogies that they have previously developed to explain voltage and current. Can they now **adapt** these analogies to incorporate ideas about resistance, and **identify the strengths and weaknesses** of these? [O2]

Extend

- Students able to progress further should **develop** an analogy of voltage, current and resistance, which can incorporate the mathematical link. [O3]

Plenary suggestions

Summarising knowledge Ask the students to write a summary **explaining** the terms 'voltage', 'current' and 'resistance' and how they relate to one another. [O1, 2&3]

Answers to Student Book questions

1. a) circuit A b) there is a smaller resistance in this circuit; so a higher current will flow
2. obstacles are the resistance in the circuit; people are the charge
3. It would be brighter; there is less resistance in platinum; which would allow a higher current to flow.
4. 9 ÷ 3 = 3 ohms
5. Change the type of material the wires are made from to one with a higher resistance; higher resistance wire would prevent electrons flowing as easily as they do through copper; so a smaller current will flow for the same voltage. Increasing the number of components would also provide a higher resistance to the flow of current.

Answers to Worksheet 2.6.13

1. Resistance is a measure of the opposition to the flow of charge.

    River analogy: a conductor is like a river with lots of water and no boulders; an insulator is like a river with very little water and lots of boulders.

    Coal truck analogy: a conductor is like lots of coal trucks travelling on a motorway with no roadworks or obstructions due to breakdowns; an insulator is like a road full of road works and traffic lights with only a few coal trucks on it.
2. The resistance is fixed so there is the same constant opposition to the flow of charge; when the voltage is increased, there is a bigger push; so the current flows faster. With a fixed resistance the increase in voltage will affect the flow of charge directly.
3. a) 2 ohms b) The current would decrease

    c) This is true; the voltage determines how much push the current is given; the resistance determines how much opposition there is to the flow of charge; the ratio between the amount of push and the amount of opposition determines the flow; which is the current.

Answers to Practical sheet 2.6.13

2. Graph should have voltage on the *x*-axis and current on the *y*-axis.

    a) a straight line graph through the origin indicates that the current is directly proportional to the voltage

    b) consistent, repeat readings confirm if the results are reliable
3. a) voltage ÷ current should be (roughly) equal for all data

    b) As the voltage increases, the current increases proportionally; when the resistance in the circuit is fixed. This is because the charges in the connecting wires are given a bigger push with higher voltages and increase proportionally in their flow. The resistance in this circuit does not alter with higher voltage.

Chapter 6: Magnetism and Electricity

6.14 Investigating factors affecting resistance

Lesson overview

Learning objectives
- Describe some uses of resistance.
- Investigate and explain factors affecting resistance.

Learning outcomes
- Describe resistance and its effect in a circuit. [O1]
- Investigate factors affecting resistance. [O2]
- Use models and analogies to explain how different factors affect resistance. [O3]

Skills development
- Thinking scientifically: analyse data
- Working scientifically: record evidence
- Learner development: collaborate effectively

Resources needed graph paper; equipment and materials as detailed in the Technician's notes; Worksheet 2.6.14; Practical sheet 2.6.14; Technician's notes 2.6.14

Digital resources Quick starter; Interactive activity: Choose the factors which increase the resistance of a wire, and those which decrease resistance; Slideshow: Using low and high resistances – A look at some factors that affects the resistance of materials

Common misconceptions Resistance is only affected by the voltage.

Key vocabulary resistor, variable resistor, filament

Teaching and learning

Engage
- **Groups** Ask groups of students to complete task 1 of Worksheet 2.6.14. They should use their ideas to prepare a short **role-play** to model what resistance is and how it affects a circuit. Select different groups to **show** their role-play. [O1]
- Now ask them to **model** being a thicker and a thinner wire – what effect does thickness have on the resistance of a wire? Discuss how their role-plays can account for this. [O1&2]

Challenge and develop
- Remind the students of the mathematical link between current, voltage and resistance. Demonstrate a fixed voltage circuit that includes a variable resistor and an ammeter – see Technician's notes 2.6.14. Discuss what the effect on the current would be if the resistance were to be increased. Select different students to **explain** this. [O1&2]

- Establish that if the voltage of the circuit is fixed and its resistance increases, the current decreases proportionally in most conductors, so long as the temperature rise does not affect the resistance. By recording the current, discuss how the students can work out the resistance mathematically. [O2]

- **Groups** Give the students Practical sheet 2.6.14 and ask them to **follow the procedure** and **investigate** how the length and (if time allows) the thickness of a wire affects its resistance. [O1, 2&3]

    You could ask lower-attaining students to investigate the effect of length, while other students could **plan** an investigation of the effect of the thickness of the wire, as suggested in task 2 of Worksheet 2.6.14.

- The students should **collect** reliable data, **record** their results and **draw a graph**. [O2]

    Higher-attaining students could also investigate the effect of material on resistance, if time allows. [O2&3]

Chapter 6: Magnetism and Electricity

Explain

- Ask the students to **prepare a presentation** of their findings and to include either a diagram or a **role-play** to **explain** their results. They can use the Student Book to help them. [O2&3]

    Higher-attaining students should use more than one model and/ or analogy to support the explanation of their results, as suggested in task 3 of Worksheet 2.6.14. [O3]

Consolidate and apply

- Ask the students to **draw** a diagram of three wires – one with a very high resistance, one with a medium resistance and one with a very low resistance. They should **explain** how the features of the wires affect their resistance. [O2&3]

    Middle-attaining students should incorporate two variables in their diagrams.

    Higher-attaining students could incorporate all three variables in their diagrams.

Extend

- Students able to progress further could **research** applications requiring very high and very low resistances – they should **identify** and **explain** how such resistances are achieved. Models and analogies should be used in their explanations. [O3]

Plenary suggestions

Just a minute Select students to **talk** for a minute on the topic of resistance without hesitation, repetition or deviation. [O1, 2&3]

Answers to Student Book questions

1. for example: the knob on a toaster, the heat settings on a hairdryer, and electric cooker settings all have a variable resistor; electronic devices such as computers and mobile phones have fixed resistors.
2. The size the of current in a circuit can be controlled carefully.
3. High resistance; the the energy can be transferred to heat as the wire gets hot due to the friction effects of the current.
4. The 12 A dryer will have a higher resistor in its circuit.
5. The length of circuit wire may be altered; so as the knob is turned the amount of wire included in the circuit becomes longer or shorter; changing the current in the circuit; for loud volumes, the resistance is kept low.
6. made of very thick wire; and of a material with a very low resistance; to keep the resistance as low as possible; because the current has to be transported over large distances

Answers to Worksheet 2.6.14

1. opposition; electrons; electrons; other atoms; higher; more; higher
2. Same length of wire; same material of wire; voltage on for the same length of time; same setting of the rheostat in each investigation. Procedure to similar to that of investigating length; but changing the thickness of wire instead.

    a) The thicker the wire, the lower the resistance.

    b) There are more charged particles in a thicker wire; it is easier for charged particles to travel in a thicker wire compared to a thinner wire.
3. Graph with thickness of wire on the *x*-axis and the mean current on the *y*-axis.

    a) appropriate line of best fit – straight line   b) resistance is directly proportional to the length of a wire

    c) Appropriate explanation suggesting that the longer the wire, the higher the resistance; and so the less current flows when the voltage remains the same; this is because there are more atoms to collide with during the flow of the charge. The thicker the wire, the lower the resistance for the same voltage; and the more current will flow; there are more charged particles; and less oppostion to their motion in a thicker wire.

Answers to Practical sheet 2.6.14

Table correctly completed with any anomalous results circled and omitted in calculation of mean values. Graph with length of wire on the *x*-axis and mean current on the *y*-axis; appropriate line of best fit.

For the thickness experiment, the graph should have thickness of wire on the *x*-axis and mean current on the *y*-axis, with an appropriate line of best fit.

Chapter 6: Magnetism and Electricity

6.15 Explaining circuits using models

Lesson overview

Learning objectives

- Describe how the voltage, current and resistance are related in different circuits.
- Use a model to explain the relationship between voltage, current and resistance.

Learning outcomes

- Use different models to describe voltage, current and resistance. [O1]
- Relate the current, voltage and resistance to the rope model. [O2]
- Compare the strengths and weaknesses of different models. [O3]

Skills development

- Thinking scientifically: use models
- Working scientifically: develop explanations
- Learner development: ask questions

Resources needed equipment and materials as detailed in the Technician's notes; Worksheet 2.6.15; Practical sheet 2.6.15; Technician's notes 2.6.15

Digital resources Quick starter; Interactive activity: Match the scientific ideas about electric circuits to the rope model analogy

Key vocabulary model, analogy

Teaching and learning

Engage

- **Small groups** Ask the students to **draw up a table** with three rows and three columns – headed 'Voltage', 'Resistance' and 'Current'. Along each row they should write the name of a model or analogy that they have used to explain how electric circuits work. This could be 'Water analogy', 'Coal truck analogy' or 'Straw analogy' – all are depicted in the Student Book. Ask the students to **explain** how voltage, current and resistance are represented in all three analogies. [O1&2]

Challenge and develop

- Work with students to build a 'big' circuit that takes up the whole room but has just one bulb and one battery (see Technician's notes 2.6.15). [O1]

- Discuss with them how quickly they expect the light bulb to go on when the battery is connected, compared with how quickly the bulb will light up in a small circuit. Discuss how the different models would predict what would happen to the light bulb. All the models used so far would predict a delay – but the students will see that the light bulb actually comes on immediately. Establish the need for a different model to explain this. [O1&2]

- Demonstrate the rope loop model with the whole class, alongside the big circuit taking up the whole room. Have different students representing the light bulb, which acts like a resistance in the circuit. Select different students to **explain** how this model represents current, voltage and resistance. [O1&2]

- **Groups of eight** Ask the students to follow the instructions in Practical sheet 2.6.15 and to **model** the circuits shown using this new model – explanations are also given in the Student Book. Each group should **try out** the model for the different circuits given and **explain** how the current, voltage and resistances are different. Select different groups to **share** their observations and explanations. [O1&2]

    Higher-attaining students should **compare the strengths and weaknesses** of the rope model with those of other models. [O3]

Chapter 6: Magnetism and Electricity

Explain

- **Groups** For each of the circuits, the students should **write an explanation** of how the rope model represents the voltage, current and resistance, and the effect of each in each of the circuits. This should be done on a table copied from Worksheet 2.6.15. [O1&2]
- Select different groups to **feed back** their ideas for discussion.

Consolidate and apply

- Ask the students to answer the questions on Worksheet 2.6.15 and those in the Student Book. [O1, 2&3]
- They could **draw** an annotated diagram of the rope representing a circuit with one light bulb and **explain** how the rope loop model works. [O1&2]

    Higher-attaining students could **identify strengths and limitations** of the model [O3]

Extend

- Students able to progress further could **make suggestions** as to how to amend the rope loop model to incorporate wires of different resistance. [O2&3]

Plenary suggestions

True/false Ask the students to **devise** their own 'true' or 'false' questions relating to the use of models to represent electric circuits. They should take it in turns to ask the class these questions.

Answers to Student Book questions

1. voltage = 9 V; resistance = 9 ohms
2. a) same   b) brighter   c) same
3. in the particles of rope
4. it opposes the flow of the rope; modelling resistance
5. One person, with the higher resistance; must hold the rope more firmly than the other.
6. hold it less tightly; use a thicker rope

Answers to Worksheet 2.6.15

1. a) *River*: i) using a waterfall   ii) kinetic energy of the water   iii) flow of the river   iv) water particles in the river
    v) boulders in the river
    b) *Coal trucks*: i) being sent from the depot full of coal   ii) the coal represents energy   iii) trucks moving along a road
    iv) each wagon is the charge   v) obstructions in the road/ traffic lights
    c) *Straw*: i) strength of the blow   ii) kinetic energy of the air   iii) flow of the air   iv) air particles   v) narrower straw
2. a) Current is represented by the pull of the rope in the circuit; voltage by the push on the rope at the 'battery'; resistance is represented by holding the rope tighter/ looser.
    b) i) harder push on the rope at the battery
    ii) tighter grip on the rope at the positions of the components
    iii) everyone holds the rope tighter
3. *Strengths* of the rope model: it can explain how the current moves instantaneously in all parts of the circuit; the charges are not made in the battery – they are already there in the wire and the battery just makes them move around, just as the rope is always there and just gets pushed around; the current does not get used up – the rope does not disppear; energy is transferred in the circuit; the teacher's hands get more tired as energy is transferred round the circuit; there is more heat at the components as friction increases due to increased resistance; current only flows in one direction in the circuit.
    Weaknesses of the rope model: it can't expain how the battery exerts a potential difference on the current at all times; there is a slight delay as the rope is being fed around the circuit; it would be difficult to demonstrate $V \div I = R$.

Chapter 6: Magnetism and Electricity

6.16 Describing series and parallel circuits

Lesson overview

Learning objectives

- Understand how voltage and current vary in a series circuit.
- Understand how voltage and current vary in a parallel circuit.

Learning outcomes

- Recognise circuits as being series or parallel and identify the features of each. [O1]
- Draw and interpret circuit diagrams for series and parallel circuits; predict the brightness of bulbs in these circuits. [O2]
- Explain why components behave differently in series and parallel circuits. [O3]

Skills development

- Thinking scientifically: ask questions
- Working scientifically: make predictions
- Learner development: collaborate effectively

Resources needed equipment and materials as detailed in the Technician's notes; Worksheet 2.6.16; Technician's notes 2.6.16

Digital resources Quick starter; Interactive activity: Choose the statements which best describe series circuits, and those which best describe parallel circuit; Slideshow: Splitters and multi-sockets – The dangers of overloading; Video

Common misconceptions The arrangement of a circuit has no effect on the components.

Key vocabulary series circuit, branch, parallel circuit

Teaching and learning

Engage

- Give small groups of students bulbs, leads and batteries. Challenge them to see if they can **find** a way to build circuits in which two bulbs are just as bright as one bulb. Give them a time limit of 2 minutes. [O1]

Challenge and develop

- Demonstrate a simple circuit using a battery, a light bulb, an ammeter and a switch connected in series. Now connect another similar circuit alongside the first, but this time connect two identical light bulbs in series. Before turning on the switch, ask the students to **recall** previous learning and **predict** what will change when the second light bulb is added – ask them to **explain** their ideas. Finally demonstrate a third circuit alongside the other two, this time connecting two bulbs in parallel. Ask the students to **compare** the series and parallel arrangements and to **describe** what differences they can see. Ask them to **predict** what will happen to the brightness of the light bulbs in the parallel configuration. Select different students to **make responses** and discuss their ideas. [O1&2]

- Introduce the terms 'series' and 'parallel'. Ask the students to complete task 1 of Worksheet 2.6.16, **drawing** circuit diagrams for the two arrangements and **predicting** what would happen if a light bulb were to be removed from the series circuit and then from the parallel circuit. [O1&2]

Explain

- Give small groups of students six bulbs, leads, switches and a battery. Ask them to **design** their own series and parallel circuits, each having three bulbs. They should **draw** the circuit diagrams and **predict** the brightness of the bulbs in each arrangement (task 2 of Worksheet 2.6.16). Allow them to **build** the circuits to **test** their predictions. [O1, 2&3]

Key Stage 3 Science Teacher Pack 2 © HarperCollinsPublishers Limited 2014

Chapter 6: Magnetism and Electricity

- The students can then **annotate** their circuit diagrams from the last task, or draw larger ones **explaining** what they think is happening to the current, voltage and resistance in each case (task 3 of Worksheet 2.6.16). [O3]
- Select different groups to **show** their annotated diagrams and discuss their ideas. Challenge any misconceptions they may have. [O1, 2&3]

Consolidate and apply

- Ask the students to answer the Student Book questions. [O1, 2&3]
- **Pairs** Ask them to **draw** circuit diagrams with a motor, bulb and buzzer connected first in series and then in parallel. Ask them to **explain** how the behaviour of the components will change in the different types of circuit. [O1, 2&3]

Extend

- Students able to progress further could **investigate** circuits that are part series and part parallel. They should **make predictions** about the brightness of bulbs in each case and **explain** what is happening to the current, voltage and resistance. [O2&3]

Plenary suggestions

Compare series and parallel circuits Ask the students to **write a comparison** of series circuits and parallel circuits – what are the main differences between them? [O1, 2&3]

Answers to Student Book questions

1. all the components would stop working; the circuit is no longer closed
2. a) Check that the circuit diagram has the correct symbols; and is drawn according to conventions.
   b) there would be no current in the circuit
3. The drawing should represent the descriptions.
   a) The voltage in the two circuits will be the same overall; because they have the same number of cells.
   b) The current in the circuit with three bulbs will be smaller than the circuit with one bulb.
   c) The three bulbs will be less bright than the single bulb.
4. a) Check that the circuit diagram is drawn correctly and according to conventions.
   b) In the parallel circuit, each bulb would be as bright as if it were the only bulb connected to the battery; in the series circuit each bulb would be much dimmer.
5. *Advantages of series*: if there is a fault with one component the current stops flowing; which can protect the other components.
   Disdvantages of series: if bulbs are connected in series and one has a fault, none of the lights will work.
   Advantages of parallel: if one light bulb is faulty, all the others will continue to work.
   Disadvantages of parallel: the battery will not last as long as it would if the components are connected in series.

Answers to Worksheet 2.6.16

1. a) i) and ii) Check that the circuit diagrams are drawn correctly; and according to conventions.
   b) i) the other bulb will go out   ii) the other bulb will stay on
2. *In series*: the three bulbs will be equally dim; and less bright than a series circuit with two bulbs.
   In parallel: the bulbs will be equally bright; and just as bright as in a circuit with just one bulb; the bulbs will also be much brighter than the bulbs in the series circuit.
3. *Three bulbs in a series circuit*: the resistance in the circuit has increased; the voltage remains the same; the current in the circuit is the same everywhere; but is lower than for two bulbs; due to the increased resistance. The amount of energy is now divided across the three bulbs, instead of two; so they are all less bright compared with two bulbs.
   Three bulbs in a parallel circuit: there are three branches; each behaving like an individual circuit; each branch has the same resistance as a circuit with one bulb; because there is only one bulb in each branch. The current across the branches is shared; but the voltage across each is the same; so the same energy is transferred as it would be for one bulb; all the bulbs light up equally brightly; as if there was only one bulb in the circuit.

Chapter 6: Magnetism and Electricity

6.17 Comparing series and parallel circuits

Lesson overview

Learning objectives

- Investigate and explain current and voltage in series and parallel circuits.
- Explain the circuits in our homes.

Learning outcomes

- Make measurements of current and voltage in series circuits and parallel circuits. [O1]
- Use models to explain what is happening to the current and voltage in series and parallel circuits; calculate the current and the voltage in series and parallel circuits. [O2]
- Make predictions about current and voltage in different circuit arrangements; explain how the domestic ring main works. [O3]

Skills development

- Thinking scientifically: use equations
- Working scientifically: interpret evidence
- Learner development: collaborate effectively

Resources needed equipment and materials as detailed in the Technician's notes; Worksheet 2.6.17; Practical sheet 2.6.17; Technician's notes 2.6.17

Digital resources Quick starter; Interactive activity: Order the circuits from the one with the highest current, to the one with the lowest

Common misconceptions The current in circuits is used up. The voltage is the same in all circuits.

Key vocabulary ring main, appliance, mains supply

Teaching and learning

Engage

- **True/false** Have a class quiz using statements such as:
  - In a parallel circuit the bulbs are arranged side-by-side. (F)
  - There is no difference in the brightness of the bulbs if they are in series or in parallel. (F)
  - Two bulbs in parallel are brighter than the same two bulbs in series. (T)
  - The battery runs out faster if the bulbs are in parallel. (T)
  - 100 bulbs in parallel will be just as bright as if there were just one bulb in the circuit. (T)

Challenge and develop

- **Small groups** The students should **set up** three series circuits – one with two bulbs, one with three bulbs and one with four bulbs, as shown on Practical sheet 2.6.17. They should **measure** the current and the voltage across one of the bulbs in each circuit and in the main part of the circuit, as shown in the diagram on the practical sheet, and **record** their results. [O1]

- The students should now use the rope model to **simulate** each of the circuits, **explaining** the values of current and voltage obtained. They can use the Student Book to help them if required. [O2]

- Next, ask them to **set up** three parallel circuits and **make measurements** of voltage and current, using the same numbers of bulbs as before, as described on Practical sheet 2.6.17. They should **record** the values and answer the corresponding questions. The students should then **model** each circuit using the rope model, to **explain** the values obtained. [O1&2]

- If possible show a video of the domestic ring main and use the 'Household circuits' section of the Student Book to help explain how it works. Discuss the advantages and disadvantages of supplying household electricity in this way. [O3]

Key Stage 3 Science Teacher Pack 2 © HarperCollins*Publishers* Limited 2014

Chapter 6: Magnetism and Electricity

Explain

- Select different groups to **demonstrate** their model of each type of circuit from Practical sheet 2.6.17. They should **explain** the values of current and voltage obtained. [O1&2]

  Ask higher-attaining students to use the rope model to **explain** to the class how the domestic ring main works. [O3]

Consolidate and apply

- Ask the students to answer the questions from Worksheet 2.6.17 and the Student Book, **calculating** values of current and voltage where appropriate. [O1, 2&3]

  Ask higher-attaining students to carry out some **research** and produce a poster about the domestic ring main. [O3]

Extend

- Students able to progress further could **design** their own circuits containing part series and part parallel components. They could **make predictions** of the values of current and voltage across different components and then **set up** the circuits to **test** their predictions. [O2]

Plenary suggestions

Circuit problems The students could draw their own series and parallel circuit diagrams with numerical values for the voltage across the battery and the current in the main circuit, and ask each other to **predict** the values for current and voltage across the components.

Answers to Student Book questions

1. it will decrease; the voltage is shared between three lights instead of two
2. Double the voltage will mean that the lights will be twice as bright; if the current in the main circuit remains at 2 A, the current in each branch will be 0.2 A.
3. add another loop with a person holding part of it; to represent the light bulb
4. In a series circuit the current would be he same; the voltage across them would be different, depending on the resistance. In a parallel circuit the voltage would be be the same; the current would be different, depending on the resistance.
5. it may be difficult to determine where a fault lies

Answers to Worksheet 2.6.17

1. *Series circuit*: the current is the same; the voltage is shared between the components.
   Parallel circuit: the current is shared between each branch; the voltage is the same across each branch.
   In a parallel circuit, the total sum of current in all the branches is the same as the current in the main circuit.
2. circuit 1: A = 9 ÷ 3 = 3 V; B = 3 A;   circuit 2: C = 9 V; D = 3 ÷ 3 = 1 A
3. a) $R = 9 ÷ 3 = 3$ ohms   b) 1 ohm   c) 4 ohms   d) $I = 12 ÷ 4 = 3$ A   e) they are the same brightness

Answers to Practical sheet 2.6.17

1. a) The current should decrease with the number of light bulbs, but it remains equal to the current in the main part of the circuit.
   b) The voltage across a bulb should decrease with increasing numbers of bulbs.
   c) The current through one bulb should be the same irrespective of the number of bulbs.
   d) The voltage should remain the same across all components in the circuit; irrespective of the number of bulbs.
2. a) The current in the circuit will be $1/5$ of the current with one bulb on its own.
   b) The voltage across one bulb will be $1/5$ of the battery voltage.
   c) The current through a bulb will be the same as it was with fewer bulbs in the circuit.
   d) The voltage will be the same as in the other cases.

Chapter 6: Magnetism and Electricity

6.18 Applying circuits

Lesson overview

Learning objectives
- Describe how circuits are arranged in common appliances

Learning outcomes
- Identify if a circuit is arranged in series or parallel or both. [O1]
- Describe different uses of series and parallel circuits. [O2]
- Explain the advantages of using either series or parallel circuits. [O3]

Skills development
- Thinking scientifically: ask questions
- Working scientifically: develop explanations
- Learner development: communicate effectively

Resources needed Christmas tree lights; Worksheet 2.6.18 (second page copied onto card)

Digital resources Quick starter; Interactive activity: Complete the sentence about series and parallel circuits; Hangman: Key vocabulary game

Common misconceptions All circuits may have the same arrangement.

Key vocabulary circuit breaker, thermostat, series–parallel circuit

Teaching and learning

Engage
- Recap series circuits and parallel circuits from the previous lesson.
- Demonstrate a set of Christmas tree lights working. Remove one of the bulbs and ask the students to **identify** if the circuit is connected in series or in parallel. Discuss the advantages and disadvantages of having the bulbs in this arrangement. [O1, 2&3]

Challenge and develop
- Show the students a circuit diagram containing a circuit breaker (Topic 6.7 in the Student Book). Remind them of what they have previously learned about how a circuit breaker works. Discuss whether the circuit is series or parallel and the advantages of this arrangement. Use the Student Book for support. [O1, 2&3]
- Use the Student Book (Figure 2.6.18b) to show the arrangement of the circuit in a hairdryer. Discuss why the circuit is arranged in this way and the advantages this offers. [O1, 2&3]

  Higher-attaining students should **discuss** the series–parallel arrangement of a car-light dimmer (Figure 2.6.18c) after reading about it in the Student Book. Ask them 'What benefits does a series–parallel circuit offer?'. [O3]

Explain
- **Small groups** Ask the students to **role-play** what is happening in a given circuit – they could use the rope model to help them. Allocate one of the examples to groups of students as follows:

  Lower-attaining groups: the Christmas tree lights

  Middle-attaining groups: the hairdryer

  Higher-attaining groups: the car-light dimmer

  They should **explain** how the circuit behaves normally and then **model** what happens if one component is faulty. [O1&2]

Chapter 6: Magnetism and Electricity

Higher-attaining students should **consider the advantages and disadvantages** of the circuit they have been given, explaining why both series and parallel parts are advantageous. [O3]

Consolidate and apply

- Ask the students to answer the questions on Worksheet 2.6.18 and the Student Book questions. [O1, 2&3]
- Ask them to **match** the circuits to the appliances using the card sort from Worksheet 2.6.18, without the support of other resources. [O1&2]

Extend

- Students able to progress further could **set up** their own series–parallel circuits and **explore** how the current and voltage change. They should **make predictions** about what will happen to the circuit when specific components are faulty.

Plenary suggestions

'Just a minute' Select individual students to **talk** for a minute, without repetition, deviation or hesitation, on the topic of series circuits and parallel circuits. [O1, 2&3]

Answers to Student Book questions

1. The lights would all be equally dim/bright; if one bulb was faulty they would all go out and it would be hard to detect which bulb was faulty.
2. If the circuit breaker was activated, only the current to the circuit breaker would be affected. Current would still be supplied to the faulty appliance; which is potentially dangerous and could cause electric shocks.
3. for example shower; washing maching; dishwasher;central heating boiler
4. Parallel; if one appliance is faulty the others are not affected.
5. Current passes through the variable resistor; and then branches through the bulbs.
6. for example dimmer switches for household lights

Answers to Worksheet 2.6.18

1. A – parallel; B – series; C – series and parallel; D – series; E – parallel
2. A – Christmas tree lights; B – circuit breaker; C – car lights dimmer; D water heater; E – hair dryer
3. *Circuit breaker*: series; a faulty appliance, which has caused the circuit to break, can be removed safely.

   Hairdryer: the parallel circuit enables the blower and the heater to work independently of each other; the blower can still blow if there is no heat.

   Water heater: series; enables the control of the water temperature; once the thermostat has reached the required temperature the heater is switched off; because it is in series, no more current is supplied to the heater.

   Christmas tree lights: parallel; if one bulb blows the rest are unaffected.

   Car lights dimmer: the variable resistor is in series with the bulbs; so the brightness of both bulbs is controlled. The bulbs are in connected in parallel; if one is faulty the other will still work.

Chapter 6: Magnetism and Electricity

6.19 Checking students' progress

The 'Checking your progress' section in the Student Book indicates the key ideas developed in this chapter and shows how students progress to more complex levels. It is provided to support students in:

- identifying those ideas
- developing a sense of their current level of understanding
- developing a sense of what the next steps in their learning are

It is designed either to be used at the end of a chapter to support an overall view of the progress, or alternatively during the teaching of the unit. Students can self assess or peer assess using this as a basis.

It would be helpful if students can be encouraged to provide evidence from their understanding or their notes to support their judgments. In some cases it may be useful to explore the difference in the descriptors for a particular idea so that students can see what makes for a 'higher outcome'.

It may be useful with some descriptors to provide examples from the specific work done, such as an experiment undertaken or an explanation developed and recorded. If marking and feedback uses similar ideas and phrases this will enable students to relate specific marking to a more general sense of progress.

Chapter 6: Magnetism and Electricity

To make good progress in understanding science students need to focus on these ideas and skills:

Students who are making modest progress will be able to:	Students who are making good progress will be able to:	Students who are making excellent progress will be able to:
Describe differences between permanent and temporary magnets.	Describe and compare different methods to make permanent magnets.	Use the domain theory to explain how materials become magnetised and demagnetised.
Describe some effects of the Earth's magnetic field.	Describe the geodynamo theory.	Explain evidence for how the Earth's magnetic field works.
Describe how to test the strength of a magnet and an electromagnet.	Design investigations to compare different methods of making magnets and testing the strength of electromagnets.	Use models and analogies to explain the factors affecting the strengths of magnets and electromagnets.
Describe different applications of magnets and electromagnets.	Explain the advantages of using electromagnets.	Compare and contrast the use of magnets and electromagnets in different applications, such as a circuit breaker.
Describe and investigate different types of batteries, including fruit batteries.	Analyse and interpret data to explain how to make the most effective fruit batteries.	Explain how a battery works, using ideas about charge.
Describe what is meant by current, voltage and resistance.	Apply a range of models and analogies to describe current, voltage and resistance.	Evaluate different models and analogies for explaining current, voltage and resistance.
Describe the relationship between current, voltage and resistance in a qualitative way.	Use data to identify a pattern between current, voltage and resistance.	Use data and a mathematical relationship between current, voltage and resistance, to carry out calculations.
Make measurements of current and voltage in series and in parallel circuits.	Use models and simple calculations to explain and compare what happens to the current and voltage in series and parallel circuits.	Use calculations to make predictions about current and voltage in series and parallel circuits.
Describe different domestic uses of series and parallel circuits.	Make comparisons between components in series and parallel circuits.	Explain the advantages of using series or parallel circuits, including the domestic ring main as an example.

Chapter 6: Magnetism and Electricity

6.20 Answers to Student Book Questions

This table provides answers to the Questions section at the end of Chapter 6 of the Student Book. It also shows how different questions assess attainment in terms of the focus and style of a question as well as its context. Question level analysis can indicate students' proficiency in approaching different aspects of scientific understanding and different types of answer.

Q	Answer	Marks available	Focus: Knowledge & understanding	Focus: Application	Focus: Evaluation of evidence	Style: Objective test question	Style: Short written answer	Style: Longer written answer	Context: Types of magnets, domain theory	Context: Applications of magnets	Context: Current, voltage and resistance	Context: Series and parallel circuits
1	c	1	x			x					x	
2	b	1	x			x			x			
3	d	1	x			x				x		
4	a	1	x			x			x			
5	Any two from: • an electromagnet requires an electric current to operate; permanent magnets don't • the magnetic effect of an electromagnet can be switched off; this can't happen in a magnet • an electromagnet is a temporary magnet; ordinary magnets can be permanent	2	x				x		x			
6	Any two from: • series components are connected one after the other; in one continuous loop • parallel components are connected separately in their own loop; between the terminals of a cell • parallel circuits have branches	2	x				x					x
7	Drawing: (see Figure 2.6.7c in Student Book) • electromagnet	1	x				x			x		
	• iron contacts, pivot and spring	1	x				x			x		
	Any two from: • normally a low current so electromagnet is not strong enough to break contacts • if there is a fault, a high current increases the strength of the electromagnet; attracting the iron contacts • the circuit breaks	2	x				x			x		

Chapter 6: Magnetism and Electricity

Q	Answer	Marks available	Focus: Knowledge & understanding	Focus: Application	Focus: Evaluation of evidence	Style: Objective test question	Style: Short written answer	Style: Longer written answer	Context: Types of magnets, domain theory	Context: Applications of magnets	Context: Current, voltage and resistance	Context: Series and parallel circuits
8	c	1		x		x						x
9	a	1		x		x				x		
10	c	1		x		x				x		
11	b	1		x		x			x			
12	• When the magnet is dropped; the domains are disturbed and fewer will be aligned with each other	1		x			x		x			
	• When placed in a strong magnetic field; the domains are realigned due to the presence of the field	1		x			x		x			
13	• Increase the voltage by making the 'boots' turn faster	1		x			x				x	
	• Increase the resistance by placing obstacles in the way	1		x			x				x	
14	Any two of the following (max. 2) for each circuit *Series circuit 1* • voltage is 3 V across each lamp • voltage is shared across components • current is 3 A • current is the same at any point	2		x				x				x
	Parallel circuit 2 • voltage = 6 V at each point • same voltage is applied to each branch • current = 1.5 A in each branch • current is divided between the branches	2		x				x				x
15	The fruit battery with the brighter light has (any two from): • bigger difference in the reactivities of the metals used • larger surface area of metal plates • metal plates pushed deeper in the fruit • one fruit juicier than the other	2			x		x				x	
16	• Graph of data in table with labels, correctly named and titled	2			x			x			x	
	• Sketch of resistance graph for an electricity distribution line wire should show resistances well below those of the wire in the table; demonstrating that the new wire has a much lower resistance	1			x			x			x	
	• The wire needs to have a much lower resistance so that maximum current can be transferred with as little energy transferred as heat as possible	1			x			x			x	
	Total possible:	30	12	12	6	8	10	12	7	7	9	7

Scheme of Work

Scheme of Work

Teaching Key Stage 3 in three years

The following pages show the full plan of the scheme of work for Collins Key Stage 3 Science Teacher Pack 2 taught over 3 years.

Teaching Key Stage 3 in two years?

If you are using the Collins KS3 Science scheme to deliver the Programme of Study in two years there are three ways you can do it:
1. Focus on the lessons shaded in the table. By so doing you will have visited all the key ideas.
2. Use the shaded lessons as a starting point but draw on ideas, activities and questions as necessary, i.e., 'swapping out' the occasional activity on an indicated lesson.
3. Use the introductory lesson and/or the 'Applying key ideas' lesson to see what students are more confident with and what time would be better spent on.

Collins Connect is our digital learning platform that offers a range of linked resources to enhance your lessons.

Scheme of Work

Chapter 1: Getting the Energy your Body Needs

Lesson	Lesson title	Overarching objectives	Learning objectives	CD-ROM resources	Collins Connect resources	Notes for two-year scheme
2.1.2	Exploring the human skeleton	The structure and functions of the human skeleton, to include support, protection, movement and making blood cells	• Identify bones of the human skeleton • Explain why we have different shapes and sizes of bones • Communicate effectively to investigate the structure and function of bones	Worksheet 2.1.2	Quick starter; Interactive activity: drag the bones to the correct part of the body; Slideshow: An introduction to the human skeleton, its evolution and uniqueness	
2.1.3	Analysing the skeleton	The structure and functions of the human skeleton, to include support, protection, movement and making blood cells	• Describe the roles of the skeleton • Explain the evidence for each of the roles of the skeleton • Estimate height using bone measurement calculations and suggest reasons for differences between people	Worksheet 2.1.3; Practical sheet 2.1.3; Technician's notes 2.1.3	Quick starter; Interactive activity: drag the functions to the correct bone(s); Video	
2.1.4	Understanding the role of skeletal joints	Biomechanics – the interaction between skeleton and muscles, including the measurement of force exerted by different muscles	• Describe the roles of tendons, ligaments, joints and muscles • Compare different joints within the human skeleton • Collaborate effectively to interpret how we use joints	Worksheet 2.1.4; Practical sheet 2.1.4; Technician's notes 2.1.4	Quick starter; Interactive activity: Drag the example of joints to the correct group; Slideshow: Introduction to the joints of the thumb, a new born baby and the pelvis; Hangman: Key vocabulary game	

Scheme of Work

2.1.5	Investigating muscle strength	Biomechanics – the interaction between skeleton and muscles, including the measurement of force exerted by different muscles	• Identify muscles used in different activities • Plan an investigation to compare strength of different muscles • Make a prediction about which muscles are stronger than others	Worksheet 2.1.5; Practical sheet 2.1.5; Technician's notes 2.1.5	Quick starter; Interactive activity: Order the muscles of the human body, from head to toe; Interactive activity: Match the actions to the muscles involved
2.1.6	Analysing muscle strength	Biomechanics – the interaction between skeleton and muscles, including the measurement of force exerted by different muscles	• Display data in a suitable graph • Analyse data to compare the force of different muscles • Explore the use of scientific ideas in identifying and treating muscle disorders	Worksheet 2.1.6a (copied onto card) and Worksheet 2.1.6b	Quick starter; Slideshow: A look at steroids and their side effects; Video
2.1.7	Examining interacting muscles	The function of muscles and examples of antagonistic muscles	• Describe antagonistic muscles and give examples • Explain how antagonistic muscles bring about movement • Evaluate a model of antagonistic muscles	Worksheet 2.1.7; Practical sheet 2.1.7 (second page copied onto card); Technician's notes 2.1.7	Quick starter; Interactive activity: Match the muscles that work together in pairs
2.1.8	Exploring problems with the skeletal system	The structure and functions of the human skeleton, to include support, protection, movement and making blood cells Biomechanics – the interaction between skeleton and muscles, including the measurement of force exerted by different muscles	• Recall some medical problems with the skeletal system • Describe treatments for some skeletal system problems • Communicate effectively to learn how treatments have changed over time	Worksheet 2.1.8	Quick starter; Interactive activity: Match the picture to the type of broken bone; Slideshow: A look at osteoporosis; Hangman: Key vocabulary game

Scheme of Work

2.1.9	Applying key ideas		• Extract ideas about skeleton and muscles from the text, including earlier sections of the chapter • Apply ideas about maintaining muscle and bone mass in relation to the effects of space travel • Suggest how understanding the effects of space on the skeleton can be applied on Earth	Worksheet 2.1.9	
2.1.10	Understanding how our muscles get energy	Aerobic and anaerobic respiration in living organisms, including the breakdown of organic molecules to enable all the other chemical processes necessary for life The word equation for aerobic respiration	• Recall the equation for respiration and describe what it shows • Explain the importance of respiration • Apply what we know about respiration	Worksheet 2.1.10; Practical sheet 2.1.10; Technician's notes 2.1.10	Quick starter; Interactive activity: Match the words that are associated with proteins or carbohydrates; Slideshow: A comparison of the two essential life processes – photosynthesis and respiration
2.1.11	Investigating respiration	Aerobic and anaerobic respiration in living organisms, including the breakdown of organic molecules to enable all the other chemical processes necessary for life The word equation for aerobic respiration	• Recall that respiration takes place in plants and animals • Describe some experimental evidence for respiration • Consider the quality of evidence for respiration	Cards from Worksheet 2.1.10 (as used in the previous lesson); Worksheet 2.1.11; Practical sheets 2.1.11a–d; Technician's notes 2.1.11	Quick starter; Interactive activity: Drag the respiration and photosynthesis phrases to the correct boxes

Scheme of Work

2.1.12	Analysing adaptations for respiration	Aerobic and anaerobic respiration in living organisms, including the breakdown of organic molecules to enable all the other chemical processes necessary for life	• Describe where in the cell respiration takes place • Explain how mitochondria are adapted for respiration • Compare and explain numbers of mitochondria in different cells	Worksheet 2.1.12	Quick starter; Interactive activity: Match the mitochondria-rich cells with their energy-consuming function	
2.1.13	Examining links between respiration and body systems	Aerobic and anaerobic respiration in living organisms, including the breakdown of organic molecules to enable all the other chemical processes necessary for life	• Describe some systems in animals and plants that are linked with respiration • Explain how some systems and respiration are dependent • Suggest the consequences of a failure in linked body systems	Worksheet 2.1.13	Quick starter; Interactive activity: Match the body systems to their function; Slideshow: A look at the importance of body systems in respiration and the role of the liver; Hangman; Key vocabulary game	
2.1.14	Exploring respiration in sport	Aerobic and anaerobic respiration in living organisms, including the breakdown of organic molecules to enable all the other chemical processes necessary for life	• Describe what is meant by anaerobic respiration • Explain why some sports involve more aerobic or more anaerobic respiration • Explain what is meant by oxygen debt	Worksheet 2.1.14	Quick starter; Interactive activity: Match the sport to the main type of respiration that occurs; Interactive activity: Place into the correct order to describe how the body obtains and stores glucose; Video	Ensure important points about the role of respiration are covered, from lesson 2.1.13

Scheme of Work

2.1.15	Understanding anaerobic respiration	The process of anaerobic respiration in humans and micro-organisms, including fermentation, and the word equation for anaerobic respiration	• Recall that microbes carry out anaerobic respiration • Describe some evidence to show that anaerobic respiration produces carbon dioxide • Construct a method to show what is produced in anaerobic respiration	Worksheet 2.1.15; Practical sheet 2.1.15; Technician's notes 2.1.15	Quick starter
2.1.16	Investigating fermentation	The process of anaerobic respiration in humans and micro-organisms, including fermentation, and the word equation for anaerobic respiration	• Describe some applications of fermentation • Identify dependent, independent and control variables in an investigation • Analyse data and identify next steps	Worksheet 2.1.16; Practical sheet 2.1.16; Technician's notes 2.1.16	Quick starter; Slideshow: A look at how humans use yeast cells; Interactive activity: Match the products which are made by fermentation with the microbe involved; Interactive activity: Drag the phrase to the correct box – does it speed up reactions, slow them down, or both?; Video
2.1.17	Comparing aerobic and anaerobic respiration	The differences between aerobic and anaerobic respiration in terms of the reactants, the products formed and the implications for the organism	• Describe some similarities and differences between aerobic and anaerobic respiration • Work responsibly within a team to summarise respiration	Worksheet 2.1.17	Quick starter; Interactive activity; Drag the correct respiration phrases into the correct groups; Slideshow: Explores the importance of enzymes in respiration; Hangman: Key vocabulary game

Scheme of Work

Chapter 2: Looking at Plants and Ecosystems

Lesson	Lesson title	Overarching objectives	Learning objectives	CD-ROM resources	Collins Connect resources	Notes for two-year scheme
2.2.2	Understanding the importance of plants	The dependence of almost all life on Earth on the ability of photosynthetic organisms, such as plants and algae, to use sunlight in photosynthesis to build organic molecules that are an essential energy store, and to maintain levels of oxygen and carbon dioxide in the atmosphere	• Identify the importance of plants to life on Earth • Use evidence to explain that plants do not use soil to grow • Evaluate secondary data to start to explain how plants make food	Worksheet 2.2.2; Practical sheet 2.2.2; Technician's notes 2.2.2	Quick starter; Interactive activity: Sort trees into the products they are used for; Slideshow: Looking at the discovery of photosynthesis; Video	
2.2.3	Exploring how plants make food	The reactants in, and products of, photosynthesis, and a word summary for photosynthesis. Plants making carbohydrates in their leaves by photosynthesis	• Identify the reactants and products of photosynthesis • Plan and predict the results of investigations • Evaluate the risks of a procedure	Worksheet 2.2.3; Practical sheet 2.2.2; Practical sheet 2.2.3; Technician's notes 2.2.3	Quick starter; Interactive activity: Rearrange the steps in a method to explain how to test a leaf for the presence of starch	
2.2.4	Looking at leaves	The adaptations of leaves for photosynthesis	• Relate the size of a leaf to the availability of light • Relate the function of the leaf to its structure and the types of cell • Evaluate the structure of a cell related to its function	Worksheet 2.2.4; Practical sheet 2.2.4; Technician's notes 2.2.4	Quick starter; Slideshow: A detailed look at the different components of a leaf; Interactive activity: Match the adaptations of the leaf to its function; Hangman: Key vocabulary game	

Scheme of Work

2.2.5	Exploring the role of stomata	The adaptations of leaves for photosynthesis The role of leaf stomata in gas exchange in plants	• Describe how stomata control gas exchange • Explain how gas exchange occurs in leaves • Analyse how stomata density is affected by different conditions	Worksheet 2.2.5a; Worksheet 2.2.5b (second page copied onto card); Practical sheet 2.2.5a; Practical sheet 2.2.5b; Technician's notes 2.2.5	Quick starter; Interactive activity: Which of the sentences about stomata are true, and which are false?	Recap on the adaptations of leaves, using key points from lesson 2.2.4
2.2.6	Investigating photosynthesis	The reactants in, and products of, photosynthesis, and a word summary for photosynthesis	• Identify the factors that can affect photosynthesis • Predict the results of the investigations • Interpret secondary data about photosynthesis	Worksheet 2.2.6a; Worksheet 2.2.6b; Practical sheet 2.2.6a; Practical sheet 2.2.6b; Technician's notes 2.2.6	Quick starter; Interactive activity: Complete the sentences about photosynthesis	
2.2.7	Exploring the movement of water and minerals in plants	Plants gain mineral nutrients and water from the soil via their roots	• Identify how water and minerals move through a plant • Explain how water and minerals move through a plant • Evaluate the cell structures that allow the movement of water and minerals through a plant	Worksheet 2.2.7a, Worksheet 2.2.7b; Technician's notes 2.2.7	Quick starter; Interactive activity: Rearrange the sentences to describe the movement of water through a plant	Refer to the role of minerals, from lesson 2.2.8
2.2.8	Investigating the importance of minerals to plants	Plants gain mineral nutrients and water from the soil via their roots	• Identify the minerals essential to healthy plant growth • Explain the effects of a deficiency in essential minerals • Evaluate the limitations of evidence	Worksheet 2.2.8a copied onto card; Worksheet 2.2.8b; Practical sheet 2.2.8; Technician's notes 2.2.8	Quick starter; Slideshow: An introduction to plant mineral deficiencies; Interactive activity: Match the mineral deficiency to its effect on a plant; Video	

Scheme of Work

2.2.9	Investigating chemosynthesis	The interdependence of organisms in an ecosystem, including food webs	• Describe how ocean vent communities survive • Describe the adaptations of tubeworms • Compare and contrast chemosynthesis and photosynthesis • Evaluate models of chemosynthesis and photosynthesis	Worksheet 2.2.9	Quick starter; Interactive activity: Which of the statements are true for photosynthesis, and which are true for chemosynthesis?; Hangman: Key vocabulary game
2.2.10	Applying key ideas		• Extract ideas about plant adaptations and nutrition from the text, including earlier sections of the chapter • Apply ideas about plant nutrition to explain evidence • Apply ideas and information about plant nutrition to propose the outcome of a situation	Worksheet 2.2.10a; Worksheet 2.2.10b	
2.2.11	Understanding food webs	The interdependence of organisms in an ecosystem, including food webs	• Describe how food webs are made up of a number of food chains • Make predictions about factors affecting plant and animal populations • Analyse and evaluate changes in a food web	Worksheet 2.2.11a; Worksheet 2.2.11b copied on to card and cut up; Worksheet (teacher) 2.2.11c; Worksheet (teacher) 2.2.11d	Quick starter; Interactive activity: Organise organisms into a food chain

Scheme of Work

2.2.12	Exploring the importance of insects	The interdependence of organisms in an ecosystem, including insect-pollinated crops The importance of plant reproduction through insect pollination in human food security	• Describe the impact of low pollination on fruit production • Explain why artificial pollination is used for some crops • Evaluate the risks of monoculture on world food security	Worksheet 2.2.12; Practical sheet 2.2.12; Technician's notes 2.2.12	Quick starter; Slideshow: A description of how bees pollinate plants and how honey is made; Interactive activity: Define the conditions required for enhancing bee populations; Video
2.2.13	Looking at other examples of interdependence	How organisms affect, and are affected by, their environment, including the accumulation of toxic materials	• Describe examples of the interdependence of organisms • Explain how organisms help other organisms to survive • Explain ideas about habitat destruction	Worksheet 2.2.13a; Worksheet 2.2.13b copied on to card and cut up	Quick starter; Slideshow: Some examples of interdependence; Interactive activity: Match the key interdependence terms to their definition; Hangman: Key vocabulary game
2.2.14	Understanding interactions in the environment	How organisms affect, and are affected by, their environment, including the accumulation of toxic materials	• Describe some effects of human activity on the environment • Explain why a range of species is endangered • Analyse and evaluate secondary data and recommend solutions for species survival	Worksheet 2.2.14	Quick starter; Slideshow: A look at some British species which are endangered; Interactive activity: Order the level of risk scientists assign to a species, from most to least threatened; Video

Scheme of Work

2.2.15	Learning about ecological balance	How organisms affect, and are affected by, their environment, including the accumulation of toxic materials	• Describe ways in which organisms affect their environment • Explain why prey populations affect predator populations • Evaluate a model of predator–prey populations and explain the importance of predators	Worksheet 2.2.15a; Worksheet 2.2.15b	Quick starter; Slideshow: A look at the predator-prey relationship between a Canadian lynx and a Snowshoe hare; Interactive activity: Sort the statements into those which refer to predators and those which refer to prey organisms	Include the impact of human activity from lesson 2.2.14
2.2.16	Understanding the effects of toxins in the environment	How organisms affect, and are affected by, their environment, including the accumulation of toxic materials	• Describe how toxins pass along the food chain • Explain how toxins enter and accumulate in food chains • Evaluate the advantages and disadvantages of using pesticides	Worksheet 2.2.16	Quick starter; Interactive activity: Match the farming chemical to its use; Slideshow: A look at bioaccumulation of mercury	
2.2.17	Exploring how organisms co-exist	How organisms affect, and are affected by, their environment, including the accumulation of toxic materials	• Describe the role of niches • Explain the concept of resource partitioning • Analyse and evaluate the role of variation in enabling organisms to co-exist	Worksheet 2.2.17; Practical sheet 2.2.17; Technician's notes 2.2.17	Quick starter; Interactive activity: Define four key ecological terms; Hangman: Key vocabulary game	

Scheme of Work

Chapter 3: Explaining Physical Changes

Lesson	Lesson title	Overarching objectives	Learning objectives	CD-ROM resources	Collins Connect resources	Notes for two-year scheme
2.3.2	Using particles to explain matter	The properties of different states of matter (solid, liquid and gas) in terms of the particle model, including gas pressure	• Recognise differences between solids, liquids and gases • Describe solids, liquids and gases in terms of the particle model	Worksheet 2.3.2; Practical sheet 2.3.2 (the last page copied onto card); Technician's notes 2.3.2	Quick starter; Interactive activity: Drag the solid, liquid or gas to the correct group when at 25°C and at atmospheric pressure; Interactive activity: Place the elements in order, from strongest to weakest forces between the elements	
2.3.3	Understanding solids	The properties of different states of matter (solid, liquid and gas) in terms of the particle model, including gas pressure	• Describe the properties of solids • Relate the properties and behaviour of solids to the particle model	Worksheet 2.3.3; Practical sheet 2.3.3 (last page copied onto card); Technician's notes 2.3.3	Quick starter; Slideshow. Explaining properties of gases, liquids and solids	The principles of the particle model from lesson 2.3.2 should underpin this and the next two lessons
2.3.4	Exploring Brownian motion	Brownian motion in gases	• Describe how theories develop • Describe and explain Brownian motion in terms of particles	Worksheet 2.3.4; Practical sheet 2.3.4; Technician's notes 2.3.4	Quick starter; Interactive activity: Re-order the statements about the movement of a drop of red dye in water	

Scheme of Work

2.3.5	Understanding liquids and gases	The properties of different states of matter (solid, liquid and gas) in terms of the particle model, including gas pressure	• Compare different properties of liquids and gases • Relate the properties and behaviour of liquids and gases to the particle model	Worksheet 2.3.5; Practical sheet 2.3.5; Technician's notes 2.3.5	Quick starter; Interactive activity: Place the fluids in order of most to least viscous at room temperature; Slideshow: Volume and compression; How much air is in a scuba tank?; Hangman: Key vocabulary game
2.3.6	Changing state	Changes of state in terms of the particle model	• Recognise changes of state as being reversible changes • Use scientific terminology to describe changes of state • Explain changes of state using the particle model and ideas of energy transfer	Worksheet 2.3.6; Practical sheet 2.3.6; Technician's notes 2.3.6	Quick starter; Interactive activity: Drag the examples of change in state to the correct group – melting, condensing or sublimation; Video
2.3.7	Understanding evaporation	Changes of state in terms of the particle model Energy changes on changes of state (qualitative)	• Investigate factors affecting evaporation • Explain the differences between boiling and evaporation using the particle model	Worksheet 2.3.7; Practical sheet 2.3.7; Technician's notes 2.3.7	Quick starter; Interactive activity: Drag the items to the correct group – boiling point less or greater than water; Slideshow: Factors affecting evaporation: Why does nail varnish remover dry more quickly than water?
2.3.8	Exploring thermal expansion	Changes with temperature in motion and spacing of particles	• Identify how heat affects the arrangement and movement of particles • Use the particle model to explain the effects of heat on expansion	Worksheet 2.3.8; Practical sheet 2.3.8; Technician's notes 2.3.8	Quick starter; Video

Scheme of Work

2.3.9	Making sense of models	A simple Dalton atomic model	• Describe the concept of a 'good enough' model • Link the particle model to elements and compounds • Evaluate the strengths and weaknesses of the particle model	Worksheet 2.3.9; Technician's notes 2.3.9	Quick starter; Hangman: Key vocabulary game	
2.3.10	Applying key ideas		• Extract ideas about changes of state, expansion and energy changes from the text, including earlier sections of the topic • Apply ideas about the particle model to explain some physical processes • Use ideas and information about particles to explain the properties of different states of matter and how changes of state can be applied	Worksheet 2.3.10; Technician's notes 2.3.10		
2.3.11	Explaining density of solids and liquids	The differences in arrangements, in motion and in closeness of particles explaining changes of state, shape and density, the anomaly of ice–water transition Similarities and differences, including density differences, between solids, liquids and gases	• Use the particle model to explain density differences between solids and liquids • Use the particle model to explain anomalies between ice and water	Worksheet 2.3.11; Technician's notes 2.3.11	Quick starter; Slideshow: What is density?; Interactive activity: Drag the items to the correct group – density less or greater than water?	May be combined with lesson 2.3.12

Key Stage 3 Science Teacher Pack 2 251 © HarperCollins*Publishers* Limited 2014

Scheme of Work

2.3.12	Explaining the density of gases	The differences in arrangements, in motion and in closeness of particles explaining changes of state, shape and density, the anomaly of ice–water transition Similarities and differences, including density differences, between solids, liquids and gases	• Use the particle model to explain differences in the density of gases • Evaluate a method of measuring density	Worksheet 2.3.12a; Worksheet 2.3.12b; Practical sheet 2.3.12; Technician's notes 2.3.12	Quick starter; Interactive activity: Place the gases in order, from highest to lowest density at standard room temperature; Video
2.3.13	Explaining concentration and pressure	The properties of different states of matter (solid, liquid and gas) in terms of the particle model, including gas pressure	• Describe what is meant by concentration and pressure. • Use the particle model to explain differences in concentration and pressure	Worksheet 2.3.13; Practical sheet 2.3.13; Technician's notes 2.3.13	Quick starter; Slideshow: Working out concentration: A fizzy drink example
2.3.14	Exploring diffusion	Diffusion in liquids and gases driven by differences in concentration Diffusion in terms of the particle model	• Use the particle model to explain observations involving diffusion	Worksheet 2.3.14; Practical sheet 2.3.14; Technician's notes 2.3.14	Quick starter; Slideshow: Observing diffusion with bromine gas; Interactive activity: Drag the items to the correct group – speeds up or slows down diffusion of particles; Hangman: Key vocabulary game
2.3.15	Conserving mass	Conservation of mass Changes of state Conservation of material and mass, and reversibility, in melting, freezing, evaporation, sublimation, condensation, dissolving	• Use the particle model to explain the Law of Conservation of Mass	Worksheet 2.3.15; Practical sheet 2.3.15a; Practical sheet 2.3.15b; Technician's notes 2.3.15	Quick starter; Interactive activity: Which of the statements about chemical reactions are true, and which are false?

Scheme of Work

2.3.16	Deciding between physical and chemical changes	Mixtures, including dissolving The difference between chemical and physical changes	• Use the particle model to explain the differences between physical and chemical changes • Recognise that mass is conserved in all changes	Worksheet 2.3.16; Practical sheet 2.3.16; Technician's notes 2.3.16	Quick starter; Slideshow: Changes that are easily reversed and changes that are not easily reversed; Interactive activity: Drag the change into the correct group – physical or chemical change?	May be combined with lesson 2.3.17
2.3.17	Explaining the properties of mixtures	Mixtures, including dissolving The properties of different states of matter (solid, liquid and gas) in terms of the particle model, including gas pressure	• Use the particle model to explain the properties of mixtures	Worksheet 2.3.17; Practical sheet 2.3.17; Technician's notes 2.3.17	Quick starter; Interactive activity: Match the terms about mixtures and changing states to their correct definition; Video	
2.3.18	Using particle models	The differences in arrangements, in motion and in closeness of particles explaining changes of state, shape and density, the anomaly of ice–water transition	• Use 'good enough' particles models to explain different observations	Worksheet 2.3.18; Practical sheet 2.3.18a; Practical sheet 2.3.18b; Technician's notes 2.3.18	Quick starter; Slideshow: A look at how sugar dissolves in water; Interactive activity: Place the events in order of how sugar dissolves in tea; Hangman: Key vocabulary game	

Scheme of Work

Chapter 4: Explaining Chemical Changes

Lesson	Lesson title	Overarching objectives	Learning objectives	CD-ROM resources	Collins Connect resources	Notes for two-year scheme
2.4.2	Exploring acids	Defining acids and alkalis	• Recognise acids used in everyday life • Describe what all acids have in common • Evaluate the hazards that acids pose	Worksheet 2.4.2	Quick starter; Interactive activity: Match the foods to the main acid(s) they contain; Interactive activity: Match the hazard to the symbol; Slideshow: What do acids have in common?; Video	
2.4.3	Exploring alkalis	Defining acids and alkalis	• Recognise alkalis used in everyday life • Describe what all alkalis have in common • Evaluate the hazards that alkalis pose	Worksheet 2.4.3	Quick starter; Interactive activity: Drag the products to the correct group: acidic or alkaline?; Slideshow: What do alkalis have in common?	
2.4.4	Using indicators	The pH scale for measuring acidity/alkalinity; and indicators	• Use indicators to identify acids and alkalis • Analyse data from different indicators • Compare the effectiveness of different indicators	Worksheet 2.4.4; Practical sheet 2.4.4; Technician's notes 2.4.4	Quick starter; Slideshow: What are indicators? A look at different types of indicator; Interactive activity: Drag the acids to the correct group – strong or weak	May be combined with lesson 2.4.5
2.4.5	Using universal indicator	The pH scale for measuring acidity/alkalinity; and indicators	• Describe what the pH scale measures • Measure and record pH values • Identify the advantages of universal indicator	Worksheet 2.4.5; Practical sheet 2.4.5; Technician's notes 2.4.5	Quick starter; Interactive activity: Match the colour given from universal indicator paper to the correct product; Hangman: Key vocabulary game	

Scheme of Work

2.4.6	Exploring neutralisation	Defining acids and alkalis in terms of neutralisation reactions The pH scale for measuring acidity/alkalinity; and indicators	• Describe examples of neutralisation • Use indicators to identify chemical reactions • Explain colour changes in terms of pH and neutralisation	Worksheet 2.4.6; Practical sheet 2.4.6; Technician's notes 2.4.6	Quick starter; Interactive activity: Match the everyday neutralisation reactions together; Video
2.4.7	Explaining neutralisation	Defining acids and alkalis in terms of neutralisation reactions Chemical reactions as the rearrangement of atoms Representing chemical reactions using formulas and using equations Reactions of acids with alkalis to produce a salt plus water	• Recall the equation for a neutralisation reaction • Explain how water is made during a neutralisation reaction • Apply a model to explain neutralisation	Worksheet 2.4.7	Quick starter; Interactive activity: Drag the chemicals to the correct group – product or reactant; Slideshow: A model for neutralisation
2.4.8	Understanding salts	Chemical reactions as the rearrangement of atoms Representing chemical reactions using formulas and using equations Reactions of acids with alkalis to produce a salt plus water	• Name examples of salts • Describe the uses of common salts • Predict the reactants used in and the salts made by different neutralisation reactions	Worksheet 2.4.8	Quick starter; Interactive activity: Match the salts to their uses
2.4.9	Exploring the reactions of acids with metals	Reactions of acids with metals to produce a salt plus hydrogen	• Describe the reaction between acids and metals • Explain the reaction between acids and metals • Compare the reactivity of different metals	Worksheet 2.4.9; Practical sheet 2.4.9; Technician's notes 2.4.9	Quick starter; Interactive activity: Drag the metal to the correct group, depending on how it reacts with acid

Scheme of Work

2.4.10	Exploring the reactions of acids with carbonates	Chemical reactions as the rearrangement of atoms Representing chemical reactions using formulas and using equations	• Describe the reaction between acids and carbonates • Explain the reaction between acids and carbonates • Write word equations for the reactions between acids and carbonates	Worksheet 2.4.10; Practical sheet 2.4.10; Technician's notes 2.4.10	Quick starter; Slideshow: Summarising the reactions of acids with carbonates; Hangman: Key vocabulary game
2.4.11	Applying key ideas		• Identify some factors that affect the pH of urine • Explain how the pH of urine can be used by medical practitioners • Apply knowledge about acids and alkalis to reactions in the body	Worksheet 2.4.11; Technician's notes 2.4.11	
2.4.12	Investigating the effectiveness of antacids	Reactions of acids with alkalis to produce a salt plus water	• Design an investigation to compare the effectiveness of indigestion remedies • Analyse data to identify a suitable indigestion remedy	Worksheet 2.4.12; Practical sheet 2.4.12; Technician's notes 2.4.12	Quick starter; Interactive activity: Place the steps of the antacid experiment into the correct order
2.4.13	Understanding the importance of acids and alkalis	Defining acids and alkalis in terms of neutralisation reactions Reactions of acids with alkalis to produce a salt plus water	• Classify common useful chemicals as acids or alkalis • Explain the importance of acids and alkalis in everyday life • Explore common misconceptions about acids and alkalis	Worksheet 2.4.13	Quick starter; Slideshow: Acids and alkalis in industry: The chlor-alkali industry; Interactive activity: Are the statements about acids and alkalis fact or fiction?; Video; Video

Scheme of Work

2.4.14	Exploring combustion	Combustion Fuels and energy resources	• Explain the terms fuel and combustion • Recall what is needed for combustion • Analyse the fire triangle and apply it to putting out fires	Worksheet 2.4.14; Technician's sheet 2.4.14	Quick starter; Interactive activity: Match the method of putting out a fire to what it removes from the fire triangle; Hangman: Key vocabulary game
2.4.15	Understanding combustion and the use of fuels	Combustion Fuels and energy resources	• Identify applications of combustion reactions • Identify fuels used in different applications • Compare the energy of different fuels	Worksheet 2.4.15; Practical sheet 2.4.15; Technician's notes 2.4.15	Quick starter; Interactive activity: Exothermic or endothermic? Drag the phrases to the type of reaction they're associated with; Slideshow: So many fuels: Fossil fuels and plants; Interactive activity: Place, in order, the fuels that you think hold the most to the least energy (in Joules/Kg)
2.4.16	Exploring the effects of burning	Combustion Chemical reactions as the rearrangement of atoms Representing chemical reactions using formulas and using equations The production of carbon dioxide by human activity	• Summarise combustion using an equation • Compare complete and incomplete combustion • Explain what is meant by the conservation of mass	Worksheet 2.4.16 (with the second page copied onto card); Practical sheet 2.4.16; Technician's notes 2.4.16	Quick starter; Interactive activity: Drag the substances to the correct group – hydrocarbon or not

Refer to reasons for selecting different fuels, from lesson 2.4.15

Scheme of Work

2.4.17	Understanding acid rain	Combustion The composition of the atmosphere	• Describe how combustion can cause acid rain • Describe the effects of acid rain • Explain the effects of acid rain	Worksheet 2.4.17	Quick starter; Slideshow: How does burning affect rain?; Interactive activity: Re-order the process of acid rain formation from sulfur dioxide; Hangman: Key vocabulary game

Scheme of Work

Chapter 5: Exploring Contact and Non-Contact Forces

Lesson	Lesson title	Overarching objectives	Learning objectives	CD-ROM resources	Collins Connect resources	Notes for two-year scheme
2.5.2	Exploring magnets	Non-contact forces: forces between magnets. Magnetic poles, attraction and repulsion	• Explain magnetic attraction and repulsion • Apply the concept of poles and laws of attraction and repulsion • Predict the effects of arrangements of magnetic poles	Worksheet 2.5.2; Practical sheet 2.5.2; Technician's notes 2.5.2	Quick starter; Slideshow: Magnetic levitation: A look at the use of magnetic repulsion and attraction in the operation of Maglev trains; Interactive activity: Drag the statements about magnets into the correct true or false groups	May be combined with lesson 2.5.3
2.5.3	Understanding magnetic fields	Magnetic poles, attraction and repulsion. Magnetic fields by plotting with compass, representation by field lines. Earth's magnetism	• Describe magnetic fields • Explore the field around a magnet • Explain the shape, size and direction of magnetic fields	Worksheet 2.5.3; Practical sheet 2.5.3; Technician's notes 2.5.3	Quick starter; Interactive activity: Complete the sentences about magnetic fields	
2.5.4	Investigating static charge	Non-contact forces: forces due to static electricity. Separation of positive or negative charges when objects are rubbed together: transfer of electrons, forces between charged objects	• Recognise the effects of static charge • Explain how static charge can be generated • Use evidence to develop ideas about static charge	Worksheet 2.5.4; Practical sheet 2.5.4; Technician's notes 2.5.4	Quick starter; Interactive activity: Drag the materials to classify them as conductors or insulators	May be combined with lesson 2.5.5

Scheme of Work

2.5.5	Explaining static charge	Non-contact forces: forces due to static electricity Separation of positive or negative charges when objects are rubbed together: transfer of electrons, forces between charged objects	• Explain static charge in terms of electron transfer • Apply this explanation to various examples	Worksheet 2.5.5; Practical sheet 2.5.5; Technician's notes 2.5.5	Quick starter; Slideshow: Atoms and ions: How electron transfer between atoms forms ions, which assemble into alternating lattices due to electrostatic attractions; Interactive activity: Arrange the sentences on static charge into the correct order; Hangman: Key vocabulary game
2.5.6	Understanding electric fields	Non-contact forces: forces due to static electricity Separation of positive or negative charges when objects are rubbed together: transfer of electrons, forces between charged objects The idea of electric field, forces acting across the space between objects not in contact	• Explain static electricity in terms of fields • Explain how charged objects affect other objects	Worksheet 2.5.6; Technician's notes 2.5.6	Quick starter; Interactive activity: Drag the sentences into the correct order, to explain why a statically charged balloon sticks to a wall
2.5.7	Applying what we know about electrostatics	Non-contact forces: forces due to static electricity Separation of positive or negative charges when objects are rubbed together: transfer of electrons, forces between charged objects The idea of electric field, forces acting across the space between objects not in contact	• Apply an understanding of static electricity to various situations • Explain how static electricity can be useful and can be dangerous	Worksheet 2.5.7	Quick starter; Slideshow: Antistatic devices: Problems (as opposed to applications) of electrostatic attraction, and practical solutions to such problems; Interactive activity: Drag the sentences into the correct order, to explain electrostatic paint spraying; Video

Scheme of Work

2.5.8	Exploring gravity on Earth	Non-contact forces: gravity forces acting at a distance on Earth and in space	• Explain the effects of gravity • Compare gravity to other non-contact forces • Use the concept of a gravitational field	Worksheet 2.5.8; Practical sheet 2.5.8	Quick starter; Slideshow: Weightlessness: Creating zero-gravity/weightlessness for astronaut training using a parabolic flight path; Interactive activity: Link the statement about gravitational fields with its correct description	Refer to applications from lesson 2.5.9
2.5.9	Applying our understanding of gravity to space travel	Non-contact forces: gravity forces acting at a distance on Earth and in space	• Apply ideas about gravity on Earth to other places • Explore how gravitational fields vary • Consider the effects of these changes	Worksheet 2.5.9	Quick starter; Interactive activity: Are the statements about space travel true or false?; Interactive activity: Complete the sentences about exploring the Earth's atmosphere; Hangman: Key vocabulary game; Video	
2.5.10	Applying key ideas		• To extract ideas about magnetism, electrostatic charge and gravity from the text, including earlier sections of the topic. • To apply ideas about magnetism, electrostatics and gravity. • To evaluate ideas in relation to magnetism, electrostatics and gravity.	Worksheet 2.5.10; Technician's notes 2.5.10		

Scheme of Work

2.5.11	Exploring pressure on a solid surface	Pressure measured by ratio of force over area – acting normal to any surface	• Explain how pressure can be applied on a solid surface • Describe some effects of varying pressure	Worksheet 2.5.11a (copied onto card); Worksheet 2.5.11b	Quick starter; Slideshow: Pressure, ice and snow: Effects of increasing and decreasing pressure on ice and snow. Applications to winter activities; Interactive activity: Drag the descriptions which represent high or low pressure; Video
2.5.12	Calculating pressure	Pressure measured by ratio of force over area – acting normal to any surface	• Identify the factors that determine the size of pressure on a solid • Calculate the size of pressure exerted	Worksheet 2.5.12; Practical sheet 2.5.12; Technician's notes 2.5.12	Quick starter; Interactive activity: Order the pressures, from highest to lowest
2.5.13	Exploring pressure in a liquid	Pressure in liquids, increasing with depth; upthrust effects, floating and sinking	• Describe how pressure in a liquid alters with depth • Explain pressure increases in relation to particles and gravity	Worksheet 2.5.13; Technician's notes 2.5.13	Quick starter; Interactive activity: Complete the sentences about pressure in liquids
2.5.14	Explaining floating and sinking	Pressure in liquids, increasing with depth; upthrust effects, floating and sinking	• Explain why some objects float and others sink • Relate floating and sinking to density, displacement and upthrust • Explain the implications of these ideas	Worksheet 2.5.14; Practical sheet 2.5.14; Technician's notes 2.5.14	Quick starter; Slideshow: Balloons: Hot-air, hydrogen and helium balloons – to emphasise that buoyancy isn't limited to water; Interactive activity: Define the key terms about floating and sinking; Hangman: Key vocabulary game

Scheme of Work

2.5.15	Exploring gas pressure	Atmospheric pressure; decreases with increase of height as weight of air above decreases with height	• Explore how the pressure in a gas varies with height • Explain the implications of this changing pressure	Worksheet 2.5.15; Technician's notes 2.5.15	Quick starter; Interactive activity: Drag the descriptions which represent high or low atmospheric pressure	May be combined with lesson 2.5.16
2.5.16	Working with pressure	Atmospheric pressure; decreases with increase of height as weight of air above decreases with height	• Give examples of how pressure affects our lives • Explain how pressure is used and managed	Worksheet 2.5.16; Practical sheet 2.5.16; Technician's notes 2.5.16	Quick starter; Slideshow: High tides and flooding: Effects of low atmospheric pressure on sea level, and the consequent effects when coupled with high tides; Interactive activity: Barometers are devices used to measure pressure. Order the statements to describe their operation; Hangman: Key vocabulary game	

Scheme of Work

Chapter 6: Magnetism and Electricity

Lesson	Lesson title	Overarching objectives	Learning objectives	CD-ROM resources	Collins Connect resources	Notes for two-year scheme
2.6.2	Looking at the history of magnets	Earth's magnetism, compass and navigation	• Summarise historical ideas about magnetism • Describe how historical ideas about magnetism have changed over time	Practical sheet 2.6.2; Technician's notes 2.6.2	Quick starter; Slideshow: Developing the compass: From a lodestone on a string to modern binnacle compasses; Interactive activity: Order the discoveries in magnetism, from the oldest to the most recent; Video	
2.6.3	Exploring magnetic materials	Magnetic poles, attraction and repulsion	• Investigate magnetism in materials • Explain magnetism using the domain theory	Worksheet 2.6.3; Practical sheet 2.6.3; Technician's notes 2.6.3	Quick starter; Interactive activity: Classify the statements into those which can magnetise or demagnetise a magnetic material	
2.6.4	Testing the strength of magnets	Magnetic poles, attraction and repulsion	• Compare different methods of testing magnets • Collect data to investigate the strength of magnetism	Practical sheet 2.6.3 (from previous lesson); Practical sheet 2.6.4; Technician's notes 2.6.4	Quick starter; Interactive activity: Order the sentences into a logical sequence, to show how to compare the strength of magnets	

Scheme of Work

2.6.5	Describing the Earth's magnetic field	Earth's magnetism, compass and navigation	• Explain evidence for the Earth's magnetic field • Explain the impact the Earth's magnetic field has on our planet	Worksheet 2.6.5	Quick starter; Interactive activity: Complete the sentences about the Earth's magnetic field; Slideshow: Solar wind: The effects on the atmosphere (aurora) and electrical storms
2.6.6	Investigating electromagnetism	The magnetic effect of a current, electromagnets	• Describe what an electromagnet is • Investigate the factors affecting the strength of electromagnets	Worksheet 2.6.6; Practical sheet 2.6.6; Technician's notes 2.6.6	Quick starter; Interactive activity: Classify the statements into those which will increase, or decrease, the strength of an electromagnet; Hangman: Key vocabulary game
2.6.7	Using electromagnets	Electromagnets	• Describe different applications of electromagnets	Worksheet 2.6.7; Technician's notes 2.6.7	Quick starter; Slideshow: Electromagnets at work: Magnetic sorting, fire-doors, MRI, Maglev and security tags; Interactive activity: Order the statements to describe the operation of an electric bell; Video

Scheme of Work

2.6.8	Exploring D.C. motors	Other processes that involve energy transfer: completing an electrical circuit The magnetic effect of a current, D.C. motors (principles only)	• Describe the magnetic effect of a current and how this is applied to D.C. motors	Worksheet 2.6.8; Practical sheet 2.6.8; Technician's notes 2.6.8	Quick starter; Slideshow: Motors large and small: Robots, trains and toothbrushes; Interactive activity: Classify the statements into those which will increase, or decrease the forces produced by an electric motor; Hangman: Key vocabulary game
2.6.9	Applying key ideas		• Extract ideas about magnets from the Student Book text, including earlier sections of the chapter. • Apply ideas about the properties of magnets to explain some of their applications.	Worksheet 2.6.9	
2.6.10	Investigating batteries	Other processes that involve energy transfer: completing an electrical circuit	• Describe the link between chemical energy and electricity. • Investigate how fruit batteries work	Worksheet 2.6.10; Technician's notes 2.6.10	Quick starter; Slideshow: Inside batteries: The similarities and differences between types of cell; Interactive activity: Complete the sentences about batteries; Video

Scheme of Work

2.6.11	Describing electric circuits	Other processes that involve energy transfer: completing an electrical circuit Electric current, measured in amperes, in circuits	• Describe and draw circuit diagrams • Explain what is meant by current • Explain how materials allow current to flow	Worksheet 2.6.11 (the second page printed onto card); Practical sheet 2.6.11; Technician's notes 2.6.11	Quick starter; Interactive activity: Match the statements about electric current	
2.6.12	Understanding energy in circuits	Other processes that involve energy transfer: completing an electrical circuit Electric current, measured in amperes, in circuits Potential difference, measured in volts, battery and bulb ratings	• Describe what the voltage does in a circuit • Explain voltage using different analogies	Worksheet 2.6.12; Technician's notes 2.6.12	Quick starter; Interactive activity: Select the statements which describe current or voltage in an electric circuit; Hangman: Key vocabulary game	
2.6.13	Explaining resistance	Potential difference, measured in volts, battery and bulb ratings Resistance, measured in ohms, as the ratio of potential difference (p.d.) to current	• Explain what resistance is and how it affects the circuit • Investigate and identify the relationship between voltage and current	Worksheet 2.6.13; Practical sheet 2.6.13; Technician's notes 2.6.13	Quick starter; Slideshow: Measuring electricity: A look at multimeters and measuring V, I and R; Interactive activity: Complete the sentences about resistance in an electric circuit	Refer to factors affecting resistance, from lesson 2.6.14
2.6.14	Investigating factors affecting resistance	Resistance, measured in ohms, as the ratio of potential difference (p.d.) to current Differences in resistance between conducting and insulating components (quantitative)	• Describe some uses of resistance • Investigate and explain factors affecting resistance	Worksheet 2.6.14; Practical sheet 2.6.14; Technician's notes 2.6.14	Quick starter; Interactive activity: Choose the factors which increase the resistance of a wire, and those which decrease resistance; Slideshow: Using low and high resistances: A look at some factors that affects the resistance of materials	

Scheme of Work

2.6.15	Explaining circuits using models	Potential difference, measured in volts, battery and bulb ratings Resistance, measured in ohms, as the ratio of potential difference (p.d.) to current	• Describe how the voltage, current and resistance are related in different circuits • Use a model to explain the relationship between voltage, current and resistance	Worksheet 2.6.15; Practical sheet 2.6.15; Technician's notes 2.6.15	Quick starter; Interactive activity: Match the scientific ideas about electric circuits to the rope model analogy
2.6.16	Describing series and parallel circuits	Series and parallel circuits, currents add where branches meet and current as flow of charge	• Understand how voltage and current vary in a series circuit • Understand how voltage and current vary in a parallel circuit	Worksheet 2.6.16; Technician's notes 2.6.16	Quick starter; Interactive activity: Choose the statements which best describe series circuits, and those which best describe parallel circuit; Slideshow: Splitters and multi-sockets: The dangers of overloading; Video
2.6.17	Comparing series and parallel circuits	Electric current, measured in amperes, in circuits Series and parallel circuits, currents add where branches meet and current as flow of charge Potential difference, measured in volts, battery and bulb ratings	• Investigate and explain current and voltage in series and parallel circuits • Explain the circuits in our homes	Worksheet 2.6.17; Practical sheet 2.6.17; Technician's notes 2.6.17	Quick starter; Interactive activity: Order the circuits from the one with the highest current, to the one with the lowest
2.6.18	Applying circuits	Series and parallel circuits, currents add where branches meet and current as flow of charge	• Describe how circuits are arranged in common appliances	Worksheet 2.6.18, the second page copied onto card	Quick starter; Interactive activity: Complete the sentence about series and parallel circuits; Hangman: Key vocabulary game

Concept teaching route diagrams

Teaching route: Cells

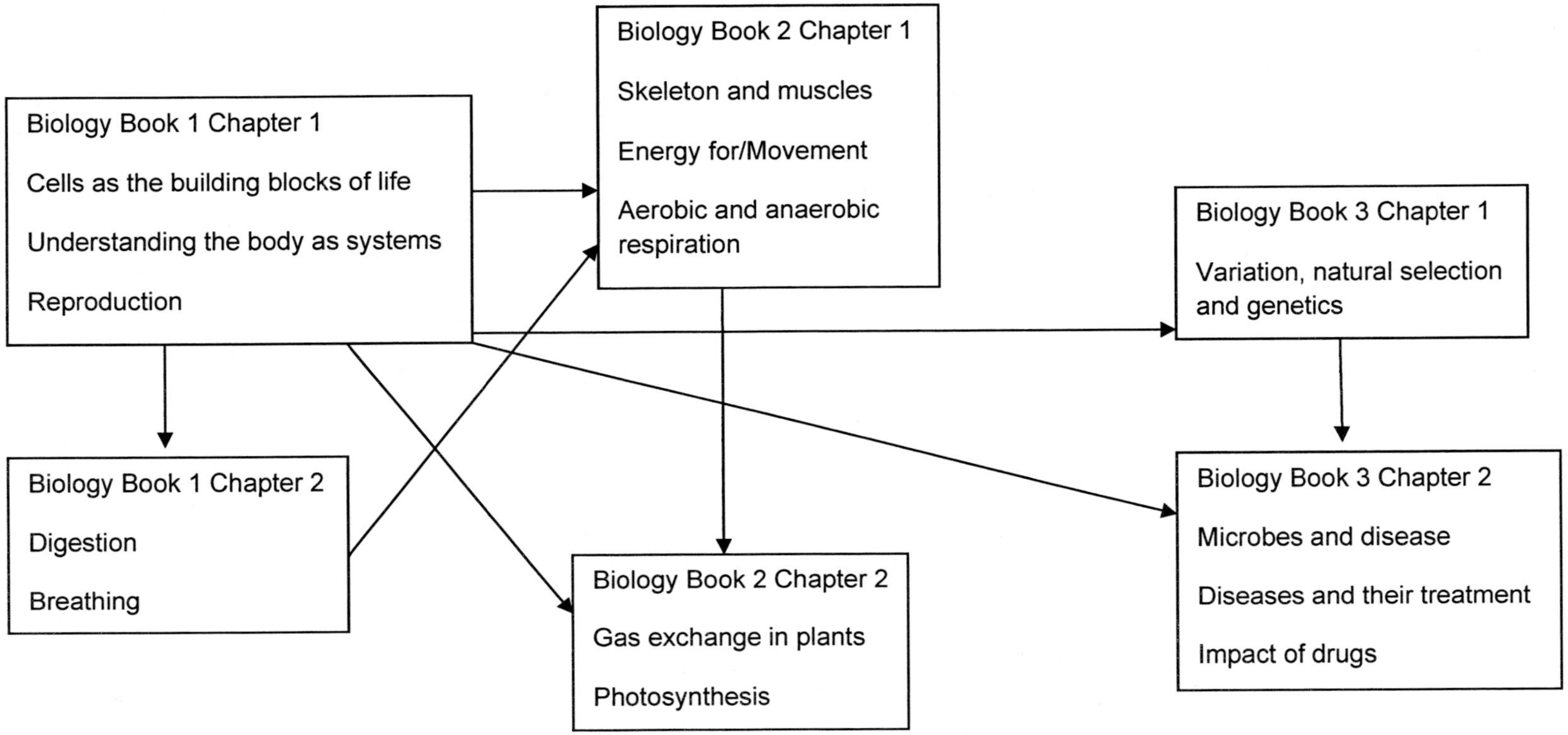

Biology Book 1 Chapter 1
Cells as the building blocks of life
Understanding the body as systems
Reproduction

Biology Book 1 Chapter 2
Digestion
Breathing

Biology Book 2 Chapter 1
Skeleton and muscles
Energy for/Movement
Aerobic and anaerobic respiration

Biology Book 2 Chapter 2
Gas exchange in plants
Photosynthesis

Biology Book 3 Chapter 1
Variation, natural selection and genetics

Biology Book 3 Chapter 2
Microbes and disease
Diseases and their treatment
Impact of drugs

Key Stage 3 Science Teacher Pack 2   269   © HarperCollins*Publishers* Limited 2014

Concept teaching route diagrams

Teaching route: Energy

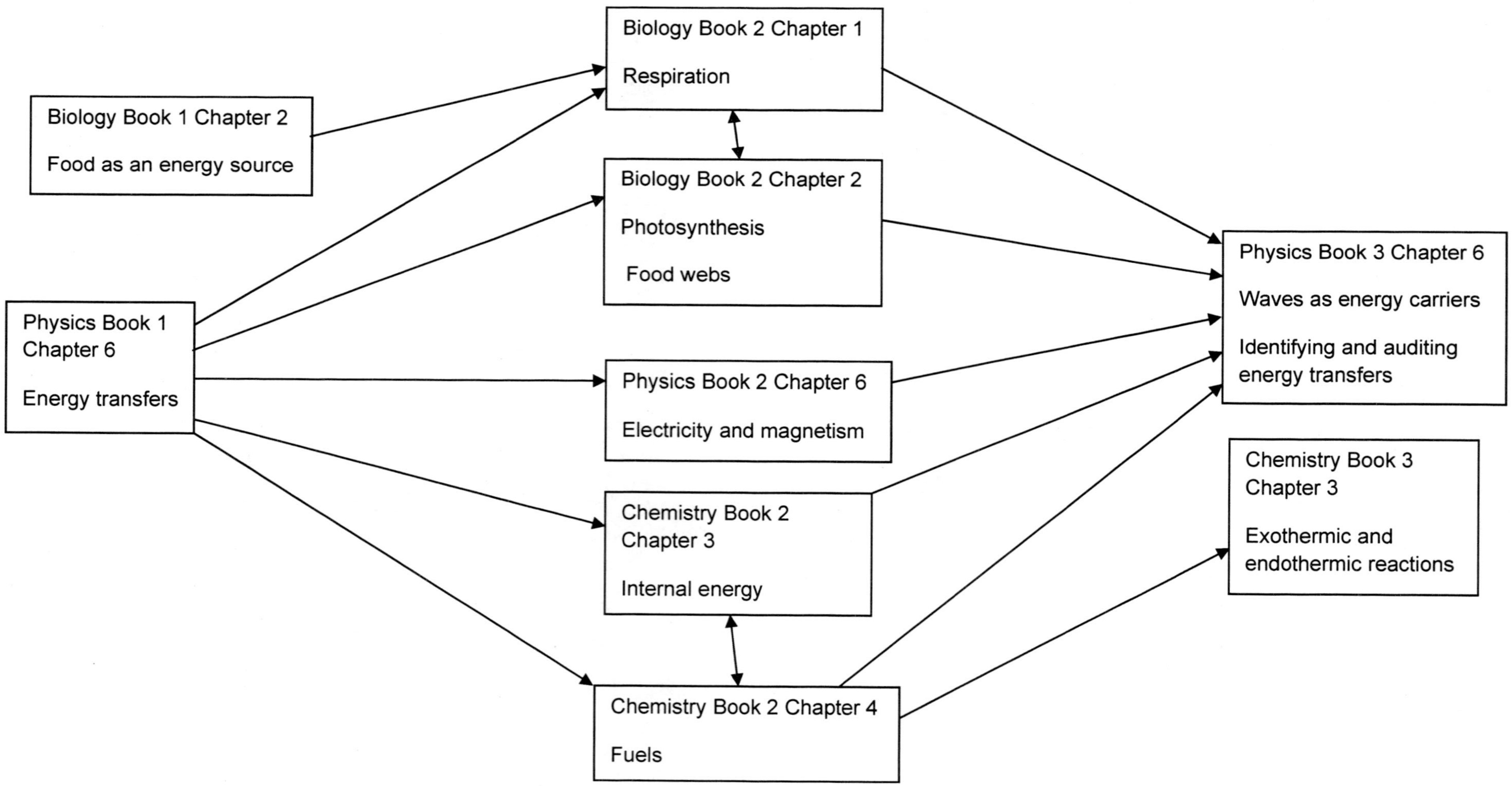

- **Biology Book 1 Chapter 2** — Food as an energy source
- **Physics Book 1 Chapter 6** — Energy transfers
- **Biology Book 2 Chapter 1** — Respiration
- **Biology Book 2 Chapter 2** — Photosynthesis / Food webs
- **Physics Book 2 Chapter 6** — Electricity and magnetism
- **Chemistry Book 2 Chapter 3** — Internal energy
- **Chemistry Book 2 Chapter 4** — Fuels
- **Physics Book 3 Chapter 6** — Waves as energy carriers / Identifying and auditing energy transfers
- **Chemistry Book 3 Chapter 3** — Exothermic and endothermic reactions

Concept teaching route diagrams

Teaching route: Forces

Physics Book 1 Chapter 5
- Contact forces and effects
- Speed
- Friction and drag
- Moments
- Stretch and compression
- Gravity

Physics Book 2 Chapter 6
- Magnetism and electromagnetism

Physics Book 2 Chapter 5
- Non-contact forces and fields: gravity, electrostatics and magnetism
- Pressure on a surface, pressure in fluids and buoyancy

Physics Book 3 Chapter 5
- Distance/time graphs
- Equilibria
- Weight and gravitational attraction
- Gravity on Earth and in space

Biology Book 2 Chapter 1
- Skeleton and muscles

Chemistry Book 2 Chapter 3
- Diffusion
- Gas pressure
- Density

Key Stage 3 Science Teacher Pack 2 271 © HarperCollins*Publishers* Limited 2014

Concept teaching route diagrams

Teaching route: Particles and elements

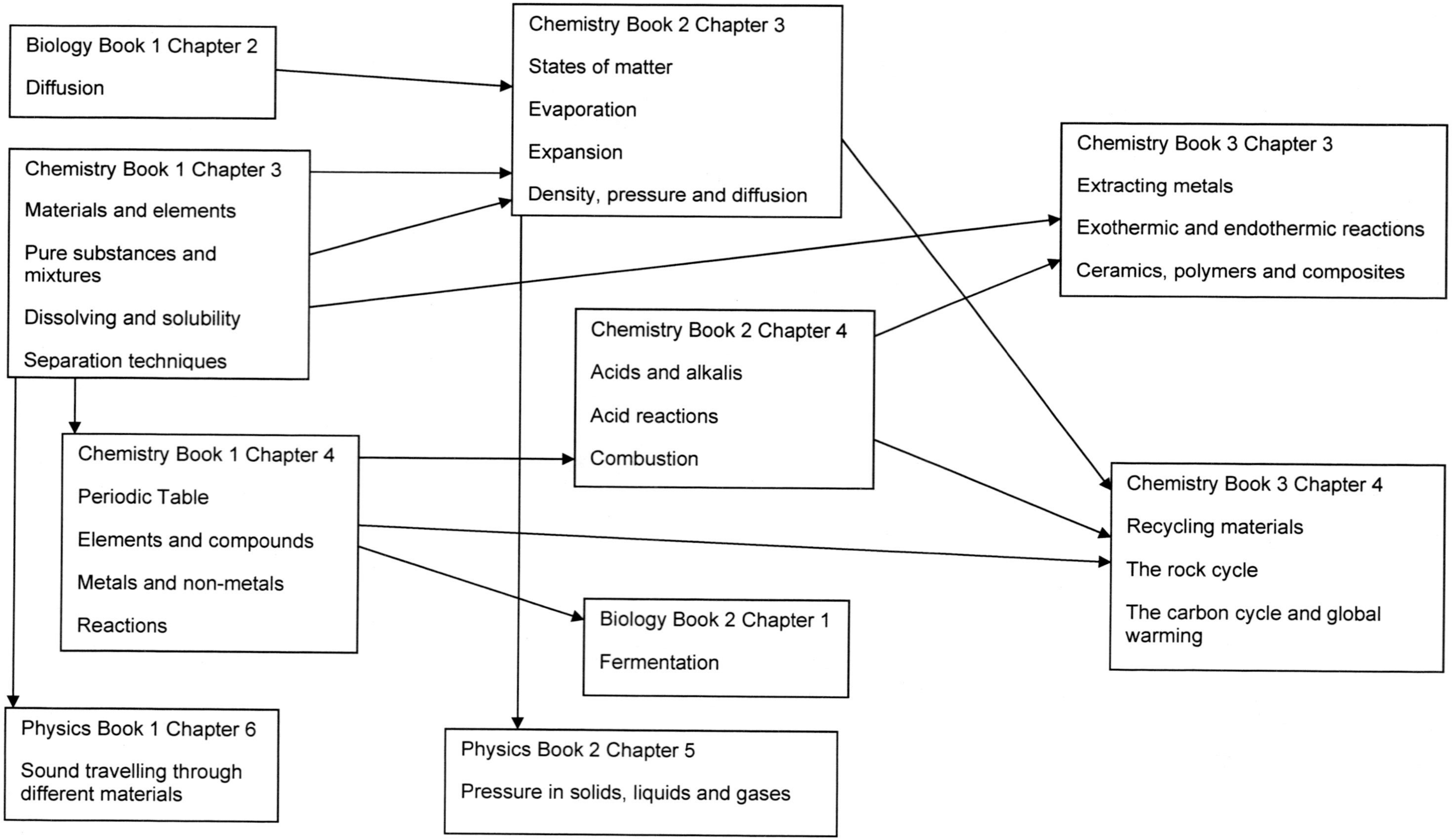

Chemistry Book 2 Chapter 3
- States of matter
- Evaporation
- Expansion
- Density, pressure and diffusion

Chemistry Book 3 Chapter 3
- Extracting metals
- Exothermic and endothermic reactions
- Ceramics, polymers and composites

Chemistry Book 2 Chapter 4
- Acids and alkalis
- Acid reactions
- Combustion

Chemistry Book 3 Chapter 4
- Recycling materials
- The rock cycle
- The carbon cycle and global warming

Biology Book 2 Chapter 1
- Fermentation

Physics Book 2 Chapter 5
- Pressure in solids, liquids and gases

Biology Book 1 Chapter 2
- Diffusion

Chemistry Book 1 Chapter 3
- Materials and elements
- Pure substances and mixtures
- Dissolving and solubility
- Separation techniques

Chemistry Book 1 Chapter 4
- Periodic Table
- Elements and compounds
- Metals and non-metals
- Reactions

Physics Book 1 Chapter 6
- Sound travelling through different materials

Key Stage 3 Science Teacher Pack 2 272 © HarperCollins*Publishers* Limited 2014

Concept teaching route diagrams

Teaching route: Interdependence

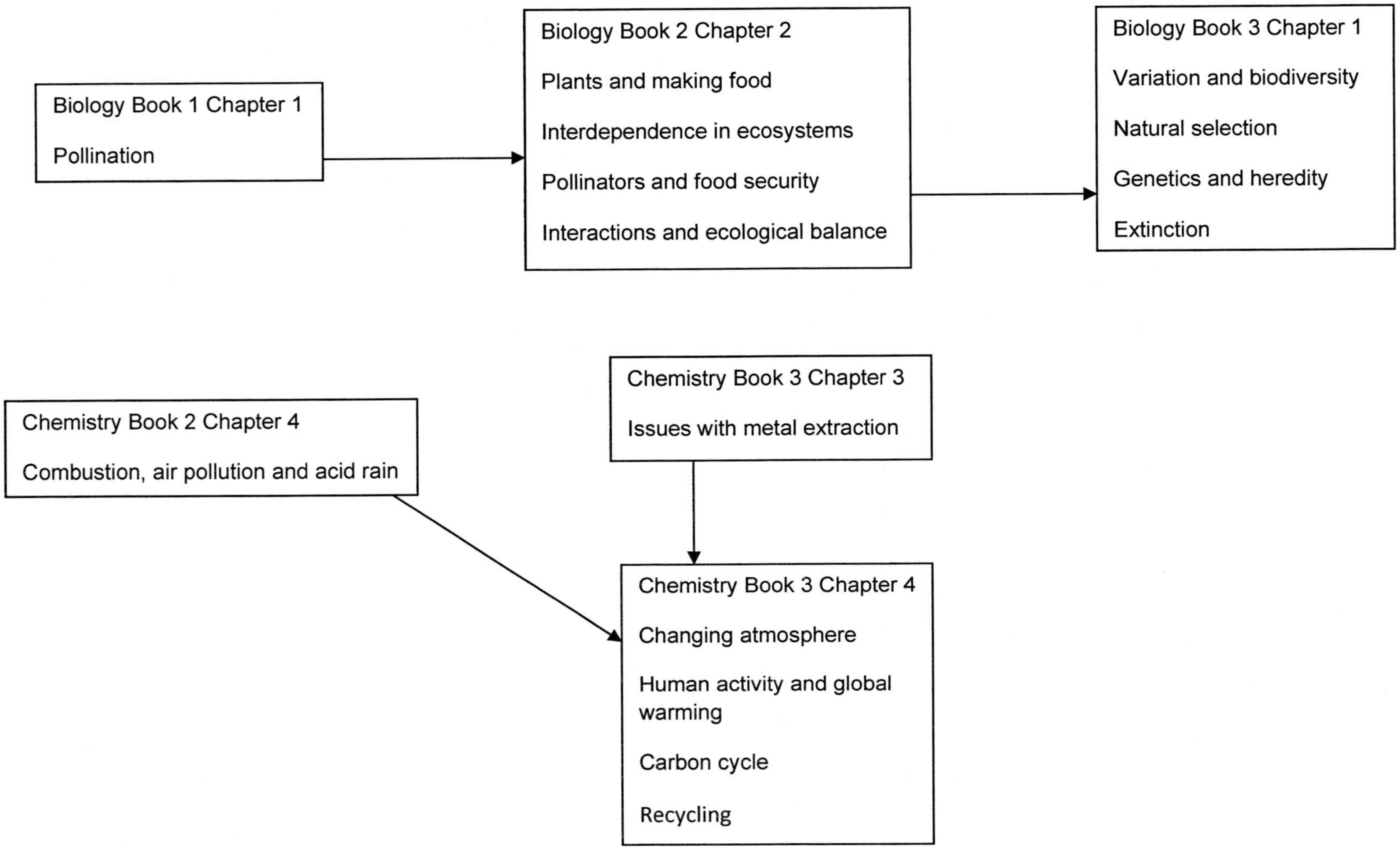

Biology Book 1 Chapter 1

Pollination

Biology Book 2 Chapter 2

Plants and making food

Interdependence in ecosystems

Pollinators and food security

Interactions and ecological balance

Biology Book 3 Chapter 1

Variation and biodiversity

Natural selection

Genetics and heredity

Extinction

Chemistry Book 2 Chapter 4

Combustion, air pollution and acid rain

Chemistry Book 3 Chapter 3

Issues with metal extraction

Chemistry Book 3 Chapter 4

Changing atmosphere

Human activity and global warming

Carbon cycle

Recycling

The Association for Science Education
Promoting Excellence in Science Teaching and Learning

Collins are proud to support the work of ASE

About us...

The ASE is the largest subject association in the UK for teachers of science. We're a powerful force to promote excellence in science teaching and learning.

Join ASE today...

ASE membership helps you bring science to life with innovative resources and expert advice that save you time, build your confidence and inspire your pupils.

Why you should join...

We help you get the basics right! Not every primary teacher has a science background, and teaching science can be a complex process. ASE journals and resources are written by some of the most exciting and experienced science educators in the UK. Our materials help you to master the principles you need to teach, and to understand how young pupils build their knowledge and understanding of science.

We help you excel as a teacher

ASE membership helps you build your skills as a teacher of science so that you can teach with confidence, generate exciting activities and inspire your pupils to explore and investigate.

Science doesn't have to be difficult – for you or your pupils. We help you to understand science – and how best to teach it.

For more details and how to join, visit www.ase.org.uk/membership

Notes

Notes